D1061793

FROM SUFISM TO AHMADIYYA

FROM SUFISM TO AHMADIYYA

A MUSLIM MINORITY MOVEMENT
IN SOUTH ASIA

Adil Hussain Khan

Indiana University Press

Bloomington & Indianapolis

This book is a publication of

Indiana University Press
Office of Scholarly Publishing
Herman B Wells Library 350
1320 East 10th Street
Bloomington, Indiana 47405 USA

iupress.indiana.edu

Manufactured in the United States of America

Cataloging information is available from the Library of Congress

ISBN 978-0-253-01523-5 (cloth)
ISBN 978-0-253-01529-7 (ebook)

1 2 3 4 5   20 19 18 17 16 15

For my parents

Contents

Acknowledgments

MANY PEOPLE HAVE contributed to the publication of this book in various capacities. I am deeply indebted to Professor Christopher Shackle, whose support and guidance shaped this project from its earliest stages. I would also like to thank Professors Paul Gifford, Kate Crosby, Oliver Scharbrodt, David Azzopardi, James Alexander Kapalo, and Sarah Stewart for their stimulating discussions and input in the direction of my research. Dr. Matthew Nelson and Huma Chughtai provided valuable insights into Pakistani politics and the National Assembly debates. Professors Ian Talbot and Avril A. Powell provided constructive feedback on earlier drafts of this project, from which I benefited greatly. I would also like to thank the editorial staff at Indiana University Press, who provided numerous suggestions for improvement and saw this project through to its completion.

The imam of London's Fazl mosque, Maulana Ataul Mujeeb Rashid, patiently dealt with and responded to endless questions on the subtleties of Ahmadi theology, especially during my first two years of research. Maulana Abdul Mannan Tahir and family were kind enough to extend their hospitality to me on a number of occasions; they also put me in touch with many notable Ahmadis in Britain, India, and Pakistan. The extended family members of Abdul Mannan Tahir guided me through Rabwah and Qadian upon my arrival and helped me make the most of my visits, which would have otherwise been far less productive had I been on my own. Maulana Sayyid Mir Mahmud Ahmad Nasir, principal of the Ahmadi seminary in Rabwah, was exceptionally kind and provided access to seminary resources in addition to granting me permission to speak freely with faculty members in Rabwah. The late Maulana Dost Muhammad Shahid graciously answered several questions both in person and through correspondence and pointed me in the appropriate direction regarding historical aspects of my research, even when our trajectories differed. I am also very grateful for the help of Dr. Navidul Haq Khan and family, whose faithful devotion to Jama'at-i Ahmadiyya left a lasting impression in my mind. Siraj and Sabah were particularly helpful and always eager to offer assistance by enthusiastically sifting through Ahmadi literature with me.

I must also thank Sabahussalaam Smith, Pasha Dougela, Tariq Sami, Syed Tayyeb Ahmad Shah, Waqar Jamil, and Ray Mynatt for their long conversations, which often challenged my developing ideas and enabled me to pursue new avenues of research, especially at the beginning of this project. The family of Jamshed and Sharaf Tirmizi warmly welcomed me into their home in Lahore, which allowed me to explore the Punjab without worry and at times provided a much-needed escape from religious controversy.

Funding from the Additional Award for Fieldwork from the School of Oriental and African Studies (SOAS) and the University of London Central Research Fund made possible trips to India and Pakistan during the spring of 2006. The Bobet Fellowship at Loyola University New Orleans helped bring this project to a close. Loyola's specialist librarian, Brian Sullivan, provided tremendous help on numerous occasions.

Chapter 4 is a revised version of my article "The Kashmir Crisis as a Political Platform for Jama'at-i Ahmadiyya's Entrance into South Asian Politics," which appeared in *Modern Asian Studies* 46:5 (September 2012). The material is included with permission from Cambridge University Press, for which I am grateful.

Lastly, but certainly not least, none of this would have been possible without the immeasurable love, support, and assistance of my family: Hina, Esa, Sana, Dean, Ameena, Musa, and Yusuf; my wife, Nasima; and most of all my parents, Khalid and Nusrat, whose prayers alone have brought me this far. Any good that may come of this is because of them.

Despite the greatly appreciated advice and efforts of many people, any errors, mistakes, or shortcomings in this book are my own.

A Note on Transliteration and Translation

THE TRANSLITERATIONS IN this book largely follow a simplified version of the system adopted by the *International Journal of Middle East Studies*. There are a number of drawbacks to adhering to this scheme strictly, however, for reasons discussed in the text. Mirza Ghulam Ahmad frequently switched from one language to another within the same work, which complicates the act of transliteration, since there are different conventions associated with each language. A given word may be spelled or pronounced differently in each language, leading to different transliterations of the same word, such as the Qur'anic concept of *khātam al-nubuwwa* and the Pakistani organization known as Khatm-i Nubuwwat. In this book, I have transliterated words based on their original context so that they may be identified as easily as possible by readers familiar with the language in question, even though this creates apparent inconsistencies in usage from one passage to another. I have also used anglicized plurals in most cases, such as *khalīfa*s instead of *khulafā*.

In rendering proper nouns that have been widely used in English, such as names or titles of individuals who regularly wrote their own names in English, I have used the preferred or most recognized spellings. In cases where names were not commonly written in English with consistent spellings, I have provided the full transliteration at the word's first appearance and used a simplified spelling thereafter. In cases where English words were rendered into Urdu script, I have used conventional English spellings instead of providing reverse transliterations.

The definitions of technical terms throughout the book reflect the context of the original passage in which they appeared, since religious terminology takes on different connotations in each language. These distinctions might not be as clear in the glossary, where most terms may be traced back to Arabic roots. I hope that this will convey a more accurate account of original passages despite apparent inconsistencies, especially for those who are not familiar with the religious undertones of each language. All translations, unless otherwise noted, are my own.

FROM SUFISM TO AHMADIYYA

Introduction

JAMĀʿAT-I AHMADIYYA, OR the Ahmadiyya Muslim Community, is one of the most controversial movements in contemporary South Asian Islam, whose members have been legally declared non-Muslim in countries such as Pakistan. This controversy over whether Ahmadis are in fact Muslims stems largely from the spiritual claims of the movement's founder, who is believed by Ahmadis to have taken on a messianic role which infringes upon mainstream conceptions of prophethood in Islam. In short, Ahmadis claim that their community was founded by the second coming of Jesus Christ, who was sent to the world by God to reform society in advance of the final judgment. This belief has shaped the development of the Ahmadiyya movement and has framed questions of legitimacy surrounding its interpretations of Islam as it continues to spread throughout the world. The transnational scope of the movement today has enabled this controversy to have lasting repercussions for conceptions of Muslim identity worldwide by helping many Muslims delineate what contemporary Islam is not. This is also true in Western European countries, such as Britain, France, and Germany, as well as in Canada and the United States, where the Ahmadiyya movement has increasingly taken root since the 1980s through the establishment of South Asian immigrant communities and converts to Islam. The impact of the Ahmadi controversy has been most evident, however, in the development of South Asian politics after India's partition in 1947, which was determined largely by religion.

Jamaʿat-i Ahmadiyya originated as an Islamic reform movement in nineteenth-century Punjab, when the Indian subcontinent was under British colonial rule. At the time, many Muslim thinkers were preoccupied with internal religious debates ranging from the ritual practices of Sufis to the role of hadith in the broader Islamic tradition. Close encounters with non-Muslims fueled interreligious rivalries with Hindus, Sikhs, and Christians, whose growing influence in the region had been facilitated by increased missionary activity under the British. These dynamics were especially important in the Punjab, where the Ahmadiyya Muslim Community was centered. The response of some Muslim intellectuals was to turn to religious reform as a means of addressing the religious and political turmoil of the colonial experience.

For Ahmadis, conditions in British India resembled those that were to herald the awaited messiah whose return had been prophesized by the Prophet Muhammad in the seventh century. The founder of Jama'at-i Ahmadiyya, Mirza Ghulam Ahmad Qadiani (1835–1908), rallied support by combining a reformist program with insights obtained from private religious experiences in order to establish a community based on his divinely guided response to changing conditions. This community sought to unite the Muslim mainstream—as well as adherents of other world faiths—under the banner of the one true religion, which is believed by Ahmadis to have been conveyed directly to Mirza Ghulam Ahmad by God himself ahead of the day of judgment. The parallels of this seemingly Islamic version of a rapture, coupled with the apocalyptic tone of Mirza Ghulam Ahmad's mystical visions, presented his role in a messianic light. Mirza Ghulam Ahmad thus launched his Islamic revival as the primary figure sent to redeem humanity from its moral deficiencies through the reformation of society along Islamic ideals. His interpretation of this scenario created a sense of controversy around his followers and skepticism about the authenticity of his claims in a way that has impacted the subsequent development of Islam well beyond nineteenth-century South Asia. Jama'at-i Ahmadiyya in this respect is a messianic movement at the margins of the mainstream revival that has gripped Islamic thought since the height of the modern era.

Since its emergence, Jama'at-i Ahmadiyya has reinvigorated the debate on Islamic orthodoxy among the Muslim mainstream. The Ahmadi controversy today converges on the question of whether Ahmadis are Muslims, which revolves around the authenticity of Mirza Ghulam Ahmad's messianic claims. Ahmadis maintain that these claims disclose Ghulam Ahmad's elevated spiritual status, which incorporates a strand of prophethood believed to be subservient to—and less in stature than—the prophethood of Muhammad. The Muslim mainstream contends that this belief presents a challenge to Islamic orthodoxy by infringing upon the finality of Muhammad's prophethood. Ghulam Ahmad's prophetic status in particular, among other Ahmadi beliefs, such as the belief in Jesus's natural death in Kashmir following his survival of crucifixion and the rejection of violent jihad, has perhaps stimulated the greatest uproar for its divergence from mainstream opinion. This has made assessing Mirza Ghulam Ahmad's career difficult, due to sharply polarized views of his legacy, as messianic savior or antichrist, where one represents pristine orthodoxy and the other represents a perverse infidelity beyond the pale of Islam.

The Ahmadi controversy has entered the public consciousness, which has enabled it to become a familiar feature of political discourse in contemporary Muslim South Asia by virtue of continued opposition to the movement over the last century. To this day, provocative headlines about Ahmadi involvement in sectarian rivalries, or in Pakistani political scandals, regularly appear in the

Urdu press. The evolution of the Ahmadi controversy is typically contextualized with key events in Pakistan's political history, including the Punjab disturbances of 1953, which led to the first-ever implementation of martial law in the country;[1] Pakistan's constitutional changes of 1974, which officially categorized Ahmadis as a non-Muslim minority;[2] and the introduction of the blasphemy ordinance of 1984, which effectively made integral aspects of Ahmadi religious life in Pakistan illegal.[3] Since 1984, a person's religious convictions found to be in violation of the penal code have been regarded as criminal, making the expression of belief in Ahmadi Islam a punishable offense, subject to fines or imprisonment.

Although these events may characterize the general resistance towards Jama'at-i Ahmadiyya in Pakistan since India's partition, they do not provide an adequate explanation for how the religious worldview of Jama'at-i Ahmadiyya became intertwined with the mainstream political discourse of modern South Asia. Mainstream politicians certainly could have allowed debates about Ghulam Ahmad's inner spiritual experiences and his hypothetical abstractions of prophecy to remain within the confines of theology, and thus limited to the realm of the 'ulamā (religious scholars). Instead, it is clear that by the time of the Punjab disturbances of 1953, Jama'at-i Ahmadiyya had already become a firmly established feature of mainstream political discourse in Muslim South Asia, which to some extent made such widespread disturbances possible. This suggests that Jama'at-i Ahmadiyya's initial thrust into the mainstream political arena must have taken place prior to 1953 and likely prior to the formation of Pakistan in 1947.

Scholars have generally paid more attention to the repercussions of the Ahmadi controversy than to its development. This approach fails to appreciate the role of Jama'at-i Ahmadiyya's rise from obscure origins through its expansion into a globalized movement at the heart of one of contemporary Islam's great doctrinal debates. To fully understand the scope of this controversy, it is necessary to consider the development of the movement's theological worldview and its politicized background within the appropriate historical context. This book traces the progression of the movement from a small Sufi-style brotherhood in nineteenth-century British India to the heavily politicized movement of today and demonstrates how sociopolitical concerns during a specific era of Muslim history in South Asia facilitated the emergence of a distinct Ahmadi religious identity. It also provides an explanation for why the Ahmadi controversy played a key role in the development of mainstream Muslim identity during the formation of Pakistan, when prospects of creating an Islamic state prompted fundamental questions about what it means to be Muslim. This line of inquiry will illustrate how the Ahmadi controversy has helped shape the discourse on orthodoxy in contemporary Islam more broadly.

Evaluating the life and claims of Mirza Ghulam Ahmad is an important part of contextualizing the religious development of Jama'at-i Ahmadiyya and its distinctive worldview. The Ahmadi interpretation of Islam is typically assumed to be the natural by-product of Ghulam Ahmad's spirituality. The development of Ahmadi Islam was not solely a religious phenomenon, however, nor was it the inevitable outcome of Mirza Ghulam Ahmad's theological claims. Rather, it was influenced in some instances by circumstances independent of religious factors. Ahmadi identity was affected by the advent of modernity and the politics of colonial subjugation as it evolved in an increasingly globalized world over the course of the twentieth century. Jama'at-i Ahmadiyya's origins in the colonial period shaped the development of its theological framework in the postcolonial period.

British rule in India initiated a reassessment of Muslim institutions and a re-evaluation of Muslim political autonomy leading up to India's partition. Jama'at-i Ahmadiyya's involvement in major political crises, such as the conflict in Kashmir since the 1930s, partition in 1947, and the Punjab disturbances of 1953, gradually led to the politicization of Ahmadi Islam. As the notion of Ahmadiyyat as a distinct expression of Islam became increasingly politicized, the formation of an Ahmadi identity took shape. Meanwhile, the dichotomy between Ahmadiyyat and Islam continued to widen. This was possible because the emergence of Ahmadi identity was influenced as much by modern South Asian politics as by modernist South Asian Islam. The interplay between religion and politics is perhaps the most striking aspect of Jama'at-i Ahmadiyya's transformation, since Jama'at-i Ahmadiyya has made meaningful contributions to both South Asian religion and South Asian politics, despite having been alienated from both in the process. This presents a challenge to previous conceptions of Ahmadi Islam, which assert that the egregiousness of Ahmadi religious interpretations somehow justified the political response against them and that religion itself dragged the movement into the mainstream political arena. We shall see in this book that Jama'at-i Ahmadiyya was not simply a religious movement in the way that it has thus far been conceived, but that it was heavily involved in political controversies alongside religious ones.

Jama'at-i Ahmadiyya's South Asian Background

In many ways, Ahmadi ideology represents a combination of medieval mysticism with modernist individualism which developed under the sphere of British colonial rule. For example, the preeminence of Mirza Ghulam Ahmad over his disciples, the esoteric ambiguity of his spiritual claims, the emphasis he placed on internal and external reform, and the exclusivity of his early community of followers are characteristics that might be associated with a medieval Sufi order. A Sufi coincidence, however, is generally emblematic of the South Asian experience of Islam, since the spread of Islam in South Asia has been intimately connected to the influence of Sufism among the mainstream. Mirza Ghulam Ahmad's mission was not unique in this respect, since numerous Sufi-style movements throughout Islamic history have been founded by charismatic leaders whose extravagant spiritual claims have been based on ecstatic experiences, esoteric insights, or mystical illuminations.

It is noteworthy that Mirza Ghulam Ahmad's modernist outlook fit comfortably within the intellectual trends of nineteenth-century Islam. This is visible through Ghulam Ahmad's rejection of traditional methodologies of Islamic scholarship in favor of individualist interpretations, including his personal experiences of the Divine. This means that Jama'at-i Ahmadiyya corresponds with modernist movements throughout the Muslim world in its rejection of the legal tradition and its disregard for the four Sunni schools of thought. Jama'at-i Ahmadiyya's unique combination of influences and its timely appearance in a particular historical context have helped determine its controversial path. These factors collectively have been incorporated in the formation of various aspects of Ahmadi religious thought and Ahmadi religious identity, which many regard as being separate from Islam.

Jama'at-i Ahmadiyya's emergence has been multifaceted. Despite its similarities to mainstream Islam, reconciling its differences presents a challenge for contemporary Muslims, even though the challenges to Islamic orthodoxy extend back beyond current formulations of the debate. It is important to recall that Jama'at-i Ahmadiyya has not always been exclusively in a state of conflict with traditional Islam, but rather Ahmadi interpretations of religion have been considered equally antagonistic towards Hindus, Christians, Sikhs, and Muslims alike. Nineteenth-century Punjab provided a setting well suited for such interreligious contestation, since a rich diversity of cultures and religious communities coexisted in close proximity. This period was conducive to religious reform for several reasons. The introduction of British colonial rule disrupted the preceding balance of power by divesting religious leaders of authority, which initiated a search for a new equilibrium between religious rivals. The realization of British dominance in the subcontinent invigorated age-old disputes among proponents of vying religious communities of Sikhs, Hindus, evangelical Christians, and Muslims. As rivalries unfolded, the establishment of British political rule presented an opportunity to restore religious authority with a renewed sense of urgency before the balance of power could be resettled. For Muslim leaders, the ensuing struggle for religious authority resulted in a scramble, as creative intellectuals and aspiring reformers sought in haste to reestablish interpretive ideologies of Islam during the period following the Mutiny of 1857.

By the end of the nineteenth century, these efforts were having a profound impact on the face of South Asian Islam, with lasting consequences throughout the twentieth century. This period saw the opening of some of the most recognizable educational institutions in contemporary South Asian Islam, including the Dār al-'Ulūm at Deoband, Sir Sayyid Ahmad Khan's Anglo-Oriental College at

Aligarh, and the Nadwat al-ʿUlamā in Lucknow. This period also fostered the growth of a number of popular movements whose influential presence is felt to this day, including those inspired by the Ahl-i Hadith and Ahmad Riza Khan's Barelwi vision of Islam. In this atmosphere, Jamaʿat-i Ahmadiyya proceeded to add yet another interpretation of Islam to a growing list of revivalist ideologies. Mirza Ghulam Ahmad represented an exception to the developing trend in that his mission depended on divine charisma, unlike most reform movements of the time. Jamaʿat-i Ahmadiyya's affinity with premodern Sufism sets it apart from other revivalist movements of the time, even though other aspects suggest a more modernist disposition, including an emphasis on personal changes that lead to social reform. While Ghulam Ahmad's notion of internal reform remained centered on purification of the heart and soul in classical Sufi style, Jamaʿat-i Ahmadiyya's notion of external reform provided an opportune reaction to the ongoing political challenges of the day, especially prior to partition. With this in mind, it was no coincidence that Jamaʿat-i Ahmadiyya consistently aligned itself with its imperial British rulers while setting out to spread the "True" teachings of Islam all over the world.

Contextualizing Mirza Ghulam Ahmad within a Sufi Framework

Mirza Ghulam Ahmad began his spiritual notoriety by claiming to be a *mujaddid* (renewer) of Islam, as well as two apocalyptic figures known as the *mahdī* (guided one) and the *masīh* (messiah). The messianic claim in particular was used to imply that his spiritual status had arrived at some level of prophethood, inferior in rank to the prophethood of Muhammad, but nonetheless commissioned by God himself for the benefit of humanity. These claims led to voluminous justifications against countless religious rivals in the form of sectarian polemics. Ghulam Ahmad's earliest publications were primarily intended to rally Indian Muslims against the rising threat of Hindu revivalist groups such as the Arya Samaj and Brahmo Samaj but were later expanded to address the threat of other rivals, such as Christian missionaries intent on offering colonized Indians salvation through Christ. In these works, Ghulam Ahmad attempted to establish Islam's superiority as a religion through the use of rationalism, logic, and argumentation. During the brief period prior to 1891, when he advanced his spiritual claims, several notable Muslims rallied around Mirza Ghulam Ahmad in support of his literary efforts against non-Muslim evangelists. By 1891, however, three years after the formation of Jamaʿat-i Ahmadiyya, Ghulam Ahmad began proclaiming his true spiritual status to the world. The implications of prophethood stemming from his messianic claims were denounced by mainstream scholars, and Jamaʿat-i Ahmadiyya fell into disrepute. Over the next fifteen years, Ghulam Ahmad focused his attention on expounding the extraordinary nature of his prophetic status and disclosing his spiritual heights to the Muslim mainstream.

Testimonials of exceptional religious experiences describing lofty spiritual heights, divinely inspired insights of unseen realms, and extravagant unveilings of hidden realities are familiar in Islamic history. Many Sufis have uttered questionable statements that have been deemed ecstatic or are understood to have taken place in a state of spiritual intoxication as an attempt to reconcile heterodox ideas with mainstream views. Abu Yazid Bistami is often credited as the founder of intoxicated Sufism,[4] but he might not be the most popular figure among nonspecialists for extravagant claims, even though his legendary presence with the Divine continues to be celebrated within intellectual circles of Sufis. Other Sufis, such as Hallaj, are better known among lay Muslims for ecstatic claims. The statement "I am the Real (*ānā al-haqq*)" famously led to his execution because it affirmed his identity with the ultimate reality of the Divine.[5] Classical memoirs such as Attar's *Tadhkirat al-Awliyā* are full of astonishing tales of Muslim mystics and devout saints who attained fantastic heights through the highest levels of divine realization.[6]

As later Sufis expanded these ideas and ecstatic experiences became an acceptable encounter along the spiritual path, a different terminology was developed to describe the stages of the mystic traveler. The *awliyā* (saints) proceeded to lay out the perils of the path in a didactic tradition that was passed down from teacher to student. Those who perfected the path reached the most advanced stages of *walāya* (sainthood), which were often characterized by special distinctions. These *awliyā* were described by terms such as *qutb* (axis), *ghawth* (helper), and *abdāl* (substitutes). There were even cases where exceptional figures would claim to be the *mahdī* himself.[7] Although this certainly was not the norm, it was not unusual either, especially among those treading the mystic path. An elitist tradition emerged in which the pinnacles of *walāya* at times began to blur with *nubuwwa* (prophethood). Since then, however, Sufis have regularly warned that the inner secrets of veiled realities may only be understood by the mystical elite who have experienced them. Although treatises were written in early Islamic history to define the boundaries of *walāya* and to safeguard those susceptible to theological deviance,[8] alternative understandings continued to appear.

There are several examples of questionable claims which have been shunned by orthodox Muslims.[9] Ruzbihan Baqli, like Mirza Ghulam Ahmad, characterized his unveilings with the term *wahy,* a type of revelation typically reserved for prophets.[10] According to Sufism scholar Carl Ernst, Ruzbihan Baqli went on to obscure the distinction between *nubuwwa* and *walāya* in a way that even most Sufis would reject, following visions in which he was told that he himself was a prophet.[11] The most prominent thinker to expand such ideas was Muhyiddin ibn al-'Arabi, who described the path of the saints as being "on the footsteps of the prophets" ('*alā aqdām al-anbiyā*). Michel Chodkiewicz's work, *Seal of the Saints,* offers western scholars insights into just how intricate these ideas may be,[12] even though Ibn al-ʿArabi might not be the best paradigm for Ghulam Ahmad's thought. A better comparison may be found in the ideas of Shaykh Ahmad Sirhindi, who shared the South Asian context with Ghulam Ahmad and proclaimed his own status as *mujaddid alf-i thānī* (the religious renewer for the second millennium) in addition to being the *khātam al-awliyā* (seal of the saints).[13] It is not surprising in this regard that Ghulam Ahmad also took the title *khātam al-awliyā* and frequently referenced the works of both Ibn al-ʿArabi and Ahmad Sirhindi. These references were clearly intended to serve as justifications for his claims by providing a precedent for his thought within the Islamic tradition, and hence giving Ghulam Ahmad's conceptualizations greater religious credibility. Jamaʿat-i Ahmadiyya has since developed a religious framework that is less intellectual and more political than either of these forerunners.

The Ahmadi religious model bears some resemblance to the early Fatimid (or early Ismaʿilis) and early Safavid dynasties, which at times have shared a sense of messianism underlying political interests, even though both comparisons are limited. There are also correlations between Jamaʿat-i Ahmadiyya and the Sufi orders of the late medieval period, such as the Nurbakhshiyya, whose founder, Muhammad Nurbakhsh, claimed to be the *mahdī* based on messianic visions.[14] The closest comparison to Jamaʿat-i Ahmadiyya in recent years is perhaps the Bahaʾi faith, whose origins in messianic Islam eventually led to the formation of a new religion grounded in seemingly universal ideals.[15] Unlike Jamaʿat-i Ahmadiyya, however, the Bahaʾi faith formalized its break with Islam, which to some extent ended questions about its orthodoxy. Both movements nonetheless have used notions of divine revelation within a messianic framework to formulate a theology emphasizing the universality of all faiths. It would be interesting to see this comparison explored further, especially if Ahmadis one day formalize their break with contemporary Islam.

It would be tempting to classify Ahmadis as religious pluralists in light of Ghulam Ahmad's claim to be the promised messiah for all faiths, were it not for the patronizing attitude of Jamaʿat-i Ahmadiyya towards other religions. Perhaps the most striking difference between Ahmadi Islam and its various sectarian counterparts is Jamaʿat-i Ahmadiyya's response to the messianic claims of Mirza Ghulam Ahmad. Whereas most Muslim movements with messianic backgrounds have either suppressed the heterodox views of their founders, or at least adopted figurative understandings of their questionable claims, Jamaʿat-i Ahmadiyya celebrates Ghulam Ahmad's prophethood and affirms a strictly literalist interpretation of his spiritual worldview.

Textual Sources: The Writings of Mirza Ghulam Ahmad

Most scholarly works on Jamaʿat-i Ahmadiyya have tended to focus on sociological aspects of Ahmadis as a persecuted Muslim minority, such as human rights issues or the growing number of refugees in Western Europe and North America. Not surprisingly, the most extensive accounts of Jamaʻat-i Ahmadiyya are found in the movement's own literary sources, which are often characterized by aggressive proselytistic argumentation. The tendency to adopt this style of writing as the primary means of communicating the Ahmadi worldview may have contributed to the overall antagonism towards the movement. Nevertheless, a style of writing based on religious argumentation has been a salient feature in Ahmadi literature, which can be seen as early as Mirza Ghulam Ahmad's first major work, *Barāhīn-i Ahmadiyya* (The Proofs of Islam).[16]

The majority of Mirza Ghulam Ahmad's works have been published in twenty-three volumes known as *Rūhānī Khazāʼin* (Spiritual Treasures) with an additional three volumes of *Majmūʻa-i Ishtihārāt* (Collected Pamphlets) and ten volumes of *Malfūzāt* (Collected Sayings).[17] Although these works tend to be organized chronologically, they do not reflect a thematic progression through Ghulam Ahmad's career. Ghulam Ahmad's writing style involved a multilingual delivery in which he frequently switched from Urdu prose, to Persian poetry, and then perhaps to Arabic revelations or Qurʼanic commentaries, all within the span of a few pages. He would also receive revelations in English or Punjabi on occasion. His long-winded discourses revolve around abstruse theological notions which are difficult to penetrate. Altogether, the combination of the level of philosophical inquiry and the multiple languages in which many of his works were written made Ghulam Ahmad's writing inaccessible to many readers by limiting his primary audience to an educated Muslim elite.

A great deal of Ghulam Ahmad's works seem to have been written in a stream of consciousness, which corresponds to his confessional style of writing. Many of his published works could easily be mistaken for secret diaries, private notebooks, or unfinished drafts in preparation. This unedited mass of loosely structured religious argumentation was published by Jamaʻat-i Ahmadiyya posthumously as an anthology of the promised messiah's writings, including several texts that appeared in print for the first time. Some of the longer works incorporated a number of discourses on unrelated themes, which appeared as unusually long footnotes extending throughout the body of the text. Some of these footnotes were later published by Jamaʻat-i Ahmadiyya as independent monographs on subject matter more neatly focused on limited theological questions. In the original texts, however, the writing may simply appear as footnotes, with footnotes to the footnotes, and sometimes even footnotes to the footnotes of the footnotes, compressed onto a single page with each note telling a unique story that extends throughout the work in question.

Several smaller texts have been translated into English while many of the most important works remain untranslated. It is unfortunate that most English translations are difficult to read since they frequently misconstrue Ghulam Ahmad's allusions or subtle religious inferences by divorcing them from the Sufi context that connects his ideas to perennial themes in the Islamic tradition. In their original form, however, the works clearly display Ghulam Ahmad's literary mastery, which appealed to familiar motifs of Muslim sentiment interwoven with intense charismatic convictions. The available translated selections of Ghulam Ahmad's works seem to lose their bombastic tone by editing away the frantic urgency with which he endeavored to deliver his message. The reverence accompanying the mythical mystique surrounding Ghulam Ahmad's uncanny approach has enabled a relationship to develop between his works and Jama'at-i Ahmadiyya which is arguably indicative of scripture. Although it is difficult to regard his works as Ahmadi scripture at this time, there remains no other source that illuminates the Ahmadi enterprise with such authoritative esteem as the works of Mirza Ghulam Ahmad.

The earliest sources, aside from Ghulam Ahmad's works, are the hagiographies and polemics produced by the movement itself, which are typical genres for sectarian movements of the time. Although these sources are essential in understanding the self-image of the early Ahmadi community, they do not provide a critical analysis of Ahmadi beliefs and doctrine. Most Ahmadi sources repeat assertions of Ahmadi ideology, dogmatically restated in different ways and at times in different languages. Likewise, the bulk of outsider literature on Jama'at-i Ahmadiyya consists of spirited rebuttals of Mirza Ghulam Ahmad or his disciples. Few academics have taken up research on Ahmadi Islam, but we may now briefly examine some of the most important studies.

Secondary Sources and Academic Surveys of Jama'at-i Ahmadiyya

One of the first and most frequently referenced surveys of Jama'at-i Ahmadiyya is a supplementary chapter in Wilfred Cantwell Smith's *Modern Islam in India,* which was first published in 1943, just prior to partition.[18] Cantwell Smith rightly placed Jama'at-i Ahmadiyya within the context of Islamic revivalist movements attempting to come to terms with modernity. Although he did not provide much commentary on Ahmadi theology, he noted that the reaction to Jama'at-i Ahmadiyya was having a greater impact on ordinary Indian Muslims than Jama'at-i Ahmadiyya itself. This reaction to Ahmadi Islam and the corresponding persecution of Ahmadis was only the beginning of Jama'at-i Ahmadiyya's politicization. Cantwell Smith commented that the exclusivist nature of Ahmadis and their "social aloofness rather than their theology (which is no more heretical than the respected Āgā Khān's) . . . occasioned the bitter antagonism between the Muslims and themselves."[19] Cantwell Smith also noted the growing influence of Jama'at-i Ahmadiyya on established religious communities in places like Africa, America, and Europe.

Most of Cantwell Smith's observations were sociological, as the subtitle of the book suggests. The popularity of the work, however, led to several misconceptions of Jamaʻat-i Ahmadiyya by later scholars. For example, Cantwell Smith noted that the voluminous works of Mirza Ghulam Ahmad, which spanned Urdu, Arabic, and Persian, were intended to address a highly literate audience. He then connected his observation to the fact that Ahmadis were known to boast astonishingly high literacy rates.[20] These comments, along with his subsequent discussion of Qadian's privately funded schools and organizational infrastructure, including a permanent *langar khāna* (free kitchen) for relief from unemployment, were often misquoted by later scholars studying Jamaʻat-i Ahmadiyya. It is clear that the early Ahmadi community in Qadian—the village of Ghulam Ahmad's birth—was largely composed of educated followers from privileged backgrounds. The population of the community at the time of Cantwell Smith's research, however, was significantly smaller than it is today. Nevertheless, one still finds lingering references to the highly educated Ahmadi elite that cite Cantwell Smith's prepartition study, even though it is no longer applicable. Excerpts from Cantwell Smith's account of Jamaʻat-i Ahmadiyya served as the basis for the main *Encyclopaedia of Islam* entry on the movement until the third edition appeared with an updated article in 2007.[21]

The next major study on Jamaʻat-i Ahmadiyya was Humphrey J. Fisher's *Ahmadiyyah: A Study in Contemporary Islam on the West African Coast*, which was published in 1963.[22] Fisher's research was limited to the spread of Jamaʻat-i Ahmadiyya in the West African context rather than the community's Indian roots, which makes it different from other surveys of Jamaʻat-i Ahmadiyya.[23] There are still occasional reminders of the subcontinent where Fisher illustrated the difficulties of being an Indian missionary in Africa by highlighting cultural barriers between imams and their congregations. For example, Fisher mentioned racial tensions between indigenous members who disapproved of black Africans following an Indian imam in prayer.[24] As such, Fisher's study is mainly centered on the African experience. His analysis of Jamaʻat-i Ahmadiyya in countries like Nigeria, Ghana, Sierra Leone, and Gambia is useful for understanding the surging population of Ahmadi diaspora communities in Africa today.

In addition, Fisher devoted part 2 of his book to "Ahmadiyyah Doctrine," providing a preliminary look at Ahmadi theology, particularly in relation to Christianity.[25] This section is especially useful as a commentary on *tablīgh* (missionary activity), a major component of Ahmadi ideology. Fisher noted that the presentation of the life and death of Jesus varied in a way that enabled Ahmadis to carefully choose arguments based on the religious orientation of the audience. Arguments challenging the divinity of Jesus were reserved for Christians, whereas arguments highlighting Jesus's natural death and denying the ascension to heaven were stressed to fellow Muslims, as a means of focusing on each respective community's tenets. This illustrates the sophistication of Ahmadi missionaries in foreign surroundings beyond South Asia. Fisher also summarized the Ahmadi account of Jesus's survival of crucifixion and his subsequent journey to

Kashmir, but dismissed Ghulam Ahmad's claim of having identified the tomb of Jesus as a gimmick.[26]

Fisher's book provides a different perspective on familiar themes regarding the Ahmadiyya community, such as its exclusivity and isolation. Although Ahmadi separatism is typically discussed in relation to other Muslims, Fisher's work addresses it in a non-Muslim setting. The similarities to Ahmadis in South Asia are apparent, which supports the notion of an emergent Ahmadi identity globally. Enforcing this identity has at times been problematic for Ahmadi officials, since West African converts, who had customarily identified themselves according to tribal affiliations, were expected to prioritize Ahmadi identity following conversion. Ahmadi identity in this respect was intended to supersede former tribal identities.[27] Identifying with Jama'at-i Ahmadiyya proved essential for those wishing to lead congregational prayers. In one case, known as the Okepopo split, legal action was taken to determine whether a non-Ahmadi could rightfully be the imam of the Okepopo mosque of the Gold Coast.[28] Local Ahmadi representatives maintained that the imam of the mosque ought to have a formal allegiance (*bay'at*) to the Ahmadi *khalīfa,* even though the mosque was frequented by all members of the Okepopo community, including non-Ahmadis from different tribal and sectarian backgrounds. Fisher noted that this demonstrated how simple participation in Ahmadi prayer services at an Ahmadi mosque was not enough to be considered an Ahmadi in West Africa.

Fisher also used conflicts with local Tijani Muslims to illuminate aspects of Ahmadi *fiqh* (jurisprudence). Apparently, one of the most visible differences between Ahmadi and non-Ahmadi Muslims in West Africa is the folding of the arms in prayer. Whereas Ahmadis fold the arms in accordance with Hanafi rulings, local Tijanis allow the arms to fall straight along the side in accordance with the Maliki school of thought, the dominant school in North and West Africa, where Fisher was based.[29] Although both methods are accepted by Sunni jurists and considered equally valid, the rigid adherence of Ahmadis to this specific practice created further tensions among West African Muslims. Fisher noted how Ahmadi missionaries would never commit to one specific school of thought, but instead would swear allegiance to the *khalīfat al-masīh* (Ghulam Ahmad's successor) and the promised messiah.[30] This is an excellent example of the much larger problem of the formulation of Ahmadi *fiqh*, which will be discussed further in this book. It may be useful to mention that Ahmadis do not actually adhere to the Hanafi school of thought like most South Asian Muslims, even though many rulings are loosely based on Hanafi methodology.

The first attempt at writing a scholarly appraisal of early Ahmadi history was Spencer Lavan's *The Ahmadiyah Movement*.[31] Lavan's history included some errors, which may have been a result of heavy reliance on secondary sources in English rather than original source material in Urdu and Arabic. For instance, a great deal of Lavan's information on Ghulam Ahmad was based on an early unfinished biography called *Life of Ahmad* by a prominent Ahmadi missionary to London who wrote the text in English.[32] In addition, Lavan's survey ends in 1936, which was before the Ahmadi controversy had surfaced in Pakistan after partition and had led to major political tensions. Still, Lavan's coverage of the period from 1908 to 1936 included a number of references to newspaper articles, government reports, and later Ahmadi and non-Ahmadi publications. Lavan's work is the first critical analysis of Ahmadi history which offers a balanced look at Ghulam Ahmad's life and mission within the scope of its broader South Asian context.

Lavan raised critical questions regarding Ghulam Ahmad's educational background and early religious influences prior to the founding of Jama'at-i Ahmadiyya.[33] This is an important line of inquiry considering Ghulam Ahmad's unorthodox mission. Lavan noted the presence of a twenty-year gap in Ghulam Ahmad's biography, which began when he finished his studies and ended when he was preparing for his mission. Lavan also commented on Ghulam Ahmad's use of Sufi metaphors and other terminology to explain Ahmadi theology by noting that "[Ghulam] Ahmad came close to what might be considered a *sūfī* conception of his own role."[34] Lavan also questioned whether Ghulam Ahmad might have received some type of specialized Sufi training.[35] Once again, the nature of early Ahmadi history makes it difficult to trace religious influences on Ahmadi theology, since Ghulam Ahmad did not openly declare allegiance to a specific Sufi order or religious institution.

Lavan's biggest contribution was perhaps his evaluation of the period from Ghulam Ahmad's death in 1908 through 1936. His book provides a reasonably detailed overview of the movement's split into Lahori and Qadiani factions. It also provides a judicious breakdown of Jama'at-i Ahmadiyya's early involvement in the Kashmir crisis and its ensuing rivalry with the Majlis-i Ahrar. Over the course of the next three decades this developed into a protracted sectarian conflict between the Ahmadi hierarchy and Ahrari officials. The key Ahrari spokesperson, 'Ataullah Shah Bukhari (1892–1961), one of India's most outspoken demagogues, eventually became the primary antagonist of the second Ahmadi *khalīfa*, Mirza Bashir al-Din Mahmud Ahmad (1889–1965). Jama'at-i Ahmadiyya's participation in the mainstream political framework of South Asia remained a steady aspect of its historical development beyond India's partition in 1947.

Until his death in 2009, chronicling the official history of the movement was the responsibility of Jama'at-i Ahmadiyya's commissioned historian, Dost Muhammad Shāhid (d. 2009). As a senior missionary who devoted his life to the task, Dost Muhammad Shahid's *Tārīkh-i Ahmadiyya* (History of the Ahmadiyya Movement) is a vital source for researching Ahmadi history in Urdu.[36] The first volume of *Tārīkh-i Ahmadiyya* appeared in 1958, but Spencer Lavan only referenced the work occasionally despite listing the first nine volumes in his bibliography. Though Shahid's voluminous work is certainly the most comprehensive source of Ahmadi history, it was not intended to provide a critical analysis of Jama'at-i Ahmadiyya. Any subsequent commentary on Ahmadi history, nonetheless, must acknowledge the authoritative accounts presented by Dost Muhammad Shahid.

During the course of my research, I had the opportunity to meet Dost Muhammad Shahid on a visit to Rabwah, Pakistan, in 2006. After a quick security screening by his secretary, we sat in his office in the *khilāfat* library complex surrounded by Ahmadi texts and old photographs of Ghulam Ahmad's *khalīfa*s, as Dost Muhammad Shahid proceeded to expound the historical development of Jama'at-i Ahmadiyya. There was a peg on the wall where he hung his turban, immaculately wrapped, and another for his *achkan* (overcoat), which dangled by the door. His advanced age and moderate celebrity status among local Ahmadis demanded a full-time staff of four or five teenage boys who promptly fetched books for him upon request from the adjoining library. In answering my questions, he would show the original passages in books, rather than simply providing references. At the end of our conversation, we briefly discussed forthcoming volumes of *Tārīkh-i Ahmadiyya,* and he boldly proclaimed that he had divulged information about Jama'at-i Ahmadiyya that even Ahmadis would not know.

The most influential work on Jama'at-i Ahmadiyya is perhaps Yohanan Friedmann's *Prophecy Continuous,* which was first published in 1989 then republished in 2003.[37] Friedmann's book places Ghulam Ahmad's interpretation of prophethood against the backdrop of medieval Islamic thought. Friedmann's greatest contribution might be his substantial research on the notion of prophecy, primarily among Sufis, prior to Ghulam Ahmad. Friedmann built upon his previous work on Shaykh Ahmad Sirhindi by further developing similar themes in an Ahmadi context. *Prophecy Continuous* provides a detailed discussion of Ghulam Ahmad's interpretation of the title *khātam al-nabiyyīn* (seal of the prophets),[38] a Qur'anic designation reserved for the Prophet Muhammad that is traditionally understood to implicate his position as the last prophet of the Abrahamic tradition. Ghulam Ahmad maintained that new prophets would continue to appear as long as they abided by Muhammad's established *sharī'a* (law). This demanded a reinterpretation of *khātam al-nabiyyīn* to mean the best rather than the last of the prophets. Friedmann showed how Ghulam Ahmad drew heavily upon Ibn al-'Arabi's distinction between legislative prophets (*anbiyā tashrī'*) and non-legislative prophets (*anbiyā lā tashrī'a lahum*).[39] In this nomenclature, legislative prophets are understood to have brought some form of scripture or legal code as part of their mission, whereas non-legislative prophets simply reinforce previously revealed scriptures. Friedmann showed how Ghulam Ahmad claimed to be a non-legislative prophet while concurrently acknowledging Muhammad's finality as the last legislative prophet, and hence the Qur'an's status as the last scripture. For this reason, Ghulam Ahmad conceded that non-legislative prophets were subservient, or perhaps inferior, to Muhammad, who would eternally remain *khātam al-nabiyyīn* (seal of the prophets).

Friedmann's work underscores Ghulam Ahmad's dependence on creative interpretations of thinkers such as Ibn al-'Arabi and Shaykh Ahmad Sirhindi to validate his position. This places the most controversial aspects of Ahmadi theology within a more appropriate context stemming from medieval mysticism. Friedmann primarily addressed fully formulated expressions of Ahmadi religious thought as a means of providing a frame of reference for Ghulam Ahmad's prophethood in Islam. Although this was certainly a worthwhile contribution, Friedmann's study is centered on the medieval background of Ghulam Ahmad's thought, rather than its religious implications. This excludes subsequent interpretations of Ghulam Ahmad's claims by the movement, which led to current formulations of the Ahmadi worldview. In contrast, this book focuses more on how Ahmadi religious thought later developed within its own framework as a means of illustrating its influence on contemporary South Asian religion and politics.

A final genre of literature about Jama'at-i Ahmadiyya is concerned with Ahmadi persecution, such as recent sanctions against Ahmadis in Pakistan. Antonio Gualtieri summarized these developments in his book *Conscience and Coercion.*[40] Since Gualtieri's account begins after partition, his treatment of the Ahmadi controversy is limited to the Pakistani context and primarily deals with the 1984 sanctions and its ramifications for Ahmadis from a human rights perspective. Gualtieri's next book, *The Ahmadis,* focuses on similar themes,[41] and includes insightful interviews with Lutfulla Mufti, then Pakistani minister of religion and minority affairs, and Marie-Andrée Beauchemin, then Canadian high commissioner in Islamabad.[42] In these interviews, Gualtieri was critical of Pakistani policies and argued that Pakistan was violating basic human rights by enforcing blasphemy laws that charged Ahmadis with posing as Muslims. Gualtieri pressed the diplomats by asking why such consistent persecution had taken place, and why such intense animosity was prevalent towards Ahmadis. Both diplomats suggested, rather disturbingly, that the overall rigidity of the Ahmadiyya movement and some of its tendencies towards Islam had instigated such harsh persecution. In the end, they dismissed the persecution and effectively vindicated previous episodes of violence by concluding that "the Ahmadis brought it on themselves."[43] Discouraged by their responses and unable to establish a meaningful dialogue, Gualtieri ended both books with his contempt for religious intolerance and a sense of despair.

Although Gualtieri affirmed his deep conviction that everyone, including Ahmadis, has the basic right of self-identification, he did not attempt to explain why such seemingly absurd allegations would be introduced, accepted, or upheld by the Pakistani government. One must construct a more complete narrative of the development of the Ahmadi controversy in order to provide convincing explanations—taboo doctrine aside—for the rise of Ahmadi persecution and its role in contemporary South Asia. Other works on Jama'at-i Ahmadiyya within this genre include Simon Ross Valentine's study of contemporary issues confronting the movement and the aftermath of Ahmadi persecution in Pakistan.[44] These contributions in many ways devote considerable attention to outlining each author's personal experiences with individual Ahmadis, rather than presenting a comprehensive analysis of the movement.

Overview of This Book

The question of whether Ahmadis are Muslims has steadily intensified into a controversy about Muslim identity in contemporary Islam where both Ahmadis and mainstream Muslims have increasingly established conceptions of orthodoxy in opposition to each other. The steady build-up of the Ahmadi controversy has taken place within a particular context unique to late-nineteenth- and twentieth-century South Asia, which has influenced its trajectory and enabled it to take shape in this way. This is to say that the development of Jama'at-i Ahmadiyya and its antagonistic relationship with mainstream Islam might have developed differently had it emerged within a different sociopolitical climate. For example, a similar movement during the medieval period might simply have been regarded as yet another Sufi order founded by a charismatic leader whose influence was bounded by localized conditions. Many such movements have emerged from, before being absorbed back into, mainstream Islam. But changing circumstances in the Muslim world, brought on by its encounter with modernity, globalization, and European colonial rule, facilitated a shift in Islamic reform ideologies which turned increasingly sectarian, in part as a response to a crisis of authority. The subsequent postcolonial period of nation building throughout the Muslim world, which saw the formation of Pakistan as an Islamic state, made it especially important to define explicitly what it meant to be Muslim. These influences helped forge a new religious identity over time known as Ahmadiyyat, which needed to distinguish itself from mainstream Islam.

This book challenges prevalent explanations of the Ahmadi controversy as being based purely on religious differences by showing how sociopolitical factors contributed to the gradual development of Jama'at-Ahmadiyya into its current politicized form. This will yield a fuller picture of the religious and political transformation of the Ahmadiyya community as well as the development of Ahmadi thought by providing a means of assessing the formalization of Ahmadi religious beliefs within their appropriate context. This book treats the notion of Ahmadi identity as an emerging phenomenon instead of as a fully formed religious ideology that suddenly appeared in the world as a necessary consequence of Mirza Ghulam Ahmad's revelations.

Chapter 1 examines Ghulam Ahmad's family background, education, and spiritual training before he made his controversial claims. Ghulam Ahmad's privileged upbringing was a result of ancestral connections with the Mughal rulers of sixteenth-century India who placed his family in charge of a budding settlement that later developed into his native Qadian. As power dynamics in the subcontinent changed, Ghulam Ahmad's family established a lasting relationship with the British government, which later proved beneficial for the family. Following the Sikh conquests of the mid-nineteenth century, the family rekindled its ties with the British in an attempt to restore its former prestige. Ghulam Ahmad was born in an uncertain climate marked by the end of the prominence enjoyed by previous generations in his family. He received a private education from personal tutors who taught him the languages necessary to pursue an Islamic education. As a young adult, Ghulam Ahmad moved to Sialkot to become a court reader, where he came into contact with evangelical Christian missionaries who were eager to expand their mission. This experience gave Ghulam Ahmad his first interaction with people who aggressively challenged his religious beliefs, allowing him to develop a taste for religious argumentation. Ghulam Ahmad began debating Christians and Hindus on religious issues and soon began writing short articles in defense of Islam. This exposure provided him with limited recognition among local Muslims and allowed him to found a small fellowship in 1889, which he called Jama'at-i Ahmadiyya. This process initiated a broader campaign which gradually led Ghulam Ahmad towards controversial claims that disclosed his messianic aspirations.

Ghulam Ahmad's prophetic claims are key to understanding the scope of his mission within the appropriate Islamic context. Chapter 2 considers Ghulam Ahmad's justifications for his prophetic status and the dependence of his mission on the rejection of Jesus's death by crucifixion. By claiming that Jesus was not alive in heaven, Ghulam Ahmad was able to assert that he himself was the second coming of the messiah. Ghulam Ahmad went to great lengths to show that Jesus died a natural death in Kashmir and argued that he himself was the promised messiah who was sent to fulfill divine prophecy. This chapter also analyzes the Sufi concepts that Ghulam Ahmad used to justify a mysterious spiritual connection between himself and the Prophet Muhammad. Ghulam Ahmad claimed that his profound love for the Prophet and his strict obedience to the Qur'an and sunna enabled him to receive prophetic insights, which he expressed in the terminology of revelation. This eventually led many Ahmadis to affirm Ghulam Ahmad's prophetic status and to distance themselves from what they believed to be antiquated interpretations of a stagnant Islamic tradition.

Ghulam Ahmad's prophethood became the subject of a heated debate within the early Ahmadi community, as members grappled with questions of authority following Ghulam Ahmad's death. This eventually led to the splitting of the movement into two camps, the Lahoris and the Qadianis, which is the focus of chapter 3. The Lahori-Qadiani split enabled the early community to formalize positions on Ghulam Ahmad's role in the Islamic tradition. This permitted the Qadiani leadership to initiate a process of institutionalization that transformed Jama'at-i Ahmadiyya into a hierarchical religious organization mediated by a *khalīfat al-masīh,* Ghulam Ahmad's political and spiritual successor. This chapter breaks down the organizational structure of Jama'at-i Ahmadiyya and looks at how its system of financial contributions was expanded following the split. In addition, we shall see how the split of the movement itself laid the groundwork for the present-day Ahmadi identity.

Chapter 4 evaluates Jama'at-i Ahmadiyya's political involvement in pre-partition India under the leadership of Ghulam Ahmad's son and second successor, Mirza Bashir al-Din Mahmud Ahmad. Communal tensions in the 1920s and the Kashmir riots in the 1930s provided Mirza Mahmud Ahmad with an opportunity to demonstrate his leadership capabilities on an international stage. This chapter looks at how Mahmud Ahmad's early political success led to bitter rivalries between Jama'at-i Ahmadiyya and the Majlis-i Ahrar. It also shows how these rivalries enabled Muslim organizations of the era to use socioeconomic issues to fuse religious ideals into a political platform. This launched Jama'at-i Ahmadiyya into the mainstream political discourse of South Asia, which aided Mahmud Ahmad in establishing the All-India Kashmir Committee. Although Mahmud Ahmad worked with influential figures, including Muhammad Iqbal, (*sher-i kashmīr*) Sheikh Abdullah, and Mian Fazl-i Husain, his unwillingness to accommodate diverse religious and political opinions became problematic. Similarly, many Muslims were unwilling to accommodate Mahmud Ahmad's political ambitions or his monochromatic vision of Islam.

The prolonged conflict in Kashmir led to a revaluation of Jama'at-i Ahmadiyya's religious worldview, which had a direct impact on the Jama'at's political platform. This is the focus of chapter 5. As the Pakistan movement gained momentum among the Muslim mainstream, Jama'at-i Ahmadiyya was forced to reassess its role in a divided subcontinent. While Kashmir remained under Dogra rule, Jama'at-i Ahmadiyya committed itself to fight alongside Pakistani troops in an Ahmadi jihad, which was seemingly contrary to Ghulam Ahmad's teachings. The ultimate failure to bring about Kashmiri independence prompted Jama'at-i Ahmadiyya's withdrawal from the political limelight, but it had already become associated with political controversies of the time. Influential members of Jama'at-i Ahmadiyya, such as Zafrulla Khan, who at the time was foreign minister of Pakistan, became the subject of open criticism and even hostility.

Within the context of ongoing political tensions of the time, the next two chapters deal with the impact of persecution on Ahmadi identity. Chapter 6 highlights how opposition to Jama'at-i Ahmadiyya began with a few isolated incidents at the turn of the twentieth century, which escalated into widespread rioting by

1953. As the political involvement of Jamaʿat-i Ahmadiyya increased, the Ahmadi identity became increasingly politicized. This chapter shows how justifications for the earliest cases of Ahmadi persecution varied considerably. It also shows how early opposition to Jamaʿat-i Ahmadiyya was not solely based on Ghulam Ahmad's controversial claims of prophethood, as most contemporary scholars portray. The politicization of the Ahmadi controversy led to gradual changes in Ahmadi identity. As partition loomed, many Muslims were willing to put aside sectarian differences and unite under a nationalist banner, which resulted in the temporary suppression of the controversy.

Chapter 7 continues the discussion of how prolonged persecution of Jamaʿat-i Ahmadiyya shaped Ahmadi identity. The opposition to Jamaʿat-i Ahmadiyya increased following the partition in 1947, at which point the Ahmadi controversy became politicized by mainstream political figures, both inside and outside the Jamaʿat. By having Muslim-majority areas of the subcontinent demarcated through the course of partition, the need to delineate Muslim identity facilitated the resurgence of the Ahmadi controversy in Pakistan, which erupted in the Punjab disturbances of 1953. The partition also led to a reshuffling of political policies within a Pakistani framework under newly emerging organizations, such as Mawdudi's Jamaʿat-i Islami. As such, religious rivalries of the past took on a different role, and the Ahmadi controversy became a question of Islamic purity, Islamization, and national identity for the newly formed Islamic state. This took the form of attacks on Ghulam Ahmad's prophethood in the public sphere. The result in Pakistan was the National Assembly decision of 1974 which declared Ahmadis non-Muslim for purposes of constitutional law. Additional changes to the constitution under President Zia-ul-Haq and the introduction of a blasphemy ordinance in 1984 forced Ghulam Ahmad's fourth successor, Mirza Tahir Ahmad, to flee Pakistan into exile and to reestablish the Jamaʿat's headquarters in London.

The conclusion retraces the development of Jamaʿat-i Ahmadiyya from its colonial past to its postcolonial present. It also shows how instigators of anti-Ahmadi sentiment over the course of the past century shared common lineages with the original opponents of Mirza Ghulam Ahmad. The leaders guiding Jamaʿat-i Ahmadiyya's institutional hierarchy have also remained tightly focused around Ghulam Ahmad's immediate descendants. Ahmadi *khalīfas* excommunicated potential dissenters and would-be rivals who challenged their views in the face of internal opposition. This process ensured that both promoters and opponents of Ahmadiyyat have remained steadfast in their respective ideologies, which over time has widened the gap between Jamaʿat-i Ahmadiyya and mainstream Islam. It is the role of this politicized persecution of Jamaʿat-i Ahmadiyya which has gradually over the course of the last century influenced a continual reassessment of Ahmadi self-identification. This has facilitated the development of an independent Ahmadi identity. Thus, it becomes clear that Ahmadi identity is not wholly based on Mirza Ghulam Ahmad's controversial claims, but is the outgrowth of multiple influences over time, including the particular South Asian context from which it emerged.

The religious beliefs and ritual practices of Jama'at-i Ahmadiyya are still undergoing a process of formalization. Jama'at-i Ahmadiyya is approaching a critical point in a religious community's formation, since it may still one day revise its theological positions in an attempt to regain acceptance from the Muslim mainstream. It could also choose to reaffirm a literalist interpretation of Ghulam Ahmad's spiritual claims and formalize its break with Islam forever. For this reason, as we embark upon an analysis of Jama'at-i Ahmadiyya's development, it must be made clear that Ahmadi identity is still in flux.

We shall see how insiders and outsiders have chosen to define and redefine Ahmadi Islam by analyzing the progression of Jama'at-i Ahmadiyya from a vague conceptualization of a charismatic leader to the institutionalized construct of today. This requires going beyond singular aspects of Ahmadi thought and looking at how Ahmadi Islam developed on the whole, from the mystical mindset of Mirza Ghulam Ahmad to a globalized movement with a supreme *khalīfa* residing in London. The political struggles of the day framed the persecution of Ahmadis in a way that led to the Ahmadi controversy becoming increasingly politicized, until the general perception developed of a natural separation between Jama'at-i Ahmadiyya and mainstream Sunni Islam.

Considerable changes needed to take place in order for the community to develop in this fashion. Subtle variations in the way that Ahmadi doctrine has been articulated over the past century correspond to different stages of development of Ahmadi identity. By mapping these changes in Ahmadi doctrine and contextualizing them appropriately, we shall gain a better understanding of Jama'at-i Ahmadiyya and its evolution over the past century, while bearing in mind that both internal and external influences on Ahmadi Islam are diverse and complex, involving a number of factors. This process will ultimately show how politics may shape religious identity and, in the case of Jama'at-i Ahmadiyya, may even form a new religion.

1 Mirza Ghulam Ahmad Qadiani before Prophethood

Mirza Ghulam Ahmad's Family Background

Accounts of the life of Mirza Ghulam Ahmad usually begin with descriptions of the Mirza'i family's sixteenth-century migration from Persian Central Asia to India. This format follows the chief source of information on his family background, located in a similarly structured autobiographical account which takes up a considerable portion of the footnotes of his *Kitāb al-Bariyya* (Book of Exoneration).[1] Ghulam Ahmad's emphasis on lineage played an important role in establishing credibility, both religiously and socially, for Jama'at-i Ahmadiyya, and it sheds light on Ghulam Ahmad's mission by characterizing the colonial context of the time. The fact that lineage has consistently been presented by Ahmadi sources as requisite for understanding the life and claims of the movement's founder should be an indication of the values of the early community and of the nineteenth-century Indian society from which it emerged.

The first recorded ancestor of Mirza Ghulam Ahmad is Mirza Hadi Beg, who was apparently a member of the Mughal Barlas tribe.[2] Ghulam Ahmad presented a genealogical tree detailing his descent from Mirza Hadi Beg, who was the first family member to migrate to India. Ghulam Ahmad claimed Persian descent throughout the course of his religious career, which played a crucial role in providing support for his broader spiritual mission. This claim makes his genealogy problematic, however, since the Barlas tribe of Central Asia was largely of Turkic origin with mixed Mongolian ancestry.[3] Ghulam Ahmad emphasized having a Persian lineage due to a hadith he interpreted to mean that the *mahdī* (messianic guided one) would be of Persian descent,[4] even though it conflicted with accepted views of the Barlas tribe being of Turko-Mongolian origin. Ghulam Ahmad acknowledged the contradiction but affirmed his ancestors were Persian, which he based purely on divine revelation. Other hadith have led Muslims to believe that the *mahdī* would be of Arab descent with a lineage emanating from the tribe of the Prophet.[5] Ghulam Ahmad was able to resolve the conflict once it was revealed to him that his paternal grandmothers—meaning the wives of his paternal grandfathers—possessed Arab ancestry, which stemmed from the Prophet Muhammad himself.[6]

The Barlas tribe was headed by Haji Beg Barlas, who lived in Kish, south of Samarqand, prior to the rise of Timur (Tamerlane). When the tribal leadership passed to Timur in the fourteenth century, members of the Barlas tribe moved west to Khurasan, where they remained until the sixteenth century. In 1530, Mirza Hadi Beg with some two hundred family members and attendants migrated to India, where they founded a village called Islampur, about ten miles west of the Beas River and roughly seventy miles northeast of Lahore. The village was part of a large tract of land (*jāgīr*) given to Hadi Beg by the imperial court of the Mughal emperor Babar,[7] who shared a tribal affiliation with the Barlas through Timur. Hadi Beg was granted legal jurisdiction over the area as a local *qādī* (Islamic magistrate), so the village came to be known as Islampur Qadi. The name of the village evolved into various forms based on cognates, until "Islampur" was dropped altogether, and it simply came to be known as Qadian.[8]

The original *jāgīr* encompassed over seventy neighboring villages, which was a sizable domain. Within the context of Mughal India, a large *jāgīr* more closely resembled a semi-independent territory than a family's oversized estate. As such, the head of the family, as the *jāgīrdār,* took on a feudal role which included relative sovereignty over the *jāgīr.* The privilege of local autonomy entailed that the old village of Qadian be a walled settlement, like others in India at the time. The fortress-style wall of Qadian had four towers. It stood twenty-two feet high by eighteen feet wide surrounding the homes of a standing militia. By the time of Ghulam Ahmad's great-grandfather, Mirza Gul Muhammad (d. 1800), who inherited the *jāgīr,* a considerably reduced force remained, including a cavalry and three large guns. Aside from references underscoring a military presence, Gul Muhammad's Qadian is portrayed as a place that fostered the growth of Islamic thought through generous endowments for Muslim intellectuals, despite external strife.[9]

As the Mughal stronghold faded, so did the influence of loyalist *jāgīrdār*s. When Gul Muhammad passed away, his son, Ghulam Ahmad's grandfather Mirza 'Ata Muhammad, inherited the *jāgīr.* During this period, the Sikh insurgency was gaining strength throughout the Punjab. The Sikhs steadily captured each village from the estate until only Qadian remained under the family's control. In 1802, Jassa Singh (d. 1803) and the Sikhs of the Ramgarhia *misal* (confederate state) seized Qadian.[10] The takeover resulted in the burning of the library, which housed a collection of Islamic texts, including Qur'anic manuscripts accumulated over previous generations. The main mosque was converted into a Sikh temple, which functions as such to this day. The surviving family members were expelled from Qadian and forced to take refuge in a nearby village, where they lived in exile for sixteen years. Hostilities continued between camps, resulting in the murder of Mirza ʿAta Muhammad, who was poisoned by rivals in 1814.

Ranjit Singh consolidated his rule of the Punjab in the following years, enabling the family to negotiate a deal with the Sikhs.[11] In 1818, the family, headed by Ghulam Ahmad's father, Mirza Ghulam Murtaza, was conditionally permitted to return to Qadian in exchange for military service. Ghulam Murtaza fulfilled his obligations alongside his brothers by enlisting in Ranjit Singh's army. Ahmadi accounts often stress that family members—especially Ghulam Murtaza—performed courageously in campaigns in Kashmir, Peshawar, and Multan.[12] Few mention, however, that these campaigns were fought against fellow Muslims rebelling against the Sikhs as *mujāhidīn* (those making jihad), which is important within the colonial context of the time. Sir Lepel Griffin noted in his survey of the Punjab's aristocracy that Ghulam Murtaza "was continually employed on active service" under "Nao Nahal Singh, Sher Singh, and the Darbar."[13] Sher Singh's forces stopped Sayyid Ahmad of Rai Bareilly—more commonly known as Sayyid Ahmad Barelwi or Sayyid Ahmad *shahīd* (the martyr)—and Shah Muhammad Ismaʿil, the grandson of Shah Waliullah Dehlawi, at Balakot in 1831.[14] Both iconic figures are believed to have been martyred en route to Kashmir via Peshawar during the battle. Although Mirza Ghulam Murtaza's role in these battles is unclear, he likely fought with Sikhs against Muslims, which might alarm many Ahmadis today, even though such incidents indeed occurred.

When the tours of duty finished, Ghulam Murtaza and his brothers were each given a pension of 700 rupees per annum. By the 1830s, the brothers' loyalty and services had been rewarded with the return of four villages from their ancestral estate, including Qadian. Altogether, the family managed to recover a total of seven villages from lost property in due course.[15] This process was made easier following the death of Ranjit Singh in 1839, which enabled the British to extend their rule over India in a relatively short amount of time after the First Anglo-Sikh War.

According to contemporary Ahmadi sources, Mirza Ghulam Ahmad was born in Qadian on Friday, February 13, 1835, in an atmosphere marred by the family's political and economic decline. The use of this date was a relatively late development, however, and its accuracy may be called into question. Estimates regarding Ghulam Ahmad's birthdate have varied from 1831 to 1840. In his own account, Ghulam Ahmad said that he was born in 1839 or 1840.[16] For several years during the reign of Ghulam Ahmad's second successor, the official birthdate was listed as 1836 until it was finally changed to 1835. The 1835 date has long since been accepted by Jamaʿat-i Ahmadiyya and currently appears in all official publications. The motivation for the change concerned the fulfillment of prophecies pertaining to the coming of the *mahdī* and the messiah. The 1835 date was settled by combining the indirect implications of Ghulam Ahmad's statements about the phase of the moon during his divinely ordained birth, and the assumption that his birth must have taken place on a Friday, which is widely regarded as the holiest day of the week in Islam.[17]

Ghulam Ahmad had a twin sister named Jannat who was born before him but died a few days later.[18] He grew up with a sense of remorse for his distressed father, who witnessed the withering away of the family's ancestral estate. Although the deterioration of social standing played a key role in Ghulam Ahmad's portrayal of his childhood as tragic, the family still maintained a respectable status in comparison to India's underprivileged classes. This attitude was common among prominent Muslim families of the Punjab throughout the period of colonial expansion, when successful campaigns of the Sikhs, and later the British, resulted in the steady decline of the Muslim aristocracy. The apathy and resentment shared by Muslim families regarding their waning influence in the nineteenth century has been captured by Ghulam Ahmad in numerous passages lamenting his family's losses. Ghulam Ahmad placed high value on his aristocratic background. There are indications of this in the way he occasionally signed his publications "Mirza Ghulam Ahmad, Chieftain (*ra'īs*) of Qadian."[19] In later publications, this signature was largely replaced with the accolade *masīh-i mawʿūd* (promised messiah). It still provides a sense of the importance of the sociopolitical title *ra'īs*, however, even if its use by Ghulam Ahmad was circumstantial following the disclosure of his spiritual claims. [20]

Education and Spiritual Training

Mirza Ghulam Ahmad began his education with private tutoring at age seven, which was typical for children of affluent families in rural Punjab. His first instructor was a local Hanafi tutor from Qadian named Fazl Ilahi, who taught Ghulam Ahmad the Qur'an and elementary Persian. At around age ten, Ghulam Ahmad began studying with an Ahl-i Hadith tutor named Fazl Ahmad from Ferozwala, District Gujranwala, who traveled to Qadian to teach Ghulam Ahmad intermediate Arabic grammar.[21] At around age sixteen, there was a small break in the lessons when Ghulam Ahmad married his maternal uncle's daughter, Hurmat Bibi, but he resumed his studies shortly thereafter with a Shiʿi tutor named Gul ʿAli Shah from nearby Batala. These lessons involved advanced Arabic grammar, logic (*mantiq*), and philosophy (*hikmat*).[22] In the early stages of the arrangement, Gul ʿAli Shah would travel to Qadian, but Ghulam Ahmad soon began traveling to Batala to continue his studies from there. In Batala, Ghulam Ahmad developed a close friendship with a classmate, Muhammad Husayn Batalwi, who was also studying with Gul ʿAli Shah. The two maintained their friendship long after their schooling had ended, even though Batalwi went on to hold a leading position in the Ahl-i Hadith movement, which has since become one of Jamaʿat-i Ahmadiyya's most enduring rivals. This explains why Muhammad Husayn Batalwi is best known among Ahmadis for his bitter antagonism towards Ghulam Ahmad, following the proclamation of Ghulam Ahmad's messianic claims.[23]

According to Ahmadi historians, the course of instruction received from these three tutors represents the entirety of Mirza Ghulam Ahmad's formal education and training. Ahmadi sources emphasize its simplicity in comparison to the curriculum for traditional Sunni *ʿulamā* in India at the time. If these reports are taken at face value, Ghulam Ahmad's education was based almost entirely on language acquisition, which only serves as the basis for traditional Islamic scholarship. This would make it useful to know the other subjects, if any, that Ghulam Ahmad studied in his youth. One cannot presume that Fazl Ilahi taught Ghulam Ahmad Hanafi *fiqh* (jurisprudence) simply because he was Hanafi, or that Fazl Ahmad taught Ghulam Ahmad hadith criticism simply because he was a member of the Ahl-i Hadith movement. Similarly, one cannot presume that Gul ʿAli Shah guided Ghulam Ahmad through the subtleties of the arguments pertaining to the coming of the *mahdī* simply because he was Shiʿa. This view of Ghulam Ahmad's Islamic education, or perhaps lack of education, is precisely the image that Jamaʿat-i Ahmadiyya maintains with firm resolve. When questioned about the inconsistencies in Ghulam Ahmad's religious education, Sayyid Mir Mahmud Ahmad Nasir, a prominent Ahmadi scholar and longtime principal of the Ahmadi seminary in Rabwah, made it clear that this background demonstrated Ghulam Ahmad was *ummī* (unlettered) in the same way as the Prophet Muhammad. He further elaborated that all prophets of God, including Ghulam Ahmad, received knowledge from Allah, who has knowledge of all things.[24]

Ghulam Ahmad was not linked to any religious institution, unlike the majority of scholars of the Muslim world, who typically underwent a period of formal study of traditional subjects commonly referred to as the Islamic sciences. In this sense, Ghulam Ahmad was simply not a traditional Islamic scholar, which may account for some of the methodological irregularities that developed later in his career. In contrast, even Ghulam Ahmad's first successor, Maulvi Hakim Nur al-Din (1841–1914),[25] spent a few years studying Islam formally with traditional scholars while traveling in the Middle East.[26] It is also important to recognize, however, that many notable figures in nineteenth-century South Asian Islam did not follow traditional courses of study and thus might not be considered traditional *ʿulamā* by those who maintain a certain standard of religious curriculum.[27] This is consistent with perceptions of nineteenth-century modernity as being associated with the decline of traditional *ʿulamā* and the rise of reformers throughout the Muslim world.[28] Although Ghulam Ahmad's fragmented scholastic background was not unusual for the time, it is unlikely that his language tutors provided the entirety of his religious education and training.

Aside from religious education, Ghulam Ahmad also studied medicine with his father, who was a notable *hakīm* (herbal and natural medicine doctor) in Qadian.[29] This tradition of herbal and alternative medicine has continued to evolve as a subculture within Jama'at-i Ahmadiyya and is connected to its holistic view of physical and spiritual healing. If this strand were more dominant, one could argue that these aspects of Ahmadi ideology bordered on the New Age. Most Ahmadi mosques today include homeopathic dispensaries with facilities for personal consultations.[30]

The years between Ghulam Ahmad's tutorials as an adolescent and the beginning of his mission are the most mysterious with regard to his religious education. The fact that Ghulam Ahmad had no links to a formal program of study with a specialist teacher makes it more difficult to trace influences on his thought. He appears to have jumped directly from being a grammar-intensive recluse to the spiritual reformer (*mujaddid*) of the age. During a gap of nearly twenty years, which is largely unaccounted for by Ahmadi biographers, little is mentioned apart from his solemn practice of reading and rereading the Qur'an in isolation. These issues were first raised by Spencer Lavan, who questioned "whether or not Ghulam Ahmad ever entered a sūfī order or received any specialized spiritual training common to almost all Muslim religious teachers of the times."[31]

It may be possible to better gauge Ghulam Ahmad's mastery of the traditional Islamic sciences by comparing his level of proficiency to that of other students with whom he studied. For example, if it was known that Muhammad Husayn Batalwi completed his religious education at the same time as Ghulam Ahmad, then it would be reasonable to conclude that Gul 'Ali Shah's lessons were fairly comprehensive, since Batalwi went on to become prominent scholar of the Ahl-i Hadith. It would have made it easier to accept the idea that Gul 'Ali Shah's lessons were sufficient to prepare both Batalwi and Ghulam Ahmad for subsequent religious careers, considering Batalwi's stature in the Ahl-i Hadith and Ghulam Ahmad's claims to be the "imam of the age."[32] Muhammad Husayn Batalwi's education did not end with Gul 'Ali Shah, however, since Batalwi went on to study for a number of years in Delhi before returning to Batala as a recognized Islamic scholar (*maulvi*).[33] This suggests that Ghulam Ahmad's education was neither extensive nor complete when he left the circles of Gul 'Ali Shah, which is consistent with Ahmadi sources that only focus on language acquisition.

It is not clear when Ghulam Ahmad abandoned his tutorials in pursuit of independent study. It is known that during the Mutiny of 1857 Ghulam Ahmad's older brother, Mirza Ghulam Qadir, was urged by his father, Ghulam Murtaza, to enlist in military service alongside several residents of Qadian. Given Mirza Ghulam Murtaza's own experiences in Ranjit Singh's army during his youth, the decision appears to have been an attempt to further family interests, which would likely have improved the family's situation in the event of a favorable outcome. Thus, the Qadiani faction, headed by Mirza Ghulam Qadir, joined General Nicholson's 46th Native Infantry,[34] earning the family financial remuneration and the lasting appreciation of the British.[35] The circumstances surrounding the family's support of the British during the Mutiny suggest that Ghulam Ahmad was too young in 1857 to have been pressured into military service by his father. According to his own account, Ghulam Ahmad said that he was sixteen or seventeen years old during the Mutiny of 1857, before his facial hair had begun to grow.[36] This might be why he was directed instead towards the civil service shortly thereafter.

Employment and Influences

Around 1864, Ghulam Ahmad was sent to work as a reader in the British-Indian court of Sialkot under the deputy commissioner, who was connected to his father. Sialkot was a much larger city than Qadian and had become a center for Christian missionary activity in Punjab during the nineteenth century.[37] The stay in Sialkot marked Ghulam Ahmad's first encounter with evangelical Christian missionaries, who appear to have influenced his religious outlook considerably. Ghulam Ahmad disliked the job but remained in Sialkot for a few years in the same capacity, despite his deficiencies in the language of empire. He did make an effort to learn English in Sialkot, where English-language courses were being offered to government employees as a means of professional development. According to Ahmadi missionary and biographer 'Abd al-Rahim Dard, Ghulam Ahmad completed the first two levels of an English course before he withdrew. Dard's account stresses that Ghulam Ahmad's English competence was only enough to enable him to read the alphabet and a few simple words. Dard also insists that Ghulam Ahmad forgot what he was taught once his studies had ended.[38]

The repercussions of the language courses may have carried over into the latter part of his mission, when Ghulam Ahmad began receiving revelations in English, which he wrote down in Urdu script.[39] Although these revelations were far less frequent than those he received in other languages—including Urdu, Arabic, Persian, and even Punjabi—they appeared miraculous to devoted followers, such as Lahori movement co-founder and Ghulam Ahmad's companion Maulana Muhammad 'Ali, who adamantly maintained that Mirza Ghulam Ahmad "did not know a word of English."[40] There is a sense of suspicion surrounding the English revelations, however, which is difficult for native speakers to ignore. These revelations were typically only a few words in length and often included phrases with questionable grammar. For example, one English revelation warned, "God is coming by His army. He is with you to kill enemy."[41] Other English revelations followed: "I love you. I am with you. I shall help you. I can what I will do. We can what we will do."[42] Ghulam Ahmad's English revelations were often supplemented with eloquent Urdu translations so he himself could understand the meaning. Without the translations, Ghulam Ahmad was forced to ask English speakers what the revelations meant. Although these examples are not intended to mock Mirza Ghulam Ahmad or to discredit what Ahmadis have come to associate with divine revelation, they do provide insight into what Ghulam Ahmad's understanding of "revelation" actually entailed. These conceptions of revelation will be important when considering Ghulam Ahmad's spiritual claims in the following chapter.

Ghulam Ahmad spent much of his personal time in Sialkot pursuing religious devotions. The Christian missionaries of Sialkot provided new prospects for religious dialogue with which Ghulam Ahmad was unfamiliar in Qadian. This exposure opened up new modes of thought for Ghulam Ahmad in his youth and enabled him to debate eschatology and salvation in an endeavor to prove the superiority of Islam as a religion.[43] The exchanges also provided Ghulam Ahmad with an opportunity to improve his communication skills by articulating his views, finessing his arguments, and formally expressing his beliefs—both verbally and in writing—for the first time.[44] These discussions were beneficial in many ways, especially since Ghulam Ahmad was still an amateur theologian, whereas his opponents were more experienced and better educated missionaries. His encounters with Christian missionaries facilitated a second period of spiritual growth, which enabled his thought to mature while he was working as a court reader full-time, since he was still not receiving any formal religious training. It is clear that these debates shaped the Ahmadi polemic against Christianity, which later came to define much of Ghulam Ahmad's mission.

Ghulam Ahmad's increased exposure to religious thinkers in Sialkot was not limited to Christians, but included leading Muslim intellectuals as well, such as Sir Sayyid Ahmad Khan (1817–1898), who had recently published a commentary of the Qur'an. Ghulam Ahmad was presented with a copy of Sir Sayyid's commentary by a friend—later to become *shams al-'ulamā*—Sayyid Mir Hasan (1844–1929),[45] who was teaching Arabic at the Scotch Mission College in Sialkot at the time.[46] Although Sayyid Mir Hasan is best known as the teacher of philosopher-poet Muhammad Iqbal (1877–1938), he was an avid admirer of Sir Sayyid and a companion of Mirza Ghulam Ahmad in Sialkot. Ironically, Ghulam Ahmad's main criticism of the commentary regarded Sir Sayyid's assertion that Jesus had died and hence was not alive in heaven, which eventually became a central tenet of Ahmadi Islam. Ghulam Ahmad actually maintained the orthodox view that Jesus was alive in heaven until relatively late in his career.[47] He also objected to Sir Sayyid's naturalism, because he felt that it diminished belief in miracles and replaced it with the determinism of modernist science.[48] Ghulam Ahmad published articles in response to Sir Sayyid and eventually wrote a book, *Barakāt al-Du'ā* (The Blessings of Prayer), which highlighted the miraculous effects of prayer.[49] Ghulam Ahmad's disputes with the Aligarh scholars continued throughout his career, even though he recanted his views on Jesus's physical ascension to heaven and adopted Sir Sayyid's position regarding Jesus's natural death.[50]

Another notable Muslim from this period whose relationship with Ghulam Ahmad is worth exploring is Maulvi Mahbub 'Alam, a prominent Sufi *pīr* of the Naqshbandi order who had apparently developed a close friendship with Ghulam Ahmad while living in Sialkot. The few accounts of their encounters in Ahmadi sources tend to minimize Mahbub 'Alam's Sufi affiliations and focus on their companionship, which is an unusual way of characterizing their relationship.[51] Although the nature of their relationship is unclear, one may question the extent to which the two developed a sense of camaraderie as insinuated,[52] considering Mahbub 'Alam's stature as an esteemed Sufi shaykh and Ghulam Ahmad's youth and incomplete religious training. Within the cultural context of the time, it would not have been common for an established shaykh of the Naqshbandi order,[53] such as Maulvi Mahbub 'Alam, to have regularly socialized, intermingled, or partaken in casual conversations with a young court clerk about their shared passion for Islam, even if these exchanges were rather engaging.

In accordance with the customary etiquettes associated with a prominent *pīr*, the only meaningful relationship that Ghulam Ahmad was capable of having with such a figure at this stage of his life was one of teacher and student. For this reason, it is more likely that Ghulam Ahmad approached Mahbub 'Alam as a student while exploring the intellectual landscape of Sialkot, although the formality of his instruction and the subject matter of his study remain unknown. Ghulam Ahmad seems to have grown fond of the shaykh while experimenting with the Sufi path under Mahbub 'Alam's guidance, perhaps without formally taking his *bay'at* (allegiance). Ghulam Ahmad's reluctance to take *bay'at* appears to have perturbed Mahbub 'Alam, who believed that a formal commitment to a teacher was necessary for further progress.[54] Maulvi Mahbub 'Alam may still have served as a spiritual guide for Ghulam Ahmad all the same, irrespective of whether Ghulam Ahmad was initiated into the Naqshbandi order. This makes the question of Ghulam Ahmad's *bay'at* with Mahbub 'Alam superfluous, since preliminary stages of Sufi training typically do not depend upon one's formal initiation into an order. This means that Ghulam Ahmad might never have been initiated into a Sufi order, as has always been claimed, despite the likelihood of his having gone to Mahbub 'Alam to learn Sufism.

These encounters with Muslim contemporaries provide further context for the subsequent development of Ahmadi Islam. In addition to closing the gaps in Ghulam Ahmad's biography, they challenge prevalent portrayals of his development by identifying potential influences on him while he was treading the path to prophethood. It is clear that Ghulam Ahmad came into contact with prominent scholars after the commencement of his mission, most of whom are given due recognition in Ahmadi literature, including those who viewed Jama'at-i Ahmadiyya unfavorably. While the interactions between Ghulam Ahmad and his rivals have been well documented by Ahmadi historians, the interactions between

Ghulam Ahmad and potential mentors have been repeatedly obscured. Ghulam Ahmad's biographers appear to have consistently concealed the names and religious affiliations of Muslims capable of influencing his mission in any way that would seem other than supernatural.

After a few years on his own, Ghulam Ahmad returned home to Qadian in 1867 upon receiving word of his mother's deteriorating health. Although he managed to leave Sialkot promptly, his mother, Chiragh Bibi, had passed away by the time of his arrival. Rather than return to Sialkot after her passing, Ghulam Ahmad remained in Qadian to help his father deal with ongoing legal battles pertaining to the recovery of the family estate. The new career path required increased travel to remote locations for extended periods of time. But the prospects of solitude provided Ghulam Ahmad with a welcome opportunity to continue his Islamic studies on his own. Ghulam Ahmad's legal success varied from case to case, which contributed in some capacity to the family's overall lack of ability to reestablish its previous influence in the region. Ghulam Ahmad's disinterest in worldly pursuits and his indifference towards establishing financial stability apparently created tension between him and his father. Mirza Ghulam Murtaza persuaded his son to study for the qualifying examination that would have enabled him to practice law, but Ghulam Ahmad failed the exam and soon lost interest.[55]

From Qadian, Ghulam Ahmad continued to cultivate relationships with accessible Muslim thinkers in the vicinity. His biographers relate that he visited nearby saintly people (*ahl allāh*) upon his return home, but again, few details are present in their accounts. Dost Muhammad Shahid mentioned a Sufi shaykh, Mian Sharaf al-Din, whose residence and instructional facility in Sum Sharif—near Talibpur, District Gurdaspur—was frequented by Mirza Ghulam Ahmad prior to the commencement of his mission. On one occasion, Ghulam Ahmad went to Sum Sharif to visit Mian Sharaf al-Din and also met another Sufi, Makka Shah, from Layl, near Dhariwal.[56] Dost Muhammad Shahid noted that Makka Shah later began traveling to Qadian to visit Ghulam Ahmad, perhaps to stress Ghulam Ahmad's relative seniority in the relationship. This was not unusual for Ghulam Ahmad, who enjoyed a number of visitors in Qadian, especially during his tenure as messiah. It seems peculiar, however, for Dost Muhammad Shahid to have mentioned Makka Shah in his section on the *ahl allāh* (a term that typically refers to pious mystics who are utterly devoted to God) in the same context as Mian Sharaf al-Din, which might imply a shared Sufi affiliation. It may also have been an attempt to signify Ghulam Ahmad's aptitude for attracting students of mysticism.

The final scholar mentioned in connection with Mirza Ghulam Ahmad's pre-messianic biography is Maulana 'Abdullah Ghaznavi. Biographical information on 'Abdullah Ghaznavi is available through various sources, including books published by his descendants.[57] Ghaznavi receives the most attention in Ahmadi sources among potential mentors of Ghulam Ahmad, even though his influence on Ghulam Ahmad has been minimized. For example, 'Abd al-Rahim Dard clarified that Ghulam Ahmad only visited 'Abdullah Ghaznavi twice, when he apparently presented Ghaznavi with gifts.[58] Ghulam Ahmad's own descriptions of the visits depict a much closer relationship with the prominent Ahl-i Hadith scholar,[59] as do the accounts of Dost Muhammad Shahid.[60] This discrepancy, however, may have less to do with 'Abdullah Ghaznavi himself, who passed away before Ghulam Ahmad could proclaim his mission, and more to do with the antagonistic relationship between Ghulam Ahmad and Maulana Ghaznavi's children and disciples, who later vehemently opposed Jama'at-i Ahmadiyya.

'Abdullah Ghaznavi was himself a controversial figure who was exiled from Afghanistan when local *'ulamā* declared him a *kāfir* (nonbeliever). This led to complications which prompted Ghaznavi's migration to India. Given his sudden departure from Afghanistan, it would be useful to examine the *fatwās* of *kufr* (infidelity) which led to Ghaznavi's exile, especially considering Ghulam Ahmad's shared trajectory and high regard for him. The internal sources of the Ahl-i Hadith only seem to mention that the *fatwās* pertained to 'Abdullah Ghaznavi's rejection of *taqlīd*, or strict adherence to the four Sunni schools of law (*madhhabs*). The rejection of *taqlīd* is a common feature of the Ahl-i Hadith and other reformist movements, which by itself would not typically warrant such a reaction. It would be interesting to see if the numerous revelations and esoteric insights attributed to 'Abdullah Ghaznavi by Mirza Ghulam Ahmad influenced the verdict of *kufr* against him.[61] Dost Muhammad Shahid mentioned that the *fatwās* of *kufr* were linked to Ghaznavi's interpretation of Sahih al-Bukhari—which is considered to be one of the most authentic books of hadith in Sunni Islam—and his rigid adherence to the sunna; but again, these explanations almost completely avoid the issue at hand by reasserting his Ahl-i Hadith views.[62] In any case, the role of *taqlīd* has certainly been contested within Muslim societies in recent centuries, including the Indian subcontinent where figures, such as 'Abdullah Ghaznavi, helped bolster support for developing reform movements, like the Ahl-i Hadith.

Before settling in Amritsar, 'Abdullah Ghaznavi studied the sciences of hadith in Delhi under the leading Ahl-i Hadith scholar of the time, Maulvi Nazir Husayn, a major proponent of the early movement in India. Maulvi Nazir Husayn Dehlawi took the title *shaykh al-kul* (the scholar of all) in reference to his scholarship, which not only implied a mastery of every subject but also his intellectual superiority over other Muslim scholars.[63] Shaykh al-Kul Maulvi Nazir Husayn Dehlawi also taught hadith studies to the sons of 'Abdullah Ghaznavi and other leading figures in the movement, including Sana'ullah Amritsari and Maulvi Muhammad Husayn Batalwi, once Batalwi had completed his studies with Gul 'Ali Shah.[64] It seems important that nearly all of Maulvi Nazir Husayn's

students opposed Ghulam Ahmad in later years.[65] In fact, this group of Ahl-i Hadith scholars under Maulvi Nazir Husayn Dehlawi spearheaded the opposition
to Jama'at-i Ahmadiyya by issuing the first *fatwā* of *kufr* against Ghulam Ahmad
in 1891.[66] The *fatwā* was a direct response to Ghulam Ahmad's publication of
Tawzīh-i Marām (Elucidation of Objectives), which explicitly elaborated his mission[67] and represented a milestone in Ghulam Ahmad's career by marking the
beginning of his estrangement from orthodox Islam.[68]

On a visit to Ghaznavi's village of Khayrdi, near Amritsar, Ghulam Ahmad
requested the maulana for special prayers concerning an undisclosed matter.
Upon receiving this request, Maulana Ghaznavi immediately went home and began to pray for Ghulam Ahmad. In the coming days after returning home to Qadian, Ghulam Ahmad received a letter from Ghaznavi relating a slight variation
of the following Qur'anic verse as a revelation which he had seen in a dream:[69]
"You are our Protector, so help us against the disbelievers (*anta mawlānā
fa'nsurnā 'alā 'l-qawm al-kāfirīn*)."[70] Maulana Ghaznavi interpreted the revelation to mean that Allah would help Ghulam Ahmad with his predicament, similar to the way in which Allah helped the companions of the Prophet Muhammad
through various tribulations.[71] The revelation, however, was almost identical to
the last verse of Sura al-Baqara (2:286). An overwhelming number of Ghulam
Ahmad's revelations have repeated Qur'anic verses, similar to this revelation of
'Abdullah Ghaznavi. In this light, it would be interesting to see how frequently
other recipients of divine revelation have repeated portions of the Qur'an and
claimed it as their own. If this format is unique, then perhaps it was first observed
by Ghulam Ahmad in the revelations of 'Abdullah Ghaznavi.

On a separate occasion, Ghaznavi saw a vision in which he described a light
(*nūr*) descending upon Qadian, but his children were being deprived of it.[72] This
particular revelation played a major role in Ghulam Ahmad's proclamation of
success following a *mubāhala* (prayer duel) in 1893 against 'Abdullah Ghaznavi's
son, 'Abd al-Haqq Ghaznavi.[73] The *mubāhala* ended when two supporters of
'Abd al-Haqq Ghaznavi publicly attested to having previously heard the revelation from Ghaznavi's father.[74] Following 'Abdullah Ghaznavi's passing, Ghulam
Ahmad saw a vision (*kashf*) in which the maulana was carrying a large sword
intended for killing the *kuffār* (infidels). In the vision, 'Abdullah Ghaznavi disclosed Ghulam Ahmad's true spiritual rank (*maqām*) and said that God would
make much use of him later in life.[75]

There are reminders of 'Abdullah Ghaznavi scattered throughout Ghulam
Ahmad's career, from the first *fatwā* of *kufr* to some of the last *mubāhala* challenges towards the end of his life. Consequently, many of Ghulam Ahmad's
publications directly or indirectly addressed scholars associated with 'Abdullah Ghaznavi,[76] which is another indication of the proximity of their relationship. Ghulam Ahmad's messianic claims may have been particularly offensive

to scholars who shared personal relationships with 'Abdullah Ghaznavi, which may have made it imperative for them to denounce Ghulam Ahmad's claims, since the bond between Ghulam Ahmad and Ghaznavi was well known among Ghaznavi's students. In contrast, had it been known on the contrary that Ghulam Ahmad was an insignificant or occasional correspondent of 'Abdullah Ghaznavi, perhaps Ghaznavi's disciples would have been willing to dismiss Ghulam Ahmad's prophetic claims as nonsense, rather than escalating the rivalry by inflating them with a false sense of credence. The extensive rebuttals of Ghulam Ahmad's character and Jama'at-i Ahmadiyya's mission should be seen as an attempt by Ghaznavi's disciples to maintain the sanctity of their public image once Ghulam Ahmad's views had begun to diverge from orthodox Islam. For scholars frequenting the same circles, distancing themselves from Ghulam Ahmad may have been the only way to safeguard their reputations.

The fierce reaction of Ghaznavi's followers to Ghulam Ahmad's claims is an indication of the evident affinity between Maulana 'Abdullah Ghaznavi and Mirza Ghulam Ahmad. In one instance, Ghulam Ahmad attempted to exploit his relationship with 'Abdullah Ghaznavi by claiming that Ghaznavi would have been an Ahmadi had he been alive. The audacity of this claim initiated a lengthy dispute in 1899 with another Ghaznavi son, 'Abd al-Jabbar Ghaznavi, and one of 'Abdullah Ghaznavi's disciples, Munshi Ilahi Bakhsh. Ghulam Ahmad's comments led to years of quarreling and several threats of *mubāhala* from both parties, though most went unanswered.[77] Munshi Ilahi Bakhsh eventually published *'Asā-i Mūsa* (The Staff of Moses) in 1900, containing his own revelations against Mirza Ghulam Ahmad.

Transition from Scholar to Prophet

The death of Mirza Ghulam Ahmad's father in 1876 marked a turning point in Ahmadi history. It was a major blow to Ghulam Ahmad, who no longer had a means of supporting his sequestered lifestyle. By then, Ghulam Ahmad had begun writing articles for local newspapers and journals from Qadian, though his publications did not provide a sufficient source of income and were not enough for his contemporaries to consider him a journalist, like other Muslim leaders of the era. Ghulam Ahmad made irregular contributions of a religious nature, including a number of Persian poems republished after his death in 1908.[78] He excelled in writing polemics against rival religious groups, including the Hindu Arya Samaj and Brahmo Samaj movements, as well as the Christians.

The Arya Samaj was a Hindu revivalist movement founded in 1875 by Swami Dayanand Saraswati (1824–1883). Dayanand had gained acceptance following the publication of his book *Satyārth Prakāsh* (The Light of Truth), in which he expounded the Vedas in a manner that was purportedly rational and consistent with modern science.[79] Ghulam Ahmad viewed the accomplishment as an attack on Islam and criticized theological issues related to the creation of the soul and the existence of God. He also disapproved of sanctioned rituals with moral implications, such as *niyoga*, a practice in which a couple experiencing difficulty conceiving sons invites another man into their relationship until the desired number of sons has been produced.[80] Swami Dayanand had personally established Arya Samaj branches in Amritsar and Lahore by 1877, which were both reasonably close to Qadian.[81] Although the Arya Samaj did not formally establish a branch in Qadian until 1887, confrontations with Ghulam Ahmad continued as a result of ongoing tension.

In 1877, a *sadhu* (wandering ascetic) came to Qadian to display his physical strength and natural abilities. His arrival was hailed by local Hindus who were convinced that he was an avatar of Shiva. When the situation was brought to the attention of Mirza Ghulam Ahmad, he had the "vagabond *sadhu*" promptly expelled from Qadian.[82] Similar incidents continued where Ghulam Ahmad confronted Aryas and Christians, whose missionary activities had dramatically changed the dynamics of religious rivalries in Punjab. It is clear that the relative success of Christianity in particular had contributed to the overall sense of Islamic decline among Muslim communities of South Asia. By the late nineteenth century, increasing numbers of disillusioned Muslims were turning to Christianity as a source of salvation, which only drew further attention to the disenchantment among the Muslim mainstream. The decline of Muslim rule and the deterioration of the Muslim aristocracy at the hands of the Sikhs and then later the British, along with the sheer magnitude of Christian missionaries overwhelming the Punjab, had led many Muslims to renounce their faith and embrace what appeared to be a socially, economically, and theologically superior religion. The struggle for religious domination was not new to India, but the manner in which religious movements were competing with each other was changing.[83]

The advent of modernity fostered a growing interest in rationalism that colored the religious arena. The use of reason, logic, and rational argumentation was increasingly seen as a credible means of approaching religion. The root assumptions of these debates, however, often remained irrational and still relied on miracles or an element of faith.[84] It had become necessary to present theological arguments in the style of scientific discourse, which was widely regarded as the preferred convention for evaluating truth claims. A key criticism regarding the role of Jesus in Islam ultimately went unanswered by the Muslim mainstream, while allegations were leveled against Muslims based on the Orientalist view that Islam had originated as a Christian heresy. Islam's confirmation of Christian beliefs pertaining to Jesus's ascension to heaven and the promise of his return had created a serious dilemma for many Indian Muslims. If Muhammad was indeed the superior prophet, then why was it Jesus whose arrival Muslims were awaiting? For Muslim lay intellectuals this question presupposed an even greater problem:

if Muhammad was indeed the superior prophet, then why was it Jesus who was alive in heaven while Muhammad lay buried in Medina?

From a theological perspective, these quandaries were perceived as embarrassments, and many Muslims were at a loss. Mirza Ghulam Ahmad composed his first and most celebrated book, *Barāhīn-i Ahmadiyya* (The Proofs of Islam) in response.[85] The publication of *Barāhīn* was made possible by donations from affluent Muslims in India who were recognized for their financial contributions in the acknowledgments of the book. The begum of Bhopal, Nawab Shah Jahan Begum, was the principal benefactor of the publication and was known for philanthropy.[86] She also funded the construction of the Woking mosque outside London, one of the earliest mosques in Britain, which was built in 1889.[87] The mosque later served as the first Ahmadi mission in Europe after it was acquired by one of Ghulam Ahmad's disciples, Khwaja Kamal al-Din, in 1912, prior to the Lahori-Qadiani split.[88] The begum's husband, Nawab Siddiq Hasan Khan, was a major figure in the early Ahl-i Hadith movement who similarly had made an initial commitment to sponsor the publication of *Barāhīn-i Ahmadiyya*. Upon receiving the text, however, he hastily returned the preordered copies to Qadian in fear that British authorities would not approve of the publication.[89]

Barāhīn-i Ahmadiyya was originally intended to appear as a series of fifty books which comprehensively addressed rationalist arguments in defense of Islam. Parts 1 and 2 were published in 1880, part 3 was published two years later in 1882, and part 4 soon followed in 1884. But the fifth and final part did not appear until 1905. Part 5 was essentially a new book altogether, despite sharing the title with the unfinished series. In the introduction, Ghulam Ahmad playfully remarked that his inability to produce the remaining forty-five books as promised was as insignificant as the zero that separates five from fifty.[90] *Barāhīn-i Ahmadiyya* carried the same polemic tone found in Ghulam Ahmad's later works, but without the controversial claims that have come to define his legacy. The series focused on defending the broader Islamic tradition in light of religious conflicts most relevant to nineteenth-century India. This motif was often overshadowed in later works by themes that emphasized or expounded the theology surrounding the implications of Ghulam Ahmad's spiritual claims.

The Rise of a *Mujaddid*

Ghulam Ahmad's first revelation concerning his divine appointment as *mujaddid* (religious renewer) of the fourteenth century AH appeared in part 3 of *Barāhīn-i Ahmadiyya,* but his status as such was not self-evident from the text of the revelation. In fact, Ghulam Ahmad did not proclaim his interpretation of the verse until much later. The revelation simply stated: "Say, 'I have been commissioned and I am the first of the believers'" (*qul innī umirtu wa anā awwalu 'l-mu'minīn*).[91] Even Ghulam Ahmad's Urdu explanation of the Arabic verse only implicitly addressed the claim, despite having been written in 1892, some years after he had defined the scope of his mission.[92] In claiming to be a *mujaddid,* a scholar is in effect asserting his status as the preeminent Muslim thinker of his generation and professing his work's superior ability to rejuvenate Muslim societies during that century of Islamic history. With this in mind, it may seem premature for Ghulam Ahmad to have advanced such a bold claim, considering his modest publication record prior to his ascent and his voluminous output afterwards. It is clear that Ghulam Ahmad's announcement marked the beginning of his religious career, rather than the end of it. After all, Ghulam Ahmad's status as *mujaddid* did not stem from peer recognition that drew on an appraisal of lifetime achievement, since the vast majority of his public efforts toward Islamic reform came after the publication of *Barāhīn-i Ahmadiyya.* The impact of *Barāhīn* was noticeable in small intellectual circles of the Punjab, but the book remained largely unread and unknown throughout the rest of the Muslim world. Ghulam Ahmad succeeded in gaining recognition nonetheless as a rising expert in formulating anti-Christian and anti-Hindu polemics.

Ghulam Ahmad began staging debates with leading members of the Arya Samaj, many of which failed to materialize. In 1883, he wrote a letter to Swami Dayanand and personally challenged him to a debate. Within months of the request, Dayanand had fallen ill from poisoning, shortly before his untimely death. The challenge was accepted by Munshi Indarman Muradabadi on Dayanand's behalf, but the debate never took place due to a breakdown in communication.[93] Ghulam Ahmad's first major debate with the Arya Samaj took place in March 1886 with Lala Murli-Dhar in Hoshiarpur,[94] where Ghulam Ahmad had just finished a forty-day spiritual retreat (*chilla*) consisting of prayer, self-imposed seclusion, and personal reflection.[95] The *chilla* was a common practice among Sufi orders, particularly Chishtis, who have been influential in South Asian Islam. In the debate, Lala Murli-Dhar attacked the miraculous nature of the moon-splitting event (*shaqq al-qamar*) described in the Qur'an,[96] while Ghulam Ahmad challenged Dayanand's defense of issues pertaining to the creation of souls.[97] As the allotted time expired with matters unfinished, the two attempted to negotiate a new format that would enable them to continue elaborating arguments in writing in which written responses could be read aloud before the audience. The two could not reach an agreement, however, and the challenge ended abruptly.

The Founding of Jama'at-i Ahmadiyya

By the end of 1888, Mirza Ghulam Ahmad was making arrangements to formalize his spiritual authority over his followers by accepting their *bay'at* (allegiance). This was over six years after the publication of his first divine appointment. Ahmadis note that his close companions, including Hakim Nur al-Din, among others, had requested Ghulam Ahmad to accept *bay'at* as early as 1883, but there is no explicit explanation of why Ghulam Ahmad waited so long to establish a formal community after already having claimed to be the *mujaddid* in 1882. There is evidence to suggest that the delay in accepting *bayʿat*—and hence the founding of Jamaʿat-i Ahmadiyya—was linked to the birth of his son, Mirza Bashir al-Din Mahmud Ahmad, which had been foretold to Ghulam Ahmad in an earlier prophecy. Spencer Lavan has suggested that fathering a son served the purpose of fulfilling the outstanding prophecy while providing greater confidence in the fate of the Jamaʿat by producing an heir apparent.[98]

Ghulam Ahmad had begun receiving revelations promising further progeny as early as 1881,[99] although many of them were not divulged until much later in his life. In 1884, Ghulam Ahmad married a second wife,[100] Nusrat Jahan Begum (affectionately known to Ahmadis as *ammā jān*), who was approximately thirty years his junior. This made her better suited for conception than his first wife, whose children with Ghulam Ahmad were fully grown.[101] In February 1886, Ghulam Ahmad published a divine prophecy announcing the impending birth of a blessed and illustrious son whose name would be Bashir.[102] When later that same year Ghulam Ahmad's wife gave birth to a daughter named Ismat, who died soon thereafter, opponents seized the opportunity to mock the *mujaddid*. The reaction of Pandit Lekh Ram (1858–1897), Swami Dayanand's successor in the Arya Samaj, was considered particularly offensive.[103] The predicament was made worse by the death of Ghulam Ahmad's next child, a boy named Bashir, who passed away in early November 1888. By this point, many of Ghulam Ahmad's supporters were losing faith in him since he had already issued a pamphlet dated August 1887 proclaiming that the previous prophecy had been fulfilled.[104] By December 1888, Ghulam Ahmad had issued an apologetic pamphlet explaining away the deaths of his children in an attempt to dispel the anxiety mounting among supporters.[105] Undeterred, Ghulam Ahmad had good reason to remain optimistic since his wife was pregnant once again. The third child, Mirza Bashir al-Din Mahmud Ahmad, was born on January 12, 1889, and the first *bayʿat* followed shortly thereafter, in March.

The childbirth prophecy is a sensitive issue about which polemics continue to be written to this day for several reasons. The eldest surviving boy following the deaths of Ismat and Bashir I from Ghulam Ahmad's second marriage was Mirza Bashir al-Din Mahmud Ahmad (1889–1965), whose health was poor throughout his childhood. Ghulam Ahmad's next child was a girl, Shawkat (1891–1892), who was followed by another boy in 1893. Apparently, the instability of Bashir al-Din Mahmud Ahmad's health produced enough apprehension regarding the fulfillment of the prophecy that when the next son was born, Ghulam Ahmad named him Mirza Bashir Ahmad (1893–1963). Bashir al-Din Mahmud Ahmad remained a "sickly child" with poor eyesight throughout his adolescence, which undoubtedly contributed to his academic underachievement, including a lackluster performance in school and eventual failure to pass the matriculation examination.[106] The fact that three of the first five children were boys named Bashir—two of whom survived beyond childhood and only one of whom reasonably fulfilled Ghulam Ahmad's prophecy—will never satisfy Ahmadi critics. Ahmadis choose to celebrate the adversity that Bashir al-Din Mahmud Ahmad faced during his youth as decisive proof of divine intervention overcoming insurmountable odds. When considering the accomplishments of Bashir al-Din Mahmud Ahmad during his *khilāfat* in conjunction with the fact that he arguably had greater influence on Jama'at-i Ahmadiyya than even his father, it is understandable why Ahmadis annually commemorate his birth as the fulfillment of divine prophecy.

Devout Ahmadis view the multiple deaths of Ghulam Ahmad's children as tests of faith, rather than a breach of prophecy. They believe that these trials and tribulations distinguished true believers from inferior followers with spiritual deficiencies unbefitting of members of the early Ahmadi community. As traditional interpretations suggest, only a select group of followers were privileged with membership in Jama'at-i Ahmadiyya by taking the first *bay'at* at Mirza Ghulam Ahmad's hand. Although in retrospect the childbirth prophecy might seem like a blunder, we can say with certainty that the remaining followers who came together to form the early Ahmadi community had developed a profound belief in the divine fulfillment of their spiritual expectations through the charisma of Mirza Ghulam Ahmad.

The timeline for the *bay'at* is as follows. Ghulam Ahmad issued a small pamphlet called *Tablīgh* (Announcement) in early December 1888, which contained a divine revelation commanding him to take *bay'at* from his supporters. The revelation declared that "those who pledge allegiance to you [Mirza Ghulam Ahmad] pledge allegiance to God. God's hand is over their hands (*alladhīna yubāyi'ūnaka innamā yubāyi'ūna 'llah; yadu 'llah fawqa aydīhim*)."[107] The Qur'anic verse in this revelation (48:10) is commonly used by Sufis in initiation ceremonies. Although Ghulam Ahmad had already expressed his intention to accept disciples in *Tablīgh*, the logistical details of the ceremony had yet to be arranged. People had been gossiping about the *bay'at* for some time, but the ambiguity of the leaflet made it worse. It was not until January 12, 1889, the day of his son's birth, that Ghulam Ahmad issued a second pamphlet, stipulating ten conditions for *bay'at*.[108] Within two months, Ghulam Ahmad left Qadian for Ludhiana, where he issued a third pamphlet, dated March 4, 1889. This pamphlet reiterated Ghulam Ahmad's intentions to accept *bay'at* and informed those who were interested in participating in the ceremony to begin making necessary travel arrangements in order to join him.[109] It is believed to have been in Ludhiana on March 23, 1889, when Mirza Ghulam Ahmad sat alone in a secluded room at the private estate of Munshi Ahmad Jan summoning his companions one by one to take *bay'at* at his hand. Nur al-Din, Ghulam Ahmad's closest companion and first successor (*khalīfat al-masīh*), was the first to be called. The second to take *bay'at* was Mir 'Abbas 'Ali, but his name is rarely mentioned, since he later abandoned the movement. A total of forty disciples are purported to have followed shortly thereafter.

There are discrepancies in the sources for both the date of the first *bay'at* and the number of participants.[110] Ghulam Ahmad's own handwritten account of the initiation, whose first page was mysteriously destroyed, begins with the ninth disciple on March 21, 1889, two days before the date presented in official accounts.[111] The variation in the date does not seem to affect the Jama'at's subsequent presentation of the event, even though the number of disciples initiated into the community on the first day may fluctuate significantly. Dard's account does not provide an exact number of disciples but implies that the figure was small.[112] The surviving pages of the original register list the names of forty-six disciples who took *bay'at* on March 21, which excludes the names of women. Thus, if we assume that the missing page began with the first eight names on March 21, as the remaining register suggests, then considerably more than forty disciples—both men and women—took the *bay'at* on the first day. But if the ceremony began on March 20 or before, then significantly fewer than forty initiates took *bay'at* on the first day. At any rate, Jama'at-i Ahmadiyya has been asserting that precisely forty people took *bay'at* on the first day ever since the second *khalīfa al-masīh*, Mirza Bashir al-Din Mahmud Ahmad, deemed it so.[113]

Towards a Controversial Messiah

In the following weeks, Ghulam Ahmad left Ludhiana for Aligarh, where he was scheduled to address scholars regarding the broader scope of his mission. The trip ended in disappointment when Ghulam Ahmad received divine instructions forbidding him to speak on account of his poor health. Despite repeated requests, Ghulam Ahmad refused to partake in some sort of dialogue. Had Ghulam Ahmad honored the requests, it would have been the first public presentation of his mission before reputable Muslim intellectuals at a recognized institution. Instead, the tenacity of his silence resulted in the aversion of the Aligarh scholars and general scorn from those who did not sympathize with his divine instructions.[114] The bitterness lingered after Ghulam Ahmad's departure and developed into somewhat of a grudge on the part of one mullah in particular, Muhammad Isma'il, whose disillusioning encounter with Ghulam Ahmad led to a jaded series of letters.[115]

The consequences of the anticlimactic journey to Aligarh were more apparent in the missed encounter with Sir Sayyid Ahmad Khan. Ghulam Ahmad's withdrawal at Aligarh made him the target of Sir Sayyid's jeering remarks, which ridiculed the financial stipulations that often accompanied Ghulam Ahmad's promises to skeptics to display divine miracles. Sir Sayyid even suggested that they travel to Hyderabad together where he "would go round singing his [Ghulam

Ahmad's] praises" as a disciple while Ghulam Ahmad showed false miracles.[116] They could then split whatever money they coerced from the unsuspecting masses. Although the two never entered into a meaningful exchange face-to-face, the impact of their relationship touched both camps. Ghulam Ahmad's resolve to remain silent and his refusal to make a public appearance enabled the opportunity to pass before he eventually made his way back to Qadian.

It is clear that the Aligarh scholars related Ghulam Ahmad's withdrawal to his inability to perform adequately before a gathering of 'ulamā. Although Ghulam Ahmad may seem to have been intimidated by the audience, it is impossible to know his inner motivations. Throughout his religious career, Ghulam Ahmad repeatedly demonstrated an overwhelming ability to sustain criticism, which at times was abusive. His unwavering conviction in his mission never prevented him from proclaiming his message, which does not necessarily mean that he should have presented his views in a public debate. Ghulam Ahmad failed in the end to exploit a rare opportunity to discuss his interpretation of Islam on an exceptionally grand stage.

The standoff at Aligarh has similarities to other instances in which Ghulam Ahmad either avoided or significantly postponed potential debates with opponents. As mentioned above, Ghulam Ahmad challenged Swami Dayanand to a debate, which was taken up by Munshi Indarman Muradabadi after Dayanand's death. But the debate never took place. On a separate occasion in 1885, Pandit Lekh Ram made the journey to Qadian, solely to confront Ghulam Ahmad in a public debate. Once again, a meaningful discourse never materialized because the two could not agree upon the procedures for distributing the monetary prize that was to be awarded to the victor.[117] In 1900, a stalemate transpired with Pir Mehr 'Ali Shah Golrawi, who traveled from Rawalpindi to Lahore for a public debate at Ghulam Ahmad's request. Again, Ghulam Ahmad never turned up.[118] In May 1892, Muhammad Husayn Batalwi pledged to bring a Sufi scholar to Qadian to debate Ghulam Ahmad. This debate never took place because Batalwi apparently refused to disclose the scholar's name.[119] In this manner, Ghulam Ahmad's behavior was inconsistent. At times, he hurled himself into religious confrontations by openly challenging anyone who denounced his claims to a mubāhala (prayer duel),[120] while at other times he balked without reason at the opportunity to vindicate his claims.

Ghulam Ahmad appears to have developed a strong preference for choosing formats which enabled him to write responses before having them read aloud by a reader. He also appears to have had a tendency to elude improvisational encounters whose arrangements required verbal responses to objections as they arose. It is possible that he may have made a conscious effort to avoid debating fellow Muslims in the early stages of his career. Yet there is no clear pattern explaining his rationale. Ghulam Ahmad's meticulous choice of opponents, like his final decision at Aligarh, is ultimately inexplicable. Perhaps Ghulam Ahmad felt that the Aligarh environment was better suited for a modernist scholar than a *mujaddid,* or perhaps he was simply obeying his revelations as he claimed. It could conceivably seem strange for recipients of divine revelation or prospective prophets of God to hold lectures at universities. It is possible that in anticipation of his claims Ghulam Ahmad wished to dissociate himself from this particular genre of scholars in lieu of something more spiritual. In any case, all that remains of the Aligarh incident is an account of Ghulam Ahmad's poor health and a divine command forbidding him to speak.

It is known that Mirza Ghulam Ahmad suffered from various chronic illnesses throughout his religious career. In 1890, the year after the *bay'at,* he became seriously ill, and rumors of his death began to circulate.[121] When he recovered from the illness, Ghulam Ahmad began writing his next series of works, *Fath-i Islām* (Victory of Islam), *Tawzīh-i Marām* (Elucidation of Objectives), and *Izāla-i Awhām* (Removal of Suspicions). The trilogy was published in 1891 as companion treatises, reflecting Ghulam Ahmad's first attempt at expounding the implications of his revelations.[122] The publication also marked the dawn of a new era of Ahmadi history, which corresponded to the launch of Ghulam Ahmad's messianic career. Ghulam Ahmad explained in these books how he was a *muhaddath,* which meant that God was speaking to him through some means of revelation. He also asserted his joint status as the promised messiah (*masīh*) and *mahdī* (guided one) sent in the spirit of Jesus son of Mary. This entailed that Jesus was not alive in heaven as the majority of Muslims believed. Ghulam Ahmad was aware that this claim in particular would elicit objections from orthodox Muslims, so he preemptively sought to clarify how the physical body of Jesus would not return as expected. Ghulam Ahmad spent the next seventeen years of his career engaged in a bitter controversy with Muslims who rejected these claims.

Although Ghulam Ahmad continued to attack misguided members of other religious traditions, Jama'at-i Ahmadiyya eventually settled into a sectarian debate with Islam. Much of the Ahmadi understanding of Islam is based on the messianic claims of Mirza Ghulam Ahmad, which thereby have had a profound impact on the development of the contemporary Ahmadi identity. We shall turn our attention at this point towards Ghulam Ahmad's messianic claims and the finer points of Ahmadi theology.

2 The Prophetic Claims of Mirza Ghulam Ahmad

Mirza Ghulam Ahmad's Primary and Secondary Claims

Mirza Ghulam Ahmad's education and spiritual training shaped the way in which he understood and expressed his religious experiences. His spiritual claims were complex, with subtle nuances that developed over the course of his life, but the controversy surrounding his claims is in many ways what makes his mission most interesting. Any serious analysis of Ghulam Ahmad's claims must account for changes in interpretation that have taken place over time. The expansion of these claims did not come to an end with Ghulam Ahmad's death, but rather continued through successive generations of Ahmadi interpreters who framed and articulated these claims differently. The ambiguous and sometimes paradoxical nature of Ghulam Ahmad's Sufi-style metaphysics has led to divergent opinions about him. His views on theological issues are often presented analytically, whereas in actuality they are difficult to assess. The controversial aspects of Ahmadi Islam are less a result of Ghulam Ahmad's primary spiritual claims and more a result of consequential inferences from—or secondary implications of—what his primary claims seem to entail. The best example of this is the case of Ghulam Ahmad's prophethood itself, which was, surprisingly, not one of his primary spiritual claims. Similarly, Ghulam Ahmad's rejection of violent jihad and his insistence upon Jesus's survival of crucifixion were consequences of his claim to be the promised messiah. To better understand Ghulam Ahmad's mission and appreciate how he became a prophet of God, one must evaluate the religious background of his primary spiritual claims alongside what they entail.

Mirza Ghulam Ahmad's claims were intended to assert his role in the world and delineate his spiritual rank. He claimed to be a *muhaddath,* someone to whom God speaks; a *mujaddid,* a renewer of Islam; the *mahdī,* a figure known as the guided one who will return in the latter days; and the *masīh-i mawʿūd,* or the promised messiah widely regarded as the second coming of Jesus son of Mary.

His joint status as the *mahdī* and *masīh* led to the most recognizable aspects of his mission with theological implications that have since defined his legacy in Islamic history. It is clear that Ghulam Ahmad understood his function in terms of the long-awaited fulfillment of divine prophecy. This served as the basis for the broader scope of his mission of spiritual purification and Islamic revival. The process of drawing connections, however, that enabled members of Jama'at-i Ahmadiyya to acknowledge, accept, and adhere to Ghulam Ahmad's claims within a familiar Islamic framework was something that needed to be developed—and then further elaborated—much later. These developments have since laid the foundation for the current Ahmadi identity, and so we shall first look at the spiritual claims as they were presented in their original form.

Jesus as the Promised Messiah

In the western Christian context, there is perhaps nothing more provocative about Ahmadi Islam than Mirza Ghulam Ahmad's account of Jesus's survival of crucifixion. By maintaining that Jesus Christ survived the crucifixion, Ahmadis conclude that Jesus could neither have been resurrected nor could he have ascended to the heavens. This stance was intended to undermine the very basis for the Christian belief that Jesus died for the sins of humanity. If Jesus did not die for the sins of humanity and is not alive in heaven, then according to Mirza Ghulam Ahmad there is no viable reason to remain Christian. Ghulam Ahmad was convinced that he could prove that Islam was superior to Christianity as a religion if he proved that Jesus survived the crucifixion.

It is important to appreciate this rationale within the context of the rivalry between Islam and Christianity in nineteenth-century India.[1] The rivalry was a major concern for Indian Muslims who felt threatened by advances of Christian missionaries, particularly in Punjab. The sociopolitical context of the colonial experience provided an appropriate backdrop for Ghulam Ahmad to fulfill his role as the *mahdī* and to metaphorically "break the cross," as many believed the *mahdī* was supposed to do. The advent of modernity had aroused interest in rationality, which undoubtedly shaped the delivery of Ghulam Ahmad's message. With this in mind, Ghulam Ahmad believed that it was possible to prove Christianity was a baseless religion and convince people of Islam's truth, purely through rational argumentation and logical proofs. It is important to recall, however, that Christianity was not his only target. Throughout his career, Ghulam Ahmad devoted considerable attention to debunking Hinduism as well. In fact, he had been using logical argumentation since his first major work, *Barāhīn-i Ahmadiyya* (The Proofs of Islam), the first part of which was published in 1880, nine years before his Jama'at was founded.

Aside from the general dismantling of a fundamental doctrine of Christianity, Ghulam Ahmad needed to prove that Jesus, as the first messiah, was not alive in heaven awaiting his final return. Otherwise, Ghulam Ahmad could not claim to be the second messiah since the first messiah was alive. This argument is equally important to mainstream Muslims who maintain that Jesus will descend from the heavens in the latter days and fight evil alongside the *mahdī*. Accordingly, Ghulam Ahmad's claim to be the second coming of Jesus depends on there being no other messiahs standing by in heaven awaiting return.

These ideas were first expounded by Ghulam Ahmad in 1891 with the publication of the trilogy *Fath-i Islām* (Victory of Islam), *Tawzīh-i Marām* (Elucidation of Objectives), and *Izāla-i Awhām* (Removal of Suspicions).[2] The details of Jesus's survival of crucifixion were first presented purely as intellectual arguments based largely on textual interpretations of the Qur'an, hadith, and the Bible. A substantial breakthrough came, however, when Ghulam Ahmad was able to identify a burial tomb in Srinagar, Kashmir, as the final resting place of Jesus. In providing an actual tomb for Jesus, Ghulam Ahmad could now show conclusively that Jesus had died a natural death and would never return in the flesh as the promised messiah of the latter days. The extraordinary journey of Jesus upon surviving crucifixion was the basis for Ghulam Ahmad's book *Masīh Hindustān Meñ* (Jesus in India), which was not published until 1908 despite its having been written in the late 1890s.[3]

The book was heavily influenced by the work of a Russian traveler, Nicolas Notovitch, who spent time studying Buddhist texts in Tibetan monasteries. This enabled Notovitch to conclude that Jesus had traveled through Afghanistan, India, and then on to Tibet prior to his crucifixion.[4] The timeline for the journey was rejected by Ghulam Ahmad and restructured around the notion that Jesus had indeed traveled to India, but only after crucifixion, and then on to Kashmir where he died at age 120. Over the past century, these arguments have been expanded considerably and are best outlined in a late-twentieth-century work by Ghulam Ahmad's fourth successor and grandson, Mirza Tahir Ahmad (1928–2003), called *Christianity: A Journey from Facts to Fiction*. This restatement of Ghulam Ahmad's original premise relies more heavily on contemporary medical evidence than obscure interpretations of scripture or ancient religious texts.

A synopsis of the current position begins with the assertion that it is impossible for any human being to physically ascend to heaven.[5] It may be worth mentioning here that most Ahmadis would also reject the physical ascent of the Prophet Muhammad to heaven during the night journey (*isrā* and *mi'rāj*). To explain the whereabouts of Jesus, Ahmadis argue that Jesus did not die from crucifixion, even though he was indeed hung on the cross and crucified. The problem with this position for many mainstream Muslims is that it appears to be a direct contradiction of the Qur'an. This can be illustrated quite clearly by comparing different translations of the Qur'anic account of the crucifixion. Abdel Haleem translates the crucifixion verse like this:

... and [they] said, "We have killed the Messiah, Jesus, son of Mary, the Messenger of God." (They did not kill him, nor did they crucify him, though it was made to appear like that to them; those that disagreed about him are full of doubt, with no knowledge to follow, only supposition: they certainly did not kill him ...)[6]

Ahmadis favor a more creative rendition of the crucifixion verse, which is most apparent in the interpretive translation by Malik Ghulam Farid:

And *for* their saying, "We did slay the Messiah, Jesus, son of Mary, the Messenger of Allāh"; whereas they slew him not, nor did they bring about his death on the cross, but he was made to appear to them like *one crucified;* and those who differ therein are certainly in a *state of* doubt about it; they have no *certain* knowledge thereof, but only pursue a conjecture; and they did not arrive at a certainty concerning it.[7]

In the Ahmadi interpretation, Jesus did not hang on the cross long enough to die from crucifixion. Ahmadis argue that death by crucifixion is a long and painful process, which is precisely why it was used by the Romans as a method of intimidation and torture. Death by crucifixion involves a process which could have easily been drawn out for several days, if not longer. A person may continue to hang on the cross for an indefinite period of time until the innards ultimately collapse and bring about an excruciating death. Ahmadis argue that if Jesus was crucified on a Friday afternoon, then he could not have died by crucifixion, since it was Jewish custom to remove the crucified bodies before the Sabbath, which begins at sunset. Consequently, Jesus could only have hung on the cross for a few hours at most, which was not enough time to bring about his death by crucifixion, thereby making it less likely that he died on the cross.[8] Similarly, Ghulam Ahmad explained that the other two men who were crucified alongside Jesus did not die either, which is why their legs needed to be broken according to the Biblical account in John 19:31–34.[9] In contrast, Jesus's legs were not broken because he was believed to be dead. Here, Ahmadis argue that Jesus was still alive, but in an unconscious state. This view is commonly referred to as the swoon theory by survival enthusiasts.

The Biblical account describes a soldier who pierced Jesus's side, prompting blood and water to gush out. According to Ghulam Ahmad, this description proves that Jesus was still alive after crucifixion, since dead bodies would not bleed profusely when stabbed once the heart had stopped beating. Instead, blood begins to congeal, which prevents it from rushing forth with the same vigor, especially following a traumatic crucifixion in which large nails through the hands and feet have allowed it to drain from the limbs on its own. Ghulam Ahmad was convinced that the way in which the Bible described Jesus's bleeding after being stabbed substantiated the fact that he was still alive with his heart still beating, even though he was unconscious and appeared dead to onlookers.

The Ahmadi translation of the next verse, which describes Jesus's ascension to heaven following the crucifixion, is also worth comparing to non-Ahmadi translations. Abdel Haleem translated the verse: "God raised him [Jesus] up to Himself (*rafa'ahu 'llāhu ilayhi*)."[10] The Ahmadi translation of the verse reads: "On the contrary, Allāh exalted him [Jesus] to Himself."[11] The traditional interpretation—as seen when comparing the two translations—is that Jesus was physically raised to the heavens. This view is consistent with the Christian account of Jesus's ascension. The Ahmadi rendition reinterprets the verse to show that Jesus was only raised in spiritual status and not raised physically to the heavens. In his commentary on the verse, Malik Ghulam Farid says:

> The Jews exultingly claimed to have killed Jesus on the cross and thus to have proved that his claim to be a Divine Prophet was not true. The verse along with the preceding one contains a strong refutation of the charge and clears him of the insinuated blemish and speaks of his spiritual elevation and of his having been honoured in the presence of God. There is absolutely no reference in the verse to his physical ascension to [the] heavens. It only says that God exalted him towards Himself which clearly signifies a spiritual exaltation, because no fixed abode can be assigned to God.[12]

The commentary on the verse reinforces the Ahmadi position that Jesus died a natural death unrelated to crucifixion. Interestingly, some non-Ahmadis have also interpreted this verse similarly and concluded that Jesus was not physically raised to the heavens. For example, Muhammad Asad states in his Qur'anic commentary:

> The verb *rafa'ahu* (lit., "He raised him" or "elevated him") has always, whenever the act of *raf'* ("elevating") of a human being is attributed to God, the meaning of "honouring" or "exalting." Nowhere in the Qur'ān is there any warrant for the popular belief that God has "taken up" Jesus bodily, in his lifetime, into heaven. The expression of "God exalted him unto Himself" in the above verse denotes the elevation of Jesus to the realm of God's special grace—a blessing in which all prophets partake, as is evident from 19:57, where the verb *rafa'nāhu* ("We exalted him") is used with regard to the Prophet Idrīs.[13]

Asad goes on to reference the prominent Egyptian reformer Muhammad 'Abduh, who held similar views regarding Jesus's bodily ascension. Other commentators on the Qur'an have also denied Jesus's bodily ascension, although most of them, including Sir Sayyid Ahmad Khan, tend to be modernists with an aversion to miraculous explanations.

Ghulam Ahmad uncovered the existence of a special medicinal ointment known as the *marham-i 'īsā* (ointment of Jesus). When Jesus was taken down from the cross and enshrouded before burial, a medicinal ointment, the *marham-i 'īsā*, was allegedly applied to his wounds. Ghulam Ahmad pondered why anyone would apply a medicinal ointment to the wounds of a dead body. Ghulam Ahmad soon became convinced that the application of the *marham-i 'īsā* to Jesus's wounds decisively showed that some disciples must have known that Jesus was still alive following the crucifixion. He cited over thirty books which mentioned the *marham-i 'īsā*, the formula for preparing its mixture, and its intended uses.[14] He also claimed that the medicine could still be used to treat boils, ulcers, and the plague.[15]

Although the notion of dressing the wounds of the dead may be counterintuitive, the historical authenticity of the *marham-i 'īsā* is difficult to verify. I was unable to find further discussion of the *marham-i 'īsā* in more appropriate sources, such as in the works of scholars of early Christianity, regarding the origins and intended uses of the *marham-i 'īsā* in relation to the crucifixion of Jesus.[16] Even though the name of the ointment suggests some link to Jesus, the original *marham-i 'īsā* might not have been used to dress Jesus's wounds after crucifixion. Many products, including miracle ointments, have been falsely attributed to great religious figures, like Jesus, in the past. It is difficult to find references to the ointment of Jesus prior to the medieval period, aside from the expected accounts of perfumes and oils routinely used in ancient burials. For this reason, there are no conclusive testimonials to substantiate the origins of the *marham-i 'īsā* and Ghulam Ahmad's claim.

Ghulam Ahmad used a number of textual sources to construct an argument which demonstrated that Jesus did not die on the cross. He also attempted to corroborate the evidence with something more substantial in plain view. Ghulam Ahmad believed that Jesus journeyed east after the crucifixion in order to escape further persecution and to reunite the lost tribes of Israel. Jesus continued traveling east through present-day Afghanistan and on to India, where he finally settled in Kashmir. Ghulam Ahmad identified the shrine of an old saint in Khaniyar, Srinagar, as the actual tomb of Jesus. Local legend apparently attributes the tomb to an ancient "Hebrew prophet" who came to Kashmir from a distant land around the time of the crucifixion.[17] The prophet buried in the tomb is called Yus Asaf, which Ghulam Ahmad believed to be a corrupted Hebrew variant of Jesus as "the gatherer of people (*jamā'at ko ikatthā karne wālā*)" in reference to a Biblical account of Jesus bringing people together.[18]

Evidently, locals in Srinagar had independently attributed the tomb to Jesus for some time, which fitted neatly into Ghulam Ahmad's crucifixion survival theory. By producing an actual tomb, Ahmadis believe that they have tangible archaeological evidence in support of the messiah's death. Once again, it would be difficult to argue that Jesus is alive in heaven while his corpse is enshrined in Kashmir. Likewise, demonstrating that Jesus died a natural death is critical for Ahmadi Islam, since the belief in Jesus's physical ascension to heaven is incompatible with Ghulam Ahmad's messianic claim. In this sense, Mirza Ghulam

Ahmad may only become the second messiah when the first messiah is known to be dead, irrespective of the authenticity of the tomb in Kashmir.

In the Footsteps of the Prophets

In claiming to be the second coming of Jesus, Mirza Ghulam Ahmad was making an intrinsic claim to prophethood. It followed that since Jesus was a prophet in his first appearance, he would remain a prophet in his second appearance unless he was somehow demoted or stripped of his prophetic status. Ghulam Ahmad's claim to be the *mahdī* did not carry the same implications, even though he argued that the *mahdī* and the *masīh* would be the same person,[19] as other Muslim scholars had done before him.[20] Ghulam Ahmad's implicit claim to prophethood was expounded at length throughout his career, but it had been present in his writings in some form since at least the early 1890s. His previous claims of receiving revelation from God were not as controversial as claiming to be the promised messiah, and hence did not elicit the same backlash from Muslim critics.

Revelation exists in many forms in the Islamic tradition. The language used to describe revelation varies from different types of divine inspiration to true dreams, none of which are considered sufficient for prophethood. Ghulam Ahmad's awareness of these subtleties made reconciling his claims more difficult for his contemporaries, since he never openly claimed prophethood in the way that one might expect a prophet of God would do. Instead of making a forthright claim, Ghulam Ahmad would either qualify his claims with elaborate explanations or contextualize his prophecy with references to themes contrary to notions of prophethood in Islam, which only added to people's confusion. Even in retrospect, making sense of the totality of these claims throughout Ghulam Ahmad's career is a challenge due to numerous contradictions, deliberate ambiguity, and the general ambivalence with which Ghulam Ahmad evasively expressed his ideas. The linguistic façade created by intermittent jumps from Urdu prose to Arabic verse to Persian poetry added yet another layer of complications. This has made English translations that adequately express the subtleties in Ghulam Ahmad's writing rather difficult, especially since each language has its own terminology with unique connotations for prophecy and revelation. It may be worth mentioning, however, that the linguistic complexity found in Ghulam Ahmad's works is as emblematic of Muslim writing in nineteenth-century South Asia as it is a display of Ghulam Ahmad's literary mastery.

In English, a prophet may be defined as someone who merely prophesizes the future. In an Islamic context, this is not the case. The terminology of revelation in the Islamic tradition denotes certain qualitative distinctions in spiritual rank, especially in certain strands of Sufism. An average Muslim may receive divinely inspired revelations that correctly prophesize the future. But this type of revelation does not entail prophethood in the traditional sense, even though one may describe it as such in English. Understanding the context of passages insinuating prophecy through the use of revelation terminology while navigating the religious undertones in Ghulam Ahmad's writing is perhaps the key to making sense of his theology. This type of technical jargon was typically only used with great care and with an appreciation for sensitive distinctions in religious symbolism. Ghulam Ahmad's writing style tended to mix specialized terms, however, and augment their traditional usages. This may have been a technique used to add literary value to his writing, but it makes analysis of his ideas less precise. We shall now look at examples of how Ghulam Ahmad made figurative imagery of religious terminology and symbolism overlap.

In *Fath-i Islām* (Victory of Islam), Mirza Ghulam Ahmad claimed to be a *mujaddid-i dīn* (renewer of the faith) similar to the other *mujaddids* (renewers) from previous centuries. In defining the role of *tajdīd-i dīn* (religious renewal), he stated that a *mujaddid* becomes the deputy (*nā'ib*) and successor (*khalīfa*) of the Prophet Muhammad, the inheritor of all the blessings of the messengers and prophets, and one whose heart is illuminated with revelation (*ilhām*) from God with guidance from the Holy Spirit (*rūh al-quds*).[21] Each trait individually represents a bold claim for any saintly Muslim, including a *mujaddid*, even if they are not presented consecutively in this fashion, which might seem somewhat ostentatious. These characteristics have distinct connotations which normally would never be combined in such a configuration. As a result, Ghulam Ahmad's conceptualization of a *mujaddid* seems rather excessive, yet it is presented as routine fact. One may choose to treat Ghulam Ahmad's presentation of the traits of a *mujaddid* as hyperbole, even though it would be difficult to defend this view within the context of the justifications for these claims throughout the body of the text. Ghulam Ahmad went on to distinguish himself from predecessors and show why his rank was higher than that of previous *mujaddids*. In the end, he proclaimed his own advent as the second messiah in the same image as the first, Jesus son of Mary.[22]

The second coming of Jesus is something that the Muslim *umma* has anticipated for centuries. Ghulam Ahmad made use of the discourse on *mujaddids* and the second coming of Jesus to introduce his claim to be the promised messiah modeled after the first messiah, Jesus. He began by elaborating hypothetical expectations of the second messiah in the third person, before proclaiming that the criteria had been fulfilled and staking his claim. Maintaining these types of ambiguities and utilizing contradictions was part of Ghulam Ahmad's writing style. Within the same footnote in which he claimed prophethood, Ghulam Ahmad rebutted his own claim and denied his prophetic status. Ghulam Ahmad would often claim to be a prophet in a context that was contrary to prophethood by advancing concepts with divergent connotations or by presenting his ideas through contradictory claims. In one example, he claimed to be both a *muhaddath* (one spoken to by God), which is a non-prophet, and the *khalīfat-ullāh* (representative of God on Earth), a term repeatedly used in the Qur'an to describe prophets, if not all of humanity. For example, in 2:30 Adam is called a *khalīfa*. In 38:26 David is called a *khalīfa*. In 27:62 the term refers to everyone collectively. Typically, an ordinary *muhaddath* would not be connected with the *khalīfat-ullāh*, since the two terms have different connotations and little to do with each other in the traditional sense.[23] Within a few pages of this early treatise, Mirza Ghulam Ahmad made a number of distinct, yet often conflicting, spiritual claims that are difficult to reconcile.

It may be tempting at first glance to dismiss Ghulam Ahmad's claims as a reflection of his unfamiliarity with the Islamic tradition, even though he was fully aware of the traditional usages of the terms. It is in part a result of this confusion that polarized views of Ghulam Ahmad's claims have always existed. Most scholars thus far have treated each claim individually under the presumption that Ghulam Ahmad claimed to be either a *muhaddath*, or a *mujaddid*, or the *mahdī*, or the messiah, or a prophet, similar to the way in which they were first presented above. This is primarily a result of similar treatment in Ahmadi sources, which tend to view each individual claim as a new stage of spiritual progress attained by Ghulam Ahmad. This approach to a large extent reflects Yohanan Friedmann's illuminating analysis of Ghulam Ahmad's claims in his seminal work, *Prophecy Continuous*,[24] where the focus is centered on providing the medieval background of Ghulam Ahmad's thought. In contrast, however, it seems more appropriate to treat these terms as a singular reflection of Ghulam Ahmad's spiritual ascent, demonstrating the sheer uniqueness of his spiritual status. I would argue that the totality of this unprecedented combination of divinely bestowed honors truly reflected Ghulam Ahmad's extraordinary self-image. He unreservedly propagated his mission and teachings in this fashion with no regard for potential inconsistencies. He saw his status as exceptional, august, and utterly unique, wholly different from those who came before him. He believed that he was the fulfillment of all previous divine prophecies of the latter days and the culmination of every true religious tradition.

Nevertheless, the condemnation of Ghulam Ahmad's claim to prophethood by the Indian *'ulamā* did not go unnoticed. It is possible that unfavorable reactions to Ghulam Ahmad's presentation of his spiritual status and divine commission may have persuaded him to soften expositions of his self-image in public. As opposition mounted, Ghulam Ahmad felt obliged to elaborate his position further. By the publication of his following book, *Tawzīh-i Marām* (Elucidation of Objectives), Ghulam Ahmad had withdrawn into a more apologetic tone. A complete reversal following such extravagant claims was problematic and would have damaged his credibility as a scholar. On the other hand, continuing to defend such unconventional claims was not an effective way of increasing his followers, even if he believed them to be true. If Ghulam Ahmad did not believe his claims to be true in the fullest sense, however, he had a responsibility to acknowledge his eccentricity and to clarify the confusion, as the title of the book suggests.

Ghulam Ahmad's awareness of the unsettled situation resulted in a detailed discussion on the prophetic rank of the second messiah. Ghulam Ahmad argued once again that since Jesus was a prophet of God during his first appearance in the world, it follows that he ought to be a prophet during his second appearance. Interestingly, in *Tawzīh-i Marām* Ghulam Ahmad treated this rationale as an objection to his being the second manifestation of Jesus. His reasoning demonstrated awareness of clear physical differences between himself and the first messiah, which also implies acknowledgment that he was not really a prophet. He began replying to this objection by mentioning that the Prophet Muhammad never explicitly made prophethood a requisite for Jesus in his second coming.[25] Ghulam Ahmad conceded that if hadith or Qur'anic verses existed referring to the prophethood of Jesus in his second coming, he would not be able to make such a claim. Next, Ghulam Ahmad went on to say that there was no doubt that God had designated Jesus in his second coming as a *muhaddath* for the *umma,* "and a *muhaddath* in one sense is actually a prophet (*awr muhaddath bhī ek ma'ne se nabī hī hotā hay*)."[26] He explained that this prophethood was not complete but was partial (*juzwī*) prophethood, since a *muhaddath* is spoken to by God and given insights about the unseen. He added that a *muhaddath* has revelations (*wahy*) which are free from satanic corruption, similar to the revelation (*wahy*) of prophets and messengers.[27] A *muhaddath* is appointed by God, knows the essence of the *sharī'a,* and must publicly proclaim his mission. Ghulam Ahmad also warned that a divine punishment was predestined for anyone who rejected a *muhaddath.*[28] In conclusion, Ghulam Ahmad proclaimed that he was that messianic *muhaddath* who had been sent by God in the image of Jesus.[29]

This is a rather elaborate way of divulging one's divine appointment and proclaiming one's prophethood. Ghulam Ahmad's reluctance to claim prophethood straightforwardly may have been a result of his awareness of the incompatibility of such a claim with orthodox Islam, even though the basic claim of being a *muhaddath* is in itself acceptable, particularly in Sufi strands of thought commonplace in the South Asian tradition. The existence of a *muhaddath* after the death of the Prophet Muhammad is not incompatible with Islamic orthodoxy, but Ghulam Ahmad's expansion of the qualities of a *muhaddath* were colored with the perfections of prophethood in such a way that they inappropriately overlapped.

Was Mirza Ghulam Ahmad a Prophet: Yes or No?

It is not surprising that by 1891, only two years after he began taking *bay'at* (allegiance) and accepting disciples, people were still confused about Mirza Ghulam Ahmad's mission and spiritual status. It is surprising, however, that more than a decade after the formation of Jama'at-i Ahmadiyya, his own Ahmadi disciples were still unsure about his spiritual status relating to prophethood. In 1901, the confusion of Ahmadis about the spiritual status of their leader prompted Ghulam Ahmad to write *Ek Ghalatī kā Izāla* (The Correction of an Error), in which he attempted, once again, to clarify his spiritual claims to followers. At present, the Qadiani branch of the Jama'at treats this short booklet as the definitive tract affirming Ghulam Ahmad's prophethood, while the Lahori branch in contrast uses *Ek Ghalatī kā Izāla* to show that Ghulam Ahmad denied being a prophet. The two branches use the same booklet to draw opposite conclusions. The only reason why this is possible is that Ghulam Ahmad's presentation of his prophetic status remained muddled with contradictions, with clear statements affirming his prophetic status and clear statements denying it.

The booklet opens with a personal anecdote of Ghulam Ahmad reprimanding one of his disciples who was confused about the claims of his mentor. When the Ahmadi disciple was confronted by a doubter with objections to Ghulam Ahmad's claim to be a prophet (*nabī*) and a messenger (*rasūl*), the disciple rejected the claim to prophethood without hesitation. Ghulam Ahmad warned that simply denying his prophetic status outright (*mahz inkār*) was wrong.[30] He explained his position by stating that his revelations contained words such as *nabī, rasūl, mursal,* and *nazīr,* which referred to prophets, messengers, and warners, and thereby affirmed his status as a prophet of God. Ghulam Ahmad went on to address the Qur'anic designation of the Prophet Muhammad as *khātam al-nabiyyīn* (the seal of the prophets),[31] which, even in the context in which Ghulam Ahmad was using it, implied that Muhammad was the last prophet of God.[32] If this is true, however, and Muhammad was indeed the last prophet, then it raises questions about how these types of prophetic revelations were possible and how Ghulam Ahmad could continue claiming to be a prophet. This was Ghulam Ahmad's response:

> The answer is precisely that without a doubt in this way no prophet, new or old, can come (*is kā jawāb yahī hay ke beshak is tarah to ko'ī nabī nayā ho ya purāna nahīñ ā-saktā*).[33]

Following a brief rejection of the popular belief regarding Jesus returning from the heavens, Ghulam Ahmad supported the orthodox position by citing the famous hadith declaring that "there is no prophet after me (*lā nabiyya ba'dī*)," in reference to Muhammad being the last prophet. He explained that all doors of prophethood were closed except one, which was *fanā fī 'l-rasūl* or annihilation of one's being through total obedience to the Prophet Muhammad.[34] It may be worth mentioning here that the concept of *fanā* (annihilation of the self) has long since been associated with Sufism but is rarely associated with Mirza Ghulam Ahmad.[35] This raises the question of whether Ghulam Ahmad's experience of *fanā* influenced the formulation of his controversial claims in ways other than those he suggested. If this were the case, then his claims of prophethood may have been no more than ecstatic statements based on euphoric mystical experiences that need not be taken literally. There is certainly a precedent for this in countless statements of intoxicated Sufis who preceded Ghulam Ahmad and notoriously claimed similar mystical experiences of the Divine. It is not surprising that Ghulam Ahmad most frequently justified his position by almost exclusively referencing Sufi scholars before him. Most notably, Ghulam Ahmad relied heavily on ideas developed by the Sufi masters Ibn al-ʿArabi and Shaykh Ahmad Sirhindi to defend his position that prophethood following the death of Muhammad was permissible in Islam.[36]

Ghulam Ahmad proceeded to describe his prophethood as *zillī* (shadowy) or *burūzī* (manifestational), which meant that it was dependent upon the prophethood of Muhammad. Ghulam Ahmad believed that it was only through his experience of *fanā fī 'l-rasūl*, resulting from complete submission to the Prophet Muhammad, that his prophethood had any meaning whatsoever.[37] In other words, by imitating the Prophet Muhammad so closely, Ghulam Ahmad identified with Muhammad's very being and thereby acquired his own prophetic status through the Prophet Muhammad. By perfecting this identity—and by virtue of receiving disclosures of the unseen (*ghayb*)—one may "call" Ghulam Ahmad a prophet. Ghulam Ahmad was only "called" a prophet in this sense because he reflected the perfections, virtues, and high moral character of the Prophet Muhammad so closely. He was the *khalīfat-ullāh*, Allah's representative on Earth.[38] In the sense that Ghulam Ahmad had no new scripture to disseminate and no new law to supplement or supersede the *sharīʿa*, he was not a prophet of God.[39] Ghulam Ahmad was only ascribed prophethood through his pure and perfect spiritual imitation (*burūz*) of Muhammad.

Ghulam Ahmad paid considerable attention in his booklet to the *khātam al-nubuwwa* verse of the Qurʾan, which famously declares Muhammad to be the seal of the prophets (*khātam al-nabiyyīn*),[40] in order to explain how the seal on prophethood had not been broken. This undue attention affirming the soundness of the verse implies that Ghulam Ahmad understood that no prophet could appear after Muhammad. As he had already explained, no prophet could exist in the world after Muhammad, including Jesus, because if Jesus were to return to the world in the way that most Muslims expected, the seal of prophethood would be broken.[41] The summation of his thoughts at the end of the tract helps to clarify his final position.

> This entire treatise is intended to show that my ignorant opponents accuse me of claiming to be a prophet or a messenger, whereas I make no such claim. In these regards, I am neither a prophet nor a messenger in the way that they think. However, in one sense, I am a prophet and a messenger in the manner

in which I have just explained. So whoever maliciously accuses me of claiming prophethood or messengership is following false and filthy persuasions. It is my manifest spiritual imitation (*burūz*) [of the Prophet Muhammad] that has made me a prophet and a messenger, and it is on this basis that God has repeatedly called me a prophet of God and a messenger of God, but in manifestational (*burūzī*) form.

(*ab is tamām tahrīr se matlab merā ye hay ke jāhil mukhālif merī nisbat ilzām lagāte hayñ ke ye shakhs nabī yā rasūl hone kā da'wā kartā hay mujhe aysā ko'ī da'wā nahīñ—mayñ is tawr se jo wo khayāl karte hayñ na nabī hūñ na rasūl hūñ—hāñ mayñ is tawr se nabī awr rasūl hūñ jis tawr se abhī mayñ ne bayān kiyā hay—pas jo shakhs mere par sharārat se ye ilzām lagātā hay jo da'wā nubuwwat awr risālat kā karte hayñ wo jhūtā awr nā pāk khayāl hay—mujhe burūzī sūrat ne nabī awr rasūl banāyā hay awr isī binā par khudā ne bār bār merā nām nabī allāh awr rasūl allāh rakhā magar burūzī sūrat meñ*).[42]

The reality of this explanation is that Mirza Ghulam Ahmad's conceptualization of his own prophetic status is complicated. Aside from contradictory statements made throughout his career, Ghulam Ahmad went to great lengths to qualify his conception of prophethood and show how he fit into the prophetic tradition. But once again, the greatest challenge for contemporary scholars is working out the semantics of the prophetic terminology within the context of Ghulam Ahmad's unique self-image. We must look at the language Ghulam Ahmad chose to express his ideas in order to get a fuller picture of his spiritual self-image. For this reason, we shall turn our attention to some of the complications surrounding Ghulam Ahmad's claims and those surrounding his presentation of them.

The Terminology of Prophethood and Revelation

The words most commonly associated with revelation and the prophetic tradition in Islam are derived from Arabic roots. They take on different meanings, however, when used in the relevant languages of scholarship within Islamic studies, despite the shared religious context. In the case of Ahmadi literature, assigning fixed meanings to words for analytic purposes based on previous usages in the religious tradition is often inappropriate because of Ghulam Ahmad's intermittent jumps between Urdu, Arabic, and Persian. To further complicate things, Ghulam Ahmad frequently switched between poetry and prose within the context of the same discussion, often switching languages as well. It appears as though he used the same word differently depending on his writing style—poetry or prose—and on the language in question—be it Urdu, Arabic, or Persian. Ghulam Ahmad blurred together the connotations of prophetic terminology and ignored the religious precedent set by the tradition. He also placed an unusual emphasis on uncommon terms, such as *burūz* (manifestation) and *zill* (shadow), which had negligible use outside a rare and exceptional genre of elitist Sufi literature.[43] These terms are virtually never used in a prophetic context aside from the ecstatic claims of a limited group of controversial figures.

Within a relatively short period of time, Jama'at-i Ahmadiyya's insistence upon maintaining an intense proselytization campaign demanded that elitist terminology be abandoned in favor of more common and less sophisticated explanations that were more easily understood by less educated Muslims. In trying to define irregular ideas with regular terminology, many Ahmadis reduced Ghulam Ahmad's claim to simply being a prophet without the additional qualifiers that routinely accompanied his own explanations. Since the vast majority of Muslims did not understand Ghulam Ahmad's prophetic qualifiers (such as manifestational, shadowy, partial, dependent, and non-law-bearing, among others) that prefixed—and hence limited—his prophethood, the standardized terminology for prophets and revelation quickly took hold. It is important to emphasize that even within the prophetic context Ghulam Ahmad's self-image was extraordinary and unique. Although his prophethood was secondary, in that it was the consequential outcome of his being a *burūz* (manifest spiritual imitation) of Muhammad, he still considered himself to be the *mahdī* and the promised messiah of the latter days who consistently received revelations from God.

Attempting to classify these revelations appropriately poses other problems as well. Similar to the jargon associated with prophethood, several words have been used to describe inspirational insights or revelatory experiences in the Islamic tradition, including, for example, *wahy, ilhām, kashf, ru'yā, futūhāt,* and *mubashshirāt.* Ghulam Ahmad also added to the list Perso-Urdu words, such as *pesh go'ī* and *khwāb,* which he used in a similar context when describing mystical experiences. It is interesting to note that he used these words interchangeably as revelation, while ignoring the theological connotations, which at times had profound implications for his claims. Even in the case of the revelations of the Prophet Muhammad himself, Muslims acknowledge that subtle distinctions in *wahy* distinguished between the Qur'an and *hadīth qudsī,* though both are unquestionably accepted as divine revelation.[44] Unlike connotations in English, where anyone who prophesizes the future may be considered a prophet, one cannot acquire prophethood through prophecy in an Islamic context. This is due in part to the notion that revelations and divine inspirations have qualitative distinctions. But if one is willing to accept that Mirza Ghulam Ahmad did acquire a contingent or shadowy (*zillī*) prophetic status as he claimed, then how should one treat his shadowy revelations? Humphrey Fisher recognized this problem and raised similar questions in his study but did not attempt to answer or expound upon what it entailed for Jama'at-i Ahmadiyya, as is done below.[45]

Mirza Ghulam Ahmad attempted to qualify his own revelations in one of his more metaphysical works, *Haqīqat al-Wahy* (The Reality of Revelation). Alongside philosophical subject matter, the book presents a thought-provoking insight into the intended significance of Ghulam Ahmad's revelations in relation to his conspicuous self-image. As one of his last major works, *Haqīqat al-Wahy* was published in May 1907, only one year before his death. It may thus be considered to have represented his final thoughts on his revelations and prophetic status after a full yet bitterly contested career.

Ghulam Ahmad organized the book into four chapters, each detailing one type of revelation. The first chapter categorizes people who have some true dreams or receive some true inspirations but have no spiritual connection to Allah. The second chapter describes people who may periodically have true dreams or true revelations while maintaining some connection to God, even if this connection is not a strong one in the sense that they do not represent the spiritually elite. The third chapter details people who have a very strong connection to Allah and receive pure revelations with great frequency that are lucid, unambiguous, and illuminating. These people were said to have been consumed by the love of God, including God's chosen prophets and messengers. The fourth and final chapter is devoted to the revelations of Mirza Ghulam Ahmad himself. It places his revelations within the aforementioned context and gives him a distinctive status as the promised messiah.[46]

It is clear that Ghulam Ahmad's concept of prophethood was intimately connected to his concept of revelation. Throughout his career, Ghulam Ahmad was consistent in asserting that by receiving revelation, he received access to the unseen, which thereby granted him access to prophethood. In terms of the act of revelation itself, however, Ghulam Ahmad never mentioned an intermediary that liaised between himself and God,[47] which represents a peculiarity in Ghulam Ahmad's revelations, considering that an intermediary is traditionally believed to be a necessary part of the experience of prophetic revelation in Islam, due to the Qur'anic verse 42:51.[48] There only appear to be two exceptions to this in the Islamic tradition where prophets received the word of God without some sort of intermediary. The first was Moses during his interlude on Mount Sinai, and the second took place when Muhammad ascended through the heavens during his night journey. This may explain why Ghulam Ahmad often took the name *kalīmullāh* (the one to whom God speaks),[49] which was given to Moses in reference to his being spoken to by God uniquely in this direct manner.[50]

Ghulam Ahmad certainly claimed to have seen and communicated with angels, but in general, he never claimed to receive revelation from them regularly in a conventional sense. On these occasions and in specific dreams, Ghulam Ahmad described angels who disclosed hidden truths, but they do not seem to have played a significant role in his day-to-day revelatory experiences. This suggests that Ghulam Ahmad's type of revelation was significantly inferior to the *wahy* of prophets like Muhammad and Jesus, who are believed to have received the word of God through the angel Gabriel. I was unable to find any indication that

Ghulam Ahmad received revelation from the angel Gabriel or through any other intermediary, which leads one to question why he insisted on calling his revelations "revelation (*wahy*)."

The ability of non-prophets to tell the future—or in other words to prophesize it—is not celebrated in traditional Islam, which may be demonstrated by the negative attitude towards soothsayers and oracles in the Qur'an.[51] Ghulam Ahmad explained:

> And then there is this one other objection which is raised in order to provoke the ignorant, they say that I have claimed prophethood, whereas this accusation is completely false. In actuality, I have made no such claim to the type of prophethood that is well known to be forbidden by the Holy Qur'an. I only claim that on one side I am *ummatī* (a devout follower of the example of the Prophet Muhammad) and on the other side I am a prophet, purely because of the bounties of the prophethood of the Holy Prophet, may the peace and blessings of Allah be upon him. And by prophet, I only mean to the extent that I receive an abundance of God's speech and conversation.
>
> (*awr phir ek awr nādānī ye hay ke jāhil logoñ ko bharkāne ke līye kahte hayñ ke is shakhs ne nubuwwat kā da'wā kiyā hay hālāñke ye unkā sar-ā-sar iftirā hay—balke jis nubuwwat kā da'wā karnā qur'ān sharīf ke rū se mana' ma'lūm hotā hay aysā ko'ī da'wā nahīñ kiyā gayā sirf ye da'wā hay ke ek pahlū se mayñ ummatī hūñ awr ek pahlū se mayñ āñ-hazrat sall-allāhu 'alayhi wa sallam ke fayz-i nubūwwat kī wajah se nabī hūñ awr nabī se murād sirf is qadr hay ke khudā ta'ālā se ba-kasrat sharaf-i mukālama o mukhātaba pātā hūñ . . . *)[52]

Although Ghulam Ahmad's position may not represent a traditional understanding of prophethood or revelation, it explains his self-image rather well. Receiving numerous communications from the Divine does not make one a prophet in Islam. One may ask why Ghulam Ahmad insisted upon using this terminology with mainstream Muslims when he knew that he intended something far more complex. It is interesting that Ghulam Ahmad attempted to justify his concept of prophethood by referring to Shaykh Ahmad Sirhindi, the Naqshbandi master who also faced intense criticism for similar unorthodox claims.[53] The glaring difference between the two is that Shaykh Ahmad Sirhindi's contribution to the Islamic tradition is firmly placed within a Sufi context, whereas Ghulam Ahmad has been distanced from both ecstatic Sufism and orthodox Islam.

Being divinely inspired and claiming extraordinary spiritual heights is a typical feature of the writings of intoxicated Sufis. Jama'at-i Ahmadiyya has long since lost touch with this context for various reasons, which we shall explore in subsequent chapters. Within the nineteenth-century framework of the subcontinent, which witnessed technological advancements alongside a decline of traditional 'ulamā, Ghulam Ahmad's claims were disseminated through the masses as popular religion. To this day, many of Jama'at-i Ahmadiyya's members fail to appreciate why taking such claims literally is problematic within orthodox Islam. As seen above, Ghulam Ahmad himself acknowledged that even nonbelievers are capable of receiving communication from the Divine, which implies that revelation in itself does not entail prophethood, irrespective of how frequent or vivid it may be. Yet, the firm commitment of Ahmadis to asserting the authenticity of Ghulam Ahmad's revelation and prophethood has developed into a distinctive feature of Ahmadi Islam. We shall see in the next chapter how the question of Ghulam Ahmad's revelation and prophethood later evolved into a question of authority.

It is easy to see how differences of opinion regarding Ghulam Ahmad's prophethood reappeared after his death and eventually contributed to the Lahori-Qadiani split. For the Qadianis—at least in terms of their theological interpretation—any type of prophethood is still recognized as prophethood, regardless of its deficiencies. At present, the Qadiani branch treats *Ek Ghalatī kā Izāla* as the definitive treatise establishing Ghulam Ahmad's prophetic status but tends to overlook later works, such as *Haqīqat al-Wahy,* which continue to qualify Ghulam Ahmad's prophethood in a similar way to earlier tracts. In reference to *Ek Ghalatī kā Izāla,* the Qadianis maintain that "for the previous ten years [Mirza Ghulam] Ahmad had been assuring the world that he did not lay any claim to prophethood and now in this leaflet [*Ek Ghalatī kā Izāla*] he definitely declared that he was a prophet of God."[54] The conventional Ahmadi understanding of Ghulam Ahmad's prophetic claim, however, is inconsistent with his later writings, since there is no sharp break in the way that Ghulam Ahmad articulated his prophetic status after 1901. In reality, he continued to make similar statements about prophethood later in life, as seen in *Haqīqat al-Wahy.*

Reconciling the Revelations of the Promised Messiah

In terms of analysis, acknowledging that Mirza Ghulam Ahmad developed a unique concept of revelation is a first step. The next step of contextualizing these revelations within the scope of the broader Islamic tradition is problematic, since it involves discerning how one ought to treat these revelations in relation to other Islamic concepts beyond the immediate scope of Jama'at-i Ahmadiyya. There has always been a general consensus within Jama'at-i Ahmadiyya that Mirza Ghulam Ahmad did not bring any new law or *sharī'a.* The Qadiani branch has emphasized this point by asserting that Ghulam Ahmad was a non-law-bearing prophet, as he often stated in his own writings. For Ahmadi theologians, the problem with acknowledging that Ghulam Ahmad was a non-law-bearing prophet is that it suggests that he himself needed to abide by the preexisting *sharī'a.* In theory, Ghulam Ahmad's status as a non-law-bearing prophet entails that no one can act upon his revelations. It also implies that if any of Ghulam Ahmad's revelations are found to be inconsistent with the *sharī'a,* then they ought to be discarded.

These questions of authority have yet to be explicitly addressed by Jama'at-i Ahmadiyya, despite implicit references in standard Ahmadi claims. Superficially, many Ahmadis might be comfortable asserting that Mirza Ghulam Ahmad was a non-law-bearing prophet while affirming that he himself was bound by the *sharī'a*. Maintaining these beliefs, however, essentially renders Ghulam Ahmad's revelations meaningless, since no one has the right to act upon them without appealing to valid forms of legal justification, as recognized by the *sharī'a*. The very act of using Ghulam Ahmad's revelations to clarify, amend, or create any rulings whatsoever would seemingly assign greater value to them than he himself intended, regardless of whether they are consistent with the *sharī'a*. This means that Ahmadi rulings ought to be subject to the same legal discretion while adhering to the same legal methodology as the classical Islamic tradition. This also entails that Ahmadi rulings ought to be subject to the same legal scrutiny from dissenting scholars who may choose to disagree with particular claims.

In actuality, however, this is not the way Ghulam Ahmad's opinions are treated within Jama'at-i Ahmadiyya. Ghulam Ahmad's opinions and revelations have already acquired a unique precedence over all other *sharī'* rulings, even though this precedence has yet to be formalized into a rigorous legal methodology. The problem has been compounded in recent years as Ghulam Ahmad's *khalīfa*s have acquired a status that is comparable to the familiar Shi'i notion of the infallible imam, in the sense that the Ahmadi *khalīfa* gives divinely inspired injunctions that may not be contravened.[55] The leadership hierarchy's contention that the Ahmadi *khalīfa* is chosen by God is steadily being accepted as doctrine by members of the Jama'at. This sentiment has been present in some form following the election of nearly every Ahmadi *khalīfa*, ever since it was first emphasized in this way following the Lahori-Qadiani split in 1914. The debate resurfaced at times, including during Mirza Bashir al-Din Mahmud Ahmad's lengthy final illness.[56] This has been problematic when opinions of two or more *khalīfa*s clash or when one particular *khalīfa*'s opinion clashes with the opinion of Ghulam Ahmad himself.

There is no doubt that Jama'at-i Ahmadiyya will one day need to grapple with the problem of forming a formal legal methodology of "*fiqh-i ahmadiyya*," which clearly establishes a framework to rank classical sources, such as the Qur'an and hadith, against Ghulam Ahmad's revelations, writings, and sayings in conjunction with opinions of the presiding *khalīfa*. Ahmadis claim to base their legal methodology primarily on rulings and principles of the Hanafi *madhhab* but reject strict adherence to any particular school of thought, which is likely a direct result of Ghulam Ahmad's Ahl-i Hadith influence. In practice, Ahmadis obey the rulings of the presiding *khalīfa* under the presumption that his living awareness, and perhaps his divine connection, makes him better suited to address contemporary issues more appropriately as they arise. The informal precedence of the presiding *khalīfa,* however, has yet to be formalized into doctrine, which poses problems for relations with other Muslims.[57]

There are two short volumes of Ahmadi legal rulings which were published relatively recently by a committee of missionaries as guidelines for basic family issues and prayer in Jama'at-i Ahmadiyya.[58] Comparatively, the process of formalization took centuries to develop in Sunni and Shi'i Islam, which devoted attention to the need for a more rigorous legal methodology only after a clear *khalīfa* or *imām* had ceased to exist. This process of formalization for Jama'at-i Ahmadiyya will require official positions on the nature of Mirza Ghulam Ahmad's prophethood and on the authority of his revelations in relation to the inspiration of his spiritual successors. This is not to suggest that Ghulam Ahmad never explicitly addressed the issue of his own legal authority. There are certainly examples which could be used to establish legal precedence in his writings.[59]

At times, Ghulam Ahmad openly stated that revelations (*ilhām* and *kashf*) received by the people of revelation (*ahl-i kashf*) are on the same level as hadith in terms of legal authority. This suggests that he had complete autonomy to make legal rulings in accordance with his discretion, however he saw fit, as an independent or unbounded *mujtahid*.[60] Although this is a clear contradiction of classical legal theory or *usūl al-fiqh*, it is sufficient for our purposes to recognize that the potential for grounding Ahmadi legal methodology has yet to be formalized.

Paths to Prophethood

If one could determine exactly what Ghulam Ahmad intended regarding his spiritual status, it would make addressing questions of authority much easier. Although the most imperative question in relation to Ghulam Ahmad's prophethood may revolve around the question of authority, there are other questions which must first be considered, since many of these issues are contingent upon a clarification of his path to prophethood. There is nothing that explicitly details how Ghulam Ahmad acquired prophethood or what type of prophethood may potentially be acquired. We saw how Ghulam Ahmad added a number of qualifiers to his prophethood by using various prefixed terms to limit his prophetic status. It is unclear whether these qualifiers were intended to create a qualitative or a quantitative distinction in his prophetic rank. When Ghulam Ahmad referred to himself as a partial (*juzwī*) prophet, he may have been making a quantitative distinction about his prophecy, which he often justified by referring to the famous hadith about true dreams being 1/46 of prophecy.[61] In this sense, Ghulam Ahmad considered his portion of prophecy qualitatively authentic but numerically incomplete. When relying on this hadith, Ahmadis often overlook that the stated proportion entails that Ghulam Ahmad's prophecy was incomplete by 45 of 46 parts or 97.8 percent.

In the original Arabic passage, Ghulam Ahmad said that this type of prophetic revelation was given to elite saints (*khawāss al-awliyā*), which is odd since the *awliyā* (saints) are not prophets.[62] It often seems as though Ghulam Ahmad's conception of *nubuwwa* (prophethood) was much closer to classical notions of *walāya* (sainthood). Quite often in Ghulam Ahmad's writings, the two appear to be indistinguishable. The importance for Ahmadis, nevertheless, is that Ghulam Ahmad's prophecy was genuine and authentic.

In other places where Ghulam Ahmad described his prophecy with terms such as *burūzī* or *zillī*, he appeared to be making a qualitative distinction about his prophethood. This suggests that he was not the same type of prophet as those who came before him, but was qualitatively a rather different one. The fact that Ghulam Ahmad drew both qualitative and quantitative distinctions about his prophethood is paradoxical, but it was this contradictory and often ambiguous use of the terminology of prophethood that enabled Ghulam Ahmad and eventually Jama'at-i Ahmadiyya to imply whatever they liked about his spiritual status. By sustaining these ambiguities indefinitely, Jama'at-i Ahmadiyya has sustained an indeterminate connection to prophethood in Ahmadi Islam.

Another question regarding the acquisition of Ghulam Ahmad's prophethood pertains to the grammatical objects of the terms *burūz* and *zill*. As we have seen above, in some accounts, Ghulam Ahmad based his claims of prophethood heavily upon the death of Jesus. Since Jesus had died a natural death and would not return from the heavens, Ghulam Ahmad had been raised by God in the image of Jesus. Given that Ghulam Ahmad was the second coming of Jesus, he had become the second messiah and acquired a prophetic status in the likeness of the first prophet, Jesus. In other accounts, Ghulam Ahmad described his absolute and complete devotion to the Prophet Muhammad by employing the Sufi concept of *fanā fī 'l-rasūl* in an unusually literal sense. Since Ghulam Ahmad had adhered to the sunna so closely and wholly devoted his life to mimicking each virtue of the Prophet Muhammad, he was transformed by God into Muhammad's *burūz* (manifestation). Ghulam Ahmad's being itself was accordingly destroyed by his intense love for the Prophet until he acquired the being of his master, Muhammad. In this explanation, Ghulam Ahmad's prophethood was a *zill* (shadow) of the prophethood of the Prophet Muhammad. This justification may also explain why many (if not most) of Ghulam Ahmad's revelations were simply verses of the Qur'an, which he claimed were re-revealed to him by God.[63]

In terms of problematizing Ghulam Ahmad's prophethood, it is clear that both scenarios are problematic for the simple reason that they appear incongruous and mutually exclusive. In the first case, Ghulam Ahmad's prophethood results from being a copy of Jesus, whereas in the second case, his prophethood results from being a copy of Muhammad. When taken together, it is not clear whom Ghulam Ahmad imitated to acquire his prophethood. These two conflicting accounts describe differing paths to prophethood, making it difficult to trace his spiritual ascent. Perhaps one possible resolution could be that Ghulam Ahmad's messiahship resulted from copying Jesus whereas his prophethood resulted from copying Muhammad. Another feasible explanation might be that the timing of his particular advent in the latter days—perhaps in some metaphysical way—allowed for the culmination of prophecy through his unique form of prophethood, which represented all previous prophets universally.[64]

There are passages in Ghulam Ahmad's works which suggest that he was indeed a manifestation of all previous prophets. In one place, when discussing the magnitude of his divine mission, he listed the names of Adam, Seth, Noah, Abraham, Isaac, Ishmael, Jacob, Joseph, Moses, David, Jesus, Muhammad, and Ahmad as prophets who were all manifest in him. He then said that his identity with Muhammad was his most perfect manifestation (*mazhar-i atamm*), which he further explained as being the *zill* (shadow) of Muhammad.[65] These explanations were far less common but nonetheless contribute towards the complication of the problem of acquisition. In any case, Ghulam Ahmad's prophethood was vicarious in nature and contingent upon at least one unrestricted and independent prophet who came before him. Since Jesus cannot return, Ghulam Ahmad appears in place of Jesus; or since his being became utterly absorbed in the being of Muhammad, he may now function on the Prophet's behalf. It will be interesting to see if Jama'at-i Ahmadiyya further develops the idea of vicarious prophethood in the future, either through Ghulam Ahmad's successors or through any other potential Ahmadi claimants to prophethood. It will be even more interesting to see whether Ghulam Ahmad's contingent prophethood serves as the basis for the prophethood of other aspiring claimants within the newly developing Ahmadi tradition.[66] It would be ironic if one day Jama'at-i Ahmadiyya concluded that prophecy ended with Mirza Ghulam Ahmad, considering the sophistication of Ahmadi prophetology, even though this position seems likely at this stage. Otherwise, Ahmadi prophetology may potentially give way to several iterations of surrogate prophets who vicariously absorb a little less prophethood than their respective predecessors. Although this already exists to some extent through the claims of competitors, none have been officially sanctioned by the Jama'at.[67] Further analysis of these claimants is largely beyond the scope of this study.

Jama'at-i Ahmadiyya soon became immersed in a debate about two conflicting ways of addressing questions of authority, which came to a head during the Lahori-Qadiani split following the deaths of Mirza Ghulam Ahmad and his first successor, Nur al-Din. For one branch of followers, authority was restricted to Ghulam Ahmad and limited by personal interpretation of Ghulam Ahmad's mission. For the other branch, authority was consigned to a formalized institution of *khilāfat-i ahmadiyya*. To see how the Jama'at interpreted Ghulam Ahmad's claims of prophethood and responded to his divine mission, it is necessary to look more closely at the chaotic period that followed Ghulam Ahmad's death. We shall see how the process of institutionalization began to formalize the ecstatic claims of the promised messiah and shifted Ahmadi theology away from the metaphysics of Sufi elitism towards the literalist conformity of mass-market religion. This process was facilitated by abandoning the Sufi context of Ghulam Ahmad's claims, which encouraged the development of literal interpretations of his Sufi-style metaphysics. Whereas in the beginning, there were only individual disciples struggling to understand the ecstatic experiences of their master, the formation of an organizational hierarchy introduced the type of consistency in Ahmadi theological interpretation that may only accompany institutionalized religion. We shall now turn our attention to how this process affected Ahmadi identity and molded the community in a way that more closely resembles the Jama'at of today.

3 Authority, *Khilāfat,* and the Lahori-Qadiani Split

The Setting for the Split

Mirza Ghulam Ahmad passed away in the early morning hours of May 26, 1908, while visiting Lahore. His body was transported back to Qadian where Maulvi Hakim Nur al-Din, a close companion and disciple, led the funeral prayer after unanimously being chosen as Ghulam Ahmad's successor by the Ahmadis participating in the procession. Although the events may have taken some time to unfold, the selection of Hakim Nur al-Din was not contested by the nearly 1,200 members in attendance, who offered him their *bay'at* (allegiance).[1] Nur al-Din had been the first person to take Ghulam Ahmad's *bay'at* in Ludhiana in 1889 and had always been regarded as one of Ghulam Ahmad's most trusted friends. During his reign as *khalīfa,* Nur al-Din did little to assert his authority over the Jama'at. His mild-mannered personality and strict adherence to Ghulam Ahmad left little room for objections. It was not until his own death six years later that the underlying differences within Jama'at-i Ahmadiyya began to emerge.

By the time Nur al-Din passed away on March 13, 1914, tension had been mounting for some time regarding the future leadership of Jama'at-i Ahmadiyya and the correct interpretation of Ghulam Ahmad's mission and claim.[2] An underlying power struggle was beginning to surface that influenced the way in which differences of opinion were being expressed. Mirza Bashir al-Din Mahmud Ahmad, the eldest son from Ghulam Ahmad's second marriage, was favored to succeed Nur al-Din as *khalīfat al-masīh* (successor of the messiah). Unlike the uncontested decision to select Nur al-Din, Mahmud Ahmad's election was controversial. Owing to cultural mores, members placed considerable value on Mahmud Ahmad's right to succession by virtue of being Ghulam Ahmad's eldest son. He was nevertheless only twenty-five years old when elected the second *khalīfat al-masīh* on March 14, 1914, the day after Nur al-Din's demise. A minority group of roughly fifty Ahmadis refrained from giving Mahmud Ahmad their *bay'at.* In the days following the ceremony, the group led by Maulana Muhammad 'Ali, another close companion of Ghulam Ahmad, openly rejected Mahmud Ahmad's authority as the next Ahmadi *khalīfa.* Maulana Muhammad 'Ali and his supporters decided to leave Qadian shortly thereafter and establish a separate organization in Lahore. From this point forward, they came to be known as "Lahoris" in contrast to the majority of the members of Jama'at-i Ahmadiyya, who remained in Qadian and retained the name "Qadianis."[3]

Maulana Muhammad 'Ali published leaflets detailing objections to Mirza Mahmud Ahmad's succession almost immediately after the election. But the first publication to provide a comprehensive account of the opposition party's grievances did not appear until January 1918 under the heading *The Ahmadiyya Movement IV—The Split,* in reference to its position as the fourth of a series of tracts on the movement in English. Since then, the book has undergone various revisions for subsequent editions which appeared under similar titles.

Causes of the Split: Theological Objections

In his book, *The Split,* Maulana Muhammad 'Ali outlined three major objections to Mirza Mahmud Ahmad's *khilāfat.* The first objection challenged Mahmud Ahmad's interpretation of a Qur'anic verse from Sura al-Saff, which describes how Jesus prophesized the coming of the next prophet. The verse reads:

> Jesus, son of Mary, said, "Children of Israel, I am sent to you by God, confirming the Torah that came before me and bringing good news of a messenger to follow me whose name will be Ahmad."[4]

In the verse, Jesus addressed the children of Israel and described his mission as a fulfillment of prophecies in the Torah. He then gave the children of Israel glad tidings of a forthcoming messenger, "whose name will be Ahmad." Muslims often relate this verse to comparable verses in the gospel of John which express a similar sentiment in order to assert that Jesus prophesized the coming of Muhammad.[5] However, the Qur'anic verse clearly stipulates that the future messenger's name will be Ahmad, rather than Muhammad.[6] Still, the overwhelming majority of Muslim commentators have traditionally agreed that both names refer to the Prophet Muhammad. This is due to the similar meanings of the Arabic words *"muhammad"* and *"ahmad,"* which were both used interchangeably in reference to the Prophet. It nonetheless is understandable why some Ahmadi commentators were eager to establish a connection between the prophet "Ahmad" from the Qur'an and Mirza Ghulam Ahmad. From the Ahmadi perspective, an explicit Qur'anic reference would certainly bolster the case for Ghulam Ahmad's prophethood.

Muhammad 'Ali accused Mahmud Ahmad of exploiting the verse in order to claim that Jesus was speaking exclusively of his father. He also attempted to counter Mahmud Ahmad by saying that the verse referred exclusively to the

Prophet Muhammad.[7] In doing so, Muhammad 'Ali endeavored to undermine Mahmud Ahmad's religious authority, discredit his capabilities as a Qur'anic interpreter, and question his competence as *khalīfa*. Muhammad 'Ali argued that Ahmadis who believed the Qur'anic reference was indeed referring to the Prophet Muhammad were directly contradicting Mahmud Ahmad, which thereby discharged them from their loyalties to the *khalīfa*. This argument presupposed that adhering to Mahmud Ahmad's interpretations of the Qur'an was a necessary part of the Qadiani belief system. Mahmud Ahmad rebutted this view by later acknowledging that the verse could be interpreted in both ways, since the Qur'an, as he affirmed, could be interpreted in many ways. He further clarified that he did not consider it wrong or sinful for someone to disagree with his interpretations of the Qur'an.[8] Mahmud Ahmad dismissed the issue as mere difference of opinion, since it did not infringe on any core beliefs of Islam or Ahmadiyyat, which thereby curtailed further debate.

It is well known that Mirza Ghulam Ahmad's prophethood has always been a problem for the Sunni mainstream. It is not well known, however, that Ghulam Ahmad's prophethood initially posed a problem within Jama'at-i Ahmadiyya as well. Ghulam Ahmad's primary spiritual claims to be the *mahdī* (guided one) and the *masīh* (messiah) were the most problematic, because they implied his status was based on a rank containing an underlying strand of prophethood. Since the split, Muhammad 'Ali consistently argued that Ghulam Ahmad never claimed to be a "real" or "perfect" prophet in the way that the Prophet Muhammad, who administered the *sharī'a*, was a "real" and "perfect" prophet. Instead, he argued that Ghulam Ahmad claimed to be a *zillī* (shadowy) or a *burūzī* (manifestational) prophet. By mimicking the perfections of Muhammad, Ghulam Ahmad achieved God's pleasure and eventually earned a status equivalent to that of the prophets. This also explained why Ghulam Ahmad never claimed to establish any new religious law, but rather reinterpreted and readministered the original laws in what he considered to be their intended form.

Muhammad 'Ali believed that Ghulam Ahmad's prophethood was imperfect. He felt, like many Sunnis today, that Mahmud Ahmad was dangerously approaching *kufr* (infidelity) by exaggerating his father's claims.[9] Mahmud Ahmad argued that attempting to pinpoint his father's specific rank overlooked the fact that he was chosen by God for his mission. According to Mahmud Ahmad, the details of his father's prophetic rank were superfluous, because only God was capable of regulating the rank of prophets and designating one's spiritual status. Mahmud Ahmad argued that it did not matter whether Ghulam Ahmad was more of a shadowy prophet or more of a manifestational prophet, since the important part was recognizing that his father's privileged status had been assigned by God himself. Ultimately, Mahmud Ahmad concluded that Ghulam Ahmad was still a prophet of God, irrespective of the particular variety of prophethood he had attained. Mahmud Ahmad believed that this was possible because his father's status had been predicated on a type of prophethood that was assigned by Allah.[10]

For Qadiani supporters of Mirza Mahmud Ahmad, Muhammad 'Ali's concerns were irrelevant. Ghulam Ahmad, in a manner of speaking, earned his prophethood through strict adherence to the sunna of the Prophet Muhammad. Since Ghulam Ahmad copied Muhammad's perfections so closely, he literally acquired the Prophet's perfections through identification with his being. Qadiani supporters considered it meaningless to suggest that one perfection was somehow better or more authentic than another, especially since they referred to the same perfections, which had only been manifested in two different people. Mahmud Ahmad believed in this sense that Ghulam Ahmad's perfections were qualitatively identical to the perfections of the Prophet Muhammad. In mirroring Muhammad's actions so closely, Ghulam Ahmad had claimed the Prophet's perfections for himself. In his own explanations, Ghulam Ahmad articulated the metaphysics of this process by employing Sufi terminology, like *fanā fī 'l-rasūl,* which in itself enabled him to acquire a prophetic identity.[11]

The Lahoris rejected this view and maintained the orthodox position that copying the Prophet Muhammad's virtuous behavior by performing the same good deeds does not make one a prophet. But since the Qadianis were utterly convinced that they had found in Mirza Ghulam Ahmad an individual who somehow managed to capture and exhibit all the spiritual perfections of the Prophet Muhammad, they chose to call him a prophet of God. From the Qadiani perspective, it was pointless to concede that Ghulam Ahmad's prophethood was imperfect, because imperfect prophethood does not exist as an attribute in itself. Rather, the notion of imperfect prophethood is contingent upon the negation of the attribute of perfect prophethood, which apparently resolved the conflict for Qadianis. From an analytical perspective, however, everyone and everything that is "non-prophet" displays characteristics of imperfect prophethood. This means that the notion of having some essential quality capable of transforming the attribute of prophethood into the "imperfect" variety is vacuous.

The Lahori-Qadiani debate revealed important aspects of the Ahmadi belief system, especially within the context of other philosophical debates in the broader Islamic tradition. Given the circumstances and rationalized manner of debating, it is difficult to avoid peripheral comparisons of Jamaʿat-i Ahmadiyya to the early Muʿtazila.[12] Jamaʿat-i Ahmadiyya's internal debate on Ghulam Ahmad's perfections and his prophethood is far more characteristic of literalist strands of Islam or speculative philosophy than of Sufism. It is likely that the finer points of Ghulam Ahmad's prophethood did not matter to those members of the Jamaʿat who were more attracted to his esoteric insights or attacks on other religions. Mahmud Ahmad's explanation of Ghulam Ahmad's prophethood in this respect was more satisfying to the non-intellectuals of the Jama'at who simply wanted to hear a yes or no. The problem of locating Ghulam Ahmad's spiritual standing among the countless prophets in the greater Judeo-Christian-Islamic tradition was simply unnecessary and largely irrelevant to lay Muslims who had recently been joining the Jama'at from rural parts of the Punjab, shortly following Ghulam Ahmad's death. Most of Jama'at-i Ahmadiyya's lay members were not looking for an intellectual debate. Rather, most wanted to share in a familiar type of spiritual satisfaction that corresponded with their folk Sufi, Sunni, Punjabi backgrounds.

Muhammad 'Ali's final objection in *The Split* was related to the status of non-Ahmadis. Mahmud Ahmad was accused of classifying anyone who did not enter into the *bay'at* of Mirza Ghulam Ahmad as a *kāfir* (nonbeliever).[13] Had Mahmud Ahmad straightforwardly declared that all non-Ahmadis were guilty of *kufr* (infidelity), he would have effectively excluded his Jama'at from the rest of the *umma* and ostensibly formed a new religion. Although there were several examples from Ghulam Ahmad's life where religious rivals had declared him a *kāfir*, his responses to allegations were inconsistent. Ghulam Ahmad initially hesitated in retaliating and appeared reluctant to issue his own declarations of *kufr*. He also declined to participate in his first *mubāhala* (prayer duel) challenges by stating that it was not proper to enter into such contests with other Muslims.[14] Muhammad 'Ali used these examples to insist that Ghulam Ahmad would never issue an unsolicited declaration of *kufr* against everyone who did not enter into his *bay'at*, even though Muhammad 'Ali was well aware that Ghulam Ahmad had later accepted *mubāhala* challenges from Muslim opponents.[15] Muhammad 'Ali treated these *mubāhala*s as special cases directed at specific groups of people who created difficulty for Ghulam Ahmad and his mission. He maintained that they were not generally intended for all Muslims, since the idea of declaring the entire Muslim *umma* as being guilty of *kufr* was absurd. This, however, was precisely the position that Muhammad 'Ali repeatedly attributed to Mahmud Ahmad, which he summarized by saying that "all those who have not entered into the bai'at [*sic*] of the Promised Messiah are outside the circle of Islam, i.e., non-Muslims."[16]

Ghulam Ahmad acknowledged that anyone who affirmed the *kalima* or basic Islamic creed was Muslim, unless they called him a *kāfir* in which case the *kufr* would revert back to them. He legitimized his position with a famous hadith from the *kitāb al-adab* (chapter of etiquette) of Bukhari, which affirms that anyone who wrongfully calls a believer a *kāfir* is a *kāfir* him- or herself.[17] Ghulam Ahmad proclaimed that even followers of the people who declared him a *kāfir* were *kāfir*s by default, especially if they continued to follow their scholars without protest.[18] For everyone else, he said that denying his mission would only lead to sin, since it was deviating from the straight path, which importantly is not *kufr.* Ghulam Ahmad defended his position by asserting that he had brought no new *sharīʿa* and was not a law-bearing prophet, because only those who denied the legislative prophets became *kāfirs*.[19] In other books, however, Ghulam Ahmad claimed that denying his mission was equivalent to denying Allah. Hence, anyone who rejected him was a *kāfir*.[20]

His rationale for this position was once again based on the implications of his status as the promised messiah, which in his estimation was the culmination of the prophetic tradition. Since Ghulam Ahmad's being itself was identical to that of the Prophet Muhammad—and his teachings matched Muhammad's teachings exactly—rejecting Ghulam Ahmad or his teachings was in reality rejecting the Prophet Muhammad. Ghulam Ahmad maintained that he had been shown divine signs in support of his mission, which were direct manifestations of God's power. With this, Ghulam Ahmad concluded that by rejecting his mission, one was rejecting divine signs that had been shown in his favor, and therefore one was rejecting Allah.[21]

In actuality, the problem of *takfīr* (deeming someone a nonbeliever) was a subset of the previous problem of Ghulam Ahmad's prophethood. If one could pinpoint Ghulam Ahmad's prophetic status with some degree of certainty, then perhaps one could gauge the status of those who rejected his mission. The case of legislative prophets is much easier for Ahmadis to evaluate, since legislative prophets by definition bring a message that is legally binding, as seen in the notion of religious law. Had Ghulam Ahmad's message been legally binding, then anyone who rejected him—or perhaps did not enter into his *bayʿat*—might be considered a *kāfir*. Since Ghulam Ahmad only claimed to be a non-legislative prophet, however, rejecting his mission should not have resulted in *kufr*. Muhammad ʿAli's explanation drew a distinction between active rejection and passive rejection of Ghulam Ahmad's mission. Actively rejecting Ghulam Ahmad entailed being familiar with his writings, his mission, and his claims, before consciously refusing to enter into his *bayʿat,* and hence denying his mission. Passive rejection of Ghulam Ahmad referred to someone who was unaware of his mission and unaware of Jamaʿat-i Ahmadiyya. Muhammad ʿAli claimed that Mahmud Ahmad deemed both active and passive rejection of his father's mission to be *kufr*.[22]

According to Mirza Mahmud Ahmad, although Ghulam Ahmad did not introduce any new religious laws, the laws endorsed by his mission were still legally binding, just as they had always been since they were first revealed to the Prophet Muhammad. Mahmud Ahmad thereby maintained that rejecting Ghulam Ahmad was equivalent to rejecting Muhammad.[23] In later years, Mahmud Ahmad revised his position by attempting to redefine the word "*kāfir.*" He claimed that a *kāfir* need not refer to a non-Muslim, since linguistically the Arabic word "*kāfir*" had broader usages including other connotations of denial. Mahmud Ahmad claimed that his use of the word "*kāfir*," in reference to anyone who did not enter into the *bay'at* of his father, only meant that they denied the promised messiah and *mahdī*, which was still a form of *kufr* but not *kufr* of Islam. Mahmud Ahmad argued that these *kāfirs* were not considered non-Muslims, but rather were only considered non-Ahmadis.[24] Analytically, however, this explanation is trivial, since Mahmud Ahmad's reasoning is circular. Of course anyone who does not enter into *bay'at* with Ghulam Ahmad is a non-Ahmadi. The argument is redundant and results in a tautology. Nonetheless, Mahmud Ahmad's interpretation prevailed and was soon adopted as the official Jama'at position on non-Ahmadis. At present, Jama'at-i Ahmadiyya maintains that non-Ahmadis are *kāfirs* insofar as they reject the imam of the age. This position inevitably makes a value judgment about non-Ahmadi Muslims by drawing into question the sincerity of their faith or—stated differently—the authenticity of their Islam.

The debates emerging from the Lahori-Qadiani split had an impact on the identity of average Ahmadis. The Jama'at's preoccupation with speculative theology by publicly entertaining questions surrounding Ghulam Ahmad's claims of prophethood was no longer limited to small groups of intellectuals, even though participation in these debates must have isolated large portions of the early Ahmadi population. Realistically, the majority of Ahmadis had a small role in the debate that was taking shape between Lahori dissenters and the Qadiani leadership. By the time the dust had settled, the Lahoris had adopted a softer position, which was more consistent with Sunni orthodoxy. The Qadianis continued to emphasize controversial aspects of Ghulam Ahmad's prophethood, which fundamentally enabled his inner religious experiences to serve as the basis of newly formulated doctrine. Over time, the Lahoris have to some extent dissolved back into Sunni Islam, although they still maintain a sense of reverence for Mirza Ghulam Ahmad. Their distinctive features as a movement at present are largely defined in reaction to the Qadianis.

The problem of Ghulam Ahmad's prophethood and his position on *takfīr* is in many ways a problem of semantics. Distinguishing the correlations between the associated ranks of a *muhaddath* (one to whom God speaks), a *mujaddid* (renewer of the faith), a *burūzī nabī* (manifestational prophet), a *zillī nabī* (shadowy prophet), a *juzwī nabī* (partial prophet), a *tashrī' nabī* (law-bearing prophet), a *lā tashrī' nabī* (non-law-bearing prophet), a *rasūl* (messenger), a *mahdī* (guided one), a *masīh* (messiah), and so forth is inherently subjective. The problem is exacerbated by the fact that most of the relevant terminology does not have an established precedent within the Qur'an and sunna. This makes it difficult to contextualize the debates within the broader Islamic tradition. It is impossible to determine the exact degree of a *kāfir's kufr* in mainstream Islam, since no one is capable of determining the spiritual rank of any person. Taken together, these uncertainties made it easier for the Lahori-Qadiani debate to develop a political dimension.

Political Dimensions of the Split

Muhammad ʿAli had initially blamed unorthodox interpretations of Ghulam Ahmad's prophetic status on Mahmud Ahmad's youth, inexperience, and excessive admiration for his father. In his earliest explanations, Muhammad ʿAli, as a faithful disciple of Ghulam Ahmad, even included an apologetic excuse for Mahmud Ahmad's incompetence. This may be an indication of his discomfort in maligning Mahmud Ahmad's reputation. Muhammad ʿAli blamed the exaggerations on a rogue Ahmadi innovator, Muhammad Zahir al-Din, who allegedly corrupted Mahmud Ahmad's perception of his father's rank. Zahir al-Din wrote two tracts in which he attributed perfect prophethood to Mirza Ghulam Ahmad.[25] The first tract, *Nabī Allāh kā Zahūr* (The Appearance of the Prophet of God), was published in April 1911. Muhammad ʿAli claimed that this was the first time that Ghulam Ahmad's name was explicitly used in a way that implied perfect prophethood. He also said that Zahir al-Din was the first member of Jamaʿat-i Ahmadiyya to entertain the heterodox view that Muhammad was not the final prophet. By July 1912, the controversy had reached Hakim Nur al-Din, who was then presiding over the Jamaʿat as the first *khalīfat al-masīh*. As a result, Zahir al-Din was excommunicated from the Jamaʿat on charges of blasphemy.[26] Within a month, the conflict had subsided, and Nur al-Din permitted Zahir al-Din to reenter the Jamaʿat in accordance with his repentance.[27]

In April 1913, Zahir al-Din published a second tract called *Ahmad Rasūl Allāh kā Zahūr* (The Appearance of Ahmad the Messenger of God), which purportedly displayed a reworded *kalima* on the title page that said "*lā ilāha illa 'llāh ahmad rasūl allāh* (there is no god but Allah; and Ahmad is the messenger of Allah)," instead of "Muhammad is the messenger of Allah."[28] As one might expect, Zahir al-Din was excommunicated for a second time. Muhammad ʿAli noted, however, that the official reason for Zahir al-Din's second expulsion was related to an unsuccessful attempt to claim the *khilāfat* for himself.[29] It is difficult to determine the extent of Zahir al-Din's influence on Mahmud Ahmad, who was still in his early twenties at the time. Mahmud Ahmad denied the allegations and denied having any close affiliation with Zahir al-Din but continued to maintain belief in Ghulam Ahmad's prophethood.[30]

The issue of Ghulam Ahmad's prophethood is certainly a critical aspect of the conflict between Ahmadiyyat and orthodox Islam. Muhammad ʿAli's criticisms of the Qadianis, however, were often presented in a way that highlighted Mahmud Ahmad's character flaws or expressed Muhammad ʿAli's disapproval of the Jamaʿat's leadership, rather than expounding the numerous theological issues at hand. Considering the commonalities between the Lahoris and the Qadianis, it seems odd that the two camps could not resolve implicit semantic discrepancies in Ghulam Ahmad's prophetic status. Muhammad ʿAli's repeated references to Mahmud Ahmad's immaturity and his ineptitude as a spiritual leader have led some to suggest that other factors may have motivated the split, such as Muhammad 'Ali's hidden desire for the *khilāfat,* which has long been the subject of speculation among Mahmud Ahmad's supporters. Although this is certainly the most popular explanation among the Qadianis, it remains an issue worth exploring.

Muhammad 'Ali was clearly a more accomplished candidate for *khalīfa* than Mahmud Ahmad, whose only relevant qualification at the time was his lineage. Muhammad 'Ali never openly solicited the position, however. His vast knowledge of Ahmadi Islam is apparent from his numerous publications both before and after the split. Muhammad 'Ali was a close companion of Ghulam Ahmad, the first editor of the Ahmadi journal, *Review of Religions,* and a translator of the Qur'an, as well as an experienced attorney and professor of English.[31] This makes it worth entertaining Qadiani insinuations that Muhammad 'Ali disapproved of the election results, but it would be inappropriate to reduce the split in Jama'at-i Ahmadiyya solely to personal problems. It seems reasonable, however, to suggest that many of the early disputes regarding the terminology of Ghulam Ahmad's prophethood could have been resolved, had they taken place between two different people.

For Muhammad 'Ali and his supporters, the differences proved to be irreconcilable. Nearly six weeks after Nur al-Din's demise, the Lahoris left Qadian for good. On May 2, 1914, Muhammad 'Ali and Khwaja Kamal al-Din, another early missionary and companion of Ghulam Ahmad, formed the Ahmadiyya Anjuman-i Isha'at-i Islam in Lahore.[32] Meanwhile, from Qadian, Mahmud Ahmad went on to become arguably the most influential *khalīfa* in Ahmadi history. He eventually took the title *muslih maw'ūd* (the promised reformer) in reference to one of Ghulam Ahmad's prophecies. Qadiani Ahmadis have always regarded his youth and inexperience during his early *khilāfat* as divine proof of his rightful authority.

The issue of *khilāfat* eventually overshadowed the Lahori-Qadiani split and displaced the discourse surrounding deeper problems relating to Ghulam Ahmad's prophethood. The split enabled the Jama'at to formalize official positions on Ghulam Ahmad's messianic claims, which initiated a process of institutionalization that provided an overt structure of authority for the community. The result was the creation of an institution of *khilāfat,* which centralized the Jama'at's authority over ordinary Ahmadis. Once the split had taken place, justifications for the newly established institution of *khilāfat-i ahmadiyya* needed to be rooted in Ghulam Ahmad's thought retrospectively, in order to provide Mahmud Ahmad's authority with a sense of legitimacy. Retracing this process and exploring how the doctrine of *khilāfat-i ahmadiyya* took hold will reveal how Ghulam Ahmad's charismatic authority was perpetuated through institutional *khilāfat.*

Al-Wasiyyat (The Will)

Although Ahmadis draw parallels between *khilāfat-i ahmadiyya* and the first caliphate in Islam following the death of the Prophet Muhammad, Ghulam Ahmad's succession developed rather differently. On December 20, 1905, Ghulam Ahmad wrote a short tract known as *al-Wasiyyat* (The Will) in anticipation of his death in 1908. The booklet was intended to announce his long-term desires for the community, including detailed instructions for community members after his demise. Ironically, different interpretations of the text led to different conceptions of Ghulam Ahmad's wishes, which in turn led to different conceptions of the Jama'at's organizational structure. These differences were manifested during the Lahori-Qadiani split. The Qadianis pursued the notion of a singular authoritarian *khilāfat* whereas the Lahoris chose to vest the community's authority in an administrative body or *anjuman.*

In addition to Ghulam Ahmad's last will, much of *al-Wasiyyat* consisted of regulations regarding inheritance shares for the creation of an endowment scheme, which was to be subsidized by assets bequeathed by Jama'at-i Ahmadiyya's religious elite. The scheme was inspired by a vision in which an angel appeared to Ghulam Ahmad and warned of his imminent death. The angel disclosed a special plot of land upon which a future gravesite was measured out for Ghulam Ahmad. Ghulam Ahmad described the dirt surrounding the gravesite as shimmering brighter than silver. He was then shown an area called *bahishtī maqbara* (heavenly graveyard) where the heaven-bound members of his Jama'at would ultimately be laid to rest.[33] The enigmatic experience prompted Ghulam Ahmad to look for a suitable plot of land, which could serve as the *bahishtī maqbara* for his Jama'at and fulfill his divine vision.

Ghulam Ahmad designated a plot of land adjacent to the family orchard in Qadian to initiate construction of the *bahishtī maqbara.* He specified that only those Ahmadis who were pure of heart (*pāk dil*) and who gave precedence to the true faith (*haqīqat dīn*) over worldliness would share in this divinely ordained scheme. He likened exceptional members of his community to companions of the Prophet Muhammad in their authenticity (*sidq*) and their detachment from the world.[34] To demonstrate this detachment, Ghulam Ahmad required potential candidates to donate at least one-tenth of their inheritable wealth and assets to the Jama'at in order to fund the propagation of Islam and carry out the teachings of the Qur'an.[35] Ghulam Ahmad included logistical details about the collection and allocation of the endowment. He then vowed that successful participants in the scheme would be buried in the *bahishtī maqbara* alongside their master, the promised messiah.

The *al-Wasiyyat* scheme represented Jama'at-i Ahmadiyya's first-ever fixed donation system, which established a benchmark for financial sacrifice. Up to this point, Ahmadis had only paid the zakat, like other Muslims. Ghulam Ahmad had previously appealed to disciples for funding on a case-by-case basis, whenever a situation arose in which revenue was required for special projects. There were no other financial obligations exclusive to Jama'at-i Ahmadiyya. The *al-Wasiyyat* scheme offered individual Ahmadis a means to participate in a divinely ordained venture whose end result provided reasonable confidence in this world that they would enter paradise in the next world.[36] Although the *al-Wasiyyat* scheme was never intended for every Ahmadi, its exclusivity contributed to the notion of a separate Ahmadi identity through distinctive religious practices. It was also the first step towards providing Jama'at-i Ahmadiyya with a continuous source of funding, which was necessary for financial independence, self-sufficiency, and lasting autonomy from non-Ahmadi resources.

Ghulam Ahmad founded an *anjuman* (committee) called the Sadr Anjuman Ahmadiyya (Executive Ahmadiyya Committee) to administer the collection and distribution of revenue generated by the *al-Wasiyyat* scheme.[37] This placed considerable authority in the hands of a singular body, even though Ghulam Ahmad personally presided over the *sadr anjuman* until his death in 1908. Ghulam Ahmad's involvement in the *anjuman* ensured his own preeminence in the committee's leadership while Nur al-Din officially occupied the most senior office of president, which postponed questions of authority until later.[38] The only problem after Ghulam Ahmad's death was determining an independent role for the *sadr anjuman* with its structure and internal hierarchy once the community, on its own accord, had decided to elect a separate *khalifa*. It is not surprising that Nur al-Din served as the first president of the Sadr Anjuman Ahmadiyya under Ghulam Ahmad before becoming *khalīfat al-masīh*. Similarly, Mahmud Ahmad was appointed head of the Sadr Anjuman Ahmadiyya by Nur al-Din, before becoming Ghulam Ahmad's second successor. At present, a trend appears to be developing in which four of Ghulam Ahmad's five successors were serving as president of the *sadr anjuman* at the time of their predecessor's death.

About two weeks later, on January 6, 1906, Ghulam Ahmad wrote an appendix to *al-Wasiyyat* in an attempt to explain procedures for the scheme. The appendix stipulated requirements for membership in the *sadr anjuman,* revealing important information regarding its intended role within the community. Considering the nature of its origins, the Sadr Anjuman Ahmadiyya had the potential to establish a system of governance for Jama'at-i Ahmadiyya in Ghulam Ahmad's absence. Section 16 of the appendix states, however, that only two members of the *sadr anjuman* must be proficient in the Qur'an, hadith, and Arabic, as well as being versed in Ahmadi literature, which seems rather low for a religiously authoritative body.[39] This could be taken to imply that Ghulam Ahmad never intended the *sadr anjuman* to function as a religiously or politically authoritative body, which may well have been reserved for *khilāfat-i ahmadiyya* as the

Qadiani branch maintains. In this case perhaps the Sadr Anjuman Ahmadiyya was intended to serve as more of an administrative arm of the true seat of authority within the Jama'at, as it did during Ghulam Ahmad's lifetime. The small size of the original committee, which only had six non-representative members excluding Ghulam Ahmad, is consistent with its purely administrative role.[40] In other passages of the appendix, such as section 13, Ghulam Ahmad presented a challenge to this notion by explicitly stating that the Sadr Anjuman Ahmadiyya would serve as his representative after his death.

> Because the *anjuman* is the representative of God's appointed vicegerent, for this reason the *anjuman* will have to be completely free from all traces of worldliness and all its affairs should be extremely pure and founded on justice.
>
> (*chūṅke anjuman khudā ke muqarrar karda khalīfa kī jā-nishīn hay is liyē anjuman ko dunyā dārī ke rangoṅ se bi-kullī pāk rahnā hogā awr us ke tamām mu'āmilāt nihāyat sāf awr insāf par mubnī honē chāhiyeṅ.*)[41]

This passage shows that Ghulam Ahmad vested considerable authority in the *anjuman* as his representative, even though the notion of *khilāfat* remains unresolved. This is the only passage of *al-Wasiyyat* in which Ghulam Ahmad used the word "*khalīfa*," and he used it in reference to himself. In contrast, he referred to the Sadr Anjuman Ahmadiyya as his *jā-nishīn*, which has similar connotations of authoritative representation within this context, especially in English translation. Although the term *jā-nishīn* does not carry the same significance as *khalīfa* in the broader Islamic tradition, the two have become almost interchangeable in South Asian Sufism, where both terms may be applied to the head of a Sufi order and his successors. Ahmadis actually infer the establishment of *khilāfat-i ahmadiyya* from a different passage in *al-Wasiyyat*, where Ghulam Ahmad made provisions for community members to accept *bay'at* on his behalf in the event of his absence, which was revealed to have been fast approaching.

> Such persons will be selected according to the opinion of the believers. So whomever forty believers agree upon as competent to accept the *bay'at* from others in my name will be authorized to accept the *bay'at*. And he ought to make himself into an example for others. God has informed me that "I will raise a person for your community (*jamā'at*) from your progeny, and I will distinguish him through his nearness [to God] and his revelations, and he will be a means to advance truth through which many people will accept truth."
>
> (*ayse logoṅ kā intakhāb mominoṅ ke rā'ē par hogā—pas jis shakhs kī nisbat chālīs momin ittifāq kareṅge ke wo is bāt ke lā'iq hay ke mere nām par logoṅ se bay'at le wo bay'at lene kā majāz hogā—awr chāhi'ē ke wo apne taī'ṅ dūsroṅ ke liyē namūna banāwe—khudā ne mujhe khabar dī hay ke mayṅ terī jamā'at ke liyē terī-hī zurrīyat se ek shakhs ko qā'im karūṅgā awr us ko apne qurb awr wahy se makhsūs karūṅgā awr us ke zarī'e se haqq taraqqī karegā awr bahut se log sachā'ī ko qabūl kareṅge.*)[42]

Inferring the establishment of some sort of *khilāfat* from this passage might seem feasible, but the creation of an institutional hierarchy is not self-evident from the text. This presents a problem for the Qadiani vision of *khilāfat*, where only one supreme *khalīfa* at a time is authorized to accept the promised messiah's *bay'at*. Ghulam Ahmad never explicitly limited the number of *khalīfas*, nor centralized their authority, as is the case with *khilāfat-i ahmadiyya*. This suggests that the broader notion of *khilāfat-i ahmadiyya* was not necessarily intended exclusively for one person at a time. Anyone who acquired the confidence of forty believers had the potential to accept the *bay'at* in Ghulam Ahmad's name. Perhaps it is worth highlighting that Ghulam Ahmad did not allow anyone to accept *bay'at* in their own name. He also did not restrict the acceptance of *bay'at* to his progeny, even though he prophesized that someone from his progeny would guide people to truth (*haqq*). The stipulation of acquiring the confidence of forty believers and the prophecy about his progeny are mutually exclusive, since the person from Ghulam Ahmad's progeny who guides people to truth does not need to be the one who accepts *bay'at*. This means that the possibility remains for several members of Jama'at-i Ahmadiyya to have been authorized to accept *bay'at* concurrently, irrespective of lineage, which may include but is not limited to Ghulam Ahmad's progeny.

The *bay'at* ceremony is a standard feature of Sufi orders in which authorized individuals who may initiate new members into the order are typically known as *khalīfas*, and at times *jā-nishīn*s, among other terms in South Asian Islam. It is common for multiple *khalīfas* to carry out the sacred teachings of the Sufi master. Within South Asian Sufism in particular, *khilāfat* often became hereditary,[43] similar to *khilāfat-i ahmadiyya*, where the only *khalīfa* to date beyond Ghulam Ahmad's family has been Nur al-Din. In this manner, Jama'at-i Ahmadiyya adopted the familiar institution of *khilāfat*, along with numerous other Sufi orders in India, but restricted authority to only one *khalīfa* at a time. By limiting the institution of *khilāfat-i ahmadiyya* to one lone individual, the Qadiani branch consolidated the leadership of the Jama'at and reduced its sphere of religious authority considerably. It seems strange, however, for such a prolific writer as Mirza Ghulam Ahmad to have reduced the exposition of arguably one of the Jama'at's most important institutions to a mere footnote in one of his shorter texts. The institution of *khilāfat*, nevertheless, became the primary seat of authority for the Jama'at while the Sadr Anjuman Ahmadiyya took on a more supplementary role within this framework.

According to *al-Wasiyyat*, the *sadr anjuman* was a centralized institution whose headquarters was to remain in Qadian.[44] In contrast, there were no geographical restrictions placed upon the *khalīfa*, who was apparently authorized to take *bay'at* from anywhere. Ghulam Ahmad described the primary function of the Sadr Anjuman Ahmadiyya as collecting and distributing funds to support the propagation of Islam, whereas he noted that those authorized to accept the *bay'at* were responsible for providing spiritual guidance and gathering people to the one faith.[45] At present, some Qadianis differentiate between the spiritual authority of the *khalīfa* and the administrative authority of the Sadr Anjuman Ahmadiyya, even though the *khalīfa* in reality remains supreme.

Ghulam Ahmad alluded to the coming of a second manifestation of God's power (*qudrat-i thānī* or *dūsrī qudrat*) after his death, which was mentioned in contrast to his own role as the first manifestation: "I am an embodiment of God's power (*mayñ khudā kī ek mujassam qudrat hūñ*)."[46] In his elucidation, he said that God always displayed two manifestations of power to dispel two false joys (*do jhūtī khūshīāñ*) of opponents.[47] He also foretold that a second manifestation would descend from the heavens at an unknown time, which was worth waiting for "because it is everlasting, and its continuity will not be broken until the day of judgment (*kyoñ-ke wo dā'imī hay jis kā silsila qiyāmat tak munqata' nahīñ hogā*)."[48] Ghulam Ahmad explained that the second manifestation was eternal and hence preferable to the first, but could not come until he had passed away.[49]

Ahmadis have interpreted these prophecies of the second manifestation to be implicit references to the institution of *khilāfat-i ahmadiyya*. By combining Ghulam Ahmad's instructions for the *anjuman,* his permission for others to accept *bay'at,* and his dual prophecies for a blessed progeny alongside the next display of manifest power (*qudrat-i thānī*), the members of Jama'at-i Ahmadiyya (both Lahoris and Qadianis) established the institution of *khilāfat-i ahmadiyya.* As such, the guidelines from *al-Wasiyyat* laid the foundation for two governing bodies in Jama'at-i Ahmadiyya, namely the Sadr Anjuman Ahmadiyya and the *khilāfat-i ahmadiyya.* This enabled the Jama'at to remain united within a shared framework throughout Nur al-Din's reign. It was not until Nur al-Din's death that underlying differences led to a debate about the legitimacy of an authoritative institution of *khilāfat,* which once again pitted Lahoris against Qadianis. In the end, the Qadianis sided with Mahmud Ahmad's *khilāfat* whereas the Lahoris preferred a sovereign *anjuman,* which resulted in the formation of the Ahmadiyya Anjuman-i Isha'at-i Islam Lahore.

Throughout the years of Nur al-Din's *khilāfat,* from 1908 to 1914, there was a consensus regarding the framework of Ahmadi leadership, which combined an *anjuman* with *khilāfat.* This enabled dissenting theological views to exist within a singular community. Once the split had taken place, this was no longer possible. Muhammad 'Ali, as head of the Ahmadiyya Anjuman-i Isha'at-i Islam Lahore, never took the title *khalīfa.* Instead, he took the title *amīr,* perhaps in an attempt to avoid the authoritarian connotations associated with *khilāfat.* As *amīr,* Muhammad 'Ali retained political autonomy but lacked the ability to enforce his religious rulings. This approach was markedly different from the original two manifestations of the Sadr Anjuman Ahmadiyya, where, respectively, Ghulam

Ahmad himself or Nur al-Din as *khalīfat al-masīh* presided over the *anjuman*'s appointed president. The divergent views regarding the roles of the *sadr anjuman* and *khilāfat-i ahmadiyya* gradually shaped both communities independently, as each side continued pointing to passages in *al-Wasiyyat* to validate its claims.

Changes in the Ahmadi Belief System: From Theory to Practice

The split in Jamaʻat-i Ahmadiyya resulted in two factions with conflicting interpretations of Ghulam Ahmad's message. Although both groups shared a common history through Ghulam Ahmad and Nur al-Din, the differences in ideology led to differences in administrative structure, which over time led to differences in identity. The problem of *takfīr* (declaring someone a nonbeliever) in practice has sociological implications. Qadiani Ahmadis began isolating themselves as a community by separating from non-Ahmadi Muslims in ritual prayer. This was due to Mirza Mahmud Ahmad's orders forbidding disciples to pray behind non-Ahmadi imams, even in exceptional cases like funerals.[50] As before, the Lahori Jamaʻat expressed its outrage by accusing Mahmud Ahmad of distorting Ghulam Ahmad's teachings and attempting to form a new religion.[51] But the physical separation was difficult to ignore. By separating themselves in congregational prayer, Qadianis turned theoretical debates into religious ritual. Unlike before, these differences were clearly manifest to both insiders and outsiders. Similar changes facilitated further separation by enabling internal differences in belief to result in external differences in practice.

Mahmud Ahmad soon placed restrictions on marriages with non-Ahmadis. Although the prohibition was more strictly enforced among Ahmadi women who wished to marry non-Ahmadi Muslim men, the ruling was applied to both genders. He stated:

> Presently, the needs of our community dictate that members neither give their women to non-Ahmadis nor accept other women in marriage.
>
> (*āj hamārī zarūrīyāt chāhtī hayñ ke jamāʻat is tajwīz par ʻamal karē ke ghayr ahmadīyoñ ko na larkī dē awr na un kī larkī lē.*)[52]

This represented a critical break in the social structure of Jamaʻat-i Ahmadiyya at the grassroots level for several families who were now displaying their new Ahmadi identities to onlookers through distinctive social practices. Previously, scholars like Peter Hardy erroneously attributed these changes to Mirza Ghulam Ahmad himself, but in actuality most began with Mirza Mahmud Ahmad.[53] Although Ghulam Ahmad certainly placed restrictions on his disciples, they were administered in a different context and were not conceived of in this way. Children born to Ahmadi parents were now being considered Ahmadis by birth, despite being too young to take *bayʻat*. This practice represents a significant departure from most Sufi orders in the subcontinent, whose members remain involved in every social aspect of Muslim civil society. A *bay'at* was typically a non-transferable allegiance between *murīd* and *murshid* (student and teacher), but with Ahmadi allegiance, Ahmadiyyat could now be passed from generation to generation, as if it was a new religion.

The (often self-imposed) isolation of Jama'at-i Ahmadiyya gave way to new Ahmadi devotional practices, which began to take precedence over those in conventional Islam. Some changes involved taking old Islamic practices and recasting them in a new light. The process of shifting priorities included taking a fresh look at the virtues of financial sacrifice, which was emphasized to members with a renewed sense of urgency. Mahmud Ahmad developed an elaborate donation system (*chandā*) to provide regular revenue for his Jama'at. Although Ghulam Ahmad's *al-Wasiyyat* scheme was firmly in place, it only provided the Jama'at with income upon the death of members who had chosen to participate in it, whereas all others were excluded. Mahmud Ahmad revised the *al-Wasiyyat* scheme to include annual donations based on income, which created a more consistent source of revenue for the Jama'at. Mahmud Ahmad also introduced numerous other subscriptions to be paid by Ahmadis during the course of his *khilāfat,* which will be examined below. Ahmadis were expected to contribute to these schemes in addition to zakat, which in practice was gradually superseded by other mandatory donations.

Similarly, the *jalsa sālāna* (annual gathering) introduced by Ghulam Ahmad was developed into an annual convention that some consider to have superseded the grand pilgrimage of hajj. In his comments on Ghulam Ahmad's failure to perform the hajj, Spencer Lavan inferred that the *jalsa* itself served as an annual Ahmadi pilgrimage.[54] This particular issue of the hajj in Ahmadi Islam is worth discussing in some detail as Mirza Ghulam Ahmad's failure to perform the mandatory pilgrimage to Mecca has become a contentious issue. In actuality, Mirza Ghulam Ahmad never left the Indian subcontinent. Lavan cited how Ghulam Ahmad was prone to chronic illness, which would have absolved him from performing the hajj, but his comments on the role of the *jalsa* were independent of this discussion.[55] Lavan's view that the contemporary *jalsa* was displacing the pilgrimage to Mecca may have overlooked recent political restrictions, which currently prohibit Ahmadis from performing the hajj as Ahmadis. Many more Ahmadis consequently attend their respective *jalsa*s than journey to Mecca for hajj. Likewise, the number of Ahmadis who travel internationally each year to attend the main *jalsa* outside London is significantly higher than those who seem to be performing the hajj.

When Ghulam Ahmad was questioned regarding his failure to perform the hajj, he said that his primary obligation, as someone appointed by Allah, was propagating his mission (*tablīgh*).[56] When Ghulam Ahmad was asked the same question on a different occasion, he said that his priority was killing the swine and breaking the cross in reference to the popularly conceived duties of the *mahdī*. Ghulam Ahmad added that although he had already killed many swine, several stubborn souls remained.[57] Ahmadis nonetheless place extraordinary emphasis on attending yearly festivals, such as the *jalsa* gatherings. It may be premature to suggest that the *jalsa sālāna* has become a substitute for hajj, even though new rituals and practices have added unique dimensions to Ahmadi life and contributed to the emergence of a distinctive Ahmadi religious identity.

As the Qadiani branch was beginning to distinguish itself, the Lahori branch was attempting to reaffirm its Sunni identity.[58] Both sides eventually abandoned the subtle nuances of Ghulam Ahmad's prophethood altogether, albeit for different reasons. Whereas the Qadianis felt more comfortable simply asserting that Ghulam Ahmad was a prophet, the Lahoris preferred to simply deny it. Current Lahori publications typically avoid making any prophetic distinction whatsoever in Ghulam Ahmad's spiritual status and instead choose to emphasize his role as a *mujaddid* (renewer of faith). When clarifying its views, the Lahori branch tends to focus its concerns on the Qadiani *khilāfat*, in which *khilāfat-i ahmadiyya* is presented as contrary to Ghulam Ahmad's thought, and Mahmud Ahmad is treated as the usurper of his father's authority.[59] In many ways, however, this accurately conveys the source of contention for Lahoris. There is little difference in reality between the Ahmadiyya Anjuman-i Isha'at-i Islam Lahore and the Sadr Anjuman Ahmadiyya with respect to their authoritative positions over their communities. This can easily be demonstrated by the fact that neither *anjuman* has ever been able to impose its religious ideology on its Jama'at, which only reinforces the primary distinction between the two groups as having been determined by the role of *khilāfat*.

The Institutionalization of Jama'at-i Ahmadiyya

Despite having undergone a number of changes and considerable expansion over the past century, the Sadr Anjuman Ahmadiyya today remains the primary administrative authority in Jama'at-i Ahmadiyya under the *khalīfat al-masīh*.[60] Mirza Mahmud Ahmad's desire for Jama'at-i Ahmadiyya to function on a global platform demanded that he streamline his power. By institutionalizing the Jama'at, Mirza Mahmud Ahmad enabled his authority as a sovereign *khalīfa* to efficiently reach local Ahmadi congregations, which he was determined to establish throughout the world. A transfer of charisma needed to take place between the divine guidance of the promised messiah and the institution of *khilāfat* formed by his successors. Within a month of his election, Mirza Mahmud Ahmad set up an advisory council (*majlis-i shūrā*), which in 1922 became a permanent part of the Jama'at's infrastructure. Each year, *majlis-i shūrā* members from local Ahmadi chapters worldwide still develop proposals which are sent to the *khalīfa* regarding their respective positions on Jama'at policy.

The echelons of authority within the Jama'at hierarchy are based on geographic boundaries, with local, regional, and national levels. Executive representatives within the hierarchy distinguish between administrative or spiritual aspects of Ahmadi life, though both are embodied by the *khalīfat al-masīh.* Ahmadi missionaries are responsible for religious leadership, including daily worship, spiritual guidance, and religious propagation. They are encouraged to remain impartial in order to resolve potential disputes between members. Typically, an Ahmadi missionary (*muballigh*) must attend a seven-year training course at an Ahmadi seminary before being assigned to local chapters, which are usually situated in major cities. These missionaries fall under the jurisdiction of the national *amīr,* who serves as a liaison between the *khalīfa*'s personal administration and each local chapter. In western countries, Ahmadi missionaries tend to avoid political involvement, whereas national *amīr*s, who typically do not have any formal religious education or training, might be heavily involved in local politics. Each local chapter has a president, who serves as the administrative leader and is elected at regular intervals by financially contributing members of the community. Members who do not or cannot contribute financially are barred from participating in elections, unless they obtain special permission from the *khalīfat al-masīh.* This route carries social stigma, however, and is apparently regarded as a humiliating process.

Whereas a missionary conveys the national or international interests of the Jama'at to local members, the president expresses the concerns of local members to the *amīr* or *khalīfa.* In local chapters without missionaries, the president is responsible for religious guidance, even though the president, like the *amīr,* rarely has any formal religious education or training. Many Ahmadi mosques fit comfortably within modernist trends in this respect, since local leaders often have reasonably high secular credentials but little knowledge of Islam's intellectual tradition. For example, they may hold university degrees instead of traditional authorizations of learning.

Mahmud Ahmad established separate auxiliary organizations for women in an attempt to give them a voice in administrative affairs. The *lajna imā'illāh* (council for the handmaidens of God) was founded in December 1922 for Ahmadi women above age fifteen. *Nāsirāt al-ahmadiyya* (female helpers of Ahmadiyya or Ahmadi female helpers) was formed in December 1938 for girls of age fifteen and under. Each auxiliary organization for women meets locally and elects its own president. Each local *lajna* president reports to a national *lajna* president (*sadr lajna imā'illāh*), who reports directly to the *khalīfat al-masīh.* This suggests that Ahmadi women have some autonomy in terms of handling their own affairs within the administration.

The men are split into three groups, also based on age. The *majlis khuddām al-ahmadiyya* (organization for the servants of Ahmadiyya, or perhaps for Ahmadi servants), an auxiliary organization consisting of young men of ages fifteen to forty, was founded in December 1938. The *khuddām* are responsible for everything requiring physical labor and are usually the first to carry out new initiatives. Like the *lajna*, each local *khuddām* chapter elects its leader (*qā'id*) and its national president (*sadr majlis khuddām al-ahmadiyya*), who like his female counterpart reports directly to the *khalīfat al-masīh*. In July 1940, the *majlis atfāl al-ahmadiyya* (Ahmadiyya children's organization) was created for boys ages seven to fifteen. The *atfāl* are largely a subset of the *khuddām*, in the sense that they fall under the jurisdiction of the local *qā'id*. The third and final auxiliary organization, *majlis ansārullāh* (organization for the helpers of Allah), was founded in the same year, in 1940, for men above age forty. The *ansār* often provide intellectual and spiritual guidance for younger members, as the elders of Jama'at-i Ahmadiyya. The *majlis ansārullāh* has a local leader (*zaīm*) along with a national leader (*sadr majlis ansārullāh*), who reports directly to the *khalīfat al-masīh*. For areas with larger Ahmadi populations, there may be additional subdivisions in ranks to alleviate workloads and provide administrative support, but the primary strata of the hierarchy remain the same.

It is no coincidence that most of the auxiliaries were formed in the 1930s when Mahmud Ahmad was heavily involved in the crisis in Kashmir, which is discussed in the following chapter. Jama'at-i Ahmadiyya's increased political involvement worldwide at the time—and its entanglement with the Majlis-i Ahrar in particular—demanded a substantial increase in funding beyond the *al-Wasiyyat* scheme.[61] In November 1934, Mahmud Ahmad created the *tahrīk-i jadīd* (new movement) fund for the expansion and propagation of Ahmadi Islam in foreign lands.[62] A committee called the Tahrik-i Jadid Anjuman Ahmadiyya was set up as a subsidiary of the Sadr Anjuman Ahmadiyya to manage the new source of funding. Ahmadis are encouraged to contribute generously to the *tahrīk-i jadīd* scheme in addition to other financial obligations. Although the tension with the Ahrar over Kashmir eventually subsided, the *tahrīk-i jadīd* scheme remained in place for charitable contributions through annual subscriptions.

Mahmud Ahmad solicited donations of both time and money for Tahrik-i Jadid. He purportedly urged Ahmadis to limit themselves to a single meal per day in order to donate the resulting savings to Tahrik-i Jadid. In an attempt to increase missionaries, Mahmud Ahmad appealed to members to offer themselves to the Jama'at as living endowments (*waqf*), enabling them to work on a voluntary basis for minimal remuneration. He compelled parents to persuade children to dedicate their lives to the Jama'at in this fashion, by enrolling them in Ahmadi seminaries for missionary training. Influential Ahmadis were asked to give lectures and compose publishable works on behalf of the Jama'at. Students were advised to seek the *khalīfa*'s counsel prior to pursing higher education, so that they would choose a course of study beneficial for the movement. Everyone was encouraged to participate in the scheme to fulfill the mission of the promised messiah however possible, whether by adopting simple lives, by volunteering services, or by donating personal property.

Since then, these schemes have been expanded and updated in various ways in accordance with the community's needs. For example, on April 3, 1987, the fourth *khalīfa*, Mirza Tahir Ahmad, launched the *waqf-i nau* (new[born] endowment) scheme, in which parents were asked to endow their children's lives for Jama'at service during infancy. Although the children's future occupations were not limited to missionary work, parents could even enlist their children before birth. As the first generation of this group has only recently come of age, it appears to have provided Jama'at-i Ahmadiyya with an unending labor force at virtually no expense.[63]

In 1958, eleven years after the partition which forced Jama'at-i Ahmadiyya to relocate its headquarters to Rabwah, Pakistan, Mahmud Ahmad launched the *waqf-i jadīd* (new endowment) scheme to generate revenue for the propagation of Ahmadi Islam in rural Pakistan.[64] Another subsidiary of the Sadr Anjuman Ahmadiyya was established to oversee the new source of income and appropriate funds. Although, the fourth *khalīfa*, Mirza Tahir Ahmad, expanded its mission in 1986 to include remote and developing areas around the world, most proceeds from the *waqf-i jadīd* scheme are still spent primarily on the subcontinent. This completed Jama'at-i Ahmadiyya's three main administrative branches: the Sadr Anjuman Ahmadiyya, Tahrik-i Jadid, and Waqf-i Jadid.[65] It is important to recognize once again that all of these branches remain well within the domain of the *khalīfat al-masīh*.

The structure of the Jama'at created a religious institution with formalized procedures that provided boundaries for individual Ahmadis. It objectified authority by substantiating a social system that could be applied to every local chapter throughout the world. Now individual Ahmadis had an acute awareness of the progression of religious authority through a clear chain of command. The hierarchy begins with the local president and moves up through the national *amīr* until it reaches the *khalīfa*, who represents God's chosen messiah and to some extent God himself. Moreover, at the local level, administrative rank created a distinction between officeholders and non-officeholders, which is implicitly used to imply religious seniority. This enables individuals in isolated areas to assess their personal role within the institutional hierarchy, and hence within the broader Jama'at.

Mirza Ghulam Ahmad's Jama'at-i Ahmadiyya was considerably different from the Jama'at of today. Although he too had complete control over his community, Ghulam Ahmad's authority was purely charismatic in the sense that it was derived entirely from God. In contrast, Mirza Mahmud Ahmad's legitimacy as *khalīfa* was contingent upon his father's charisma. Mahmud Ahmad drew upon his father's charisma to substantiate his reign through the creation of institutional *khilāfat*, which was made possible by redefining the role of the Sadr Anjuman Ahmadiyya. He facilitated this process by persistently publicizing his father's prophecies from *al-Wasiyyat*, which referred to a member of Ghulam Ahmad's progeny who would someday lead people to truth.[66] In addition, Mahmud Ahmad utilized other prophecies pertaining to Ghulam Ahmad's progeny to reinforce his right to *khilāfat*.[67] Recognizing *khilāfat-i ahmadiyya* in itself was no longer enough. Ahmadis now needed to accept the *khalīfa*'s divine appointment. This became a central theme in Ahmadi Islam from the time of the Lahori-Qadiani split, which has since been endorsed by each subsequent successor of Mirza Mahmud Ahmad.[68]

The Qadiani branch perceived the structural changes in the Jamaʿat as fulfillment of divine prophecy. On February 20, 1944, before a gathering in Hoshiarpur, Mirza Bashir al-Din Mahmud Ahmad cemented his position in Ahmadi history by formally declaring that he was indeed the *muslih-i mawʿūd* (promised reformer) that Ghulam Ahmad had prophesized over half a century before.[69] The date marked the fifty-eighth anniversary of Ghulam Ahmad's first publication of the prophecy regarding his blessed son. This placed an exceptional burden on Lahori opponents, who had difficulty explaining away Mahmud Ahmad's lineage and his charisma. Even though Mahmud Ahmad happened to be the *khalīfa*, it was the institution of *khilāfat* itself that in reality embodied Ghulam Ahmad's charisma by spreading it throughout the new structure of Jamaʿat-i Ahmadiyya. This enabled each officeholder to participate in the transfer of charisma, making it possible for individual Ahmadis to share in the fulfillment of divine prophecy personally. Whereas ineffable experiences, enigmatic prophecies, and Sufi-style mysticism were all esoteric aspects of Ghulam Ahmad's charisma, Mahmud Ahmad transformed them into exoteric offices with administrative titles. The bureaucratization of charisma meant that spirituality itself could be derived from obedience to—or at times participation in—the structural hierarchy (*nizām*) of the Jamaʿat, which was welcomed by Ahmadis as a manifestation of God's favor.

Breaking down the layers of authority in *khilāfat-i ahmadiyya* is an exercise in institutional representation. Ghulam Ahmad as the *mahdī* and the *masīh* represents the correct interpretation of God's law and message, the *khalīfa* represents the promised messiah, the *amīr* represents the *khalīfa*, and the president represents the *amīr*. All claim that their positions are authorized by divine will. In practice, few members, if any, have any formal religious education or training, which is fascinating for a religious hierarchy. Members of the hierarchy, like the *khalīfa*, substantiate their legitimacy purely through Ghulam Ahmad's institutionalized charisma. Each individual Ahmadi is personally linked to some vague sense of charisma through the institution of *khilāfat*, even though s/he may have little or no contact with the *khalīfat al-masīh*. Paradoxically, the *khalīfat al-masīh* is the keystone that binds the Jamaʿat together, even though he too is bound by the same institutionalized charisma in a similar fashion.

Beyond the Split and Towards an Ahmadi Identity:
The Early Years, 1914–1925

The series of events beginning with Mirza Ghulam Ahmad's death, followed by the death of Hakim Nur al-Din, which culminated in the splitting of Jama'at-i Ahmadiyya, placed extraordinary strains on community members and their leadership. The years immediately following Mahmud Ahmad's election have been regarded as some of the most trying in Ahmadi history. The general uncertainty and overall confusion in the movement left many Ahmadis disoriented, as they looked to their leadership for a sense of stability. But the instability itself provided Mahmud Ahmad with the flexibility needed to change the direction of the movement without adverse reactions from disciples. Once the split in the movement became final, the time for dissent had passed. Those who had chosen to remain with Mahmud Ahmad were obliged by his discretionary decisions to display a renewed sense of fidelity. The multiple changes in leadership had raised new questions regarding the developing identity of the Jama'at, which prevented the community from normalizing itself by settling the fluctuations in its evolving identity. It was not until the mid-1920s that the young *khalīfa,* Mirza Bashir al-Din Mahmud Ahmad, gained the confidence and foresight necessary to define for his members what he thought the future of Ahmadiyyat ought to be. For this reason, throughout the formative period of Ahmadi Islam, many of the Jama'at's efforts were exerted in coming to terms with changes in leadership, reconciling the ensuing fallout from the split, and resettling the Ahmadi identity into a state of equilibrium that was consistent with Mahmud Ahmad's vision.

Through the early stages of the Jama'at's development, variations in leadership were correlated with variations in sentiment regarding Ahmadi identity. This period represented a time of inner exploration for the community. The turmoil resulting from continuous changes forced individual Ahmadis to confront broader questions of Ahmadi identity more directly than had been done in the past. The obvious question of identity had become the most difficult to answer. What exactly does it mean to be an "Ahmadi"? For the earliest members of the movement, an intuitive answer was perhaps most appropriate, such as taking the *bay'at* of Mirza Ghulam Ahmad. For them, simply being a disciple of Mirza Ghulam Ahmad was sufficient to designate one as an Ahmadi. Accordingly, as the leadership of the community ventured through different manifestations following Ghulam Ahmad's death, the response to the principal question of identity needed to be delineated.

In 1889 when Ghulam Ahmad initially invited people to join his mission by taking his *bay'at* in Ludhiana, he published a list of conditions for those aspiring to become disciples. The *bay'at* itself was clearly intended as a privilege for the spiritually elite and for those who wished to join their ranks. At the time, being an Ahmadi was largely contingent upon Ghulam Ahmad's assessment of one's successful efforts to adhere to his requisite conditions. The conditions of *bay'at* defined the Ahmadi identity by making explicit Ghulam Ahmad's expectations of his followers. The very notion that the *bay'at* was conditional suggests that it could potentially have been revoked. The ten requisite conditions of primary concern upon which Mirza Ghulam Ahmad chose to base his movement may be abbreviated as follows:[70]

1. Abstaining from *shirk* (associating partners with God)
2. Abstaining from dishonesty, adultery, and lustful transgressions
3. Strict observance of the five daily prayers with an additional special emphasis on voluntarily offering the *tahajjud* (late night/predawn) prayer, seeking forgiveness, and invoking blessings in praise of the Prophet
4. Abstaining from verbally or physically abusing anyone or anything while maintaining a general sense of compassion towards everyone, especially other Muslims
5. Maintaining ultimate trust in and dependence on God through both good times and bad times
6. Abstaining from un-Islamic behavior by using the Qur'an and sunna as a model for one's life
7. Abstaining from pride and arrogance by adopting a general sense of humility
8. Giving precedence to Islam over everything, including one's wealth, honor, and loved ones
9. Maintaining a sincere commitment to the service of all of God's creation, especially service to humanity
10. Remaining faithful and obedient to Mirza Ghulam Ahmad in an exemplary manner that transcends ordinary relationships

Note that only the tenth of the ten conditions listed above resembles something inherently Ahmadi. The first nine conditions are all general Islamic principles which presumably any pious Muslim would willingly prioritize. Similarly, the final condition was a legitimate stipulation, which only prioritized Mirza Ghulam Ahmad's religious discretion over that of other spiritual teachers, as the *murshid* (spiritual guide) of his disciples. Although the provision is distinctly Ahmadi, it seems reasonable to impose such expectations upon one's spiritual disciples (*murīds*). For instance, had the name of any other Sufi *pīr, murshid,* or *shaykh* been substituted for Mirza Ghulam Ahmad in the tenth condition, the list would lose its Ahmadi identity. The ten conditions in this sense could easily have been requirements for initiation into any Sufi order in the broader Islamic tradition.

Considering that none of the conditions for joining the Ahmadi community presented a challenge to Islamic orthodoxy, the extraordinary aspect of Ghulam

Ahmad's list may not be visible in what is present, but rather in what is missing.[71] The absence of what are currently considered distinctive features of Ahmadi Islam is more significant than what amounts to Ghulam Ahmad's ten guidelines for spiritual development. There is no mention of Ghulam Ahmad's controversial claims, nor of those advanced by his successors. There are no references to Ghulam Ahmad's role as a *mujaddid, muhaddath, mahdī,* or the *masīh,* Jesus son of Mary. And there are no references to the implied consequences of these claims, which culminated in his prophetic rank and unique spiritual status. There is nothing to indicate that the Prophet Muhammad is anything other than the last prophet, since there is no indication of Ghulam Ahmad's interpretation of the Qur'anic verse declaring Muhammad to be the *khātam al-nabiyyīn* (seal of the prophets).[72] There are also no statements condemning violent jihad. And lastly, there are no allusions to Jesus's survival of crucifixion or his subsequent journey to his final resting place in Srinagar, Kashmir. In short, the characteristics commonly associated with Ahmadi Islam at present are conspicuously absent from the list of conditions for joining the movement in Ghulam Ahmad's 1889 treatise. One may argue that Ghulam Ahmad did not fully elaborate the details of his religious claims until much later. He also never revised the conditions upon which he accepted *bay'at,* which suggests that the list accurately embodied the values that Ghulam Ahmad prioritized to his earliest followers.

In returning to the notion of identity, the ten conditions of *bay'at* demonstrate that the earliest members of Jama'at-i Ahmadiyya identified more closely with the broader Islamic tradition than the sectarian-style movement of today. This suggests that a shift has taken place, which obviates the use of the same criteria to construct the religious identity of Ahmadis in the contemporary Jama'at. Most scholars at present unassumingly narrow distinguishing features of Ahmadi Islam to three controversial doctrines without questioning how or why they came into being. They are Ghulam Ahmad's interpretation of *khātam al-nubuwwa,* the survival of Jesus after crucifixion, and strict adherence to nonviolent jihad.[73] This shift in religious identity has left a gap between the early community and the Ahmadiyya movement of today, which continues to broaden as a result of complex factors that will be explored in subsequent chapters. In the meantime, we shall look at the role of the conditions of *bay'at* in historical context.

Until his death in 1908, being Ahmadi hinged exclusively upon Ghulam Ahmad's willingness to accept a candidate's *bay'at.* If he decided to refuse, reject, or revoke a disciple's *bay'at,* then considering that person Ahmadi would have been problematic.[74] After Ghulam Ahmad's death, however, the face of Jama'at-i Ahmadiyya changed. The unresolved issues that perpetuated the Lahori-Qadiani split, along with the actual splitting of the movement itself into two geographically separate camps, led to more elaborate responses to the primary question of identity, which yielded new understandings of what it meant to be Ahmadi.

Although the original ten conditions of *bay'at* remain unchanged to this day, they no longer exclusively represent the conditions for one's induction into Jama'at-i Ahmadiyya. At present, the initiation process includes an official Ahmadi "declaration form," which ameliorates the ten conditions of *bay'at* with explicit testimonies of faith that affirm one's belief in *khātam al-nubuwwa*, Mirza Ghulam Ahmad's status as the *imām mahdī* and promised messiah, and a vow of loyalty that pledges faithful obedience not only to the *khalīfat al-masīh*, but to the institution of *khilāfat-i ahmadiyya*.[75] These additions are far more consistent with what one might expect to find in a document that lists the terms for joining Jama'at-i Ahmadiyya. But this in itself does not provide a sense of how the addendum is viewed in comparison to the original ten conditions, nor the emphasis placed upon it by the Jama'at.

In practice, maintaining belief in Ghulam Ahmad's role as the promised messiah and *imām mahdī* in a way that implies his prophetic status appears to have overshadowed the previous dependence upon the original ten conditions of *bay'at*. This emphasis is in part why these tenets have become associated with popular conceptions of Jama'at-i Ahmadiyya. It also provides a sense of how restructuring Jama'at-i Ahmadiyya as an institutionalized religious organization fostered the emergence of a new Ahmadi identity based on supplementary beliefs, including *khātam al-nubuwwa*, Jesus's survival of the cross, and *khilāfat-i ahmadiyya*. For some reason, the new criteria still exclude an explicit reference to nonviolent jihad. In comparison to the original ten conditions of *bay'at*, the commitment to nonviolent jihad has increasingly been imbued with new social and political significance, particularly for Ahmadis living in the West in a post-9/11 era. During the course of my fieldwork, I was unable to find ordinary Ahmadis who had committed the ten conditions of *bay'at* to memory. This may provide an indication of their relative importance to the contemporary Ahmadi identity. Ahmadis are certainly familiar with the ten conditions of *bay'at*, but memorizing them or strictly adhering to them in daily practice is not a part of their religious self-image in a way that would contribute to self-identification. Within the community, little attention is given to memorizing or—perhaps more importantly—to implementing these conditions in daily practice. There is a discrepancy between the theory presented in Ahmadi texts and the lived religious practices of ordinary members of the community. Perhaps these observations may also apply to some extent to the "declaration form." At present, the "declaration form" is invariably accompanied by a third document, which carries considerable weight within the day-to-day lives of ordinary Ahmadis. This third document is used to determine a new initiate's prescribed financial contributions (*chandā*) to the Jama'at. The obligation to maintain regular financial contributions might not be formally stipulated in writing as expected. Contributing financially to the movement, however, is an essential part of remaining in good standing with the leadership, with few exceptions determined on a case-by-case basis. May it suffice to say that a detailed anthropological study of Jama'at-i Ahmadiyya's beliefs and practices would be a welcome contribution to the field.[76]

The procedure for the *bay'at* ceremony in Jama'at-i Ahmadiyya has been uncoupled from its sacred origins in Sufi initiation. The methods employed today more closely resemble the banal process of filling out an application form as opposed to the solemn Sufi expression of allegiance to one's spiritual mentor. The annual Ahmadi convention (*jalsa sālāna*) is the only exception where remnants of the Sufi ceremonial *bay'at* still linger today. Each year in London, thousands of Ahmadis gather to renew their *bay'at* at the hand of the *khalīfat al-masīh.* In a moving display, the *khalīfa* stretches his hand as each disciple surrounding him from every direction does the same to join him. Those beyond the inner circle place their right hand on the shoulder of the person in front of them creating an unbroken chain that leads directly to the *khalīfat al-masīh.* Aside from this annual exception, the Ahmadi *bay'at* ceremony has become wholly divorced from the deep expression of initiation rooted in the heritage of Sufi Islam. The community has largely abandoned the hallowed procedure of tradition, where the physical joining of hands serves as a demonstration of the spiritual connection between *murshid* and *murīd,* and instead replaced it with the signing of a piece of paper.

The shift in Ahmadi identity was a slow process that quietly evolved over successive generations during the first century following Ghulam Ahmad's death. The movement needed to refashion itself into a mold that was more conducive to the intense demands of proselytization, which surpassed those of a much smaller and less globalized Ahmadi community. The original organizational structure of the Jama'at was intended for the elitist membership of the earliest disciples, where recruits either kept in direct contact with Ghulam Ahmad or possessed the educational background to purchase, read, and comprehend his complex literary works. This structure lacked an institutional hierarchy, which was not suitable for the Jama'at of the future, when mass membership was destined to come from sections of the Punjab's rural population. The exclusivity of the early community and its sense of religious elitism were replaced with a more accommodating brand of religion that bureaucratized spiritual rank through the creation of a structural hierarchy.

Mahmud Ahmad was clearly aware of the logistics of mass conversion, which is why he took steps to adapt the configuration of the Jama'at appropriately. With a stabilization period following the split that enabled changes in leadership to settle down, the foundations for subsequent changes in ideology and structure were well established by the 1920s. But changes in communal identity following Mahmud Ahmad's succession to *khilāfat* and the split in the Ahmadiyya movement were not inevitable. The split only served as a catalyst for further changes by bringing the question of Ahmadi identity to the forefront, while Mahmud Ahmad's vision for his movement allowed changes to take place more smoothly and largely unopposed, following a purge of the Jama'at's Lahori members. In fact, it was the circumstances surrounding subsequent events which little by little honed the identity of the movement with gradual change. We shall now turn our attention to key events that punctuate Ahmadi history in an attempt to offer suggestions as to why the Ahmadi identity became so heavily politicized.

4 Politics and the Ahmadiyya Movement under Mirza Bashir al-Din Mahmud Ahmad

The "*Rangīlā Rasūl*" Incident: The "Playboy" Prophet

By 1925, Mirza Bashir al-Din Mahmud Ahmad had missionaries diligently setting up Ahmadi centers all over the world. Ahmadi Islam had touched virtually every continent through the establishment of local chapters in Western Europe, North America, both East and West Africa, Mauritius, Syria, and Palestine. It was the communal tensions back home in India, however, that were creating the greatest stir. Hindu-Muslim tensions had been building steadily before they came to a head in the late 1920s. Polemic pamphlets blaspheming religious rivals were popular on both sides when a spirited Arya Samajist published the *Rangīlā Rasūl* booklet in 1924, attributing a number of sexual exploits to the Prophet Muhammad.[1] The publication managed to capture the attention of Muslim India. The Arya polemicist responsible, Rajpal, was initially convicted under section 153A of India's penal code in an attempt to keep communal tensions under control. This amounted to a sentence of eighteen months in prison and a 1,000-rupee fine. But the Punjab High Court overturned the decision in June 1927 and acquitted Rajpal of the charges. In addition, the high court's Hindu justice, Dalip Singh, imprisoned the editor of Lahore's *Muslim Outlook* for expressing outrage following the acquittal, which only exacerbated the situation from the perspective of Punjab's Muslims. Defending the Prophet quickly became the focus of ordinary Muslims throughout India as a result.

Historically, few things have united Muslims as successfully as the defamation of the Prophet Muhammad. Jama'at-i Ahmadiyya, under Mirza Bashir al-Din Mahmud Ahmad, responded to the attack as mainstream Muslims followed its lead.[2] Mahmud Ahmad printed a poster with a picture of Mirza Ghulam Ahmad and a lengthy retort to the anti-Islamic remarks.[3] The poster circulated the *khalīfa*'s response, which roused support and clarified the limits of Muslim tolerance until the deputy commissioner ordered that it be torn down. It is possible that the Jamaʿat's response to the attacks materialized at the expense of softer paths to reconciliation with Hindus. Spencer Lavan argued that Ahmadi reactions, such as the polemic poster, further contributed to "creating the hostile climate of opinion" that prevailed throughout the *Rangīlā Rasūl* incident.[4] Nonetheless, the newly developing organizational structure of the Jamaʿat, coupled with the resolve of a young *khalīfa,* enabled the Muslim mainstream to find its voice during a brief period of communal discord. Many Punjabi Muslims benefited from Jamaʿat-i Ahmadiyya's streamlined institutional hierarchy and organizational framework, which by now was largely in place and ready to deploy a global network of missionaries at the *khalīfa*'s command.

The high court's failure to administer a punishment provoked an increase in anti-British sentiment throughout India beyond the Punjab. Many Muslims blamed the government for its weak response to the tract about the Prophet Muhammad. Mahmud Ahmad ordered the London mission to protest to the British secretary of state for India about what he labeled injustices abroad, including the imprisonment of the editor of the *Muslim Outlook.* The Ahmadi missionary responsible for fulfilling the *khalīfa*'s orders in London was ʿAbd al-Rahim Dard, one of the biographers of Mirza Ghulam Ahmad. Dard wrote a series of letters publicizing the event and informed British government officials that "Muslim leaders like the Head of the Ahmadiyya Community, Qadian, Sir Abdul Qadir and Sir Mohammad Iqbal [were] doing their best to keep the [Indian] masses under control."[5] The message was clear. Dard conveyed that the Ahmadiyya community would continue offering its loyalty to the British Raj during the strife. The Ahmadi mission in London followed up its correspondence with a petition that secured over five hundred signatures, including those of such notable figures as Sir Arthur Conan Doyle.[6] The reputation of the dignitaries who signed the petition appears to have compelled the British Parliament to respond.[7] The impact of the petition became clear when the signatures of Sir Arthur Conan Doyle and Sir William Simpson were named in the official response to Dard's letter as justification for action.[8] Jamaʿat-i Ahmadiyya's network successfully raised awareness about dysfunctional communal relations in India and prompted external action by Britain, due to its organizational structure, resolute missionaries, and excellent contacts with members of high society.

Locally in the Punjab, similar efforts were being made by Mahmud Ahmad, who found himself at the helm of a major pan-Islamic campaign that was no longer limited to Ahmadi disciples in Qadian. The defense of the Prophet Muhammad generated widespread support from the Muslim masses, including eminent leaders, with little opposition. This enabled local protests in the Punjab to take shape as grassroots movements by attracting large numbers of the Muslim population. Muslim solidarity was short-lived, however, as internal rivalries resurfaced. It is clear that sectarian differences were (perhaps grudgingly) ignored just long enough to retaliate against the attacks on the Prophet, which in this case benefited Jama'at-i Ahmadiyya. In her influential work, *Self and Sovereignty,* South Asian historian Ayesha Jalal noted:

> With the Ahmadis under Bashiruddin Mahmud taking a lead in propagating the way of life, and the work and character of the Prophet, there was no immediate danger of Muslims collectively turning upon enemies within. Individual Sunni Muslims might resent Ahmadis spearheading the veneration of the Prophet, but with one of Punjab's most indefatigable public speakers, Ataullah Shah Bukhari [co-founder of the Majlis-i Ahrar-i Islam], temporarily in jail for creating a breach of the peace, there was for the moment no prospect of a concerted popular campaign against the Qadian faction.[9]

Mirza Mahmud Ahmad had temporarily canvassed his way to the forefront of Muslim India's inner circle of political activists. This was not the last time that Mahmud Ahmad would allow religio-political activism to dominate his agenda. Given the historical context of the late 1920s, Jama'at-i Ahmadiyya's response was understandable and consistent with the views of most Muslims of the time. The *Rangīlā Rasūl* incident represented the degraded state of Hindu-Muslim relations at a difficult time in modern India's history. It served as a distraction from internal debates which had come to dominate India's Islamic scene by enabling sectarian Muslims to band together as defenders of the Prophet. It also demonstrated the political potential of Jama'at-i Ahmadiyya, which Mahmud Ahmad perceived as a sign of the Jama'at's ability to participate in worldly endeavors.

Although the second *khalīfa,* Mirza Mahmud Ahmad, may not have single-handedly prevented the situation from "degenerating into violence" in the way that Ahmadis fondly remember,[10] his role was significant, considering that the community contributed towards the intensification as well as the resolution of the conflict. The *Rangīlā Rasūl* incident marked a turning point in Ahmadi history. The perceived success encouraged Mahmud Ahmad to pursue political activism in anticipation of other opportunities that would soon present themselves in Kashmir.

Prelude to the Riots

Muslim rule in Jammu and Kashmir extends back before the Mughal period. A Muslim-majority population has dominated the Kashmir valley for several centuries under various forms of government. There was a brief interlude of Sikh rule during the Ranjit Singh era, which lasted nearly three decades but ended soon after his death in 1839. At this point, the British consolidation of India led to the signing of successive treaties in 1846, first in Lahore and then in Amritsar, which resulted in the transfer of the state of Jammu and Kashmir to the loyalist

Dogra chieftain, Gulab Singh, in exchange for a relatively small payment. Kashmir historian Mridu Rai notes that this enabled the British to avoid the logistical formalities of rule while maintaining an active influence in the region through a reduced role of "firm supervision."[11] Since the Dogra maharaja and his successive heirs were Hindu, Kashmiri Muslims developed the tendency of looking to co-religionists on the other side of the border for support from the Punjab whenever political tensions intensified. Punjabi Muslims had likewise taken to assessing their own state of affairs under the British by comparing it to the state of Muslims in Kashmir. In 1909, Punjabi Muslims held the Kashmiri Muslim Conference in Lahore in conjunction with the growing popularity of the independence movement.[12] The inception of the organization, however, was more of a symbolic gesture than a radical call to action. It took nearly twenty years of almost complete dormancy before the committee was revived with widespread recognition and mass publicity.

By the early 1930s the Dogra maharaja of Jammu and Kashmir, Hari Singh, had developed a reputation for highhanded treatment of his Muslim-majority subjects. The growth of political dissent in Muslim areas coincided with severe economic decline internationally, whose effects Kashmir could not escape. Heavy taxation resulting from the government's false appraisal of agricultural production left many families in hardship. More and more qualified Kashmiris were finding themselves without suitable work, which added to the perception of Muslim victimization. Opportunities for Kashmiri Muslims were diminishing on many levels, and halfhearted attempts to remedy the situation had failed. Only recently in 1927 a state-sponsored scholarship committee, consisting entirely of Hindu members, determined that eleven out of twelve possible awards would be given to Hindu students, leaving only one scholarship for a Muslim candidate. The selection was defended by government officials as being based entirely on "merit," which fueled a sense of inequality among Muslims. This led many to believe that the government was committed to truncating opportunities for Muslims before they entered the workforce.[13] Still, Kashmiri Muslims contested their situation with "remarkably little organized resistance" until the summer of 1931, when things began to change.[14]

Panic on the Streets of Srinagar: The Kashmir Riots

The underlying tensions that had been building steadily for decades reached their boiling point on June 5, 1931, when a Hindu head constable of police reportedly ordered a subordinate Muslim constable to stop reading the Qur'an. After allegedly calling the recitation nonsense (*bakwās*), the head constable proceeded to snatch the Qur'an from the hands of the subordinate officer and throw it into the dustbin.[15] The rumors about the incident alone were enough to provide the Punjabi press with ample material to provoke an international controversy.[16] Newspapers with colorful accounts of the event served as a catalyst for Muslim political mobilization. The sociopolitical climate of pre-partition Kashmir facilitated the notion of widespread Hindu favoritism, which polarized the population and made Muslims receptive to articles depicting them as "downtrodden slaves" of Dogra rule.[17] Advocates of India's Muslim population were livid, which led Punjabi protesters to stream across the border as the demonstrations began.

Towards the end of June 1931 a "European's cook" named 'Abd al-Qadīr was arrested for making a seditious speech at Srinagar's *khānaqāh mu'allā*.[18] Government reports indicate that the speech involved inciting listeners to violence by directing them "to kill Hindus and burn their temples."[19] The government tried to control the hype surrounding the trial by conducting the proceedings secretly within the Srinagar jail, where 'Abd al-Qadīr was being detained. The *darbār* (royal government) believed that a swift, closed trial would prevent public excitement and contradict what India's newspapers claimed was taking place. When whisperings of a "secret trial" leaked out the night before the arraignment, however, disaster became unavoidable. Thousands of demonstrators arrived at the Srinagar jail on July 13, 1931, to protest the proceedings inside.

It is understandable in retrospect why so many people believed that a secret trial was simply another Dogra conspiracy to continue oppressing Muslims. The police were summoned in the early morning hours, but did not arrive until the afternoon. The ill-preparedness of police was later attributed to the failure to appreciate the magnitude of the situation and to the overall lackadaisical attitudes of officers.[20] As the protest intensified, the anger of the crowd apparently escalated into belligerence. Irascible protesters surrounded the prison and began hurling stones and bricks at the guards. They proceeded to shake the telephone lines furiously, until they were finally cut off. The guards intermittently fired warning shots with minimal effect, but the crowd responded by trying to set fire to the prison. The guards opened fire, killing ten immediately, which successfully dispersed protesters away from the prison. The mob then carried the bodies back to the city, shouting slogans and waving banners soaked in the blood of the dead. Upon arrival, rioters devastated the Maharaj-ganj bazaar, located in the Hindu quarters of Srinagar, and looted a number of shops.[21]

The riots marked the beginning of three long years of strife, disturbances, and political unrest throughout the state of Jammu and Kashmir. Muslim shopkeepers declared a *hartāl* (strike) in the weeks that followed by refusing to open for business, bringing much of Srinagar's daily commerce to a standstill. Muslims continued their noncompliance by refusing to take part in the official Riot Enquiry Committee, despite repeated requests from the *darbār*. On September 23, 1931, a crowd of fifteen thousand dissidents armed with staffs and axes amassed at the house of Sa'd al-Din, a local Muslim who had recently risen to prominence for refusing to take part in the Riot Enquiry Committee. This time rioters apparently had "no quarrel with Hindus, but [rather] ha[d] declared Jehad [*sic*] against His Highness' government."[22]

An ordinance was passed the following evening, September 24, which gave ordinary members of the military and police extraordinary powers to control "turbulent persons" by making arrests and seizing property without warrant.[23] The ordinance also incorporated a clause which made "dissuading" others from military enlistment a prosecutable offense punishable by one year in prison, flogging, or both.[24] Angry responses led to retaliation from both sides. Following the Friday prayers on September 25 in the town of Shopian (south of Srinagar), a mob of Muslims attacked a subinspector and eight constables who were "watching the prayers," resulting in the death of one head constable. When the requested military reinforcements arrived and opened fire, another person was killed and at least seven more were injured.[25] Meanwhile, the British resident in Kashmir was led to believe that a "rapid improvement" of troop morale was taking place under the looming threat of the new ordinance. This only lasted until local "Europeans" began complaining that Hindus were abusing their newly acquired powers. Some Hindu officers apparently interpreted the ordinance to justify thrashing any Muslim who failed to say "*mahārājā sāhib kī jay*! [victory to the maharaja]" whenever they passed a member of the military or police. Indeed, this behavior was corrected as soon as possible, but some Muslims in Srinagar had already been "severely" beaten.[26]

From 1931 to 1934 communal disturbances in Kashmir displaced diplomacy as a preferred means of expressing political dissent.[27] The instability produced by the circumstances enabled a new Muslim leadership to emerge out of the broader movement for independence. Leaders identified the symbolism of India's Islamic cause in Kashmir, making the crisis a paradigm for Muslim independence. From a certain perspective, the Kashmir crisis exemplified both the tyrannical subjugation of Muslims and an idealized spiritual resistance that bordered on outright jihad. The new political leadership emerging from the center was eager to use the crisis as a means of substantiating its political vision in the event of a favorable outcome. The mainstream perception of the crisis in Kashmir provided an opportune moment for emerging Muslim leaders to demonstrate how their party's Islam was capable of transforming society in the manner in which they had claimed. Furthermore, the Kashmir crisis coincided with a time that was sufficiently removed from the failures of the Khilafat Movement, enabling India's aspiring leaders to substantiate their claims (once again) through seemingly new courses of action.[28]

Jama'at-i Ahmadiyya and the Revival of the All-India Kashmir Committee

Kashmir has always played a significant role in Ahmadi explanations of Jesus's survival of crucifixion.[29] Mirza Ghulam Ahmad himself wrote a tract in which he argued that both Jesus and Mary traveled to Kashmir after the crucifixion to escape further persecution.[30] Jama'at-i Ahmadiyya has subsequently produced an extensive amount of literature pertaining to Jesus's journey to Kashmir and his burial in a particular Sufi shrine in Srinagar, which Ghulam Ahmad identified as the actual tomb of Jesus.[31] In addition, Maulvi Hakim Nur al-Din, Ghulam Ahmad's closest companion and first successor (*khalīfat al-masīh* I), served as chief royal physician (*shāhī tabīb*) to the maharaja of Jammu and Kashmir for fifteen years, under Hari Singh's two predecessors.[32] Due to its importance to the community, Mahmud Ahmad visited Kashmir on a number of occasions, both before and after his ascension to *khilāfat* in 1914. With this in mind, it is not surprising that Jama'at-i Ahmadiyya was pursuing an aggressive missionary campaign in Kashmir prior to the outbreak of the riots.

Soon after the riots, on July 25, 1931, the Lahore-based Kashmiri Muslim Conference held a meeting in Shimla to determine its course of action. Many notable dignitaries were present, including Sir Muhammad Iqbal; Sir Mian Fazl-i Husain; the nawab of Malerkotla, Sir Muhammad Zulfiqar 'Ali Khan;[33] *shams al-'ulamā* Khwaja Hasan Nizami of Delhi, and Khan Bahadur Shaykh Rahim Bakhsh, as well as several other nawabs, a Deobandi professor, and high-ranking administrators from both the *Siyāsat* and *Muslim Outlook* newspapers. On Iqbal's nomination, the members unanimously chose Mirza Bashir al-Din Mahmud Ahmad as president, with his missionary disciple, 'Abd al-Rahim Dard, as secretary, of what they now called the All-India Kashmir Committee.[34]

The inaugural meeting at Shimla was important for several reasons, considering that the group's motivations for political mobilization were still the same, and the circumstances surrounding the Kashmiri Muslim Conference's former period of impotence had not really changed by 1931. The newly founded All-India Kashmir Committee still had no clear grounds for agency, in the sense that there was no official sponsorship from any of the three governments (Kashmiri, Indian, and British) involved. Likewise, there were no definitive goals, no explicit reasons for its existence, and no Kashmiri lobby officially asking for its help. For all intents and purposes, the All-India Kashmir Committee was no different than it had always been during its quieter years during the earlier part of the twentieth century. Prior to the meeting at Shimla, the committee was little more than an unorganized group of influential Muslims, predominantly from the Punjab, who were understandably upset about the conditions of their co-religionists in Kashmir. Nonetheless, sympathy did not translate into power on the other side of the border in Kashmir.

Shimla marked the beginning of changes which altered the role of both the committee and the Muslim struggle for independence in Kashmir. In light of the fact that the meeting took place in Shimla, instead of somewhere more convenient, such as the committee's previous headquarters in Lahore, the All-India Kashmir Committee had already taken on a more national appearance, which extended beyond the Punjab.[35] The new members at Shimla, and those who joined soon thereafter, were more representative of an "All-India" organization, which now stretched from the Frontier in the west to Bengal in the east. The augmented geographic boundaries represented a step towards establishing credibility. Now, at the very least, the All-India Kashmir Committee could produce non-Punjabi members who held meetings in one of the nation's capitals.

The Emergence of Key Players in the Crisis

A young Kashmiri named Sheikh Mohammed Abdullah (1905–1982) was among the Muslim activists to emerge following the riots.[36] Sheikh Abdullah was an unemployed master's graduate of Aligarh at the time who was making a name for himself by delivering impassioned speeches in protest. His continued involvement in political activism eventually earned him the laudatory title *sher-i kashmīr* (the Lion of Kashmir) as well as the opportunity to serve as the state's chief minister from 1975 until his death in 1982.[37]

The Kashmir crisis also marked the emergence of the recently formed Majlis-i Ahrar-i Islam, an organization that was trying to establish itself in opposition to the Ahmadi-administered All-India Kashmir Committee.[38] From its inception, the Ahrari defense of Islam was reactionary in nature. It unapologetically incorporated anti-*darbār*, anti-British, anti-Sikh, anti-Hindu, and anti-Ahmadi sentiments all on a single platform.[39] The Ahrar's stance was reinforced through a militant enterprise, which involved wielding *jathā*s (gangs) who threatened to infiltrate the Kashmiri border at a moment's notice.[40] Sir Mian Fazl-i Husain described them as the "riff-raffs" among the Muslims.[41] Although the Ahrar's tactics appeared crude in the earliest days, they nevertheless may have provided suitable opposition for Mahmud Ahmad, who was considered by Ayesha Jalal to have been "running the local administration [in Qadian] on the lines of an Ahmadi mafia."[42]

Mahmud Ahmad's objectives were to find "Ahmadi" solutions to a set of sophisticated political problems. Leading a successful lobby on behalf of the All-India Kashmir Committee from India was a challenge, but ensuring that it had an impact on the streets of Kashmir was a different matter. Mahmud Ahmad knew that utilizing local Kashmiris would be more beneficial than bringing in outsiders. He needed to mobilize Kashmiri Muslims against the Dogra government, while warding off attacks from the Ahrari opposition, and neither task was easy. Had the *darbār* been willing to respond to civil sentiment, either through the implementation of changes in public policy or perhaps by initiating a plan to bring about these changes in the near future, it is probable that a great deal of social anxiety could have been avoided. Reconciliation was no longer a viable option, however, once the crisis had begun and mainstream members of Kashmiri society had taken to rioting en masse. Several Kashmiri Muslims were weary of the government and unwilling to entertain diplomatic negotiations. Both the severity of the violence and the widespread consent expressed by the masses during communal disturbances made it difficult to stop the crisis by finding a compromise solution. Furthermore, reconciliation needed to take place against a backdrop of groups like the Ahrar, who specialized in rousing communal hatred.

Mirza Bashir al-Din Mahmud Ahmad's Strategic Response to the Crisis

Mahmud Ahmad's method for resolving the conflict in Kashmir was to utilize Jama'at-i Ahmadiyya's excellent contacts in the region and its institutionalized structure for political leverage. The institutional framework itself gave Mahmud Ahmad an advantage over his opposition,[43] since it was different from any other Muslim group of the time with the exception of the Isma'ilis. Considering that Mahmud Ahmad was personally responsible for setting up the Jama'at's organizational structure, it makes sense that he was quick to use it to enter into an international crisis. Mahmud Ahmad had always intended for his Jama'at to compete for the dominant leadership of the Muslim world, thereby enabling the Ahmadi *khilāfat*—which is to say, his own *khilāfat*—to reign supreme over the *umma*. This is why Mahmud Ahmad never fully supported the Khilafat Movement, since doing so would have undermined his own claim to *khilāfat*.[44]

The All-India Kashmir Committee needed the approval of Kashmiri Muslims in order to have lasting effects in Kashmir. Mahmud Ahmad also needed to balance the support of the Kashmiri mainstream with the logistics of an international resistance. He established a publicity committee whose only function was to bombard the Indian press with news coverage of the internal situation in Jammu and Kashmir. The committee publicized issues throughout the subcontinent among Muslims who were unaware of either internal developments in Kashmir or the All-India Kashmir Committee's response to the crisis.[45] Mahmud Ahmad then ordered the establishment of Kashmiri independence offices—otherwise known as reading rooms—throughout Jammu and Kashmir, but shrewdly forbade his Ahmadi disciples to hold positions of leadership in them.[46] This further created the impression of an organized resistance taking shape internally, with Muslims coming together from within the state's borders. His strategy was intended to beguile onlookers who were attempting to assess the threat of Kashmiri Muslims by showing them the borrowed framework of an organized institution that was already in place. In doing so, Mahmud Ahmad hoped that government officials would be thoroughly dismayed by the unified network of reading rooms that had simply been nonexistent in the weeks prior to the riots, but were now seemingly popping up throughout the state. From the government's perspective, this should not have been possible without previous warning signs. No one had anticipated that the leaders of the uprising would be capable of organizing themselves as rapidly and competently as they had done in Kashmir.

The unfolding situation presented the *darbār* with a disgruntled Muslim population transforming into a collective resistance with remarkable efficiency. Realistically, however, the underlying structure of Jamaʿat-i Ahmadiyya had taken nearly forty years to establish. Dogra officials were nevertheless left wondering how such a highly organized network of Muslims had materialized virtually overnight. Mahmud Ahmad was keenly aware that the mere threat of organized resistance pervading the state had damaging consequences for officials, who now appeared isolated from their Muslim subjects. From the government's perspective, the inability to anticipate this type of resistance signified multiple failures on various levels, including repeated disregard of indicators pointing towards the potential unraveling of the state.

Sheikh Abdullah's Pact with the *Khalīfa*

With the infrastructure of resistance beginning to take shape, Mahmud Ahmad began searching for a Kashmiri spokesperson to be advanced for the cause. He summoned some fifteen to twenty candidates to Qadian for personal interviews in order to get a better idea of whom he would be working with in the future.[47] Once the meetings were complete, Mahmud Ahmad asked the Kashmiri delegation if they knew of other potential leaders who had not joined them in Qadian. The entourage concurred that there was a Sheikh Mohammed Abdullah of Srinagar who could not risk leaving Kashmir in fear that the *darbār* would not permit him to return. This response piqued Mahmud Ahmad's interest, so he made arrangements to meet Sheikh Abdullah at the border town of Garhi Habibullah. In a truly Bollywood-style masquerade, ʿAbd al-Rahim Dard smuggled Sheikh Abdullah—who was hiding under a blanket in the backseat of the carriage—across the Indian border into Garhi Habibullah to meet the All-India Kashmir Committee's new president. When the meeting with Mirza Mahmud Ahmad was over, Sheikh Abdullah was smuggled back into Kashmir in the same manner in which he arrived.[48]

The scheme was a success and the agreement was simple. Sheikh Abdullah was to set up an office in Srinagar from which he could devote full-time attention to the independence movement. He was entrusted with establishing a periodical to disseminate information and publicize the resistance internally, which resulted in the founding of the *Islāh* newsletter. The *Islāh* was a rare Muslim mouthpiece within the borders of Kashmir that was created purely to promote the independence movement. Mirza Mahmud Ahmad was aware that it was inappropriate for him to intervene as the *khalīfa*, since most Muslims in Kashmir were not his Ahmadi disciples. In addition, the All-India Kashmir Committee at this point was more of a façade for Jamaʿat-i Ahmadiyya than an inclusive umbrella, despite its influential membership.

A newspaper was an important organ for communicating ideas throughout the subcontinent in this historical context. Periodicals were one of the few means by which major leaders of the era could spread ideas beyond their immediate vicinities, which were often limited to crowds that emerged from local mosques following the Friday prayers.[49] For this reason, Sheikh Abdullah's easy access to the press instantly made him a major player in the eyes of government observers tracking the development of the situation. In fact, the impact of Sheikh Abdullah's ideas circulating through the Kashmiri press may have been more influential than Mahmud Ahmad had anticipated, due to circumstances surrounding the press at that time.

Mridu Rai noted that in the early years of the conflict, Kashmir's reinvigorated press was taking advantage of the Dogra rulers' 1932 relaxation in the censorship of Muslim publications.[50] Sheikh Abdullah fulfilled his obligations during the early 1930s by publishing articles that made explicit appeals to the All-India Kashmir Committee and effectively begged for its intercession. This alone provided Mahmud Ahmad with legitimacy as a political leader and enough leeway to enfranchise his political platform on behalf of the All-India Kashmir Committee from neighboring India. Now, Mirza Mahmud Ahmad possessed the freedom to pursue matters in Jammu and Kashmir as he saw fit, while acting as the rightful president of the All-India Kashmir Committee. In return for internal publicity and public appeals for intervention, Sheikh Abdullah, who did not come from an affluent background and hence lacked personal resources, received the necessary funding to sustain his independence office in Srinagar. The initial amount agreed upon at Garhi Habibullah was a base allowance of 238 rupees per month with a potential for increase as needed.[51] This was a generous figure for the time.

Sheikh Abdullah was so convincing in aligning himself with the All-India Kashmir Committee that he spent the rest of his career facing accusations of being "Qadiani" from opposition parties, who sought to malign his reputation whenever the opportunity for political advancement arose. This posed a problem for *darbār* officials who were still trying to identify key players in the crisis. Consequently, local authorities now had to waste time trying to determine if Sheikh Abdullah really was a "Qadiani." It took months until 'Abd al-Rahim Dard clarified the issue on a visit to the resident in Kashmir.[52] Even so, doubts remained and periodically reemerged as a hazard for unassuming Kashmiris who were caught in the fallout of political opportunists exploiting the latest scandal. There are examples of this in Sheikh Abdullah's memoirs:

> Unfortunately, the Mirwaiz [Maulvi Yusuf Shah] became embroiled in their [Majlis-i Ahrar's] intrigues. On 30 January 1932, he delivered a sermon at Khanqah-e-Naqshbandia in which he accused me of being a Qadiani. Everyone knew that I was a Sunni, of the Hanafi sect. This event took place in the dead of winter when most Kashmiris do not leave their houses without their *kangris* [braziers]. During the altercations which followed his allegation, these *kangris* were freely used as trajectories, injuring a number of people.[53]

Being labeled a Qadiani in the 1930s was equivalent to slander. The allegations that he was associated with Jama'at-i Ahmadiyya created difficulties for Sheikh Abdullah in Kashmir, even though he clearly benefited from Ahmadi publicity on other occasions. The title *sher-i kashmīr* (the Lion of Kashmir) itself was purportedly coined by Mahmud Ahmad, who incessantly published sensationalized articles about Sheikh Abdullah referring to him as the *sher-i kashmīr*. As other papers became acquainted with the *sher-i kashmīr* title, and Sheikh Abdullah's contributions to the Kashmiri cause were substantiated over time, *sher-i kashmīr* eventually became synonymous with Sheikh Abdullah.[54]

The affinity between Mirza Mahmud Ahmad and Sheikh Abdullah developed gradually as both remained true to the agreement and honored their commitments. The details of each specific project varied, but the underlying premise was always the same. On May 23, 1932, Mirza Mahmud Ahmad—this time on behalf of Jama'at-i Ahmadiyya—established a new scholarship fund for Muslim students studying in Kashmir. With an additional 200 rupees per month, Sheikh Abdullah was able to establish a suitable boardinghouse with a full-time cook, which enabled twenty promising candidates to pursue higher education each year.[55] Although this may seem like a small figure at first, it was considerably larger than the number of Muslim students included in the government's offer of 1927, which created a stir and was followed by accusations of Hindu favoritism. The new scholarship fund consisted of enough awards to woo Muslim favor in Kashmir and increase positive publicity for Jama'at-i Ahmadiyya at a reasonable price.

In reality, increasing revenue was never a problem for Mahmud Ahmad, who had constructed a fund-raising industry that was beginning to perpetuate itself. There was a circular return as funds were channeled back into the same system from which they emerged. Sheikh Abdullah's frequent displays of public approval for the All-India Kashmir Committee's initiatives had loosened the pockets of the committee's wealthier members, which sparked an increase in donations as well as a broader "All-Indian" membership to expand its roster. Likewise, growing numbers of underprivileged Kashmiris were willing to support a movement that was having a visible impact on the ground, including stipends for families of the deceased and medical provisions for those injured in the riots.[56] Consequently, the increased confidence of lower-class Kashmiris in the All-India Kashmir Committee attracted even more donors from above.

Jama'at-i Ahmadiyya's Devotional Support for the All-India Kashmir Committee

Mahmud Ahmad appropriated funds to the Kashmiri cause from every accessible channel, including Jama'at-i Ahmadiyya. As *khalīfat al-masīh* II, he established the Kashmir Relief Fund, a mandatory charitable donation (*chandā*) levied upon each wage-earning Ahmadi within his Jama'at. These Ahmadis were required to give at least one *pāī* (¹⁄₁₉₂ of a rupee) on every earned rupee per month,[57] which the Jama'at continued to accrue for decades after the riots.[58] Still, many Ahmadis likely considered the Kashmir crisis a worthy cause and donated to the relief fund openhandedly.

Many Ahmadis worked anonymously behind the scenes, contributing to the hidden labor force of the independence movement under various banners, such as the All-India Kashmir Committee and the numerous reading rooms. Unskilled laborers, however, were not the only Ahmadis compelled by their *khalīfa* to volunteer time and effort for the Kashmiri cause. Mahmud Ahmad instructed skilled Ahmadis to contribute professional services to Kashmiris as well. Throughout the stormiest years following the riots, major cities like Srinagar were occasionally subjected to bouts of martial law. The communal tensions and revolutionary threats had raised concerns among members of the military and police. The violent implications of the ordinance of September 24, 1931, discussed earlier, reflected the heightened state of paranoia regarding national security. In consequence, an inordinate number of Muslims were falsely arrested and detained under pretexts that were precariously linked to various offenses.

With the internal situation deteriorating, Kashmir did not have an independent judicial system in place to determine whether those incarcerated were being held on legitimate charges. In addition, the *darbār* had been using the ordinance to justify the acquisition of property from those indicted, since the ordinance permitted action to be taken based solely on suspicion.[59] When such cases went to trial, they invariably came down to one person's word against the word of another. The All-India Kashmir Committee sent teams of attorneys to Kashmir to assess the situation and defend those who had been wrongfully detained or whose property had been wrongfully confiscated. Although there were also several cases where wealthy Kashmiris had property or businesses seized, the majority of cases appear to have involved lower-class Kashmiris with no recourse to legal counsel. This could also suggest that property was confiscated under genuine suspicion, since less fortunate people are less likely to own considerable property.

The lawyers went to major cities in Jammu and Kashmir at their own expense as volunteers of the All-India Kashmir Committee. This involved several prominent Ahmadis who were primarily responding to their *khalīfa*'s instructions. The All-India Kashmir Committee's legal team included Shaykh Bashir Ahmad (who later became a high court justice in Lahore), Chaudhry Muhammad Yusuf Khan, Shaykh Muhammad Ahmad Mazhar (who authored numerous lexicons pertaining to Ghulam Ahmad's linguistic theory),[60] Chaudhry Asadullah Khan (the younger brother of Zafrulla Khan), and others. Dost Muhammad Shahid has recorded the details of many of these cases whose defendants were acquitted or whose convictions were overturned due to the efforts of the All-India Kashmir Committee's legal team throughout the early 1930s.[61]

Some of the All-India Kashmir Committee's internal support and services, such as the legal contributions, medical relief, and scholarship funds, were meaningful in the sense that their interface with the Kashmiri public was deeply rooted enough to impact those who were presumably the most affected. Mahmud Ahmad also had a number of other influential contacts within the All-India Kashmir Committee with whom he was collaborating to support initiatives. Iqbal's sentimental connection to Kashmir is well known and often attributed to his family's Kashmiri background. His lifelong contributions and poetry about the struggles of the Muslims of Kashmir and the wider subcontinent have been well documented.[62] Similarly, it is known that Mian Fazl-i Husain's influence played an important role in stabilizing support for the All-India Kashmir Committee.[63] As with Iqbal, Mian Fazl-i Husain's contributions to the independence movement have been recognized by the historians of South Asia,[64] although his personal relations and social contacts are often overlooked with respect to his professional affiliations. Within an Ahmadi-specific context, Mian Fazl-i Husain claimed to have a "great regard" for Maulana Muhammad 'Ali of the Lahori branch of Jama'at-i Ahmadiyya.[65] He had also been mentoring the young Chaudhry Muhammad Zafrulla Khan (1893–1985) for some time, a devoted Ahmadi disciple who entered the movement at the hand of Mirza Ghulam Ahmad.

From 1930 to 1932, Zafrulla Khan participated in all three round table conferences in London, where discussions were held about constitutional reforms as a step towards independence. About five months after the riots, in December 1931, Zafrulla Khan was elected president of the All-India Muslim League. He held the post until June 1932, despite Ahrari protests,[66] when he resigned to fulfill his next task. Mian Fazl-i Husain had been a member of the Viceroy's Executive Council from 1930 to 1935, but his declining health forced him to take a four-month leave of absence during the summer of 1932. Upon his recommendation, Zafrulla Khan took Fazl-i Husain's place on the Viceroy's Executive Council throughout the summer months,[67] which was a bold move considering Zafrulla's age, inexperience, and lack of seniority. In his diary, Mian Fazl-i Husain admitted: "If it comes off, it will be a startling appointment."[68] Zafrulla Khan's political aptitude had been developing rather quickly, and his proximity to eminent personalities provided an opportunity to discuss the Kashmir matter personally with the viceroy in the early 1930s.[69] Zafrulla Khan represents one of Jama'at-i Ahmadiyya's most successful political leaders. As such, he was an invaluable asset to Mirza Mahmud Ahmad and the All-India Kashmir Committee during the crisis, and perhaps even more so following partition.

Towards Visions of Independence

Several factors came together for Jama'at-i Ahmadiyya during the crisis in Kashmir in the 1930s, which amounted to a transnational network of support with vast resources to apply pressure on the relevant governments (Kashmiri, Indian, and

British) involved. As a result, the inability to identify the role of key figures in the Muslim leadership frustrated the response of government officials. This enabled Mahmud Ahmad to exercise various levels of control over how the crisis was portrayed by voicing similar concerns through dissimilar outlets. He was thus able to influence a broader constituency than he would normally have been able to reach. His connections with revolutionary demagogues such as Sheikh Abdullah, who represented the Muslim sentiment of a country, and with idealized literary icons such as Iqbal, who has come to represent the Muslim sentiment of an era, enabled Mahmud Ahmad to exert influence throughout the region. Mahmud Ahmad now had the ability to meet with the viceroy personally and threaten him with various courses of action,[70] including increased civil disobedience, like the mass boycott by shopkeepers (*hartāl*) of August 1931.[71] Mahmud Ahmad recognized the implications of the delicate balance between action and inaction. He also attempted to intimidate government officials by threatening to resign as All-India Kashmir Committee president and requesting supporters to comply with Ahrari objectives, which would likely have resulted in a more violent conclusion to the crisis.[72]

In his capacity as president of the All-India Kashmir Committee, Mahmud Ahmad applied whatever pressure was at his disposal upon the British and Indian governments to intervene in Kashmir, since he was convinced that British intervention was the best political solution to the conflict. Mahmud Ahmad believed that British intervention would displace Dogra rule and eventually give the Muslims of Kashmir the best chance at gaining independence. Although this was an indirect route to Kashmiri independence, it might have been a reasonable strategy considering the enduring violence in Kashmir to this day. Despite Mahmud Ahmad's efforts, the British were determined to let Kashmiris settle their own disputes, while intervening sparingly and only when necessary. This attitude eventually exacerbated the ideological conflict between Mahmud Ahmad and his opponents, as well as Sheikh Abdullah, who from the beginning had insisted upon the creation of an independent Kashmir.

The Rise of Opposition: The Majlis-i Ahrar

As popular as the All-India Kashmir Committee had become, it did not win the support of every Muslim in Kashmir. The Muslim opposition to the All-India Kashmir Committee was centered on the newly formed Majlis-i Ahrar-i Islam.[73] Mahmud Ahmad initially attempted to attract Ahrari sympathizers by repeatedly publishing appeals for All-India Kashmir Committee supporters to cooperate with the Ahrar on Kashmir. Mahmud Ahmad also sent Muhammad Ismaʿil Ghaznavi, the nephew of Ahrari co-founder Maulana Da'ud Ghaznavi,[74] as an emissary to the Ahrari leadership, bearing his offer to resign as president if the Ahrar agreed to collaborate with the All-India Kashmir Committee.[75] Janbaz Mirza has chronicled the Ahrar's perspective in an eight-volume history illustrating the profound skepticism of Ahrar members towards Mahmud Ahmad's offers, which appeared in popular newspapers, such as the *Inqilāb*.[76] The Ahrar in reality questioned the motivations of nearly every organization other than itself. In the end, neither group was willing to work with the other towards common goals, despite dramatic calls for Muslim unity emanating from both camps. After a slow start, the Ahrar made significant contributions to the people of Kashmir on its own terms. Although the details of these contributions are largely beyond the scope of this book, they are worth mentioning in brief.

The most celebrated member of the Ahrar's leadership was *amīr-i sharī'at* (as he was frequently called) 'Ataullah Shah Bukhari. Bukhari was considered a mesmerizing speaker who captivated Punjabi audiences and mobilized the masses. Prior to the riots, the founders of the Ahrar had seceded from the Congress Party in protest to pursue their own political objectives. Even after they committed themselves to founding a new organization, it took years before Ahrari leaders could benefit Kashmir in the ways they intended. The initial campaign may have served more as an annoyance to government officials than a serious threat, but it still altered the dynamics of the conflict. The criticisms expressed by Ahrari leaders represented the views of Muslims who had reservations about peaceful solutions to the crisis. As articulate as he may have been, 'Ataullah Shah Bukhari did not need to be a gifted speaker to convince many of his stance, since similar ideas had already penetrated rural South Asia beforehand. This gave leaders like Bukhari a considerable advantage. His no-nonsense approach to regime change in South Asia reflected the exasperation of a Muslim population that was no longer willing to wait for diplomacy to take its course.

When Ahrari *jathās* (gangs) began crossing the Kashmiri border from Sialkot in the summer of 1931, local officials mistakenly presumed that they had the situation under control. Once the ordinance of late September 1931 took effect, police had the authority to use harsh measures against agitators. The *darbār*, however, did not anticipate that so many Muslims would not be intimidated by the consequences. Police continued making arrests until Kashmir's prisons reached their capacities. Defiant Ahrari supporters proudly filled the jails, which escalated diplomatic negotiations rather abruptly. But the Ahrar soon exhausted its resources and could not afford to support Punjabi volunteers, who had been camping on mountainsides exposed to the elements. The weather itself forced most *jathā* volunteers to return home once the punishing conditions of the Kashmiri winter months appeared.

The Majlis-i Ahrar did not have at its disposal the institutional framework, financial resources, or labor force that Mahmud Ahmad had in Jama'at-i Ahmadiyya. This did not discourage Ahrari leaders. The Ahrar arranged to solicit regular donations (*chandā*) from volunteers,[77] but the urgency of the crisis did not leave time for collections. The logistics of establishing an adequate infrastructure demanded that the majority of the Ahrar's funds be spent on stabilizing the new organization. In the beginning, even Sheikh Abdullah acknowledged the forbearance and physical hardship of Ahrari volunteers, but concurrently noted that he had not received a single rupee from the movement.[78] By 1939, Sheikh Abdullah's messages had changed from mild irritation to utter frustration, as he advised the Ahrar to stay out of Kashmiri affairs.[79] The Ahrari leadership faced a number of problems in attempting to organize a sustainable movement aside from securing a steady source of funding. By the time the movement stabilized, the riots had long passed and partition was fast approaching.

The Disbanding of the All-India Kashmir Committee

After two years of Mirza Mahmud Ahmad's leadership and services, the All-India Kashmir Committee was prepared to move on to the next stage of its development. Mahmud Ahmad had helped to establish the All-India Kashmir Committee as a viable organization which had acquired a sense of legitimacy in the eyes of government officials. There were still a number of logistical issues that members needed to address, even after having achieved meaningful results in Kashmir. The All-India Kashmir Committee had yet to formally define its objectives, which was a necessary part of moving forward as an organization, since the committee had initially been formed in reaction to the riots in Kashmir. The All-India Kashmir Committee in some ways was still a group of elitists who shared concerns for fellow Muslims in Jammu and Kashmir. After two years, however, this group was beginning to resemble a formal organization in that it had an elected leader and was successfully lobbying three governments on an international scale.

In order to sustain itself beyond the aftermath of the riots, the All-India Kashmir Committee needed to solidify its organizational façade by explicitly defining its aims in writing. In 1933, the All-India Kashmir Committee still had no formal constitution, no formal objectives, and no formal procedures for carrying out its implicit goals. In reality, Mahmud Ahmad had complete control of the All-India Kashmir Committee, much like his own Jama'at, albeit for different reasons. Thus, there was a sense of validity to Ahrari criticisms that were beginning to resonate throughout the region, which often highlighted the potential for an Ahmadi conspiracy. Many feared that Mahmud Ahmad was exploiting the situation in Kashmir to expand Jama'at-i Ahmadiyya. The only reasonable course of action for the committee's advocates was to consolidate the All-India Kashmir Committee in a way that would formalize its agenda and turn it into a self-sufficient organization. The process of building an institution was in some respects Mahmud Ahmad's specialty, since it was exactly what he had done with his own Jama'at following the Lahori-Qadiani split.[80]

Mahmud Ahmad must have been aware that people both inside and outside the All-India Kashmir Committee had problems with his approach. He never denied his high hopes for the Muslims of Kashmir whenever he was questioned about proselytization,[81] even though he preferred to avoid the issue. His explanations often depicted a romanticized image of Kashmiri Muslims embracing Ahmadiyyat after seeing the tremendous effort of individual Ahmadis in the way of Islam. This vision conflicted with the views of the remaining non-Ahmadi supporters of the All-India Kashmir Committee, however. Mahmud Ahmad's acute awareness of the situation suggests that he feared creating a rift within the All-India Kashmir Committee, which might have damaged his credibility as a leader and perhaps tainted his Jama'at's ongoing efforts in Kashmir. Mahmud Ahmad knew that his disciples would follow him, irrespective of outside opinion, but it was not prudent for him to cut ties with the All-India Kashmir Committee. Once again, labor and funding had never been a problem for Mahmud Ahmad. Instead, he needed the recognition of fellow non-Ahmadi Muslims in order to achieve political goals. Conversely, the non-Ahmadi members of the All-India Kashmir Committee relied on the benefits of Jama'at-i Ahmadiyya's funding and infrastructure, which intrinsically accompanied Mahmud Ahmad's membership.

In May 1933 at Lahore's Cecil Hotel, the All-India Kashmir Committee decided to remedy the outstanding problems. Mahmud Ahmad resigned as president, largely in response to external pressure,[82] which was beginning to polarize the committee's internal roster.[83] Following what was described by Dost Muhammad Shahid as a dignified ceremony, the committee selected Iqbal as an interim president to oversee the next election and to initiate the process of writing a constitution.[84] During the interim period, Iqbal recommended that Ahmadis be prohibited from serving as president, due to the inherent conflict of interest. Members were concerned that another Ahmadi president of the committee would only take orders from the *khalīfat al-masīh*,[85] which was a criticism that Mahmud Ahmad did not dispute. Mahmud Ahmad's resignation was a problem for the committee's ambivalent members on both sides. It was no secret that the majority of Ahmadis who supported the committee did so out of obedience to their *khalīfa*. Had the committee revoked the membership of Ahmadis altogether, it would essentially need to reestablish itself once again without an Ahmadi infrastructure, which was something its leaders had failed to do for the twenty years prior to 1931. Not only would this adversely affect the committee's source of Ahmadi funding, it would also diminish its international pool of Ahmadi laborers.

It appears as though the Ahmadi withdrawal from the All-India Kashmir Committee and its subsequent incarnations under similar names took several years to become final. Periodically, there were halfhearted attempts to keep both factions of the committee working together on the Kashmiri front, but each side eventually pursued its own interests. Mirza Mahmud Ahmad's resignation and subsequent break with the committee did not prevent his Jama'at from being involved in the ongoing crisis in Kashmir. The sole support of Jama'at-i Ahmadiyya itself was enough to provide Mahmud Ahmad with a platform to continue working towards Kashmir's independence without the aid of the committee's more distinguished members. After various phases under different names, the All-India Kashmir Committee settled back into a similar role to the one it had played before the riots, an ineffective body of well-known Muslims without any real power.

This evolved into an unexpectedly awkward situation for Mahmud Ahmad because it forced community leaders, such as Iqbal and Sheikh Abdullah, to state their official positions on Ahmadi Islam. Mahmud Ahmad's non-Ahmadi collaborators were not members of Jama'at-i Ahmadiyya for a reason, which is not to say that they despised Ahmadis, because they were clearly willing to interact with them socially, politically, and religiously on a number of occasions. Nevertheless, they ultimately disagreed with Ahmadi interpretations of Islam on some level. This was most often reduced to the problem of *takfīr* (accusing someone of being a nonbeliever), which resulted from Mahmud Ahmad's presentation of his father's prophethood. Although Mahmud Ahmad's contacts maintained relations with him, they were forced to distance themselves publicly from Ahmadi Islam and openly denounce the Ahmadi practice of *takfīr*. It is interesting to note that the issue of Ghulam Ahmad's prophethood did not dominate criticisms of Jama'at-i Ahmadiyya until much later. The process of dissociating from Mahmud Ahmad and Jama'at-i Ahmadiyya was centered more on a public display of alienation, rather than breaking private contacts with individual Ahmadis. It appears as though Iqbal, Fazl-i Husain, and Sheikh Abdullah still met with, sat with, and prayed with Mahmud Ahmad as Muslims who shared common political interests but maintained conflicting perspectives on Islam. This was different from rival groups such as the Ahrar, who fiercely opposed Jama'at-i Ahmadiyya from the outset.[86]

Due to pressures of pragmatism, many of India's political elite had shown a willingness to cooperate with Mahmud Ahmad in hope of establishing the image of Muslim unity. Once deviations in his theological worldview became politicized, however, they abandoned him by removing him from the limelight. The fact that Mahmud Ahmad's sectarian outlook sanctioned *takfīr* and hence encouraged further divisions in Islam was problematic for this type of politics, because opposing a particular party in Muslim South Asia could be perceived as opposing Islam.

Mahmud Ahmad could no longer represent the face of Muslim politics in any capacity whatsoever, except as *khalīfat al-masīh*. It seems as though Mahmud Ahmad understood the implications of his actions and willingly accepted his new role as a follower of Indian politics rather than a leader. This process was made easier by the political achievements of some of his more prominent disciples following India's partition. As the Ahmadi controversy continued to erupt with greater frequency in the coming years, Ahmadis still managed to attain high-level political positions. They included Zafrulla Khan, who became the first foreign minister of Pakistan before going on to have a successful career in the United Nations, where he served as president of the General Assembly and president of the International Court of Justice. Interestingly, Zafrulla Khan's accomplishments in international politics did not enable him to receive public recognition for his religious affiliations, which is ironic considering Mahmud Ahmad's political aspirations. To better understand these developments and the extent of Jama'at-i Ahmadiyya's political involvement in South Asia, one must look at the changing role of Jama'at-i Ahmadiyya in the years preceding partition.

5 Religion and Politics after Partition
The Ahmadi Jihad for Kashmir

Partition and Kashmir

With the presidency of the All-India Kashmir Committee behind him, Mirza Bashir al-Din Mahmud Ahmad continued his campaign in Kashmir as head of Jama'at-i Ahmadiyya. This involved a temporary transformation of his image to that of a less political *khalīfa*. Despite attempts to maintain his affiliation with the All-India Kashmir Committee, the relationship proved to be irreconcilable. Internal support from Jama'at-i Ahmadiyya was nonetheless enough to provide Mahmud Ahmad with a sufficient platform to continue working towards Kashmir's independence on his own. As this transition unfolded in subsequent years, Jama'at-i Ahmadiyya began moving in a different direction from the All-India Kashmir Committee, while other changes beyond Mahmud Ahmad's control continued to take place on the Kashmiri front. By 1939, Sheikh Abdullah had shifted the discourse away from sharp communal polemics that highlighted internal differences, towards an inclusive Kashmiri nationalist movement intended to unite the people of Kashmir. This may be illustrated by the name change of his All Jammu and Kashmir Muslim Conference to the All Jammu and Kashmir National Conference, as noted by Mridu Rai. The new platform incorporated Hindus and Sikhs, in addition to Muslims, as victims of the Dogra government's oppression of its people and marked a new approach to both Kashmiri politics and identity.[1]

The political dynamics of South Asia changed rapidly in the 1940s once Britain announced conditions for India's partition. It was initially unclear whether princely states like Jammu and Kashmir would fall within the boundaries of India or Pakistan, since it was plausible that some states might remain independent, resulting in little change in the case of Kashmir. Sheikh Abdullah responded by launching the Quit Kashmir Movement (*kashmīr chhor do*) in anticipation of the celebrations planned for the centennial anniversary of the Treaty of Amritsar of 1846, as a means of denouncing a hundred years of unwelcome Dogra rule in

Jammu and Kashmir. The Quit Kashmir Movement demanded that the maharaja leave Kashmir immediately and allow Kashmiris to set up whichever form of government they desired.

By the following year, when partition was finalized in 1947, local Kashmiri factions began an insurgency to reclaim the state from Dogra rule. Shortly thereafter, Muslims from neighboring frontier regions and Afghanistan began pouring into the state to assist locals with the removal of the maharaja. In response, the *darbār* acceded to India as many Muslims had feared and requested Indian troops to intervene in order to quell the insurrection. When India's military crossed Kashmir's border with armored vehicles to attack Kashmiri guerrillas, the newly formed government of Pakistan sent troops to counter the assault, beginning the Indo-Pakistani War of 1947 (or the First Kashmir War).

Meanwhile, Jama'at-i Ahmadiyya was tangled in the web accompanying partition, along with the rest of the Muslim population whose homes fell on the Indian side of the border. The community's theological worldview prevented it from abandoning Qadian altogether, since Mirza Ghulam Ahmad had ordained it sacred based on divine revelations described in *al-Wasiyyat*.[2] Mirza Bashir al-Din Mahmud Ahmad initially instructed members of Jama'at-i Ahmadiyya to remain in Qadian during the upheaval of partition, while he himself withdrew to Pakistan to make arrangements for the community's future. However, he was forced to send large trucks across the border to collect his disciples, once conditions in Qadian became too dangerous for ordinary Ahmadis residing in or around the village.[3] Mahmud Ahmad also instructed 313 Ahmadis to stay in India as defenders of Qadian and conferred on them the title *darveshān-i qādiyān* (the dervishes of Qadian). He equated the merit of the *darveshān-i qādiyān* to the merit of the 313 companions of the Prophet Muhammad who participated in the Battle of Badr, the first major battle in Islamic history, which symbolizes victory of the faithful against insurmountable odds. The remaining members of the Jama'at, who constituted the majority of Ahmadis in Qadian, migrated to Pakistan to seek out new prospects. Most Muslims entering Pakistan from the Indian Punjab, including Mirza Mahmud Ahmad, first went to Lahore as refugees until the summer of 1948, by which point Mahmud Ahmad had managed to secure a permanent location for his disciples. Jama'at-i Ahmadiyya purchased an empty plot of land from the Pakistani government on the west bank of the Chenab River opposite the village of Chiniot and between the present-day cities of Faisalabad and Sargodha. There they founded a new village called Rabwah in connection with the Qur'anic description in 23:50 of a hillside where God granted Jesus and Mary refuge.[4]

The fresh start in Pakistan proved to be a challenge for Jama'at-i Ahmadiyya, as the community struggled for some years with logistical issues involving the development of a relatively isolated tract of barren land. But Mahmud Ahmad's professional network, which consisted largely of personal contacts, did not disappear following the migration to Pakistan. For example, Zafrulla Khan held a senior position in the new administration as the country's first foreign minister, which he retained for seven years (1947–1954) under Muhammad 'Ali Jinnah's successors. In addition, some Ahmadis were serving as highly decorated generals in the Pakistani army. This enabled Mahmud Ahmad to maintain a close connection to Kashmir, especially through Zafrulla Khan, who had been directly involved in diplomatic efforts accompanying the military conflict as the leader of Pakistan's first delegation to the United Nations.

Zafrulla Khan's Recollection of India, Pakistan, and Kashmir

A valuable collection of interviews with Sir Zafrulla Khan details his recollection of the deliberations at the United Nations in the years following partition.[5] According to Zafrulla Khan, India took its case regarding the status of Kashmir to the UN Security Council in early January 1948. Following a preliminary meeting in New York, both India and Pakistan had agreed that the future accession of Jammu and Kashmir should be determined directly by the people through "a free and impartial plebiscite to be held under the auspices of the United Nations."[6] The secretary of state for commonwealth relations, Philip Noel-Baker, had come to New York as the British representative to the UN Security Council. Zafrulla Khan felt that Noel-Baker had worked diligently to find a reasonable solution, which in this case entailed an immediate ceasefire followed by a plebiscite under fair and impartial conditions. British prime minister Clement Attlee intervened from London, however, by sending a "disastrous telegram" that redirected British interests and disrupted Noel-Baker's progress.[7] The reason for the interruption was apparently that Attlee had independently received threats from India, warning that the proposed plebiscite would "push India into the arms of the USSR."[8] The fear of communism was a serious problem for western powers, such as Britain, within the newly developing Cold War context of the conflict in Kashmir. The proposed Security Council resolution of February 6, 1948, had six sponsors, who were about to vote on terms of agreement when India withdrew for further consultation.[9] When the Security Council reconvened on April 26, 1948, it adopted a much weaker resolution.

The following week, British general Sir Douglas Gracey, who at the time was serving as the commander in chief of Pakistan's army, received intelligence reports that India was preparing to launch a military offensive in Kashmir in opposition to the Security Council resolution. In response, Pakistan deployed troops in early May 1948 to counter the anticipated Indian offensive.[10] Another commission was set up to oversee the implementation of the previous resolutions and take action to stop the fighting. According to Zafrulla Khan, the commission began working on potential solutions, which were never rejected solely by Pakistan, until an agreement was reached at the end of December 1948. The ceasefire went into effect on January 1, even though the resolution was dated a few days later, on January 5, 1949.[11] The commission reconvened once again in an attempt to negotiate a final truce agreement. The first condition of the resulting truce stipulated that all tribal insurgents who had come to Azad Kashmir with intent to fight must leave immediately. Shortly after the ceasefire, the commission certified that this condition had been met. The second condition stipulated a complete withdrawal of Pakistani troops but only a withdrawal of the majority of Indian troops, so that a UN plebiscite administrator could carry out the final duties of the referendum related to agreed-upon election procedures. The process stalled at this stage, and the truce agreement was never settled. The commission disbanded and an official representative was appointed in its place to carry out the remaining process of demilitarization.[12]

The first UN representative to be appointed in lieu of the commission, in April 1950, was Sir Owen Dixon, an Australian High Court judge who went on to become chief justice. After several failed attempts at settling an agreement and numerous trips between Delhi and Karachi, Sir Owen Dixon offered a new suggestion in which the proposed outcome involved "certain areas of the State [of Jammu and Kashmir] contiguous to India which had a clear non-Muslim majority acceding to India and the Azad Kashmir territory with its solid Muslim population acceding to Pakistan, leaving the future of the rest of the State, including the Valley, to be determined by a Plebiscite."[13]

The religious demographics of the Kashmir valley of the time indicate that 93.6 percent of the population was Muslim while 4 percent was Hindu.[14] Although Pakistani prime minister Liaquat 'Ali Khan reluctantly accepted the proposal, to Dixon's surprise Indian prime minister Jawaharlal Nehru rejected it, despite early indications to the contrary. According to Zafrulla Khan, the proposal ultimately fell through when Dixon refused, among other things, to declare Pakistan as the aggressor in the conflict, since he claimed that he was not authorized to do so by the UN Security Council. Dixon's successor was a U.S. senator from North Carolina, Frank Graham, who continued to try to find an acceptable solution to the problem of demilitarization. By 1951, India had set up a constituent assembly in Kashmir in order to begin the process of framing a new constitution and settle the problem of accession. The Security Council had already made clear, however, that any resolution made by Kashmir's new constituent assembly would not absolve India of its obligations resulting from the previous UN Security Council resolutions.[15]

India nonetheless created a constituent assembly and named Sheikh Abdullah prime minister in exchange for cooperation on the issue of accession to India. Although Sheikh Abdullah was prepared to acknowledge the current position of Kashmir's status under Indian dominion, he assumed that Kashmir would remain autonomous while working towards a plebiscite that provided an option for independence.[16] This was considered unacceptable by the Indian government, so Sheikh Abdullah was arrested in 1953 under fraudulent charges and spent most of the next eleven years in prison. When he was finally released in 1964, he remained in police custody for several years as hearings took place before the case went to trial. Long before partition, Sheikh Abdullah had already developed a reputation for repeatedly going to prison on behalf of the Kashmiri cause. This extended period of incarceration solidified his reputation as the *sher-i kashmīr* (Lion of Kashmir), Kashmir's premier freedom fighter.

Mirza Bashir al-Din Mahmud Ahmad's Jihad for Kashmir

The stalemate in Kashmir following partition provoked some Muslims to take action in direct support of Pakistani troops, which typically amounted to military intervention by non-military personnel. The justifications presented by Muslim leaders for such actions usually involved explicit comparisons of the crisis in Kashmir to jihad. The jihad analogy was problematic for Ahmadi sympathizers, however, due to Mirza Ghulam Ahmad's long-standing condemnation of violent jihad (*jihād bi'l-sayf*). Some Ahmadis were nonetheless reconsidering the need for a military campaign in Kashmir. From an ideological perspective, Jama'at-i Ahmadiyya was faced with the dilemma of choosing between Ghulam Ahmad's disapproval of violent jihad and fighting in the conflict alongside fellow Muslims whose struggle they had supported for decades. This was a major theological issue, because reinterpreting Ghulam Ahmad's position would overturn a direct injunction of the promised messiah that had always been central to Ahmadi religious thought.

While Zafrulla Khan was assiduously pursuing a diplomatic resolution of the conflict in Kashmir, Mahmud Ahmad was exploring alternative options. Soon after his migration to Lahore in 1947, Mahmud Ahmad called a council (*shūrā*) of top advisers in which he announced that the promised messiah's era of suspending violent jihad (*yaza' al-harb*) was coming to an end. Then, he instructed members of the Jama'at to start preparing for a violent jihad (*jihād bi'l-sayf*).[17] Immediately following intelligence reports from the Pakistani army of an impending Indian offensive towards the end of May 1948, Mahmud Ahmad made arrangements to establish his own Ahmadi militia for deployment in Kashmir. By June 1948, the Furqan Battalion, also known as the Furqan Force, was formed.

The Furqan Force set up camp on the Kashmiri border with permission from the deputy commissioner of Sialkot. The first unit consisted primarily of forty to fifty highly proficient ex-military officers under the command of retired colonel Sardar Muhammad Hayat Qaysrani. The battalion suffered minor losses in air raids and scuffles with the Indian army. A more adequate force was set up shortly thereafter under the administrative leadership of Mirza Mahmud Ahmad's eldest son, Mirza Nasir Ahmad, who eventually succeeded his father as *khalīfat al-masīh* III. The purpose of the battalion was to offer permanent support to the

Pakistani army. Dost Muhammad Shahid split members of the Furqan Battalion into four categories, which may be summarized as follows:

1. Elite officers from the Pakistani army—either retired or active officers who were forced to take temporary leave from military service with a reduction in pay before being eligible for service in the Furqan Battalion
2. Employees of Jama'at-i Ahmadiyya—such as missionaries and students who were training to become missionaries, totaling approximately 125
3. Unpaid volunteers with military or police training—lower-ranking officers who may have been actively involved in military or police service but received no financial compensation, unlike the first two groups
4. Unpaid volunteers with no military or police training—ordinary Ahmadis who volunteered with no prior commitment or obligation to the military and no financial dependence on Jama'at-i Ahmadiyya, totaling approximately 3,000[18]

Members of the Furqan Battalion received limited training through the summer of 1948 before being armed and deployed on the Kashmiri front in September, as a volunteer battalion serving "under Commander MALF."[19] Commander in Chief Sir Douglas Gracey wrote a glowing letter of recognition showing his appreciation for the battalion's services:

> Your B[attalio]n was composed entirely of volunteers who came from all walks of life, young peasants, students, teachers, men in business; they were all embued with the spirit of service for Pakistan; you accepted no remuneration, and no publicity for the self sacrifice for which you all volunteered. . . . In Kashmir you were allotted an important sector, and very soon you justified the reliance placed on you and you nobly acquitted yourself in battle against heavy enemy ground and air attacks, without losing a single inch of ground.[20]

Sir Douglas Gracey disbanded the Furqan Battalion on June 17, 1950, after almost exactly two years of service, which extended well beyond the ceasefire agreement of January 1949. From the perspective of Ahmadis, these soldiers are remembered as *mujāhidīn*. Thus, those who died in active service are believed to possess the highest level of martyrdom. I was fortunate to speak to a few of the aging members of the Furqan Battalion who currently reside in London. They speak of their experiences with nobility and a sense of pride. Ahmadis who are aware of their contributions treat them with great respect at local mosques.

The Religious Implications of an Ahmadi Jihad

Aside from Mahmud Ahmad's extensive political involvement in Kashmir, the case of the Ahmadi militia, the Furqan Battalion, raises a number of theological questions for Ahmadi Islam, which must be addressed by Ahmadi theologians. Long before the partition of India, Mirza Ghulam Ahmad had created a stir in legalist circles by categorically condemning violent jihad against the British Raj.[21] Although Islamic scholars have debated various interpretations of the doctrine of jihad for centuries and questioned its validity in countless hypothetical special cases, Ghulam Ahmad's opinion was more contentious than the opinions of his predecessors, since he appeared to abolish violent jihad forever.[22] The problem with reconciling his claim from Jama'at-i Ahmadiyya's perspective was that unlike some of Ghulam Ahmad's other disputed claims—such as his claim to prophethood—Ghulam Ahmad expressed his justifications for condemning violent jihad in clear, straightforward, and unambiguous language. Ghulam Ahmad's condemnation of violent jihad underlies a great deal of his writing and is a recurring theme in Ahmadi literature. One of the more concise examples of his view on jihad is a *fatwā* written as a poem called *dīnī jihād kī mumāna'at kā fatwē masīh-i maw'ūd kī taraf sē* (the promised messiah's legal opinions prohibiting war in the name of religion). A few lines from the beginning and end of the poem have been reproduced in an attempt to illustrate Mirza Ghulam Ahmad's rhetoric:

> Now friends, leave the idea of jihad
> Wars and fighting in the name of religion are forbidden now
> (*ab chhor do jihād kā ay dosto khayāl*
> *dīn ke līye harām hay ab jang awr qitāl*)

> Now the Messiah has come as the leader in religion
> All religious wars are finished now
> (*ab ā-gayā masīh jo dīñ kā imām hay*
> *dīñ kē tamām jangoñ kā ab ikhtitām hay*)

> Now from the heavens descends the light of God
> To sanction war and jihad is foolish now
> (*ab āsmāñ se nūr-i khudā kā nuzūl hay*
> *ab jang awr jihād kā fatwā fuzūl hay*)

> Now he who performs jihad is an enemy of God
> Only one who rejects the Prophet maintains this belief now
> (*dushman hay vo khudā kā jo kartā hay ab jihād*
> *munkir nabī kā hay jo yē rakhtā hay e'tiqād*)

> Oh People, why do you leave the traditions of the Prophet?
> Abandon as wretched, whoever abandons them . . .
> (*kyoñ chhortē ho logo nabī kī hadīs ko*
> *jo chhortā hay chhor do tum us khabīs ko*) . . .

> . . . Just tell people that this is the time of the Messiah
> Now wars and jihad are forbidden and disgusting
> . . . (*logoñ ko ye batā'e ke waqt-i masīh hay*
> *ab jang awr jihād harām awr qabīh hay*)

Friends, I have fulfilled my mandate now
And if you still do not understand, then God will make
    you understand [on the day of judgment]
(*ham apnā farz dosto ab kar chukē adā*
ab bhī agar na samjho to samjhāegā khudā)²³

In contrast to the above poem expressing Ghulam Ahmad's formal opinion on the matter, which was written in 1900, Mahmud Ahmad expressed his opinion in a couplet in 1946 just prior to sending the Furqan Battalion to Kashmir:

The blessed hour for Islam's wars has come
Commence it I may, but only God knows its end

(*hay sā'at-i sa'd āyī islām kī jangoñ kī*
āghāz to mayñ kar dūñ anjām khudā jānē)²⁴

Within traditional Sunni legal thought, any *fatwā*, irrespective of its purpose, must adhere to certain criteria in order to be considered valid. This means that each *fatwā* invariably pertains to specific conditions, in which a particular scholar may offer an opinion corresponding to specific circumstances. Ghulam Ahmad's *fatwā* on jihad notoriously caused alarm due to the universality of its application, which appears to go beyond the particular circumstances pertaining to British rule in India and categorically abrogate violent jihad in Islam forever. This was confirmed by Mahmud Ahmad's sensitive treatment of doctrinal issues surrounding the notions of *yaza' al-harb* (suspending wars) and *jihād bi'l-sayf* (literally, jihad with the sword) with his advisory council in Lahore mentioned above.²⁵ Permanently repealing violent jihad in Islam is impossible without nullifying key aspects of the *sharī'a*. For this reason, when Ghulam Ahmad's opinion of jihad is considered alongside his ambiguous implications of possessing a prophetic status, two possibilities arise. Either Mirza Ghulam Ahmad was in fact abrogating violent jihad, which thereby alters immutable aspects of the *sharī'a* and contradicts his status as a non-law-bearing prophet, or everyone, including Mirza Mahmud Ahmad, misunderstood Ghulam Ahmad's opinion, which alternatively must have depended upon the unique circumstances of the world at that particular point in Islamic history. In this case, Ghulam Ahmad's rejection of violent jihad is no longer applicable since these special circumstances no longer exist.

It is clear that Ghulam Ahmad's contemporaries interpreted his *fatwā* as being universally applicable, which was one of the main reasons they criticized his views and condemned him as someone who was changing Islam rather than reviving—or even reforming—it in the conventional sense. Mirza Mahmud Ahmad's comments to his advisory council in Lahore indicate that he himself understood Ghulam Ahmad's opinion to be eternally binding, yet his military actions in Kashmir and his poetry at the time represent a departure from this view. This raises the question of whether Mahmud Ahmad's decision to overturn Ghulam Ahmad's ruling was itself a special case, which was only applicable in Kashmir at that time, or whether it was a general ruling that permanently reauthorized violent jihad in Ahmadi Islam.

The lucid and unambiguous language of both opinions makes it difficult to reconcile the contradiction. At face value, arguing that either opinion referred to a special case seems unconvincing and apologetic. At present, ordinary Ahmadis maintain that violent jihad is an incorrect interpretation of the "True" understanding of jihad in Islam, which would be better described in terms of an inner spiritual struggle, as is commonly emphasized in strands of Sufism. This means, however, that Ahmadis are in danger of forgoing the religious implications of the Furqan Battalion's contributions on the battlefield by maintaining such an inflexible position on violent jihad. Denying violent jihad in this context diminishes the spiritual merit of the mission and undermines the role of the Ahmadi battalion as *mujāhidīn*. In other words, this would recast the Furqan Battalion's sacrifices in a different light by substituting the notion of *mujāhidīn* with the secular connotations of Pakistani soldiers. Interestingly, the Furqan Battalion is mentioned by neither Yohanan Friedmann nor Spencer Lavan in their important studies on Jama'at-i Ahmadiyya.[26] Accordingly, the implications of the Ahmadi jihad in Kashmir for Ahmadi theology have yet to be expounded in existing literature on Ahmadi Islam.

Jama'at-i Ahmadiyya's current position recognizes that Ghulam Ahmad could not abrogate jihad, but argues that sufficient changes in the world since the advent of the promised messiah have ensured that the prerequisites for violent jihad no longer exist. Jama'at-i Ahmadiyya also asserts that the conditions of the world will not revert back to a situation that warrants violent jihad prior to the day of judgment. With this explanation, members of the Jama'at's hierarchy argue that the notion of violent jihad is inconceivable but not necessarily impossible to justify in the contemporary world, which is purportedly consistent with Ghulam Ahmad's claim of preserving the entirety of the *shar'īa* without adding or subtracting from it.[27] This argument treats the Furqan Battalion as a special case, however, and ignores the apparent contradiction expressed in the provocative language of the two *fatwās* mentioned above. This is an example within Ahmadi Islam where two claimants of divine charisma, namely the *masīh maw'ūd* (the promised messiah) and the *muslih maw'ūd* (the promised reformer), advanced conflicting truth claims, both of which were alleged to have been eternally binding. Perhaps the Jama'at will one day reconcile the contradiction by developing a more convincing explanation. For now, a duality exists where ordinary Ahmadis maintain that members of the Furqan Battalion were indeed *mujāhidīn*, yet equally, conventional volunteers who simply supported the Pakistani army, when addressing the relevant theological implications of their contributions. Hence, a paradox exists.

Within traditional Sunni Islam, dissenting views from majority legal opinions, or disagreements between scholars, are not as problematic as in Ahmadi Islam. In Sunni Islam, conflicting opinions are typically reconciled through a systematized legal tradition known as *fiqh* (jurisprudence). This has given rise to a separate discipline of Islamic legal studies known as *usūl al-fiqh*, which explicitly defines the methodology and principles used to establish legal precedents and authority within the sources for interpretation. Ultimately, it is acceptable for scholars to disagree about a ruling within certain limits, as long as the scholars in question use the appropriate legal methodology consistently, as it has come to be defined by the tradition. The notion of disagreement is widely accepted in mainstream Sunni Islam, because a legal scholar's opinion is typically not binding, unless the scholar has political backing from some statelike apparatus capable of enforcing the rulings. Furthermore, and perhaps more importantly, disagreement is permissible because mainstream Sunnis do not presuppose the divine origins of legal rulings, since a jurist does not possess divine charisma. This methodology has enabled trends to develop over time, which distinguish strong legal opinions from anomalies based on the general consensus of scholars throughout the broader Islamic tradition. Without this type of flexibility, it becomes difficult to accommodate legal disagreements and diversity of opinion, as in the case of the opposing views of Mirza Ghulam Ahmad and Mirza Mahmud Ahmad, which appear to produce an embarrassment for Ahmadi religious thought. If one day Ahmadi theologians attempt to reconcile such differences of opinion, they will either need to revise their understanding of Ghulam Ahmad's legal authority, or revise their understanding of the institution of *khilāfat-i ahmadiyya*.

The Use of Religion to Facilitate Political Support

Until the international conflict in Kashmir unfolded, Jama'at-i Ahmadiyya had avoided becoming deeply involved in politics. This pattern is to some extent what makes the political history of modern South Asia so interesting, since it was the leaders of religious organizations who stepped forward to influence the development of the political scene. It is inappropriate to think of Muslim South Asia at the time as maintaining a sharp dichotomy between religion and politics, since political leaders, such as Sheikh Abdullah, were influenced by religious concerns, and religious leaders, such as Mirza Mahmud Ahmad, were preoccupied with politics. Nationalism itself, and thus national identity, were mixed with religious identity, as reflected in the name "*pāk-istān*" which represents a pure and holy (*pāk*) land for Muslims.

Considering the high value South Asian politics has placed on religious issues, addressing religious concerns has become part of political life in the subcontinent. This is due in part to the repeated use of religion in provoking broader political discussions, which at times have involved religious digressions that might not correspond to the public's primary concerns.[28] With this in mind, one can see how Mahmud Ahmad was as much the leader of a new political party, Jama'at-i Ahmadiyya, as he was *amīr al-mu'minīn* (commander of the faithful), the *khalīfat al-masīh*. As such, his contemporaries treated him accordingly, with a sense of religious reverence fused with political esteem. In fact, the extensive list of invitations to the All-India Muslim Conference in Delhi in 1928 listed Mirza Bashir al-Din Mahmud Ahmad among prominent Muslim leaders of the Punjab, while listing one his most trusted missionaries, Mufti Muhammad Sadiq, under a different heading of "Leaders of Muslim Political Parties," as a representative of the "Ahmadiyya Association."[29] This duality enabled Muslim leaders like Mahmud Ahmad to utilize religious fraternalism to solicit support for political platforms.

At the time, Mahmud Ahmad was truly in a unique position in virtue of his network of highly influential contacts that was based largely on the reputation of his father. Mirza Ghulam Ahmad developed a distinctive spiritual orientation and scope of influence, which was grounded in theology. Mahmud Ahmad employed his father's religious reputation in pursuit of political objectives. This shift was facilitated by the fact that political activism in South Asia during the nineteenth and twentieth centuries demanded an intimate connection to religion, such that those who wished to enter into politics were first expected to disclose their religious affiliations. For this reason, nearly all of Mahmud Ahmad's high-profile relationships had some connection to his father.

It is easy to confuse the cultural context in which Ghulam Ahmad's Muslim contemporaries read his theology with today's dogmatic perceptions of his mission. Underneath the sharp polemics of Ahmadi Islam is an unexpectedly ecumenical message of religious unity from a person who claimed to be the messiah for all faiths. At times, the universality of Ghulam Ahmad's message was appreciated by his contemporaries, especially those within proximity of the Punjab with spiritual leanings towards inclusive ideologies. Acknowledging a calculated degree of tolerance towards Hindus, Sikhs, and Christians by accepting the divine origins of their faith—albeit with an inherent favoritism towards Islam— was an appealing concept, which won favor with many mystically inclined Muslims of South Asia who had an affinity for political activism grounded in a desire to bring about civil reform. This meant that some of the leaders of Muslim India's most influential movements prior to partition had close ties to Mirza Ghulam Ahmad. This was not due to the influence of his controversial theology, but rather to the general perception of his mission, which conveyed a broader message of Indian unity for many people.

Mirza Ghulam Ahmad managed to attain tacit support from sympathizers, despite the aura of controversy. There are several prominent non-Ahmadi Muslims connected to Ghulam Ahmad who illustrate this point. Both Maulana

Muhammad 'Ali and Shawkat 'Ali are renowned for formative contributions to the Khilafat Movement and the Muslim League. It is not well known, however, that their elder brother, Zulfiqar 'Ali Khan, was a faithful disciple of Mirza Ghulam Ahmad.[30] On occasion, Maulana Shawkat 'Ali would visit his elder brother and Mahmud Ahmad in Qadian, which made it possible for Mahmud Ahmad to establish influential contacts without ever leaving his rural home.[31] Similarly, Iqbal's father and brother, Shaykh Nur Muhammad and Shaykh 'Ata Muhammad, were members of Jama'at-i Ahmadiyya. Iqbal himself allegedly took Mirza Ghulam Ahmad's *bay'at* (allegiance) in the 1890s even though he clearly distanced himself from Ahmadi theology towards the end of his life.[32] There is an indication of Iqbal's early sympathies towards the Jama'at in the fact that he sent his eldest son, Aftab Iqbal, to the Ahmadi-administered *ta'līm al-islām* high school of Qadian.[33] Sir Mian Fazl-i Husain also had a long-standing relationship with Jama'at-i Ahmadiyya and met Ghulam Ahmad just prior to his passing in 1908.[34] In 1927, the *Review of Religions* proudly pictured Mian Fazl-i Husain at the newly built Fazl mosque on a visit to London, although he does not appear to have had a clear familial connection to the community.[35] When Mian Fazl-i Husain's son, Na'im, passed away during his studies at Cambridge University, he was buried in the Muslim cemetery near the mosque at Woking.[36] The Woking mosque and cemetery at the time were administered by Khwaja Kamal al-Din, the trusted companion of Ghulam Ahmad who helped establish the Lahori branch of the Jama'at following the Lahori-Qadiani split.[37] These examples show how Mahmud Ahmad maintained an extensive network of contacts who considered his father to be neither a heretic nor a messiah. Mahmud Ahmad used this to his advantage alongside support from disciples who regarded him as their *khalīfa*.

Mahmud Ahmad was much better at organizing and managing the existing reality before him than he was at recreating a new South Asian reality through revolution, reformation, or some other radical departure from conventional religion and politics of the time. Mahmud Ahmad skillfully mastered the art of manipulating the Punjabi press during his tenure as *khalīfa*. He consistently used his international network of disciples—whose organizational infrastructure he himself had created—to publicize contemporary issues around the world with great ingenuity. Somehow, Mahmud Ahmad ensured that the local Punjabi press refrained from publishing news bulletins detailing the whereabouts of political leaders who visited him in Qadian. This enabled famous leaders to visit Qadian privately and in confidence that they would not be maliciously associated with a heterodox sect by the press.[38] By the late 1930s and early 1940s being labeled a Qadiani was insulting. As mentioned in the previous chapter, these allegations caused Sheikh Abdullah difficulty in Kashmir, although he benefited from Ahmadi publicity on other occasions. At present, it is difficult to think of Sheikh Abdullah as anything other than the *sher-i kashmīr* (Lion of Kashmir), an epithet which was apparently coined by Mahmud Ahmad as a means of promoting the ongoing campaign in Kashmir. Mahmud Ahmad's mastery of public relations gave him enough control over his public image and the image of his non-Ahmadi associates to facilitate the smooth development of political relationships. Had Mahmud Ahmad's contacts been stigmatized by the press—or denounced as heretics in public—it would have further strained the development of his professional relations.

Cultural Influence in Muslim South Asia and Early Ahmadi Politics

There is still the lingering question of why so many influential Muslims were willing to work with the leader of such a controversial organization. Although many Muslims at the time considered Jama'at-i Ahmadiyya to be a valid representation of Islam, a sense of taboo still surrounded the community. Ultimately, it is not clear why Muslim leaders established such close relations with Mahmud Ahmad, but we may consider the role of cultural context as a contributing factor. Non-Ahmadi admirers of Mirza Ghulam Ahmad would have held Mirza Mahmud Ahmad in high regard based purely on their fondness for his father. Within the South Asian Sufi tradition in particular, there is an inherent value placed upon family lineage, which at times may seem analogous to the reverence for the *ahl al-bayt* in Shi'i Islam. There are many cases in South Asian Islam where descendants of the *awliyā* (saints) inherited the religious rights of their predecessors and became hereditary spiritual successors by assuming positions of authority as the keepers of important burial shrines. Similarly, the semblance of respect and religious authority accorded to Mahmud Ahmad beyond Jama'at-i Ahmadiyya was undoubtedly a result of this cultural context, which ensured the impression of a certain social standing—almost like a birthright—based on his father's acclaim. Most non-Ahmadi Muslims in the Punjab who were familiar with Ghulam Ahmad, his teachings, or his disciples, yet refused to label him a *kāfir* (nonbeliever), would likely have regarded him as some sort of village *walī* (saint) whose mystical visions of spiritual ecstasy were misunderstood. Even if non-Ahmadi Muslims did associate Ghulam Ahmad with a sense of controversy, those who did not consider him a *kāfir* would simply presume that he was the local *buzurg* (sage) of Qadian. This rationale would also apply to people who knew nothing about Mirza Ghulam Ahmad, but only saw Mahmud Ahmad as the head of a major religious movement. In this sense, there was a certain cultural intuition among Muslims in rural Punjab, which entailed that whoever he was, Mahmud Ahmad was important.

This point is critical to understanding Mahmud Ahmad's image in the eyes of his non-Ahmadi contemporaries. The magnitude of Ghulam Ahmad's claims and their theological consequences made it difficult for non-Ahmadis to reconcile the two extremes of *kāfir* or *walī*. Only a small group of scholars was willing

to engage with the subtleties of Ghulam Ahmad's claims or deal with the theological complexities of their repercussions. For most Muslims, intellectualizing
the finer points of prophecy or assiduously determining the correct stance in this
debate was a painstaking effort, well beyond everyday Islam. Classifying hypothetical abstractions at the heart of the Ahmadi controversy, which presumed
distinctions in the supposed spiritual rank of various unnamed messengers of
God in comparison to the prophets Muhammad and Jesus, all within the latter-
day context of the advent of the *imām mahdī*, was not a pressing issue in early-
twentieth-century Islam, especially in South Asia. Ordinary mainstream Muslims in India simply did not care enough about speculative religious philosophy
to invest the time necessary to enter into such high-level debates, which were otherwise irrelevant to daily Islamic practice. For this reason, non-Ahmadi Muslims
with minimal exposure to Mirza Ghulam Ahmad or his followers did not see
much difference between Ahmadi religious practices and their own. The aura of
controversy surrounding Ghulam Ahmad's claims nevertheless made it unrealis-
tic to maintain that he was an ordinary Muslim. Ghulam Ahmad's image became
polarized between the two extremes as a result: he was either a fraudulent, delud-
ed *kāfir* or a pious yet misunderstood *walī*. For most unassuming Muslims, this
was an easy choice to make, since it was far too risky to mistakenly call someone
a *kāfir* in traditional Sunni Islam.[39] The only alternative was to tolerate Ghulam
Ahmad's notoriety and accept Mahmud Ahmad as his son and legitimate heir.

Of course, there were exceptions to this rule, such as Maulana Zafar 'Ali
Khan, who led a virulent campaign against Jama'at-i Ahmadiyya from the beginning,[40] but in a gesture of good faith most respectable non-Ahmadi Muslim
political leaders treated Mahmud Ahmad as the revered leader of the Ahmadiyya
community. These initial inclinations were often validated by personal contact
with Mahmud Ahmad, which enabled outsiders to observe his genuine Islamic
behavior, his sincere concern for the well-being of the *umma,* and his resolute
determination to follow through with charismatic convictions. It is probable
that many of Mahmud Ahmad's colleagues, like Sheikh Abdullah, never knew
the details of Ahmadi theology, even after several years of political partnership.
Mahmud Ahmad's lineage made him a legitimate Muslim leader in the eyes of
his contemporaries despite the controversy surrounding his movement, which
did not preclude the right to disagree with his spiritual or political vision. For
this reason, customary etiquette and the underlying mores associated with South
Asian gentility legitimized Mahmud Ahmad's authority. It may be worth mentioning that this explanation lies in sharp contrast to the rationalizations typically presented by Ahmadis today, which are rooted in the veracity of theological
arguments pertaining to Ghulam Ahmad's prophecies of an "illustrious son."[41]
Correspondingly, the cultural context—and not his father's religiosity—won
Mahmud Ahmad favor in the eyes of his non-Ahmadi admirers. His appeal as

the head of a large Muslim Jama'at created a lasting impression among an inner circle of political activists in pre-partition India. This was reinforced in some cases by vague perceptions of an underlying theology that encouraged religious unity with Islamic themes. Mirza Mahmud Ahmad was still the leader of one of the Punjab's premier self-sufficient religious organizations, which at least superficially urged Muslims to embrace the notion of unity. Mahmud Ahmad had from birth the inherent potential to excel in India's political scene by virtue of his father's reputation.

The relationship between Mahmud Ahmad and his colleagues in politics was mutually beneficial. Both sides sought to create the image of Muslim unity in colonial India, albeit for different reasons. The reciprocal relationship enabled Mahmud Ahmad to develop a political platform for his movement and gain access to political participation for his disciples. This was used to disseminate religious ideology, attract support from outsiders, and collaborate with activists whose motivations were largely political. Ironically, it was Mahmud Ahmad's theological interpretations that ultimately drove them away. In the early days of the Kashmir crisis, Mahmud Ahmad was in an optimal position for political advancement, considering that so many of his father's sympathizers either played important roles in the independence movement or held key positions within the Muslim leadership prior to partition. In addition, Ghulam Ahmad's broader message of Muslim unity was perceived as politically empowering. Mahmud Ahmad was left isolated, however, by his interpretation of the problem of *takfir* (declaring someone a nonbeliever), which was seen as stemming from the exaggerated significance of his father's role in the broader Islamic tradition. This prevented Mahmud Ahmad—and eventually Jama'at-i Ahmadiyya—from gaining the sympathies of mainstream Muslims, who had been looking for a message of pan-Islamic unity rather than obstinate sectarianism.[42]

Mahmud Ahmad appeared far more accepting of other political attitudes than of other interpretations of Islam. Still, one must recognize his role as an influential political leader nearing the end of British colonial India. From the perspective of politics, Mirza Mahmud Ahmad's leadership and vision was exceptional, especially when considering how few people had the capacity and resources to follow through with such grandiose schemes. His contributions to Muslim politics in South Asia were meaningful, even though his legacy beyond Jama'at-i Ahmadiyya remains tarnished by his questionable theology. From the perspective of religion, however, Mahmud Ahmad's contributions were considerably less notable than those of his father, especially beyond his disciples. Mahmud Ahmad's religious thought represented a significant departure from Ghulam Ahmad's spiritual worldview, which he not only expressed but also emphasized. In comparison, Mirza Mahmud Ahmad lacked the mystical insights, esoteric abstractions, and eclectic metaphysical creativity present in his father's religious conceptualizations. The intellectual sophistry that characterized Ghulam Ahmad's proofs was uninterestingly presented by Mahmud Ahmad as doctrinal dogma. In the end, Mirza Mahmud Ahmad's narrow view of Islam and his simplistic reduction of his father's prophethood led to reckless *fatwās* of *kufr* whose implications undermined the very basis of Muslim unity. In contrast, however, Mahmud Ahmad's interpretations broadened the concept of revelation in order to reinforce his own charismatic authority.

A conflict of interest gradually developed between Mahmud Ahmad and his political contemporaries, who did not want or need another visionary politician. Instead, they hoped to convey to outsiders the image of solidarity by inspiring South Asian Muslims to come together for the greater good through shared visions of national independence. Ghulam Ahmad's underlying message had the potential to offer this image under the leadership of a single *mahdī*, who had come—as *mahdī*s always do—to unite the *umma* against oppressive and unjust rulers.

Lessons from Kashmir: Distinguishing Religion from Politics

Over the years, the Kashmir crisis served as a testing ground for political parties and Muslim leaders, which facilitated the emergence of a new leadership in Muslim South Asia following partition. The continued strain of communal tensions coupled with the need for socioeconomic reform provided a backdrop for Muslim leaders and their organizations to prove their claims by implementing political policies. Mirza Mahmud Ahmad's involvement in communal politics and in the formation of modern South Asia's political machinery added a new political dimension to the Ahmadi identity. As Jama'at-i Ahmadiyya abandoned the other-worldliness of Ghulam Ahmad's Sufi metaphysics, it began to move away from the elitist circles affiliated with the upper classes towards a populist approach that offered this-worldly gains for average Indian Muslims.

In this way, Jama'at-i Ahmadiyya was no different from any other Muslim political party of the time, in that it condoned the notion of an implicit connection between political success and religious authenticity. By attributing sociopolitical accomplishments to a religious worldview, a Muslim political party substantiated both its political platform and its interpretation of Islam. Correspondingly, this was used to demonstrate its religious superiority to rivals and, in the case of Jama'at-i Ahmadiyya, to expand its mission. Unfortunately for Jama'at-i Ahmadiyya, the espousal of politics and religion could conversely be used to imply that the reverse was also true. For this reason, the ultimate failure of Jama'at-i Ahmadiyya to bring about Kashmiri independence quietly encouraged the general perception that Ahmadi Islam was hollow.

Factors contributing to the politicization of Jama'at-i Ahmadiyya took place long before partition as part of a gradual process, which was initiated by events, such as the Kashmir crisis, that were forged within a mixed religious and political framework. As individual Ahmadis became more accustomed to civic involvement, self-promoting publicity campaigns, and political activism throughout the various crises of the 1930s and 1940s, Jama'at-i Ahmadiyya's role in public affairs became a firmly established feature of South Asian religion and politics. Familiarity with the Ahmadi presence in South Asian politics contributed to the politicization of Jama'at-i Ahmadiyya, which ultimately influenced subsequent events in Pakistan's early history, including the Punjab disturbances of 1953. Although these events today are commonly included in the public discourse on Ahmadi Islam, they are rarely contextualized with regard to the two preceding decades of conflict in Kashmir, upon which the Ahmadi political platform was predicated. The subsequent presence of Jama'at-i Ahmadiyya in South Asian politics following partition cannot be divorced from its lengthy development prior to partition, which relied heavily on the political platform that was constructed over the course of the crisis in Kashmir, as a means to disseminate Ahmadi Islam in South Asia. To see a fuller picture, however, it is necessary to look at how the political discourse surrounding Jama'at-i Ahmadiyya changed in the face of mounting opposition following partition.

6 Early Opposition and the Roots of Ahmadi Persecution

Understanding Ahmadi Persecution

Jama'at-i Ahmadiyya has steadily been attracting international attention for reasons other than its founder intended. The harsh treatment of Ahmadis in South Asia and beyond has stimulated a wave of humanitarian interest in the modernist messianic movement. This demands a basic overview of Ahmadi theology, which unavoidably emphasizes distinctive features of the movement by highlighting the differences between Ahmadi Islam and the Muslim mainstream. Consequently, Ahmadis themselves have become rather effective at pointing out religious differences, while rather ineffective at recognizing similarities to other Muslim communities in a way that could potentially diffuse sectarian tensions. Over the second half of the twentieth century, the negative perception of Jama'at-i Ahmadiyya has developed from a tolerably controversial movement, as seen in the heyday of the Kashmir struggle, to a persecuted minority movement whose connection to Islam is often reduced to little more than its historic roots. The social stigma associated with Ahmadi identity in some ways no longer represents mere differences of opinion within a single religious tradition, but arguably different religious traditions altogether. The long-standing treatment of Ahmadiyyat by non-Ahmadi Muslims as something other-than-Islam has had a profound impact on how Ahmadis perceive themselves. This has influenced how Ahmadis locate themselves in relation to the Muslim mainstream, since Ahmadis have gradually become more comfortable distinguishing their views from those of mainstream Muslims. It appears as though Ahmadis may have contributed to the process of disengagement by slowly dissociating the notion of Ahmadiyyat from its Islamic context, as if it were an emerging religious tradition distinct from contemporary Islam. To gain a better understanding of this process, we shall consider how this transformation corresponds to the community's persecution in a postcolonial setting.

Most accounts of Ahmadi persecution have adopted a historical approach, which aims to establish a chronology of specific cases of Ahmadi persecution in order to demonstrate the severity of the social injustices that Ahmadis face. In documenting the frequency of events, this approach endeavors to substantiate the need for action by making a moral appeal to outsiders based on the persistence of Ahmadi religious persecution, the gravity of individual cases of maltreatment of Ahmadis, and their collective implications. The persecution of Ahmadis is a weighty issue, which at times pertains to matters of life and death.

The focus of this book is somewhat different. The aim here is to emphasize how religious persecution has contributed to the emergence of a politicized Ahmadi identity, rather than to provide a comprehensive account of anti-Ahmadi activities. For this reason, there will be no theoretical analysis of the concept of persecution, no attempt to provide a working definition of religious persecution, and no examination of the ethical or legal "justifications" for the numerous cases of Ahmadi persecution over the past century, even though these areas of interest are certainly worthy of scholarly attention. Instead, we shall focus our attention on how persecution has influenced the precarious nature of the Ahmadi identity by altering the movement's theological worldview. This involves looking at potential causes for persecution and Ahmadi responses to hostilities, and providing explanations for how the most intense cases of persecution have influenced Ahmadi identity.

The Beginnings of Persecution

Mirza Ghulam Ahmad's controversial claims have always provoked skepticism and distrust from the Sunni scholars of South Asia. Hence it did not take long for theological objections to Jama'at-i Ahmadiyya to be made manifest in a violent response. The first cases of Ahmadi persecution date back to the early 1900s, during Mirza Ghulam Ahmad's lifetime. The details of these accounts vary considerably, even though they yield the same conclusions. A Muslim scholar and intellectual named Sahibzada 'Abd al-Latif (1853–1903), of Khost, Afghanistan, had a prominent position in the Afghan court of Amir 'Abd al-Rahman Khan (circa 1840–1901).[1] In 1893, 'Abd al-Latif was sent to negotiate the border between British India and Afghanistan as a member of the amir's delegation. The demarcation of the boundary resulted in the Durand line, named after Sir Henry Mortimer Durand (1850–1924), which controversially split the Pashtun tribal lands on each side of the border.[2] During the negotiations, 'Abd al-Latif met an Ahmadi named Chan Badshah from Peshawar, who was working as a staff member of the British delegation. Chan Badshah presented 'Abd al-Latif with a copy of Mirza Ghulam Ahmad's recently published *Ā'ina-i Kamālāt-i Islām* (Reflections of Islam's Perfections), which sparked an interest in 'Abd al-Latif.[3]

'Abd al-Latif's curiosity prompted him to send his own disciples to Qadian in order to investigate the teachings of the author further. The students of 'Abd al-Latif included Maulvi 'Abd al-Rahman, Sayyid 'Abd al-Sattar Shah, Maulvi 'Abd al-Jalil, and Ahmad Nur Kabuli.[4] Each visit must have lasted some months, given the distance between Kabul and Qadian, and 'Abd al-Latif's desire for his students to have adequate opportunity to grasp Ghulam Ahmad's teachings. During one such visit, Ghulam Ahmad was preoccupied with writing a tract condemning jihad. With the topic fresh in his mind, he managed to convince 'Abd al-Rahman that violent jihad against the British was un-Islamic.[5] Upon his return to Kabul, Maulvi 'Abd al-Rahman stopped briefly in Peshawar, where he met Khwaja Kamal al-Din, the devoted disciple of Ghulam Ahmad who subsequently co-founded the Lahori branch of Jama'at-i Ahmadiyya. 'Abd al-Rahman's encounter with Khwaja Kamal al-Din only reinforced his inclinations regarding the impermissibility of violent jihad. It appears as though by this point Maulvi 'Abd al-Rahman must have already taken Ghulam Ahmad's *bay'at,* because he was openly preaching his Ahmadi views upon his return to Kabul. The Afghan amir allegedly had Maulvi 'Abd al-Rahman imprisoned for disobedience, and he was strangled to death in prison shortly thereafter, in 1901.[6] It is not clear whether Maulvi 'Abd al-Rahman's death was an official execution sanctioned by the state or whether he was simply murdered in prison. Irrespective of the circumstances surrounding his death, Ahmadi sources are clear in attributing his arrest to the public denunciation of jihad, which resulted from his Ahmadi convictions. Thus, Maulvi 'Abd al-Rahman is considered the first martyr of Ahmadi Islam.

In October 1901, the amir of Afghanistan, 'Abd al-Rahman, died, leaving his throne to his son, Sardar Habibullah Khan (1872–1919). The coronation of the new amir was reported by a British engineer who attended the event. Even though the account does not mention 'Abd al-Latif by name, it describes him placing the turban on the head of the new Amir Habibullah at the Juma Masjid.[7] One year later, in 1902, 'Abd al-Latif sought Amir Habibullah's permission to leave Afghanistan in order to perform the hajj in Mecca. The amir honored the request by funding the expedition for 'Abd al-Latif and a small entourage of students. For unknown reasons, the group began the journey traveling southeast to Lahore, presumably to fulfill prior commitments. However, restrictions had been placed on pilgrims traveling to Mecca through India due to the outbreak of plague, which prevented 'Abd al-Latif from completing his pilgrimage and performing the hajj. Rather than returning to Kabul immediately, 'Abd al-Latif decided to visit Ghulam Ahmad at his home in Qadian, which was within reasonable proximity of Lahore. 'Abd al-Latif remained in Qadian for some months, which enabled him to spend meaningful time with Mirza Ghulam Ahmad and Hakim Nur al-Din. During his stay, 'Abd al-Latif took Ghulam Ahmad's *bay'at* and related having several visions and dreams, which shaped his impression of the visit.

Once the pilgrims returned to Kabul, 'Abd al-Latif began proclaiming his revised views of the death of Jesus and the impermissibility of jihad against the British. Amir Habibullah consequently had 'Abd al-Latif imprisoned for infidelity, and the case went to trial. For several weeks, 'Abd al-Latif remained in prison, where he continued arguing his case and attempting to convince others of his Ahmadi interpretations, which at times took the form of writing. In the end, 'Abd al-Latif's interpretations of Islam were deemed unacceptable, and he was stoned to death in a public execution in July 1903 for refusing to recant his views. Ghulam Ahmad declared the ordeal to be the fulfillment of divine prophecies and went on to write a confessional tract commemorating the passion of the martyrs.[8] Ahmadi sensitivities regarding the martyrdoms of Maulvi 'Abd al-Rahman and, especially, Sahibzada 'Abd al-Latif have largely been shaped by Ghulam Ahmad's grieving response to the executions and his poignant retelling of the story. These two martyrs are undoubtedly among the most revered figures in early Ahmadi history. Ghulam Ahmad argued at length about how 'Abd al-Latif's sacrifice "may even surpass the sacrifice by Hadhrat Imam Hussain," who is unquestionably the quintessential martyr of the broader Islamic tradition.[9]

The martyrdom of Sahibzada 'Abd al-Latif is unique, considering his high social standing in Afghan civil society, which may also be one of the reasons why he attracts so much attention among Ahmadi historians. It may be difficult to ascertain his scope of influence as a dignitary and religious scholar, even though there is enough information available from the accounts of surviving family members to provide a broader perspective of his execution. 'Abd al-Latif devoted his attention to the pursuit of religious education. This demanded extensive travel to various institutions of learning, including those in Muslim centers such as Delhi, Lucknow, and Peshawar, where he managed to visit luminaries in India. During his journeys, 'Abd al-Latif studied under Maulvi 'Abd al-Hayy Lakhnawi (d. 1886), the renowned hadith scholar of the Farangi Mahall.[10] 'Abd al-Hayy Lakhnawi maintained a Sufi affiliation with the Qadiri order, but also developed good relationships with leading members of the Ahl-i Hadith movement, such as Nawab Siddiq Hassan Khan of Bhopal.[11] The Qadiri affiliation may have influenced 'Abd al-Latif to take the *bay'at* of 'Abd al-Wahhab Manki upon returning home to Khost after completing his studies in India, before his transfer to Kabul.[12] 'Abd al-Wahhab Manki was a prominent *khalīfa* of the Qadiri shaykh 'Abd al-Ghafur, the *akhūndzāda* of Swat. Swat's marginal location on the border of Afghanistan and British India made it prone to political unrest over various disputes concerning the boundaries of the frontier, which had taken place for decades. It has been noted by Afghan scholar Senzil Nawid that 'Abd al-Ghufar's *khalīfa*s, including 'Abd al-Wahhab Manki, "were active in spreading the gospel of jihad throughout the region."[13]

In reality, Afghanistan had been under military threat from Britain in the east and Russia in the north for the greater part of the nineteenth century. Skirmishes had been taking place since the beginning of the First Anglo-Afghan War in 1838. This dissuaded 'Abd al-Rahman from enthusiastically pursuing diplomatic relations with Britain, even though his own installation as amir of Afghanistan was arguably a direct outcome of British influence at the end of the Second Anglo-Afghan War (1878–1880). Within this context, Amir 'Abd al-Rahman had successfully managed to exploit the idea of jihad as a means of forging unity among rival Afghan tribes against non-Muslim invaders and internal dissenters who sought to spark a rebellion.[14] The underlying threat of revolt from religious leaders moved 'Abd al-Rahman to seize the traditional source of income of the *'ulamā* by nationalizing the *awqāf* (endowment) funds under a central administration.[15] If members of the *'ulamā* questioned his motivations or alleged favoritism, he would have them tortured or executed.[16] Senzil Nawid noted:

> Amir 'Abd al-Rahman tried to repress the activities of the tribal clergy by transferring the authority to declare jihad to the state. To justify the usurpation, he ordered books written asserting that no one but the caliph, amir, or sultan was authorized to declare jihad. At the same time, the amir enhanced his image as a pious amir, or sultan, possessing religious and secular powers—the imamate and the amirate. Heresy, even contact with "infidels," was severely punished.[17]

This suggests that Maulvi 'Abd al-Rahman and Sahibzada 'Abd al-Latif's rejection of violent jihad posed a serious threat to the amir of Afghanistan at a time of armed hostility. The amir would likely have seen the rejection of violent jihad as an attempt to undermine his authority. The notion of waging jihad against a common imperialist enemy of infidels was a major factor in binding the otherwise independent tribes of Afghanistan into a single unified nation. Otherwise, the nationalistic idea of uniting Afghanistan's tribal regions under a single political banner—as "Afghans" purely for the sake of "Afghanistan"—was largely a foreign concept, which to some extent was irrelevant in the era before colonialization. This suggests that the executions of 'Abd al-Rahman and 'Abd al-Latif were probably motivated by multiple factors rather than purely by their heretical views. Ahmadis may have been singled out for undermining the authority of the amirs and threatening the stability of a vulnerable state. It is difficult to speculate, however, about whether 'Abd al-Rahman and 'Abd al-Latif would still have been executed or imprisoned simply for being Ahmadi under different political circumstances. In any case, both amirs, 'Abd al-Rahman and Habibullah, chose to make examples of their opponents, which left two Ahmadis dead as instigators of sedition.[18]

For Jama'at-i Ahmadiyya, the emblematic martyrdom of Sahibzada 'Abd al-Latif set the standard for pious integrity, resolute conviction, and forbearing tolerance in the face of abuse. It also introduced the general perception among

Ahmadis that non-Ahmadi *mullās* are the enemy.[19] The narratives of the martyrdoms of Sahibzada ʿAbd al-Latif and Maulvi ʿAbd al-Rahman have since been immortalized in a legacy that befits the first martyrs of a developing religious tradition. From a different perspective, the martyrdom was also regrettable because Sahibzada ʿAbd al-Latif was one of few members of Jamaʿat-i Ahmadiyya who had the potential to shape the community even more in life than in his untimely death. Although he might not have been influential beyond his immediate circle of Afghani religious thinkers, ʿAbd al-Latif held respectable credentials from studying under some of the more distinguished Muslim scholars of the subcontinent at the time. His spiritual lineage was impressive and consisted of private lessons from authorized scholars in the traditional manner, including the notable hadith master ʿAbd al-Hayy Lakhnawi of the Farangi Mahall. Similarly, his (albeit brief) mystical training at the hands of the Sufi shaykh ʿAbd al-Wahhab Manki, following his induction into the Qadiri order, was unparalleled within the limited scope of Ahmadi intellectuals. It may be worth recalling that virtually none of the early members of the community, including Mirza Ghulam Ahmad himself,[20] had such an extensive background in the traditional Islamic sciences, perhaps with the exception of Maulvi Hakim Nur al-Din, who spent several years prior to his *bayʿat* with Mirza Ghulam Ahmad studying at the sacred mosques of Mecca and Medina, where he too was initiated into the Naqshbandi order at the hands of one Shaykh Shah ʿAbd al-Ghani. He also studied with Maulvi Nazir Husayn Dehlawi and a disciple of Sayyid Ahmad Barelwi.[21] It may have been the early Ahmadis' lack of emphasis on possessing traditional conceptions of sacred knowledge—or on Islamic education in general—that enabled such a smooth transition away from the Islamic sciences toward the divine charisma of an implicitly infallible *khalīfa*.

By the 1920s, nearly ten Ahmadis had been stoned to death in Afghanistan. Once the precedent had been set, the perception of Ahmadiyyat as a heresy deepened. The Afghan penal code introduced from 1924 to 1925 stipulated that being Ahmadi was a capital offense.[22] Meanwhile, the Jamaʿat's administration continued pushing forward with its agenda for proselytization around the world. Oddly enough, Jamaʿat-i Ahmadiyya faced its most bitter opposition within the Muslim world rather than from Christendom, although a main objective of the promised messiah was to "break the cross." The explanation for this involves complex Islamic legal injunctions dealing with apostasy (*irtidād*) and infidelity (*kufr*). This makes it useful to examine further the relationship between Islamic law and the overall perception of Jamaʿat-i Ahmadiyya within the context of its presentation of Ghulam Ahmad's mission.

Converting the Arabs

Ahmadis have had some contact with the Arab world from almost the very beginning. Mirza Bashir al-Din Mahmud Ahmad toured the Middle East and performed hajj in 1912 at age twenty-three, two years before becoming the second *khalīfa*. Although the Ahmadi mission in Britain was established in 1912, proselytization efforts in the Arab world did not materialize until the 1920s.[23] The first Ahmadi missionaries to the Middle East, Sayyid Zayn al-'Abidin Waliullah Shah and Jalal al-Din Shams, were dispatched to Damascus in 1925 by the second *khalīfa*, where they established a functional base to expand religious activities in the region. Around the same time, Maulvi Abu'l-'Ata (born as Allah Ditta) Jalandhari was sent to Jerusalem. The missionaries were able to travel to nearby cities, including Haifa, Beirut, and even Cairo, as well as smaller sections of Syria and Palestine, while spreading the Ahmadi mission. The report in the *Review of Religions* acknowledged difficulties in Damascus, but assured readers that the mission was a success since "many [had] joined the movement."[24] At some point between Mahmud Ahmad's hajj in 1912 and Jalal al-Din Shams's arrival in Syria in 1925, Zayn al-'Abidin Waliullah Shah acquired a lectureship at Sultania College in Damascus, perhaps just prior to Shams's arrival. Although his teaching specialization remains unclear, the appointment suggests that the reception of Ahmadis in Damascus was not completely hostile.[25]

When Zayn al-'Abidin Waliullah Shah returned to Qadian, Jalal al-Din Shams was left alone in Damascus. The aforementioned account in the *Review of Religions* goes on to describe opposition to Jalal al-Din Shams, which included the refusal of service from local shops and the publication of sarcastic cartoons in local newspapers mocking the missionary. The resentment towards Shams apparently escalated when "bigotted [sic] Mullahs" got involved and issued disparaging statements about Ahmadi interpretations of Islam.[26] At the height of tensions in December 1927, Jalal al-Din Shams was stabbed by a local fanatic. By January 1928, the French authorities in Syria had Shams promptly expelled from the country out of concern for his own safety.

The British government records provide a fuller account of the circumstances surrounding the missionary's departure than the bulletins in the *Review of Religions*. Jalal al-Din Shams's expulsion from Syria in 1928 was motivated by a number of unrelated factors. Both British and French authorities in Syria had become concerned with Shams's safety towards the end of 1927. Although Shams was eager and willing to leave Syria much earlier, Mirza Mahmud Ahmad refused to grant him permission to leave Damascus. For this reason, local authorities expelled Shams as a courtesy following the attack once it was determined that he would not be able to leave Damascus voluntarily as long as Qadian refused to recall its missionary. The French authorities concluded that the only way to ensure public order and Shams's personal safety was to expel him from the country. In fact, when Jalal al-Din Shams finally managed to leave Damascus, he was dispatched directly to Haifa instead of being permitted to return home to India. In a letter drafted by Ahmadi missionary Mufti Muhammad Sadiq, Mirza

Mahmud Ahmad protested the decision from Qadian and demanded that Shams be given the same rights and security measures as those awarded to other missionaries in the region, such as the Christians. The official response of the British undersecretary to the government of India stated that

> the French authorities in ordering the expulsion of Maulvi Jalal-ud-din Shams was based on considerations of public order and the Maulvi's own personal safety as it was felt that the activities of Maulvi Jalal-ud-din Shams which differed from those of other missionaries in Damascus in that they were a dissemination of a new religion rather than the ministration to adherents of established religions, were of a nature to provoke disturbances.[27]

A letter from another British official reiterates this sentiment, stating that

> the missionaries of other denominations are . . . in a somewhat different position from that of the Ahmadi[s], as they are considered to provide for the spiritual welfare of an established community, whereas Jalal-ud-Din Shams was engaged in creating a new one.[28]

This perception of the Ahmadi mission is telling, since British administrators were certainly not in a position to determine what constitutes Islam. They may likely have been repeating the allegations of Syrian *'ulamā*, who were trusted and considered better suited to evaluate the authenticity of the Islamic tradition. For our purposes, one of the most intriguing aspects of the correspondence with Qadian is that Mufti Muhammad Sadiq found it necessary to note that the opposition to Jalal al-Din Shams was focused specifically on the Ahmadi interpretation of jihad.[29] This is markedly different from the numerous objections to other theological issues disputed by Ahmadis today regarding Mirza Ghulam Ahmad's prophethood.

It is difficult to speculate about the intensity of the opposition to Jalal al-Din Shams in 1920s Damascus. Similarly, it is difficult to assess the claims of success in disseminating Ahmadi interpretations of Islam. However, a letter published nearly five years later by the *Review of Religions* indicates the level of adversity towards Jama'at-i Ahmadiyya. This letter was written by Muhammad Hashim Rashid, a local *khatīb* (one who delivers sermons) of Damascus, who according to the editors of the *Review of Religions* spearheaded the opposition against Jalal al-Din Shams.[30] The letter does not convey a belligerent tone, but rather praised the commonalities between Ahmadis and other Muslims while expressing what might be considered legitimate grievances based upon a valid religious disagreement. In his letter, Rashid wrote:

> Members of the Ahmadiyya Community! You have no disagreement with the Muslims in most of their beliefs and religious practices. You are at one with the orthodox Muslims in fighting the false doctrines of the God-head of Jesus

Christ and other similar polytheistic beliefs. I, therefore did not like the statement recorded by you in your tract made by a certain person to the effect that the *Ulema* of Islam look askance at the evangelistic activities of Ahmadiyya preachers. This statement is a lie and a libel against the Muslim Ulema. Disagreement in our views regarding the death of Jesus Christ cannot stand in the way of our presenting a united front to the preachers of false beliefs and in demolishing the edifice of totally wrong and erroneous doctrines. [I] have written these few lines to show that my unqualified and unreserved sympathy and support go with you in your discussions with the up-holders of idolatrous and polytheistic doctrines and in your endeavours to establish the true belief of the One-ness of God and to refute and to repudiate the doctrine of the Divinity of anybody else beside Him. I request and hope that you would send me 15 or more copies of *'ain-uz-zia* that I may distribute them among Muslim brethren [*sic*] so that they may like me know of your great services in the cause of Islam and recognize and appreciate them.[31]

The tone of Rashid's letter is inconsistent with the tone of someone advocating the murder of Ahmadi missionaries or spearheading the opposition against them. Furthermore, as a local *khatīb* in Damascus, Rashid did not necessarily occupy an influential position among the *'ulamā*. His theological concerns in any case appear to be focused on the death of Jesus, which he was willing to ignore nevertheless. It is fascinating that neither Rashid nor Mufti Muhammad Sadiq mentioned *khātam al-nubuwwa* (finality of prophethood) as a contributing factor of the Ahmadi-Sunni divide, with the exception of an ambiguous statement briefly mentioned in an earlier part of Rashid's letter whose meaning in relation to prophethood is inconclusive. It appears—perhaps surprisingly—that the biggest theological differences between Ahmadis and mainstream Muslims were centered on jihad and to some extent on the death of Jesus. One must recognize that the focus on Mirza Ghulam Ahmad's prophethood did not play as critical a role as it does today in justifications for Ahmadi persecution. With this in mind, Maulvi Abu'l-'Ata Jalandhari wrote in the foreword of his 1933 tract, *The Cairo Debate,* that his foremost duty as an Ahmadi missionary "in the Arab Lands has been both to defend Islam against the onslaughts of Christian missionaries and to regenerate the true spirit of Islam among the Muslims."[32] These objectives make no mention of *khātam al-nubuwwa* or of Mirza Ghulam Ahmad's advent as the promised messiah and *mahdī*, which presumably should have been crucial information for fellow Muslims.

The attack on Jalal al-Din Shams may have involved non-theological factors. It was nevertheless a serious incident which effectively deterred Ahmadis from pursuing further proselytization efforts in Syria. It also contributed towards the negative perception of conventional Islam within Jama'at-i Ahmadiyya by instilling fear of fellow Muslims. Ahmadi missionaries in the Middle East have since remained largely confined to Haifa with few exceptions. In the more than a century since Mirza Ghulam Ahmad's death, Jamaʿat-i Ahmadiyya has expanded its mission considerably, but not in Muslim lands beyond rural India, Pakistan, and more recently Bangladesh. There are certainly Ahmadis in Muslim Africa, Malaysia, and Indonesia, but the numbers do not rival those of South Asia, though they are currently increasing. Most Muslim-majority countries that constitute the greater Middle East, including Afghanistan, Iran, and Turkey, as well as the countries of North Africa and Southeast Asia, such as Indonesia and Malaysia, rejected almost entirely the efforts of Ahmadi missionaries through the twentieth century, especially in comparison to South Asia, North America, and Western Europe.[33]

There may, however, be alternative explanations for the failure of Jamaʿat-i Ahmadiyya's mission in the Muslim world beyond South Asia. A lack of urgency in spreading Ahmadi ideology to Muslim lands might reflect a different outlook of the early members of the Jamaʿat, who may have identified more closely with mainstream Sunni Islam and hence had different priorities than contemporary Ahmadis. This would raise a problematic issue, however, in that one cannot convert to "Ahmadiyyat" from Islam unless "Ahmadiyyat" is its own religion or otherwise separate from Islam. This notion of early Ahmadi identity in conjunction with early cases of hostility towards Ahmadis might have been enough for Jamaʿat-i Ahmadiyya to relax its push towards furthering missionary activities in Muslim-majority countries beyond India. Since the 1930s, Ahmadi missionaries have restricted their efforts almost exclusively to non-Muslim lands or to Muslims with whom they have personal contact much closer to home.

The experiences in Afghanistan and the Middle East influenced the attitude of Jamaʿat-i Ahmadiyya's leadership towards the broader Muslim community. The violence directed towards Ahmadis thwarted further missionary activities in the Muslim world and triggered a reevaluation of the Jamaʿat's approach towards propagating the Ahmadi interpretation of Islam to other Muslims. Jamaʿat-i Ahmadiyya's hierarchy unofficially revised its regulations for proselytization by including administrative warnings to take added precaution when approaching other Muslims. Over the years, this attitude has filtered its way down through the ranks into the Jamaʿat, but has only had limited impact on Ahmadi identity. As unsettling as it may have been for ordinary Ahmadis to make sense of the martyrdoms and subsequent acts of aggression, these events remained for the time being isolated incidents of individual Ahmadis in conflict with fellow Muslims. Acts of violence and harassment beyond the subcontinent certainly contributed towards the reassessment of Ahmadi identity, but they appear to have resulted in little more than an added element of vigilance when dealing with unfamiliar Muslims. As incidents increased, so did the precautions, but the mood of the movement remained reasonably unchanged. Most Ahmadis still saw themselves as Muslims occupying a legitimate part of the global *umma*. Jamaʿat-i Ahmadiyya did not emerge in isolation from its surroundings, however. The early attacks on Ahmadis were taking place within the broader context of globalization and political change. By considering the broader context of the persecution, we shall see how outsider perceptions of Jama'at-i Ahmadiyya and the internal self-identity of the movement gradually changed.

Jama'at-i Ahmadiyya's Confrontation with Pan-Islamism

By 1912, Khwaja Kamal al-Din had stationed himself in Woking, southwest of London, as a barrister turned missionary. At the time, Kamal al-Din's personal relations with non-Lahori Ahmadis were quite strong, since both camps remained united within a single Ahmadi community until the split in 1914. The base in Woking facilitated a smooth transition for the young Zafrulla Khan, who arrived in Britain as a law student. International pressures were rising in Europe in anticipation of the First World War, while Muslims around the world were beginning to mobilize in accordance with pan-Islamic sympathies. When war broke out in 1914, Muslims at Kamal al-Din's Woking mission attempted to rally support for the Ottomans against popular opinion and, perhaps more importantly, against Britain.[34] In retrospect, this was a bold move for an immigrant community in Europe at that time.

In comparison to Kamal al-Din's efforts at Woking, Mirza Bashir al-Din Mahmud Ahmad was rallying support for Britain back in Qadian. Many Ahmadis felt obliged once again to volunteer services and support for Britain upon the request of their *khalīfa*. A letter of appreciation from the lieutenant governor of the Punjab addressed to Mahmud Ahmad acknowledged receipt of a "generous offer" of 5,000 rupees on behalf of Jama'at-i Ahmadiyya, which was a sizable contribution in 1918.[35] Such fervent acts of fidelity to the British Raj were incomprehensible to many Muslims, and frankly still might seem a little surprising today. This does not mean that South Asian Muslims defected from British involvement in the war, since British troops, including Indian regiments, certainly participated in combat, given the underlying prospects of independence. The number of Muslims deployed to the Middle East, however, was disproportionately lower than to other regions.[36] The political atmosphere in India was such that many prudent Muslim loyalists preferred to remain silent on the issue, rather than openly campaign for the British against fellow Muslims. The British authorities in colonial India certainly made it possible for smaller dissident groups, like the Ahmadis and Isma'ilis, to pursue religious objectives without the fear of a backlash from mainstream Muslims. Jama'at-i Ahmadiyya valued this protection under the British and often showed its support in public. Over the years, such issues have given way to a slew of elaborate conspiracy theories regarding the inner motivations of Mirza Ghulam Ahmad or other leading figures of Jama'at-i Ahmadiyya.[37]

Ahmadi relations with the mainstream only worsened after the war, once the Muslims of South Asia became preoccupied with the Khilafat Movement.[38] The Khilafat Movement was attractive to both activists and *'ulamā* alike, since it incorporated religious values and political aspirations that were deeply rooted in Islamic symbolism.[39] It also provided Muslims in the region with the opportunity to express their extraordinary confidence in the ability of pan-Islamic ideology to prevent the imminent dissolution of the Ottoman Empire, which for many amounted to the dismantling of the last Sunni *khilāfat*. Jamaʿat-i Ahmadiyya only offered partial support to the movement for various reasons. Mirza Mahmud Ahmad was keenly aware that the notion of retaining a unified *khilāfat* was a key feature of his own Islamic vision. It was problematic, however, for him to support someone else's right to *khilāfat* in conjunction with his own divine appointment, as manifest through the fulfillment of his father's prophecy.[40] From Mahmud Ahmad's perspective, only the Ahmadi *khalīfa* could legitimately claim the right to *khilāfat*, since the Ahmadi *khalīfa* was appointed by God. Had Mahmud Ahmad supported someone else's claim to *khilāfat*, such as in the case of the Khilafat Movement, it would have undermined his own authority and the basis for the Jamaʿat's structural hierarchy.

It may be useful to consider the religious implications of what might have happened if Mahmud Ahmad had offered his full support to the Khilafat Movement. Firstly, his support would have provided Jamaʿat-i Ahmadiyya with a precedent for dissent, which is otherwise absent from *khilāfat-i ahmadiyya*. The institutional hierarchy has no means of accommodating difference of opinion, which leaves dissenters within the hierarchy with no ostensible voice within the framework of *khilāfat-i ahmadiyya*. This means that Jamaʿat-i Ahmadiyya's support of the Khilafat Movement could have opened the door for a debate about the scope of Mahmud Ahmad's charismatic authority and the legitimacy of rival claims. But since Jamaʿat-i Ahmadiyya never fully supported the Khilafat Movement, this door has remained shut.

This posed a political problem for Mirza Mahmud Ahmad. Outwardly, he needed to present the Jamaʿat as being in support of the Khilafat Movement in order to avoid looking like the only Muslim leader who opposed Muslim unity. He also needed to preserve the integrity of his claim of being the *khalīfat al-masīh*. Mahmud Ahmad attempted to justify his own position as *khalīfa* by taking advantage of the pan-Islamic sentiment of fellow Muslims in the mainstream, which proved to be a complicated task. At its heart, Mahmud Ahmad supported the notion of a supreme *khalīfa* who enjoyed absolute sovereignty over the global Muslim *umma*. It was his contention, however, that he was that *khalīfa*. Mahmud Ahmad's Islam represented God's final message to the promised messiah and *mahdī*, which could only be divided into Ahmadi and non-Ahmadi, where one was superior to the other. Thus, in a halfhearted display of Muslim unity,

Jama'at-i Ahmadiyya officially endorsed the aims of the Khilafat Movement with noted reservations. Zafrulla Khan elaborated the official view as follows:

> I did not take any active part in the Khilafat Movement myself. For one thing, I was rather young at that time; and for another, from the religious point of view, the Ahmadiyya Movement did not look upon the Turkish Sultanate as representing the Khilafat. Nevertheless, in one of the Khilafat Movement Conferences in Allahbad, an Ahmadiyya delegation, which was led by me, made it quite clear that we were in full support of the objectives of the Movement without accepting the claim or the position of the Sultan as spiritual head of Islam.[41]

With this stance, a major theological contradiction was averted in lieu of a minor one, which resulted in Mahmud Ahmad's paradoxical support for the Khilafat Movement without its *khilāfat*. Most interpreted this as rejection of the movement altogether, which is why scholarly accounts of Jama'at-i Ahmadiyya have condoned a somewhat simplistic reduction of Mahmud Ahmad's view. This includes Yohanan Friedmann's work, which simply asserts that Mahmud Ahmad opposed the Khilafat Movement.[42] All the same, some may still consider this to be a fair interpretation of the Ahmadi view, even though Mahmud Ahmad would not have articulated it in this way. The consequence of supporting this position was that Jama'at-i Ahmadiyya was seen as one of the few organized movements, if not the only one, in Muslim South Asia that effectively opposed the grand unification of global Islam. Other prominent Khilafatists with divergent outlooks included Abu'l-Kalam Azad, Zafar 'Ali Khan, 'Inayatullah Khan Mashriqi (Khaksar Tahrik), Muhammad Ilyas Khandhalwi (Tablighi Jama'at), and even the Aga Khan (Isma'ili) himself. Mahmud Ahmad's rigidity regarding his status and his hesitation in offering support to the movement undoubtedly left many Khilafatists bitter and distraught, which only intensified in 1918 when wartime celebrations in Qadian marked the British defeat of the Ottoman Empire.[43]

Political Dimensions of Persecution

The fragmentation of the Khilafat Movement in 1924 following the abolition of the Ottoman sultanate posed another problem for Jama'at-i Ahmadiyya. This meant that what had become an influential monolithic platform for South Asian Muslims would subsequently be subdivided into a number of non-Ahmadi alternatives. Given the political turmoil of the time, this raises the question of whether Mahmud Ahmad's withholding of support led ex-Khilafatists to develop a distrust of other Ahmadis in general. The lack of support followed by the Khilafat Movement's ultimate failure may have raised concerns regarding Ahmadi loyalties, which in turn justified a sense of apprehension towards the Jama'at.

In the coming years, the opposition to Jama'at-i Ahmadiyya was championed by two organizations in particular, namely the Majlis-i Ahrar-i Islam and

Jama'at-i Islami. Despite their differences, the groups shared important similarities. First, both groups were founded by ex-Khilafatists, including 'Ataullah Shah Bukhari, Mazhar 'Ali Azhar, and Muhammad Da'ud Ghaznavi from the Ahrar, and Sayyid Abu'l-'Ala Mawdudi from Jama'at-i Islami. Second, both groups engaged with Jama'at-i Ahmadiyya differently than others had done in the past, in that both were politically oriented. It may also be worth mentioning that both organizations represented new political parties in South Asian Islam, as opposed to new religious perspectives. This means that neither group claimed to represent a new school of thought (*madhhab*) or a new sectarian movement (*firqa*). Each organization accordingly shunned the notion of sectarianism yet shared ideological ties to political Islam. This of course is in sharp contrast to Jama'at-i Ahmadiyya, which claims to represent a new apolitical sect of Islam.

Under these circumstances, Jama'at-i Ahmadiyya responded to the Dogra government's inequitable treatment of Muslims following the outbreak of riots in Kashmir in 1931. Although Mirza Mahmud Ahmad may initially have led the opposition to the *darbār* as president of the All-India Kashmir Committee, many Muslim leaders reluctantly offered support. Even this form of outward political collaboration proved to be too much for the Majlis-i Ahrar. The motivation for noncompliance stemmed from deep misgivings underlying the Ahrar's perception of Jama'at-i Ahmadiyya, which was grounded in what many believed to be legitimate concerns unrelated to the handling of the crisis. It now seems clear that Muslim rivalries, such as those between the All-India Kashmir Committee and the Ahrar, hurt Kashmiris more than they helped them and stemmed from a combination of religious and political concerns. The failure to resolve these issues diplomatically gradually facilitated the transformation of communalism into fanaticism.

The Development of an Anti-Ahmadi Platform

Before returning from his tour of London as a participant of the round table conferences, Zafrulla Khan was elected president of the All-India Muslim League in December 1931, just months after rioting had erupted in Kashmir. Zafrulla Khan rushed back from London to Delhi, where he accepted the party's nomination and delivered an inaugural speech. Ahrari protesters objected to the appointment by waving black banners at the train station,[44] which did not prevent him from assuming the post, albeit for only a few months. By the summer of 1932, Zafrulla Khan had resigned as president of the Muslim League in order to join the Viceroy's Executive Council in place of Mian Fazl-i Husain, who could not fulfill his duties due to illness.[45] Zafrulla Khan's rapid ascent through the political ranks, from a round table conference delegate, to president of the Muslim League, and then member of the Viceroy's Executive Council, was enough to validate the suspicions of Ahrari loyalists in an increasingly suspicious environment. Given the instability of the time, it seemed reasonable to conclude that for someone in his thirties to attain such lofty honors without a conspiracy was an extraordinary feat. Needless to say, Zafrulla Khan was an extraordinary individual. But many began to reconsider Jama'at-i Ahmadiyya's role in South Asian Islam and Muslim politics with a renewed sense of skepticism.

For most of the period from 1931 to 1933, both Jama'at-i Ahmadiyya and the Majlis-i Ahrar were kept occupied with the unfolding crisis in Kashmir. In the beginning, the Majlis-i Ahrar was forced to invest considerable time and resources in establishing an organizational infrastructure, as a means of keeping pace with the All-India Kashmir Committee, the Muslim League, and Jama'at-i Ahmadiyya. As the organizational apparatus began to stabilize, members of the Ahrar were able to carry out anti-Ahmadi activities more regularly. In October 1934, the Ahrar planned to hold a *tablīgh* conference in Qadian, as a means of refuting Ahmadi doctrine. The government of Punjab was obliged to intervene in order to avert public disturbances by banning the conference from taking place in Qadian and restricting its associated processions from passing through the village. The Ahrar cleverly made arrangements to move the event to the grounds of the Dayanand Anglo-Vedic High School in the neighboring village of Rajada, about a mile away.[46] In response, Mirza Mahmud Ahmad called upon 2,500 Ahmadi volunteers from the greater Punjab region to report to Qadian for security duty. As the conference date approached, it was reported that large stores of sticks and spears were being gathered in Qadian in anticipation of altercations.[47] Three days before the conference, the Punjab government ordered Mahmud Ahmad to suspend his plans, not realizing that he had already withdrawn his call for outside assistance on the previous day. The Ahrar proceeded with the arrangements, and the conference took place on October 21, 1934. It was reported that at the event, *amīr-i sharī'at* 'Ataullah Shah Bukhari engaged a crowd of thousands in a five-hour tirade vilifying Jama'at-i Ahmadiyya and spouting professions of peace, which "alternat[ed] with abuse and wit of a very low order."[48] The risk of violence remained high, even though procession routes had been determined by the government. This led officials to summon an additional four hundred policemen and two superintendents to Qadian as a precautionary measure.[49] The outcome of the conference was interesting.

> Bukhari was prosecuted for this speech and convicted at the conclusion of a sensational trial which created more interest and anti-Ahmadiya feelings than the speech itself. Since then every Ahrar speaker of note has been saying one thing or another against the Ahmadis, their leaders and their beliefs.[50]

'Ataullah Shah Bukhari's conference was a great success in terms of launching an anti-Ahmadi campaign. The mere fact that thousands of people were willing to assemble in opposition to Jama'at-i Ahmadiyya was troubling to government officials. Nearly three hundred *maulvīs* had come from as far away as

Deoband, even though the vast majority of participants hailed from local areas in the vicinity of Qadian.[51] One might be inclined to think that people closest to Qadian, who presumably had the most interaction with Ahmadis—and thereby were most familiar with Ahmadi religious practices—would be most sympathetic towards the Ahmadi predicament, but this was not the case. Those within closest proximity to Jama'at-i Ahmadiyya's headquarters were leading the opposition. Many of the Ahrar's leaders themselves were originally from areas near Qadian. Mazhar 'Ali Azhar was from Batala, and both Maulana Da'ud Ghaznavi and 'Ataullah Shah Bukhari shared ties to Amritsar. The anti-Ahmadi platform appealed to many local Punjabis for some reason. C. C. Garbett, chief secretary of the Punjab, observed that "there is no doubt that many orthodox Muslims, who are ordinarily opposed to the Ahrars, are in sympathy with this side of their activities."[52] Garbett noted in his explanation of the phenomenon that "the Government often had received complaints from non-Ahmadi residents of Qadiyan that they had been harassed by Ahmadis."[53] This harassment is probably a reference to aggressive Ahmadi proselytization techniques, which may at times have appeared argumentative.

The Ahrar's political platform had many faces in the early 1930s, from British withdrawal to Kashmiri independence. The sensitivity of the Ahmadi issue, however, was now being presented in a way that revolved around the dignity and stature of the Prophet Muhammad, which struck a chord with mainstream Muslims. These issues were rather different from justifications of early opposition to Ahmadis in Arab lands. This suggests that opposition to Jama'at-i Ahmadiyya was based on a variety of factors, which, contrary to common belief, were not limited to Ghulam Ahmad's messianic claims. The Ahmadi controversy had gone through a number of phases since Ghulam Ahmad's death. Over the years, adverse reactions to Ahmadi Islam helped shape Jama'at-i Ahmadiyya by enabling the Ahmadi identity to crystallize slowly under the pressures of persecution. As the Ahmadi controversy continued to unravel, movements in opposition to Jama'at-i Ahmadiyya steadily gained momentum. To see the full effects of this opposition on Jama'at-i Ahmadiyya, one must see how the dynamics of the controversy developed after partition.

7 Persecution in Pakistan and Politicization of Ahmadi Identity

The Politics of Partition

Mirza Bashir al-Din Mahmud Ahmad, *khalīfat al-masīh* II, remained immersed in the Kashmir crisis throughout the 1930s, which led to a sustained rivalry with the Majlis-i Ahrar. By the 1940s, both organizations had diverted their attention to the Second World War, which enabled tensions to simmer in the background for the next few years. By the end of the war, the political priorities of community leaders had shifted once again towards gaining independence from Britain. This meant that there was a greater sense of urgency among organizational leaders to voice concerns about the prospects for self-governance currently under consideration. As the push for independence gained momentum in the public discourse, India's community leaders went from entertaining proposals to finalizing schemes.[1] Although the earliest proposals dated back well into the nineteenth century, by the mid-1940s only two models of governance dominated the debate. The first viable option was rooted in conceptions of Indian nationalism, while the second was rooted in religious separatism. India's nationalists backed the creation of a single state, represented by a unified India, whereas religious separatists sought the creation of independent states based on religious affiliations. As plans for independence materialized, it became increasingly clear that India would be partitioned along religious grounds. Most separatists, however, still did not want religion to dominate public policy. On the contrary, religious affiliations were primarily intended to serve as a means of determining international boundaries. This made mixed-population states, such as Punjab, problematic for advocates of partition, due to the rich complexity of its religious heritage and the varied distribution of its religious demographic.[2] As a result, quarreling about population distributions created confusion which postponed the demarcation of international borders until late in the process.

Mirza Mahmud Ahmad, like many others, held various conflicting positions as the politics of partition evolved. In the earliest stages, Jama'at-i Ahmadiyya favored the notion of an undivided India, which initially had widespread support. Once it became clear, however, that the viability of a unified India was unlikely, Mahmud Ahmad revised his position. For at least a brief period shortly before partition, Mahmud Ahmad lobbied for the establishment of a separate princely state of Qadian, but he was forced to abandon the idea once its impracticality was made clear. This must have been disappointing for Mahmud Ahmad, considering how common princely states had been in preceding centuries, including the era of colonial expansion.

Once this was ruled out, Mahmud Ahmad thought that the state of Punjab would likely remain in India after partition, so he began rethinking his options within the framework of a divided India. This led to his petitioning for representation in government by making the case for separate Ahmadi electorates, which were intended to be distinct from those reserved for Muslims. Mahmud Ahmad argued that the consignment of separate electorates for Jama'at-i Ahmadiyya made sense, since the Parsis had also been granted separate electorates, although their numbers were half those of Ahmadis.[3] This rationale reflects the ambiguity of Punjab's status—whether it would fall in India or Pakistan—which created uncertainty among Ahmadi leaders about the status of Qadian and made it difficult to identify and articulate Ahmadi interests. Once it became clear that Punjab itself would be partitioned, Mahmud Ahmad was forced to withdraw his request for separate electorates. By this point, Hindu community leaders had already exploited the discrepancies in the Ahmadi position to argue for the inclusion of Qadian in East Punjab—along with the rest of District Gurdaspur—in hope that disputed territories would remain on the Indian side of the border. According to their reasoning, the Ahmadi demand for separate electorates from Muslims indicated that Ahmadis did not identify with Islam.[4] Justice Muhammad Munir, who co-authored *The Munir Report* following the 1953 disturbances, commented on the inconsistencies in the Ahmadi stance:

> Some of their [Ahmadi] writings from 1945 to early 1947 disclose that they expected to succeed to [*sic*] the British [as self-sovereigns of Qadian] but when the faint vision of Pakistan began to assume the form of a coming reality, they felt it to be somewhat difficult permanently to reconcile themselves with the idea of a new State. They must have found themselves on the horns of a dilemma because they could neither elect for India, a Hindu secular State, nor for Pakistan where schism was not expected to be encouraged. Some of their writings show that they were opposed to the Partition, and that if Partition came, they would strive for re-union. This was obviously due to the fact that uncertainty began to be felt about the fate of Qadian, the home of Ahmadiyyat, about which several prophesies had been made by Mirza [Ghulam Ahmad] Sahib. Provisional Partition had placed Qadian in Pakistan, but Muslims in the district of Gurdaspur in which Qadian was situated were only in a majority of one per cent, and the Muslim population in that district was mostly

concentrated in three towns including Qadian. Apprehensions about the final location of Qadian, therefore, began to be felt, and since they could obviously not ask for its inclusion in India, the only course left for them now was to fight for its inclusion in Pakistan.[5]

In July 1947, when the Punjab Boundary Commission was able to hear the Jama'at's case, Mirza Mahmud Ahmad revised his position once again. This time he made the case for Qadian's inclusion in Pakistan. Given the imminence of partition, it is likely that Mahmud Ahmad was simply trying to realign his community with mainstream Muslims in terms of both religion and politics. In addition, the Ahmadi advocate who represented the case before the boundary commission, Shaykh Bashir Ahmad, placed considerable emphasis on the logistical difficulties of collecting revenues in Qadian from disciples in Pakistan, which suggests that this was one of Mahmud Ahmad's main concerns.[6] These positions had implications for the development of the political discourse on Ahmadis in Pakistan, where Ahmadis have since 1974 been declared non-Muslims for purposes of constitutional law. With this in mind, one could argue that Jama'at-i Ahmadiyya's initial support of separate electorates from other Muslims delegitimizes its current objection to being classified as non-Muslims with separate electorates by the constitution of Pakistan, as discussed below. This reasoning is simply by virtue of Mahmud Ahmad's voluntary support for Ahmadis being counted separately from Muslims when it suited his Jama'at's interests, which at the time focused on provisional plans of transforming Qadian into a semi-sovereign state.

As the logistics of partition were being developed, Mirza Mahmud Ahmad opposed the allocation of Muslim-majority lands to Pakistan in favor of having Hindu-majority lands apportioned to India. He believed that this would invariably assign the state of Punjab to Pakistan, due to its Sikh and Ahmadi populations. Instead, the Sikhs, as non-Muslims, were allotted to India, rather than as non-Hindus to Pakistan. Thus, when Punjab was ultimately divided between India and Pakistan, large contestable tracts of land were forfeited to India. This decision had a considerable impact on District Gurdaspur, which once again included large numbers of Sikhs and Ahmadis, as well as the town of Qadian. The final decision to assign District Gurdaspur to India left Ahmadis just beyond the Pakistani border. But still, the criteria for making this division may have been based on reasonable grounds. It is important not to overlook the fact that Muslims, mainly through the Muslim League, were the strongest supporters of partition, as opposed to the rival Indian National Congress party, which only wanted independence from Britain but not from Islam.[7] Hindus, of course, would have had a comfortable majority within an undivided India and hence did not need to exclude any religion to maintain democratic dominance. Thus, it was difficult to convince non-Muslims of Mahmud Ahmad's reasoning, as there was no incentive for non-Muslim support, especially since the Congress party did not sponsor the notion of a Hindu state.

The subtleties of this controversy to some extent subdued negative responses to Jama'at-i Ahmadiyya on the part of Muslim activists who supported partition and the formation of Pakistan. Many Muslim activists who backed the Pakistan solution were apathetic towards sectarian platforms, such as the anti-Ahmadi polemics being propagated by the Ahrar. Many feared that a major controversy involving the mass excommunication of Jama'at-i Ahmadiyya from the global Muslim *umma* could have detrimental effects on the partitioning of Punjab. As a result, many proponents of Pakistan were quite comfortable overlooking religious differences when confronted with the questionable features of Ahmadi Islam. The fear of losing the Punjab to India was compounded by ambiguities surrounding the size of Jama'at-i Ahmadiyya's membership, which was difficult to assess, considering that exaggerated figures had been circulated by the Jama'at since its inception.[8] In addition, Mahmud Ahmad's involvement in the Kashmir crisis since the 1930s had been carried out rather efficiently, which demonstrated the Jama'at's capacity to sustain organizational subsidiaries without a bureaucratic breakdown, such as an interruption in finances or volunteers.

These circumstances produced conditions in which the uncertainty of the size of Jama'at-i Ahmadiyya and ambivalence towards Ahmadi Islam discouraged political leaders from pursuing sectarian debates. Most Muslim political leaders appreciated the ability of sectarianism to erode the solidarity of Muslims at a time of political crisis. It was also known that minor fluctuations in the religious demographic could sway Punjab in either direction. Meanwhile, individual efforts by Ahmadis reflected positively on the Jama'at's leadership, such as with Zafrulla Khan, whose unqualified support for Pakistan played an important role in raising the call for the Muslim state. These issues nonetheless became irrelevant once partition was complete and the division of countries became final. After partition, intolerant leaders were free to excommunicate as many Muslims as they desired without having to deal with a political backlash from pan-Islamic sympathizers, who had all but lost their influence by the end of 1947.

Ahrari Disillusion and Regrouping

Nationalist parties that opposed the Pakistan movement, such as the Majlis-i Ahrar, had hoped to see the formation of an independent, yet unified, India. The identity of the Majlis-i Ahrar during the first two years of the Kashmir crisis was based largely on its unqualified opposition to the Ahmadi-inclined All-India Kashmir Committee. Once the All-India Kashmir Committee disbanded in 1933 and Mirza Bashir al-Din Mahmud Ahmad resigned from the committee's leadership, the Ahrar were left without an ideological adversary. There was a brief interlude following the crisis in Kashmir when Ahrari leaders flirted with the notion of forming an alliance with the Muslim League. Some even considered helping Muhammad Iqbal and Muhammad 'Ali Jinnah set up the league's parliamentary board in the Punjab. In August 1936, however, the Ahrar officially severed relations with the Muslim League after refusing to pay the election fee and demanding that the league declare Ahmadis non-Muslims.[9] Despite previous differences, the Ahrar continued to support the nationalist ideology of the Congress party through occasional contact with Maulana Zafar 'Ali Khan, the editor of the *Zamīndār* newspaper, but they still had difficulties curbing internal bickering in the years leading up to partition.

On November 29, 1941, Maulana Da'ud Ghaznavi issued a statement announcing the Ahrar's decision to reunite with Congress. Soon thereafter, in 1943, the Ahrar passed a resolution officially declaring itself against partition,[10] which posed a problem in that it put the Ahrar in direct opposition to the Muslim League. The Ahrar introduced a sectarian element into its objections by portraying Jinnah as an infidel in an attempt to discredit his reputation. Mazhar 'Ali Azhar scoffed at Jinnah's marriage to a Parsi woman in a couplet, which is still famously quoted as an example of how easily the Ahrar made *takfīr* (declaring someone a *kāfir*, nonbeliever).

> He abandoned Islam for a non-Muslim woman
> Is he a "great leader" or is he a "great infidel"?
>
> (*ek kāfira ke vāste islām ko chhorā*
> *ye qā'id-i a'zam hay, ke hay kāfir-i a'zam?*)

As partition drew near, three Ahrari candidates stood in the 1946 elections against Muslim League candidates, but all were defeated.[11] Each attempt to salvage the notion of a unified India failed as partition became inevitable. Once the partition of India had taken place in 1947 and the Punjab had been divided by an international border, members of the Ahrari leadership were left with little choice but to move to Pakistan. Of course, Qadian also remained on the Indian side of the border, which meant that the Ahmadi headquarters had to be relocated to Pakistan as well.

The partition was a disconcerting experience for South Asians on many different levels, but it was especially disillusioning for members of the Ahrar. The setbacks from partition were too great to allow a return to normalcy for both Jama'at-i Ahmadiyya and the Majlis-i Ahrar. The Ahrar's primary political goal of preventing partition had failed, which made it seem as if the party would be no more. In December 1947, a meeting was held to discuss prospects of continuing organizational activities in which various options were proposed, from joining the Muslim League to dissolving the party altogether. The only consensus reached revolved around a collective desire to continue activities by taking steps to create an All-Pakistan Majlis-i Ahrar. This decision was a bit puzzling, since it meant a realignment of Ahrari objectives as a pro-Pakistan movement, which involved an overlap with the Muslim League. At the next meeting, in June 1948 in Lahore, the Ahrar affirmed its loyalty to Pakistan but rejected the notion of joining the Muslim League, due to the league's tolerance of Ahmadis. This was the same month in which Mirza Mahmud Ahmad commissioned the Furqan Battalion, the voluntary force of Ahmadis, for deployment in the escalating conflict in Kashmir. In the next general meeting, held in January 1949, again in Lahore, the Majlis-i Ahrar announced its decision "to cease functioning as a political party and to continue their future activity as a religious group."[12] In many ways, this countered nearly two decades of Ahrari political activism. But after independence it must have seemed pointless to continue pursuing the antiquated politics of pre-partition India.

In 1948, the Ahrar attempted unsuccessfully to organize communal demonstrations, which resulted in the arrest of leading members. In 1949, members of the Ahrar—after turning completely to religion—began to focus activities on denouncing Zafrulla Khan, who was then serving as Pakistan's first foreign minister. The personal attacks on Zafrulla Khan were beginning to resonate with the Pakistani public, ever since he made headlines for refusing to participate in the funeral prayer of Muhammad 'Ali Jinnah.[13] Many Pakistanis found his abstention from the prayer unsettling, especially since it was known that Zafrulla Khan and Muhammad 'Ali Jinnah had developed a close professional relationship. It soon became clear that Zafrulla Khan's motivation for avoiding the funeral prayer ultimately reduced to the Ahmadi doctrine of *takfīr*. There was, however, another reason why Zafrulla Khan refrained from joining the congregation for this funeral prayer in particular. The antecedents for Zafrulla Khan's withdrawal from Jinnah's funeral are rooted in the stoning of Sahibzada 'Abd al-Latif in Afghanistan nearly fifty years prior.

Zafrulla Khan and Jinnah's Funeral

In accordance with the legal precedent set in 1903 by the trial of Sahibzada 'Abd al-Latif, the execution of Ahmadis continued intermittently in Afghanistan through the 1920s. As isolated incidents developed into trends, apostasy trials in Afghanistan received increasing publicity in the Indian press. Media coverage of executions of Ahmadis peaked in 1924 with the stoning of Ne'matullah Khan, which took place around the same time that Mirza Mahmud Ahmad was discovering the power of propaganda in rallying support for his mission. The stoning of Ne'matullah Khan was criticized by prominent Indians, including Maulana Muhammad 'Ali and Shawkat 'Ali, who spoke out publicly against the execution. Divergent public opinion led to a minor controversy about the punishment for apostasy in Islam,[14] which was encouraged to some extent by the developing relationship between the *'ulamā* of India and Afghanistan. This was especially the case with regard to Ahmadis, since Afghans had been soliciting approval of Indian scholars to bolster religious support for executions. These efforts resulted in the production of a booklet by a prominent Deobandi scholar, Maulana Shabbir Ahmad 'Usmani (1886–1949), who upheld the view that Ahmadis were apostates and worthy of execution (*wājib al-qatl*). The booklet, however, remained largely unknown and unread for nearly three decades until Ahrari leaders obtained 'Usmani's permission to issue a reprint, which appeared in the early 1950s.[15]

By the time of partition in 1947, 'Usmani had attained political prominence among religious contemporaries, owing largely to his support for the creation of Pakistan. This was a departure from most other Deobandi *'ulamā*, who supported a united India. 'Usmani's popularity was also linked to his role as the first president of the Jam'iyyat-i 'Ulama-i Islam, a party established in 1945 as a pro-Pakistan response to the Jam'iyyat-i 'Ulama-i Hind, which served as the Muslim wing of Congress and opposed partition. The Jam'iyyat-i 'Ulama-i Islam had a mixed leadership that was backed by the Muslim League and—oddly enough—attracted Deobandis and Barelwis alike.[16] The affiliation between the Jam'iyyat-i 'Ulama-i Islam and the Muslim League may have been the deciding factor in having Shabbir Ahmad 'Usmani lead the funeral prayers for Jinnah when he died in 1948. Zafrulla Khan's disapproval of the imam, as illustrated by his refusal to pray behind 'Usmani, in this light was not arbitrary. Zafrulla Khan's voluntary self-exclusion from the funeral prayer nevertheless had lasting repercussions on Jama'at-i Ahmadiyya's public image. In the aftermath of Jinnah's death, when sensitivities ran high, publicity of the event focused on an Ahmadi refusing to join in Qa'id-i A'zam's funeral prayer, which was regarded by ordinary Muslims as very insulting.

Towards the Disturbances

In May 1949, the Ahrar began making public appeals for Ahmadis to be legally classified as part of the non-Muslim minority in Pakistan, which was merely a continuation of their previous efforts in India prior to partition. The Ahrar organized additional *tablīgh* conferences on a near-monthly basis from November 1949 onward, which again proved rather successful. As expected, the themes of the conferences included personal attacks on Mirza Ghulam Ahmad, Mirza Mahmud Ahmad, and Zafrulla Khan. At times, supporters carried iconic representations of Ahmadis, which were dramatically abused in effigy. Due to Zafrulla Khan's centrality in government, the Ahrar began campaigning for his removal from the cabinet. Ahmadis responded with their own conferences, one of which ended in violence in January 1950.[17] Ahrari protesters hurled bricks and stones at the Ahmadis, until finally "the police had to resort to a mild lathi [*lāthī* (club)] charge," to disperse rioters, but the Ahrar reassembled a short distance away and began making demands on a loudspeaker.[18]

Incidents involving violence began to increase steadily. In October 1950, some Ahmadis had gone on a proselytizing mission to Chak Number 5, near Okara, District Lyallpur (now Faisalabad), when they were assaulted by locals and chased out of the village. The next day, a villager pursued an Ahmadi named Ghulam Muhammad and stabbed him to death.[19] In May 1951, an Ahmadi mosque was burned down while worshippers were pursued and beaten.[20] The Ahrar increased anti-Ahmadi propaganda in the Punjab, often resorting to elaborate conspiracy theories involving high-ranking Ahmadis and the British or Pakistani governments. Although speeches were increasingly taking place in urban venues, the violence remained confined largely to rural areas. The home secretary of Pakistan had been considering banning the Majlis-i Ahrar since early 1950, but never acted on the recommendations out of fear that it would exacerbate the situation by provoking a public reaction.[21]

The Sadr Anjuman Ahmadiyya announced that it would hold a public conference from May 17 to 18, 1952, at Jahangir Park, Karachi, where Zafrulla Khan was to deliver a keynote speech at the conclusion of the event. On the first day, demonstrators disrupted the meeting by throwing stones at the audience. Although the agitators were arrested, which enabled the proceedings to continue, fifteen police constables were injured in the process. On the second day, Zafrulla Khan addressed the crowd as advertised and clarified that Ahmadis fully believe in the notion of the Prophet Muhammad being *khātam al-nabiyyīn*. He explained that no new law or messenger could ever abrogate or supersede the Prophet Muhammad's final message. He also asserted that Mirza Ghulam Ahmad had been commissioned by God for the renewal of religion (*tajdīd-i dīn*).[22] In conclusion, Zafrulla Khan affirmed that without Ahmadiyyat, "Islam would no longer be a liv[ing] religion but would be like a dried up tree having no demonstrable superiority over other religions."[23] Following the speech, a belligerent crowd surrounded the audience and needed to be dispersed with tear gas. A gang of rioters regrouped following the tear gas encounter and proceeded to central Karachi. In the city center, rioters vandalized buildings and commercial properties owned by Ahmadis, including the Shehzan Hotel and Shahnawaz Motors, whose windows were broken. There were also attempts to set fire to the Shehzan Hotel and an Ahmadi-owned furniture store, which housed the owner's personal library of Ahmadi literature.[24]

In the aftermath of the riots, Zafrulla Khan's speech was widely condemned by the Pakistani press well beyond Karachi. Many found it inappropriate for a government minister to endorse Jama'at-i Ahmadiyya publicly in this fashion. Many also believed that it proved that Jama'at-i Ahmadiyya was colluding with the government of Pakistan. Some insisted that the riots were a pro-British plot, while others accused the United States of involvement in the region as a means of serving postwar interests.[25] Analogies were made in the press to the protracted conflict in Kashmir, where Zafrulla Khan was blamed for failing to resolve the crisis.[26] In addition, Zafrulla Khan was often attacked personally and accused of numerous character flaws.

Preserving the Mantle of the Prophet

During the transitional period after partition, when the Ahrar had espoused a more religious role, 'Ataullah Shah Bukhari began expanding the Ahrar's activities through various sister organizations under different names. Some were localized, with weak connections to the Ahrar's leadership. Others maintained strong relations with Bukhari, which facilitated a more prominent role in the fight against Jama'at-i Ahmadiyya worldwide. The most successful affiliate to emerge from Ahrari ideology under Bukhari's discretion was the Majlis-i Tahaffuz-i Khatm-i Nubuwwat (Organization for the Preservation of "the Finality of Prophethood").[27] It is not clear precisely when Bukhari founded the organization, but the movement appears to have functioned informally for some time, until a separate leadership could be established. It may be worth recalling that at this point Bukhari himself was in his sixties and no longer capable of maintaining the vigorous lifestyle of his youth. The Majlis-i Tahaffuz-i Khatm-i Nubuwwat took on many of the Ahrar's objectives, especially since the Ahrar had renounced its previous political agenda following partition. Bukhari made efforts to give the organization a more focused mission with an autonomous appearance, while retaining a symbolic leadership role. The same Ahrari network remained intact, enabling the Majlis-i Tahaffuz-i Khatm-i Nubuwwat to receive similar support, including extensive publicity in the *Zamīndār*. By this point, however, the anti-Ahmadi slant of the *Zamīndār* had passed from Maulana Zafar 'Ali Khan to his son, Maulana Akhtar 'Ali Khan, who was now serving as editor of the paper and was responsible for promoting the organization.[28]

After some weeks, the reverberations of the press's reaction to Zafrulla Khan's speech and to the agitation in Karachi had subsided. In the summer of 1952, Ahrari leaders and associates congregated in Karachi, where they decided to hold an All Muslim Parties Convention in Lahore the following year. The conference agenda was to focus on protecting the doctrine of *khātam al-nubuwwa*. It also included explicit demands to declare Ahmadis non-Muslims, to end Zafrulla Khan's tenure as the country's foreign minister, and to remove Ahmadis from high-ranking posts in Pakistan. An advertisement was placed in the *Zamīndār* of July 3, 1952, calling upon all *'ulamā, khatībs, pīrs,* and *sajjāda nishīns* to attend the convention. Personal invitations were sent to Muslim leaders, including representatives from Jam'iyyat-i 'Ulama-i Pakistan, Jam'iyyat-i 'Ulama-i Islam, Jam'iyyat-i Ahl-i Hadith, Majlis-i Tahaffuz-i Khatm-i Nubuwwat, Majlis-i Ahrar, and the promising new reform movement, Jama'at-i Islami, which was headed by Sayyid Abu'l-A'la Mawdudi (1903–1979).

Mawdudi, like many of his contemporaries, had his first serious encounter with political activism in the Khilafat Movement, which brought him into contact with many of India's leading *'ulamā* at a relatively young age. Despite his youth, however, from 1924 to 1927 Mawdudi was permitted to serve as the editor of the *Jam'iyyati*, the monthly mouthpiece of India's pro-Congress Muslims who were affiliated with the Jam'iyyat-i 'Ulama-i Hind.[29] The exposure enabled Mawdudi during the 1930s to make connections with Muslim leaders, including Iqbal, who helped Mawdudi secure the funding necessary—despite maintaining a different outlook—to establish a revivalist religious school based on political ideology.[30] By the end of August 1941, Mawdudi was formally able to establish Jama'at-i Islami, which at that time was intended to serve as a political rival to the Muslim League by opposing partition. Once partition was complete in 1947, in defiance "the Jama'at[-i Islami] forbade Pakistanis to take an oath of allegiance to the state until it became Islamic."[31] Mawdudi even opposed government action in Kashmir by claiming that a covert war was not a proper jihad. Mawdudi subsequently served two years in prison on charges of sedition, which led Jama'at-i Islami into disrepute, since the Pakistani public did not approve of anti-government detractors.[32]

Mawdudi's release from prison in 1950 coincided with a rise in anti-Ahmadi agitation. The Ahrar attempted to reach the Muslim masses of the Punjab and polarize the political landscape by arguing that Jama'at-i Ahmadiyya was the source of elitist politics in Pakistan. Mawdudi seized the opportunity to align himself with Ahrari leaders, despite differences of opinion concerning political Islam. This may have been an attempt to facilitate his revivalist agenda through greater exposure to Ahrari patrons, which appears to have resulted in a difficult alliance for Mawdudi, who did not see himself as a populist preacher. Hence, when Ahrari leaders formed the Majlis-i 'Amal (Action Committee) in response to Zafrulla Khan's speech, Mawdudi initially joined but then withdrew on account of his apparent disdain for vigilantes.[33] But the prospect of an open debate on redrafting an Islamic constitution for Pakistan was intriguing enough to draw Mawdudi back into the conversation, even if the debaters were fixated on the Ahmadi controversy. With this in mind, it is no coincidence that Mawdudi chose this period to write his *Qādiyānī Mas'ala* (The Qadiani Problem), which conveniently discharged his religious responsibility to warn the *umma*.[34]

The Punjab Disturbances of 1953

In January 1953, the Majlis-i 'Amal met outside the Punjab in Karachi, which is located in Sindh. The course of action was to apply pressure on then prime minister, Khwaja Nazim al-Din, by presenting him with an ultimatum to address grievances regarding the status of Ahmadis and their role in the country. By February 22, 1953, about a month after presenting the prime minister with demands, the deadline for the ultimatum had expired. A few peaceful days followed. Then the committee decided to have five representatives march on the prime minister's residence with placards listing its demands. These five protesters were instructed to remain at the prime minister's residence until the demands were met. If arrested, the protesters were to be replaced with five additional volunteers. Orders were sent from Karachi to major centers of the Punjab to initiate a program of civil disobedience on Friday, February 27, that would lead to public disturbances. With news of arrests on the following day, hostile crowds began to assemble in Lahore, Sialkot, Gujranwala, Rawalpindi, Lyallpur (now Faisalabad), and Montgomery (now Sahiwal). By early March, "streams of [Ahrari] volunteers had now started pouring into Lahore by rail and by road."[35] Across the country, gossip had been spreading about concessions between Ahmadis and the agitators, which further stirred public sentiment. In one such case, Maulana Akhtar 'Ali Khan of the *Zamīndār* gave an inflammatory speech at the Wazir Khan mosque of Lahore in order to dispel false rumors that he had abandoned the Khatm-i Nubuwwat movement, resulting in a crowd of ten thousand people the same evening.[36] By this point, the Wazir Khan mosque had become a bastion for activists and dissidents, which made it possible for Lahore's mullahs to take advantage of its reputation as a hub for launching the next riot. The government curfews that were put in place during the disturbances were of little avail. By March 4, 1953, aggressive crowds were routinely becoming militant, which occasionally led police to fire on them, as the situation continued to get worse.[37]

Rioters managed to fragment urban areas throughout the Punjab, while regional violence brought the legal system to a standstill. Pakistan was facing its first domestic crisis since its formation as a new country following partition. Government buildings and post offices were burned, shops were looted, and some Ahmadis were openly lynched in public. A number of Ahmadis were compelled to renounce their faith under the threat of violence.[38] Even some unfortunate non-Ahmadis were brutally beaten for attempting to dissuade angry mobs from violence.[39] Shaykh Bashir Ahmad, a prominent attorney and the *amīr* of Jama'at-i Ahmadiyya Lahore, fired upon rioters as they advanced upon his home. He was acquitted of charges, however, when the case was brought to trial, which provides an indication of the ambivalence of Pakistan's judiciary at the time.[40]

On Thursday, March 5, 1953, Maulana Mawdudi declared that the deteriorating situation was a "civil war" between the government and its people, suggesting that the unrest was bordering on anarchy.[41] At this stage, the government had lost control of the situation and was determined to bring the disturbances to an end quickly. Government officials had already balked at the opportunity to meet public demands, however, which left no clear resolution to the conflict. In addition, government officials were anticipating that the situation would get worse on the next day, which was a Friday. The chief minister of Punjab, Mian Mumtaz

Daultana, called Karachi requesting military support in what appears to have been a state of panic. A statement was prepared conceding to the demands of the Majlis-i 'Amal, which was read in mosques during the Friday prayer. Although Daultana never intended to meet the demands, he hoped that the announcement would pacify protesters and restore public order.[42] The military arrived by prayer time, and martial law was declared at 1:30 PM on Friday, March 6, 1953, for the first time (of many) in Pakistan's turbulent history.

Developments between the Disturbances: 1953–1974

The upheaval of 1953 had religious and political implications. The imposition of martial law was in many ways a victory for the Khatm-i Nubuwwat movement, since grassroots protesters had successfully brought down the government of the Punjab, even though the demands of the Majlis-i 'Amal were never actually met. This meant that politicians had ceded power to mullahs, who had largely been excluded from the political process until now. Many Muslim Leaguers had broken ranks during the disturbances and announced support for Khatm-i Nubuwwat. Mawdudi was apprehended and sentenced to death by military tribunal for sedition, but the sentence was reduced through a series of appeals when civil law returned. He was released in 1955, after serving only two years of the original sentence.[43] Although the military managed to quell the disturbances, rioters had effectively seized political power in Pakistan. When coping with the fallout of the 1953 disturbances, political leaders were forced to recognize the dangers of being seen as adverse to the doctrine of *khātam al-nubuwwa,* which had become a politically empowering idea. In the coming years, the notion of *khātam al-nubuwwa* served as a catalyst for Islamization in Pakistan, while the notion of being "Ahmadi" had taken on a new meaning synonymous with "anti-Muslim."

As Jama'at-i Islami made strides in the political arena, Mawdudi was finally granted an opportunity to assist in drafting the 1956 constitution, which was due in part to his long-standing relationship with the then prime minister, Chaudhri Muhammad 'Ali. Middle East scholar Seyyed Vali Reza Nasr, who has published important works on Jama'at-i Islami, has noted:

> Acceptance of the constitution as Islamic paved the way for the Jama'at[-i Islami] to become a full-fledged political party. In 1957, despite reservations in some quarters within the party, Mawdudi directed the Jama'at[-i Islami] to participate in the national elections of 1958. The constitutional victory was short-lived, however. The armed forces of Pakistan, under the command of General Muhammad Ayub Khan (d. 1969), and with a modernizing agenda that opposed the encroachment of religion into politics, assumed power in 1958 and shelved the constitution.[44]

The military intervention in government in the 1950s was a major setback for proponents of political Islam, such as Mawdudi. The military's stamp on the political process compelled many religious activists to forge new political alliances with unlikely allies, which led to ideological concessions. Non–Muslim Leaguers nonetheless were making progress towards Islamization, albeit at the expense of Ahmadis and other religious minorities.

In looking beyond the disturbances, it is not surprising that Pakistan's economic situation leading up to the riots of 1953 was less than stable.[45] Food shortages in the summer of 1952 had produced disenchantment with Pakistan's bureaucracy. Concurrently, opposition leaders discovered that religious controversies were an effective way of capturing the attention of large segments of the uneducated masses.[46] This enabled opposition leaders to facilitate discussions on broader political issues in Pakistan by voicing religious concerns, such as those pertaining to the Ahmadi controversy. With partition complete, the time was right for Jama'at-i Ahmadiyya to emerge as a new enemy of state, since Hindus, Sikhs, and British colonials were finally out of the picture. One government official described the speeches of the Ahrar as follows:

> The significant feature is that after attacking the Ahmadis, most of the speakers run down the Government and accuse it of inefficiency, corruption, food situation, etc. This inclines one to the view that the anti-Ahmadi agitation is used as a device for mobilising public opinion with a view to ultimately arousing contempt and hatred against Government.[47]

By scapegoating a controversial sectarian movement, such as Jama'at-i Ahmadiyya, former anti-Pakistan activists from the pre-partition era managed to recapture a share of political influence in their new Pakistani constituencies. This transformation was ironic in that it only became possible once partition was complete. After 1947, anti-partition activists, such as Ahrari leaders and Mawlana Mawdudi, who had reluctantly migrated from India, were forced to reformulate political platforms in a nationalistic light. This strategy was antithetical to previous policies, but still capable of carrying the banner of Islamic authenticity, which was necessary by virtue of Pakistan being an Islamic state. The politicization of the Ahmadi controversy is primarily what shifted the balance of power away from the pro-partition Muslim Leaguers towards their ex-Congress rivals for the first time. It is not surprising in this light that the most effective Ahrari arguments revolved around the perception of political threats from Ahmadi conspiracies and the various governments in question, whether British, Indian, Pakistani, Kashmiri, Israeli, or American. For whatever reason, conspiracy theories involving Ahmadis were the most convincing arguments for many Pakistanis, so the Ahrar repeatedly used them to mobilize the masses, especially in rural South Asia. This was also the case in the Karachi demonstrations following Zafrulla Khan's speech, which ultimately served as a catalyst for the riots. Similarly, conspiracy theories were also used as justification for subsequent anti-Ahmadi actions, as reflected in the Majlis-i 'Amal's demands of 1953. In this case, each demand was underlined by an implicit fear of Ahmadis using political influence to exploit the country's resources at the expense of non-Ahmadis. These concerns importantly have nothing to do with what many Muslims consider to be theological shortcomings at the heart of Ahmadi *'aqīda* (creed).[48]

By the mid-1950s, the commotion had settled down as conditions began returning to a state similar to what had existed before the imposition of martial law. By the late 1950s, Ayub Khan was beginning to implement a series of secular reforms, which benefited religious minorities, including Jama'at-i Ahmadiyya, by encouraging a temporary suspension of sectarian hostilities over the next decade. Unresolved issues surrounding the status of Ahmadis nonetheless continued to underlie the political discourse of Pakistan, as public opinion remained largely unsympathetic towards Jama'at-i Ahmadiyya. Consequently, the atmosphere of aggression following the disturbances in conjunction with public aversion towards Ahmadis was enough to stimulate internal changes within the Jama'at. After the disturbances, even unassuming Ahmadis were made aware of the risks posed by menacing individuals on a regular basis, especially in the Punjab.

Failed Assassination Attempt

It was only a matter of time before an overzealous fanatic attacked the *khalīfa*. By this point, Mirza Bashir al-Din Mahmud Ahmad was surrounded by professional Ahmadi bodyguards who accompanied him at all times. On March 10, 1954, a local boy from nearby Lyallpur named 'Abd al-Hamid, who was about fifteen years old, stabbed Mirza Mahmud Ahmad following the late afternoon prayers. The knife penetrated deep into his neck, but missed the most vital areas. Rather than killing the *khalīfa*, the wound led to chronic medical complications for the remaining eleven years of his life.[49] Mirza Mahmud Ahmad initially remained in Rabwah under the care of local physicians, but was eventually forced to seek further treatment abroad in London. His mental faculties purportedly remained intact, even though Mahmud Ahmad spent the remainder of his days confined to personal quarters, where he often lay, retired on a large stiff board that aided his comfort, while continuing to receive visitors in private.[50]

The attack posed a serious problem for Jama'at-i Ahmadiyya's institutional apparatus until Mahmud Ahmad's death in 1965, since the Jama'at was stuck in a state of limbo with a charismatic leader who had seemingly lost his charisma. Allegedly, Mahmud Ahmad continued to be consulted about the most dire issues confronting the Jama'at. The face of Jama'at-i Ahmadiyya, however, was increasingly represented by his eldest son, Mirza Nasir Ahmad, who eventually succeeded his father as *khalīfat al-masīh* III in due course, but was not officially recognized as such for the decade following the attack. The duality in leadership brought to light theological ambiguities in Ahmadi Islam which had not previously been addressed by the Jama'at. If the *khalīfa* had been appointed by Allah, as many believed, then was it possible for him to abdicate the *khilāfat*? Moreover, since Mirza Nasir Ahmad was acting with the full confidence of his ailing father, many wondered whether he too embodied the charisma of the *khalīfat al-masīh*. Mian Nasir (as most Ahmadis called him before his ascent to *khilāfat*) avoided further controversy by maintaining a low profile while formally acting as the official representative of his father. Consequently, this entailed receding from the political spotlight whenever possible. Whereas Mahmud Ahmad had diligently thrust his Jama'at into any political conflict he could successfully publicize in rural Punjab, Mian Nasir took a more cautious approach, especially in the years between 1954 and 1965, which preceded his reign as *khalīfa*. This period largely corresponded with the Ayub Khan era, whose administration took a tougher stance on Pakistani dissidents, which made it easier for Mian Nasir to avoid undue attention.

Reclaiming *Khilāfat-i Ahmadiyya*

From an outsider's perspective, one could argue that this period was characterized by a bitter power struggle beneath the surface of *khilāfat-i ahmadiyya*. Mian Nasir's sudden accession to the most elevated position within the Jama'at was not received without internal opposition. The dubious nature of the transference of authority following the attack on Mahmud Ahmad was questioned by key members of the Ahmadi hierarchy. The rivalry apparently surfaced when family members began questioning Mahmud Ahmad's competence as *khalīfa* and the legitimacy of Nasir Ahmad's right to succession. Although such criticisms had typically remained within the confines of the family since the Lahori-Qadiani split, the lack of clear authority presented an occasion for debate. Some Ahmadis felt that Nasir Ahmad's half brothers were better suited to occupy the position while Mahmud Ahmad's condition was fully assessed. Other Ahmadis believed that the most qualified candidates to succeed Mahmud Ahmad were among the sons of the first *khalīfat al-masīh*, Hakim Nur al-Din.

The context of this rivalry is worth exploring further. The fate of Nur al-Din's progeny has been treated as an unspoken secret by Ahmadi historians, whose silence on the issue itself speaks volumes. Many Ahmadis would be surprised to learn that Nur al-Din married three times during the course of his life and fathered over twenty children. The whereabouts of Nur al-Din's descendants is consistently absent from Ahmadi biographical sources, with few exceptions. Only rarely are 'Abd al-Mannan 'Umar and Abd al-Wahhab 'Umar—two sons from Nur al-Din's marriage to Sughra Begum—mentioned.[51] This observation alone is hardly enough to draw meaningful conclusions about Ahmadi succession. However, in comparison to the inexhaustible literature on Mirza Mahmud Ahmad's progeny and the commemorative nature in which it is presented, the lack of source material on competing Ahmadi lineages is striking.

The majority of Nur al-Din's children, meaning his sons in particular, seem to have left the Jama'at fairly early in Ahmadi history. This must have taken place sometime before 1950, if not much earlier, assuming that the children were brought up as Ahmadis following the split. With the exception of daughters who married Ghulam Ahmad's descendants, virtually none of the other children— aside from 'Abd al-Mannan 'Umar and 'Abd al-Wahhab 'Umar—appear to have had significant ties to the hierarchy, which is unusual considering the status of their father. Unlike the others, 'Abd al-Mannan 'Umar and 'Abd al-Wahhab 'Umar seem to have followed in their father's footsteps by demonstrating enduring loyalty to Jama'at-i Ahmadiyya with heartfelt devotion, which may be illustrated by the important leadership roles they occupied prior to this period. 'Abd al-Mannan 'Umar held senior positions at the Ahmadi seminary, including principal, for over ten years, which may be an indication of his status among members of the Jama'at hierarchy. This appointment may also reflect the soundness of his religious views in the eyes of the *khalīfat al-masīh,* who must have trusted 'Abd al-Mannan 'Umar to instill conceptions of Ahmadi orthodoxy in aspiring missionaries. This makes it difficult to determine when the divergence between the families occurred, if indeed this reflects a larger issue dating back to the split. It is known that in December 1954, 'Abd al-Mannan 'Umar was invited to give a public speech at the annual *jalsa* (convention) in Rabwah.[52] In addition, the offices of the *tahrīk-i jadīd* held "tea parties" in his honor as late as 1956.[53]

Meanwhile, as pressures were mounting, Mirza Mahmud Ahmad continued to occupy the role of *khalīfa,* despite his weakened condition and visible decline in demeanor. There were rare instances when he became paralyzed temporarily, causing alarm throughout Rabwah.[54] Mahmud Ahmad was clearly perturbed by the uncertainty of his predicament and did not seem to appreciate the lack of confidence being expressed by some of his closest relatives and companions. Mahmud Ahmad issued a stark warning to "mischief mongers" who questioned his rule, before departing Rabwah in pursuit of medical treatment abroad. He made it clear that any dissension during his absence would not be tolerated, even if it originated from his own "kith and kin."[55] The Jama'at hierarchy continued issuing statements asserting that the *khalīfa* was divinely appointed, which apparently prevented him from abdicating the *khilāfat* under any circumstances.[56] Similar notions of divine authority had been associated with the *khalīfa* both implicitly and explicitly during the Lahori-Qadiani split. It appears, however, that these positions were only now becoming core aspects of Ahmadi doctrine.

Apart from the internal unrest, the Karachi press had been speculating about Mian Nasir's intent to consolidate authority in his father's absence, which would thereby ensure a smooth transition to his own *khilāfat.* These reports created even greater apprehension within the Jama'at. To ease internal suspicion, the *Review of Religions* published a response reassuring readers that Mian Nasir did not have any ambition whatsoever to become the *khalīfa*.[57] As allegations persisted from all sides, the Ahmadi hierarchy—centered primarily on Mirza Nasir Ahmad—decided to hold the sons of Nur al-Din responsible for the dissent. As a result, both sons were expelled from the Jama'at shortly thereafter. Typically, matters relating to expulsion would ultimately have fallen under the jurisdiction of Mahmud Ahmad, due to the religious aspects of excommunication. Within this context, however, a discretionary decision was likely made by Mian Nasir while fulfilling the duties of the *khalīfa* at the time. Since then, ad hominem attacks on the integrity of 'Abd al-Mannan 'Umar's character, presupposing corrupt inner motivations, have been circulating within the Jama'at as justifications. It may or may not be worth mentioning that there is little historical basis for such claims.[58]

Constitutional Islam: 1974 and 1984

By the late 1960s and early 1970s, the Pakistani electorate was captivated by the charm of Zulfikar Ali Bhutto, the founder of the newly formed Pakistan People's Party (PPP). The promise of a more liberal and relatively more secular Pakistan inspired many Ahmadis to support the party in its quest for a new regime. At the institutional level, many members of the Jama'at hierarchy openly campaigned for the PPP by urging subordinate Ahmadis to support the candidacy of Zulfikar Ali Bhutto in the general elections of 1970, whose contested outcome resulted in Bhutto's indirect path to the presidency. Mirza Tahir Ahmad (1928–2003), the younger half brother and successor of Mirza Nasir Ahmad, first met with Bhutto as a Jama'at representative in the 1960s before his own ascent to the *khilāfat*. He appears to have forged a strong political relationship with Bhutto during the campaign, as the two continued to meet on a monthly basis following the elections.[59] Ironically, the first anti-Ahmadi legislation was passed in 1974 under Bhutto's tenure as prime minister of Pakistan, which implemented constitutional changes declaring Ahmadis to be non-Muslim. This was due in part to pressure from religious opposition parties, whose influence remained strong, despite significant gains by the PPP in a short amount of time under Zulfikar Ali Bhutto's leadership. The influence of religious opposition parties in the early 1970s increased to some extent as a backlash from the war in 1971, which led to East Pakistan's independence as the new secular state of Bangladesh. Nonetheless, appeals to religious purity frequently stemmed from the ability of the Ahmadi controversy to unify the mainstream and stir civil unrest once again.

In spring 1974, news reports of violent clashes between students at Rabwah's train station spread through the nation, rekindling the ongoing debate. Bhutto was initially reluctant to respond, but opposition parties staged a walkout from the National Assembly, which prompted immediate action.[60] The popular support for the anti-Ahmadi movement was remarkable, especially considering that

Jama'at-i Islami, the single largest religious opposition party of the time, only had four seats in the National Assembly, which provides an indication of its limited political appeal.[61] On June 30, 1974, the National Assembly of Pakistan appointed a special committee to determine the status of those who did not believe in the finality of the prophethood of Muhammad (*khātam al-nubuwwa*).[62] This special committee met with various representatives from both sides, including the presiding *khalīfa*, Mirza Nasir Ahmad, and the head of the Ahmadiyya Anjuman-i Isha'at-i Islam Lahore. Deliberations concluded on September 7, 1974, when all 130 members of the National Assembly of Pakistan unanimously moved to amend Article 260 of the constitution with the following clause:[63]

> (3) A person who does not believe in the absolute and unqualified finality of the Prophethood of Muhammad (Peace be upon him) the last of the Prophets, or claims to be a prophet, in any sense of the word, or of any description whatsoever, after Muhammad (Peace be upon him), or recognizes such a claimant as a prophet or a religious reformer is not a Muslim for the purposes of the Constitution or law.[64]

This effectively designated all Ahmadis, both Qadiani and Lahori, as non-Muslims according to Pakistan's constitution. From a legal perspective, the amendment only involved relabeling the movement for classification purposes with minimal juridical implications. In many ways, however, rather than bringing the debate to a close, it opened avenues for increased Ahmadi persecution. This was in part because agitators perceived the constitutional changes as state-sponsored justification for the mistreatment of Ahmadis, who were no longer legally Muslim. This yielded interesting consequences by virtue of the mixed religious and political nature of the decision.

From an Islamic law perspective, the constitutional changes raise several causes for concern. The first problem is that the National Assembly of Pakistan lacks religious authority. Prior to the Ahmadi controversy, the National Assembly refrained from making religious injunctions of this sort. In subsequent years, the most serious disputes pertaining to the relationship between Muslim personal law and the state were referred to the Federal Shariat Court, which was not established until 1980.[65] The act of legislating matters of religious law or perhaps issuing verdicts related to the *sharī'a* has never fallen directly within the jurisdiction of the National Assembly. The National Assembly in this sense is no more representative of a *qāḍī* than the president is *khalīfa*. This is because the National Assembly is simply not a religiously authoritative body capable of issuing a *fatwā* of *kufr*, even if solely "for the purposes of the Constitution or law."

Proving that someone is guilty of *kufr* in accordance with the Islamic legal tradition is not a straightforward task. This means that demonstrating Ahmadis—or members of some other heterodox movement for that matter—are guilty of *kufr* is a bounded endeavor. At most, one could show that an individual

Ahmadi maintains heretical beliefs. In such cases, one must recognize that if an individual Ahmadi is found guilty of *kufr*, the ruling cannot be generalized and hence applied categorically to all members of Jama'at-i Ahmadiyya, even if that individual was Mirza Ghulam Ahmad himself. This means that when the leader of a community is deemed a *kāfir* (infidel) or a *murtad* (apostate), the designation does not inherently filter down to each member of that community, unless it can be shown on a case-by-case basis that each member willfully shares the same heretical views.

Let us suppose for the sake of argument that a contemporary *qāḍī* (judge charged with issuing religious rulings that are legally binding within a given jurisdiction) retroactively declares Mirza Ghulam Ahmad an apostate (*murtad*) after his death, based on previous publications. This ruling would only apply to Ghulam Ahmad himself within the relevant jurisdiction of the *qāḍī* in question. It could not be applied blindly to every subsequent member of Jama'at-i Ahmadiyya, especially when considering the fact that many Ahmadis at present were born into the Jama'at. For this reason, it is imperative to distinguish between Muslims who converted to "Ahmadiyyat," and those who were born into the Jama'at due to the religious conversion of parents or members of a previous generation. Only Muslims who deliberately converted to "Ahmadiyyat" on a voluntary basis, while being conscious of critical deviations from orthodoxy, would thus be liable for charges of apostasy, since Ahmadis born into the Jama'at would never really have been considered Muslim anyway. In this case, each Ahmadi who converted to "Ahmadiyyat" from Islam would be subject to trial individually, irrespective of the rulings of a *qāḍī* against Mirza Ghulam Ahmad. The *qāḍī* would then need to determine whether each convert purposefully intended to maintain heretical beliefs or was somehow innocently misled. Once again, those born into "Ahmadiyyat" would be exempt from accusations of apostasy. In order to charge all Muslim converts to "Ahmadiyyat" with apostasy, a verdict of *kufr* would need to be firmly established by an authoritative body capable of providing collective rulings for the global *umma,* which does not exist at this time. These rulings would ultimately amount to something similar to a traditional notion of consensus (*ijmā'*) in classical legal theory (*uṣūl al-fiqh*), which would thereby enable non-scholars to deduce that anyone affiliated with Jama'at-i Ahmadiyya was non-Muslim.[66]

From a logistical perspective, these conditions are difficult, if not impossible, to satisfy and even harder to implement in contemporary Muslim societies. The National Assembly of Pakistan does not possess the requisite religious qualifications to make judgments that are theologically binding, especially since elected officials rarely hold religious credentials. This further highlights the fact that the 1974 ruling only represents a constitutional change made by one country's National Assembly, purportedly out of political concerns for order and classification. This is not to say that the National Assembly's stance on Ahmadis is unsound or untrue, but simply that it is nonbinding and hence inapplicable in a traditional Islamic context. It follows that National Assembly rulings do not constitute *ijmā'*, since they are religiously invalid. To this day, the 1974 decision has the potential of being reversed by any subsequent government of Pakistan at any time, unlike a theological consensus (*ijmā'*), which would henceforth remain unchanged and irreversible forever.

These issues aside, the government of Pakistan went on to clarify section 295A of the penal code with this statement:

> A Muslim who professes, practises or propagates against the concept of the finality of the Prophethood of Muhammad (Peace be upon him) as set out in clause (3) of Article 260 of the Constitution, shall be punishable under this section.[67]

The wording of this amendment is contradictory in that it explicitly refers to those who do not believe in the "absolute and unqualified finality of the Prophethood of Muhammad" as Muslims. In any case, these changes to the constitution altogether should have granted Ahmadis the right to separate electoral representatives in the National Assembly, alongside those of other non-Muslim minorities. Ahmadis, however, have never taken advantage of this opportunity, since it involves an acknowledgment of their status as non-Muslims. Only one such attempt was made in 1976 by Bashir Tahir, who ran as an Ahmadi candidate in pursuit of an Ahmadi seat, but he was excommunicated from the Jama'at by *khalīfat al-masīh* III Mirza Nasir Ahmad shortly following the nomination.[68] Since Nasir Ahmad firmly maintained that Ahmadiyyat was the true expression of Islam, in accepting the candidacy Bashir Tahir was declared an apostate of Ahmadiyyat. Consequently, no further attempts have been made to claim Ahmadi seats.

In July 1977, the government of Zulfikar Ali Bhutto was overthrown by a military coup upon the National Assembly's failure to appease opposition parties, which was followed once again by martial law. The new government, headed by Bhutto's commander in chief, General Muhammad Zia-ul-Haq, favored Islamization, which led to more stringent sanctions on Jama'at-i Ahmadiyya involving additional prohibitions and punishments. In late April 1984, President Zia-ul-Haq passed Ordinance XX, as an amendment to the penal code of Pakistan, which added punitive measures that were largely limited to members of Jama'at-i Ahmadiyya. Technically, the 1974 amendment only classified Ahmadis as non-Muslims with relatively minor legal implications. In contrast, however, the 1984 ordinance made most aspects of Ahmadi religious life in Pakistan illegal. The ordinance also made it exceedingly difficult for members of civil society to maintain a laissez-faire attitude towards ordinary Ahmadis. From a political perspective, the government's stance on Jama'at-i Ahmadiyya led to continual and often unprovoked harassment of Ahmadis who were otherwise disinterested in the political process. Section 298C of the ordinance states:

> 298C. Person of the Quadiani group, etc., calling himself a Muslim or preaching or propagating his faith.
> Any person of the Quadiani group or the Lahori group (who call themselves "Ahmadis" or by any other name) who, directly or indirectly, poses himself as a Muslim, or calls, or refers to, his faith as Islam, or preaches or propagates his faith, or invites others to accept his faith, by words, either spoken or written, or by visible representations, or in any manner whatsoever outrages the religious feelings of Muslims, shall be punished with imprisonment of either description for a term which may extend to three years and shall also be liable to a fine.[69]

As a legal stipulation, the word choice of this section of the ordinance is rather loose and ambiguous, especially considering the severity of the consequences. For example, any action that "outrages" Muslim sentiment is punishable by up to three years' imprisonment and a fine. Legislating sentiment is problematic for many reasons, not least of all because it is impossible to determine by law which actions qualify as reprehensible "outrage" for any given Muslim. The classical Islamic legal tradition in comparison recognized the absurdity of distinguishing between hypocrites who merely "pose" as Muslims and genuine Muslims, which thereby removed the responsibility of making such distinctions from legal authorities. It is important to note that in traditional conceptions of Islamic jurisprudence (*fiqh*), the notion of hypocrisy, or perhaps insincerity, is significantly different from determining a *murtad* or a *kāfir*, which is a question neither of sincerity nor of *fiqh*, but rather a question of *'aqīda* (creed). Within the broader Islamic tradition, anyone who takes *shahāda* (the declaration of faith) is legally Muslim for purposes of Islamic law, unless they adopt unsound *'aqīda*, which is determined through a lengthy case-by-case process, as mentioned above. The notion of establishing the religious authenticity of a Muslim—as opposed to one who simply poses as a Muslim—is beyond the scope of both *fiqh* and *'aqīda*. In this sense, ascertaining sound *'aqīda* is considerably different from ascertaining whether someone is posing as a Muslim. This complexity is part of the broader theological problem surrounding Jama'at-i Ahmadiyya, since many mainstream scholars believe that Mirza Ghulam Ahmad adopted unsound *'aqīda*.

To clarify the law, other aspects of the ordinance explicitly defined outrageous actions. These included Ahmadis who give the "*azan* [adhān (call to prayer)]," refer to their mosques as "*masjids* [masjids (mosques)]," or affix the saying "*Razi Allah Anho* [radī allāhu 'anhu (may God be pleased with him)]" to the names of anyone other than the Prophet Muhammad, his companions, or his caliphs.[70] Since 1984, outrageous offenses have also included saying the standard Muslim greeting, *al-salāmu 'alaykum* (peace be upon you), or even reciting the *kalima* (there is no god but Allah [God] and Muhammad is his messenger).[71] This example is unusually problematic, since the very utterance of the *kalima* is precisely what causes one to leave one's former religion and enter into Islam. This is why Muslims have tended to hail the utterance of the *kalima* by non-Muslims, and perhaps even the greeting of *salām* (peace) for different reasons. Pakistani legal authorities attempted to resolve the paradox by insisting that Ahmadis who recited the *kalima*, and thereby took *shahāda*, were insincere and simply "posing" as Muslims.

London Return

The combination of dramatic changes in the political discourse of Pakistan, internal ambiguities in the administrative hierarchy of the Jama'at, and the overall shuffling of the Jama'at's leadership further destabilized the Ahmadi identity. Mirza Nasir Ahmad *khalīfat al-masīh* III passed away on June 9, 1982, eight years after the first constitutional changes had taken place. On the next day, his younger half brother, Mirza Tahir Ahmad, was elected as his successor, *khalīfat al-masīh* IV. The timing of the election was extraordinary, since on April 26, 1984, Zia-ul-Haq's Ordinance XX went into effect, within two years of Mirza Tahir Ahmad having assumed control of the *khilāfat*. Within days, on April 30, 1984, the newly elected fourth *khalīfa* fled Pakistan forever, seeking asylum in London.[72] Ahmadis often compare the story of his escape from Pakistan to the *hijra* (emigration) of the Prophet Muhammad from Mecca to Medina. By establishing a new base in London, the *khalīfa* was better positioned to recast the Ahmadi controversy in a new light. From Britain, he discovered an avid western audience whose sympathies were drawn to a fresh and fervent consciousness that had steadily been evolving into a movement for human rights.

The re-centering of the *khilāfat* in London was different from the previous move from Qadian to Rabwah for many reasons. The migration of Ahmadis from India to Pakistan in 1947 coincided with the flow of the Muslim mainstream, whereas in moving from Pakistan to Britain Ahmadis left an Islamic state in search of refuge with non-Muslims. For Jama'at-i Ahmadiyya, the success of the transition depended upon the ability to convince European hosts that Ahmadis were indeed a persecuted minority, which had become a reality for many Ahmadis in Pakistan, owing to the constitutional changes of 1974 and 1984. There were unforeseen consequences for Ahmadi identity, however, which must not be overlooked. The formation of diaspora communities of Ahmadis consisting largely of asylum seekers was understood as a natural outcome of the dichotomy between Ahmadiyyat and mainstream Islam. This was especially the case in Western Europe and North America, where obtaining immigration status by conventional means was difficult. For this reason, the establishment of a new headquarters of *khilāfat-i ahmadiyya* required an explanation both for outsiders and for Ahmadi disciples, who watched curiously as the fourth *khalīfa* apparently became better poised to fulfill the mission of the *imām mahdī* from central London. These explanations inevitably returned to the notion of a fundamental incompatibility between Ahmadis and non-Ahmadi Muslims, even though such an incompatibility has never existed. The notion of Ahmadis being incompatible with non-Ahmadis has increasingly taken root in the Ahmadi identity since the implementation of the constitutional changes in Pakistan. This has impacted the self-image of Ahmadis and outsider perceptions of Jama'at-i Ahmadiyya, both of which share in the construction of identity.

One can only speculate how Ahmadi identity might have developed differently, had the *khalīfa* stayed in Pakistan, or in any other Muslim-majority country, instead of departing for London. Perhaps an Islamic setting would have influenced Ahmadi self-perceptions differently, despite imposing potential constraints upon the *khalīfa,* who would likely have remained under the continual threat of imprisonment in countries such as Pakistan. It is clear that the escape to London encouraged a restatement of the Ahmadi worldview in a different context. This was perhaps most noticeable in Mirza Ghulam Ahmad's attack on Christian theology, which was suddenly reinvigorated by the western context as a timely religious debate. The new setting also sidelined other important objectives of Jama'at-i Ahmadiyya's early mission, such as dated disputes with religious rivals, including the Hindu revivalist Arya Samaj and Brahmo Samaj movements. Moreover, the predominantly non-Muslim surroundings placed high value on differentiating between Ahmadi and non-Ahmadi Islam as a cursory explanation for persecution. Some insiders of the Jama'at themselves have expressed concern that Ahmadis have begun to treat fellow Muslims as though they follow another religion.

The intellectual argument for retaining a western headquarters has become questionable in recent years, as diplomatic relations between India and Pakistan gradually improve. For the first time since 1947, the fifth *khalīfa,* Mirza Masroor Ahmad (b. 1950),[73] who currently presides over the Jama'at, may have the opportunity to return the center of operations of Jama'at-i Ahmadiyya to Qadian with minimal restrictions. This, however, would involve forgoing the worldly benefits of heading a transnational organization from London. It will be interesting to see whether Mirza Masroor Ahmad or any future successors succumb to religious concerns and return the Jama'at's headquarters to the sacred village of Qadian where Mirza Ghulam Ahmad's remains lie in waiting. Perhaps one day the lure of building a magnificent shrine in the consecrated lands of the *bahishtī maqbara* with a domed mosque surrounding the tomb of Mirza Ghulam Ahmad—as is so commonly done in South Asian Islam—will become too great for Ahmadis to ignore. In the meantime, there are no government restrictions to prevent this from happening, or from being postponed any further, since the political situation in India at the moment is stable enough to support an Ahmadi *khalīfa* who may choose to return at any time.

Conclusion

Beyond South Asia

The Jama'at of today has been altered by its experiences of religious persecution, mainly in South Asia. This has forced communities of contemporary Ahmadis in recent decades to develop under the ubiquitous threat of persecution. The awareness of persecution in South Asia is also prevalent in western countries where increasing numbers of Ahmadis now reside.[1] The largest communities of asylum seekers have formed near urban centers in Western Europe and North America where better employment opportunities cater to newcomers who arrive with different vocational skill sets or levels of training. The availability of options for incoming Ahmadis accommodate professionals as well as unskilled laborers from less privileged backgrounds in rural South Asia. This has led to the formation of diversified communities of western Ahmadis who represent an array of socioeconomic backgrounds. The internal diversity of each Ahmadi community, however, depends upon the immigration policies of the country in question, since all Ahmadi immigrants have not arrived in the West as asylum seekers. There are also indications that an increasing number of affluent Ahmadis have voluntarily elected to pursue career paths abroad rather than facing the perils of the South Asian workforce, where corruption and discrimination are commonplace for members of marginalized communities. These developments have created a distinction between Ahmadi communities in the West and those in South Asia, which continue to exhibit more conventional socioeconomic distributions within local congregations and lesser concentrations of Ahmadis from more affluent backgrounds on the whole.

There were a number of attempts by the fourth *khalīfat al-masīh*, Mirza Tahir Ahmad, to adopt a more progressive outlook of westernized reforms. This did not necessarily represent a major shift in ideology as much as a shift in priorities, which needed to address the impending challenges of coping with a new environment. Some of the biggest developments included expansion projects aimed at establishing a religious infrastructure for Jama'at-i Ahmadiyya in western countries, which largely amounted to a steady proliferation of mosques. There are Ahmadi mosques in most major cities in Western Europe and North America, even though Ahmadi congregations often remain relatively small. In some cases, Ahmadi venues in the West may represent little more than a vacant house that has been converted into a mosque to accommodate a limited number of worshippers during the Friday prayer. In other cases, large purpose-built facilities have been constructed in anticipation of long-term growth, such as the Baitun Nur mosque of Calgary, which opened in 2008, and the Bait ur Rahman mosque of Vancouver, which opened in 2013. These construction projects serve many purposes for Jama'at-i Ahmadiyya and provide an indication of organizational expectations regarding the establishment of a stronger presence in western countries in years to come. This transition to the West is part of the Jama'at's continuing response to ongoing challenges of persecution in South Asia.

In order to meet the anticipated needs of future Ahmadis, Mirza Tahir Ahmad introduced the *waqf-i naw* (new[born] endowment) scheme in 1987.[2] The scheme revolved around the notion of Ahmadi parents dedicating the lives of their children to the Jama'at. The *waqf-i naw* scheme has been conventionally understood as a means of broadening the number of Ahmadi missionaries worldwide, but primarily beyond South Asia. This scheme has also permitted skilled Ahmadis, especially in the West, to dedicate professional services to the Jama'at whenever their services are needed to fulfill its objectives. The demand for more missionaries has always been central to Jama'at-i Ahmadiyya's ideology of proselytization, but since 1984 the need to produce missionaries acclimated to western linguistic and cultural sensitivities has become urgent. This is not to say that the majority of Ahmadi missionaries in western countries have surpassed mainstream Muslim imams in terms of adapting to western environments, but only that Mirza Tahir Ahmad appears to have been aware that Jama'at-i Ahmadiyya needed to bridge the cultural gap as an organization for it to flourish in the future.

These efforts have been supplemented by the construction of Ahmadi seminaries near major western centers, including Frankfurt, London, and Toronto, in addition to various African and Southeast Asian locations where the Jama'at continues to spread. This has involved developing a revised curriculum in European languages, such as English or German, since most incoming students lacked the literary fluency in Urdu needed to tackle Ghulam Ahmad's works. As a result, seminary (*jāmi'a*) students are taught Urdu as a second language along with other subjects in order to fulfill the expectations of the Jama'at. The curriculum also emphasizes aspects of the Qur'an and hadith related to Ghulam Ahmad's mission, which to some extent has broadened the gap between Ahmadi missionaries and mainstream Muslim imams, who generally have a more comprehensive understanding of classical Islamic texts in their broader historical context. The need to focus on Ghulam Ahmad's mission has shaped—and perhaps even hindered—the progress of Jama'at-i Ahmadiyya's intellectual tradition, since Ahmadi missionaries inevitably view Islam from a nineteenth-century South Asian perspective as a means of justifying Ghulam Ahmad's relevance. Maintaining a romanticized view of nineteenth-century South Asia under the influence of Mirza Ghulam Ahmad as the *mahdī* and promised messiah has shaped the subsequent development of Jama'at-i Ahmadiyya's self-image. This means that second- and third-generation Ahmadis in western countries who enroll in Ahmadi religious training institutions develop a rather narrow perspective of the historical development of Islam in general, and South Asian Islam in particular.

The new seminary campuses are somewhat isolated despite their relative proximity to major cities with larger Ahmadi congregations. For example, the Toronto seminary (opened in 2003) is located in Mississauga, the Germany seminary (opened in 2012) is located in Riedstadt, and the UK seminary has moved from its original location in London (opened in 2005) to a new complex in Haslemere, Surrey (opened in 2012). This reinforces the development of uniqueness by limiting contact with outsiders and hence limiting distractions, which is a strategy used by many institutions of higher learning. A more fundamental problem with this model of higher education is the internal isolation of seminary students from other western Ahmadis who possess advanced degrees in secular disciplines. The education gap between recent missionary graduates and their Ahmadi congregations in the West is most notable among younger Ahmadis and university-educated second- and third-generation immigrants. There has been some effort in recent years to offset the discrepancy through the implementation of a more comprehensive curriculum. In other words, younger Ahmadi missionaries who are educated in the West face the danger of being further alienated from both their congregants and from other Muslims. This is one of the many challenges facing the newly formed institutions and may only be a fleeting problem that is resolved in due course, but should be noted nonetheless for the time being.

The Face of the Jama'at Today

The transition to western countries has made Jama'at-i Ahmadiyya increasingly aware of its global public image. As a result, the face of Jama'at-i Ahmadiyya has been represented more and more through professional-caliber media outlets intended to disseminate Ahmadi Islam to a globalized community. In 1994, Mirza Tahir Ahmad established an international satellite channel known today as Muslim Television Ahmadiyya (MTA) International, which is currently available in Europe through the British satellite broadcaster Sky. Although the channel was initially conceived as means for the fourth *khalīfa* to maintain contact with Ahmadi disciples in South Asia, it has since been expanded as a prime outlet for disseminating Ahmadi views and religious interpretations. MTA currently provides coverage of nearly every major Ahmadi event of religious importance, from global tours of the *khalīfa* to the *jalsa sālāna* (annual gathering) in the United Kingdom. The channel was expanded by the fifth and current *khalīfat al-masīh*, Mirza Masroor Ahmad, whose Friday sermons are broadcast on a weekly basis. This had made it easier to preserve a consistent narrative of the movement's background and history in a globalized world. It also keeps Ahmadis connected to the *khalīfa*, despite his continual travel, including in 2005 the first visit to Qadian by an Ahmadi *khalīfa* since partition. For many outsiders, this has become the face of Jama'at-i Ahmadiyya today and the primary source of information on the movement.

Since 2007, MTA has launched an Arabic-language channel known as MTA Al Arabiya, which includes original programming for broadcasts throughout the Middle East and North Africa. Some programs enable Arabic-speaking callers to pose questions to Ahmadi missionaries while live on the air. This has reintroduced Ahmadi missionaries to parts of the Muslim world and has reopened avenues for dialogue without the immediate threat of persecution. MTA keeps Ahmadis connected to other Muslims around the world, even if only as debate partners in the Arabic language. This is rather different from traditional interactions with Arabs, which at times led to hostilities between Ahmadi and non-Ahmadi Muslims. The threat of persecution remains at the forefront of Jama'at-i Ahmadiyya's global interactions, whether as an explanation for recent migration patterns to the West, or as a means of reshaping global dialogue with other Muslims. The threat of persecution remains a reality for Ahmadis worldwide, as does the liveliness of the Ahmadi controversy. With this in mind, it may be useful to consider other explanations for Ahmadi persecution today, which conceptually recognize both its historical development and its mixed religious and political composition.

Unconventional Explanations: The Case of the Common Lineage

We have seen how religious persecution has existed in various forms since the beginnings of Ahmadi history for different reasons. However, a satisfactory explanation has yet to be given as to why this persecution persists with such intensity over a century after Mirza Ghulam Ahmad's death. The only exception to this deficiency has been the preceding discussion of how the Ahmadi controversy has been intertwined with the development of aspects of South Asia's religious politics. It is important here to distinguish between causes of controversy and causes of persecution. Ahmadi interpretations of Islam have at times differed considerably from those of mainstream Muslims, but this is no different from several other messianic movements throughout the history of the broader Islamic tradition, including the Isma'ilis and the Baha'i, whose differences are less politicized on the whole for various reasons.[3] Although Ahmadi interpretations of Islam are clearly controversial, it is still not clear why such subtle distinctions in tangential themes of Islamic theology became so heavily politicized in the mainstream discourse of Muslim South Asia. Surely, the subtleties regarding the spiritual status of the *mahdī*, the true fate of Jesus shortly after his crucifixion, and the circumstantial rejection of violent jihad are at best peripheral concerns in the daily practice of most ordinary Sunni Muslims. We have also seen that even among the most contested issues, a precedent was set for the reinstatement of violent jihad by the second *khalīfa*, Mirza Mahmud Ahmad, in 1948 with his deployment of the Furqan Force in Kashmir. In addition, non-Ahmadi Muslims have shared similar, if not the same, interpretations as Ahmadis about the natural death of Jesus, which can be seen in the commentaries of other modernist interpreters of the Qur'an, who like Ahmadis no longer consider Jesus to be physically alive in heaven. The only remaining dispute of interest pertains to *nubuw-wa* (finality of prophethood). However, demystifying the Ahmadi doctrine of *khātam al-nubuwwa*, like other Ahmadi beliefs, is not a straightforward task, since Jama'at-i Ahmadiyya does not reject the notion of *khātam al-nubuwwa* outright, but rather interprets its meaning in an unusual and potentially un-Islamic way. Nevertheless, even if Mirza Ghulam Ahmad's interpretation of *khātam al-nubuwwa* amounts to *kufr* (infidelity), it still does not justify the persecution of Jama'at-i Ahmadiyya that continues to this day.

It may seem somewhat striking that despite their differences so many influential Muslim political leaders have been willing to collaborate with prominent members of Jama'at-i Ahmadiyya in the past, including Ahmadi *khalīfa*s and their representatives. This background has only contributed to a greater sense of skepticism towards the Jama'at, especially for conspiracy theorists. Beyond conspiracies, however, it seems reasonably clear why political leaders might seek to align themselves with highly organized religious institutions, particularly through the late nineteenth and early twentieth centuries, when centralized religious orders and government may have been the most influential organizations in the subcontinent. This again raises questions about why some community leaders were so tolerant while others were so intolerant.

It is worth drawing attention to the fact that many opposition leaders who instigated early anti-Ahmadi activities had close personal ties to Jama'at-i Ahmadiyya. For example, the first *fatwā* of *kufr* against Mirza Ghulam Ahmad was written in 1891 by Maulvi Nazir Husayn Dehlawi, in response to Ghulam Ahmad's publication of *Tawzīh-i Marām*.[4] Maulvi Nazir Husayn's willingness to invest the time and effort necessary to prepare a calculated response to Ghulam Ahmad must have been influenced by their previous relationship. This form of condemnation is rather different from a situation in which an arbitrary scholar incidentally decides to publicize a theological dispute with another. In this case, the significance of Mirza Ghulam Ahmad's proximity to the opposition, including Maulvi Nazir Husayn Dehlawi, has been overlooked by previous studies on

Jamaʿat-i Ahmadiyya. The extent of Nazir Husayn's role as a religious teacher of Ghulam Ahmad seems to have extended beyond the classroom, considering that Nazir Husayn performed the second marriage of Ghulam Ahmad, who traveled to Delhi from the Punjab for the occasion. These connections are difficult to ignore when assessing the way in which the dispute unfolded.

Writing a *fatwā* of *kufr* against a religious rival in the subcontinent was not altogether uncommon during the era of modernist Islamic reform. The act of ostracizing one's opponents or publicly castigating the views of those who maintained unconventional expressions of Islam was to some extent indicative of how many thinkers in nineteenth-century South Asian Islam handled dissent. A *fatwā* of *kufr* in this context certainly did not carry the weight that it could have carried within a different historical or cultural context or a different period of Islamic history. Thus, it is not surprising that other students and supporters of Maulvi Nazir Husayn from the Ahl-i Hadith were equally antagonistic towards Ghulam Ahmad's mission.

One such student of Maulvi Nazir Husayn Dehlawi was Maulvi Muhammad Husayn Batalwi. Batalwi is frequently quoted in early Ahmadi literature as an opponent of Ghulam Ahmad's mission. As mentioned earlier, Batalwi was a longtime classmate and friend of Mirza Ghulam Ahmad. It is not unreasonable to suggest that Muhammad Husayn Batalwi's personal relationship with Mirza Ghulam Ahmad influenced his response to Jamaʿat-i Ahmadiyya. The added conflict between Ghulam Ahmad and Batalwi's principal teacher, Nazir Husayn, would likely have contributed to Batalwi's disdain for Jamaʿat-i Ahmadiyya. Other prominent opponents of Jamaʿat-i Ahmadiyya who were trained by the Ahl-i Hadith master Maulvi Nazir Husayn Dehlawi included Sana'ullah Amritsari (1870–1943) and the sons of Shaykh ʿAbdullah Ghaznavi.[5] This connection may have spurred enmity between Ghulam Ahmad and ʿAbdullah Ghaznavi's sons—most notably ʿAbd al-Jabbar and ʿAbd al-Haqq Ghaznavi—which periodically led to *mubāhala* (prayer duel) challenges between the two camps.[6]

In the case of the Ghaznavis, Ghulam Ahmad had developed a close relationship with both Maulvi Nazir Husayn Dehlawi and ʿAbdullah Ghaznavi. This meant that the threat of being associated with Ghulam Ahmad was intensified, since Ghulam Ahmad was affiliated with both their teacher and their father. The personal ties provide insights into the lasting bitterness between the Ghaznavi brothers and Jamaʿat-i Ahmadiyya, which appears to have been more than a mere theological disagreement, as has previously been conceived in studies of Jamaʿat-i Ahmadiyya. It is possible that the Ghaznavis felt vulnerable to external criticism due to their dual proximity to Mirza Ghulam Ahmad, which could easily have triggered outspoken responses. The need to respond promptly and harshly probably stemmed from the fear that silence could be misconstrued as tacit approval of Jamaʿat-i Ahmadiyya, which would have reflected poorly on the family by tainting the legacies of their father and teacher. This explains why the animosity expressed towards Jama'at-i Ahmadiyya was overstated in an attempt to preserve the sanctity or nobility of the family's spiritual heritage. Offering a virulent response also served as a preemptive means of salvaging their own reputations by distancing themselves from Mirza Ghulam Ahmad, who shared similar ties. The alienation of Ghulam Ahmad from former teachers and spiritual mentors exaggerated negative perceptions of his mission by portraying him as a rogue student. The adversity did not end with opponents of Ghulam Ahmad but rather intensified through successive generations, enabling deeply personal rivalries to enter into the religious and political mainstream.

The politicization of the anti-Ahmadi movement was in many ways a direct reaction to the politicization of Jama'at-i Ahmadiyya itself. This process was largely initiated by the second khalīfa, Mirza Mahmud Ahmad, during the crisis in Kashmir. This implies that Ahmadi persecution was to some extent an indirect outcome of the politicization of Jama'at-i Ahmadiyya and of anti-Ahmadi activities being promulgated by its rivals. Prior to the politicization of Jama'at-i Ahmadiyya, the Ahmadi controversy remained largely unknown. The Majlis-i Ahrar was mainly responsible for turning the anti-Ahmadi stance into a communal priority for South Asian Muslims. This in itself warrants further investigation into the backgrounds of the founders of the Majlis-i Ahrar and their personal affiliations in an attempt to identify motivations for placing such emphasis on what at the time was a rather obscure messianic movement of rural Punjab.

The most dedicated members of the Ahrari leadership included 'Ataullah Shah Bukhari, Mazhar 'Ali Azhar, and Maulana Muhammad Da'ud Ghaznavi. Da'ud Ghaznavi was the eldest son of 'Abd al-Jabbar Ghaznavi, who of course was the eldest son of Maulana 'Abdullah Ghaznavi.[7] 'Abdullah Ghaznavi appears to have mentored Ghulam Ahmad and may have served as his spiritual guide. The connection between the two was formalized through the marriage of 'Abdullah Ghaznavi's son, 'Abd al-Wahid Ghaznavi, to Umama, the daughter of Ghulam Ahmad's closest companion and first khalīfa, Nur al-Din. Although the marriage occurred before Ghulam Ahmad announced his controversial claims, at least one of the couple's four children, Muhammad Isma'il Ghaznavi, was raised as an Ahmadi,[8] despite 'Abd al-Wahid Ghaznavi's steadfast opposition to Jama'at-i Ahmadiyya.[9] This connection may illuminate the rationale of Mirza Mahmud Ahmad in sending Isma'il Ghaznavi on behalf of the All-India Kashmir Committee to negotiate with his uncle, Da'ud Ghaznavi, who represented Majlis-i Ahrar.[10] Although Da'ud Ghaznavi was born in Amritsar, he too studied under Maulvi Nazir Husayn in Delhi for some time.[11]

The personal connection between Mirza Ghulam Ahmad and 'Ataullah Shah Bukhari, the dominant spokesperson for Majlis-i Ahrar, is reasonably consistent with other opponents already discussed. 'Ataullah Shah Bukhari was born in 1891 in Patna, Bihar, but eventually relocated to Punjab in pursuit of Islamic studies. Bukhari established himself in Golra District, where he studied under the renowned Chishti master Pir Mehr 'Ali Shah (1859–1937), whose shrine still stands at Golra Sharif in Pakistan, between present-day Islamabad and Rawalpindi. In 1915, 'Ataullah Shah Bukhari took the *bay'at* of Pir Mehr 'Ali Shah Golrawi and thus became his spiritual disciple *(murīd)*.[12] Prior to this, Pir Mehr 'Ali Shah and Mirza Ghulam Ahmad took part in a number of heated exchanges between 1899 and 1902.[13] Pir Mehr 'Ali Shah wrote two books, *Shams al-Hidāya* and *Sayf-i Chishtiyā'ī,* in direct response to Ghulam Ahmad and his messianic claims, in addition to smaller pamphlets, posters, and notices.[14] Ghulam Ahmad's written contribution to the debate included *Tohfa Golrawiyya, Arba'īn,* and *I'jāz al-Masīh.*[15] Ghulam Ahmad also challenged to a *mubāhala* Mian Allah Bakhsh Sangari, the *sajjāda nishīn* of Sulayman Taunswi. Sulayman Taunswi was the teacher of Shams al-Din Siyalwi, who was one of the teachers of Pir Mehr 'Ali Shah. This connection is not likely to have improved their relations, as the rivalry between Mirza Ghulam Ahmad and Pir Mehr 'Ali Shah continued to deepen.[16]

Although numerous challenges were made from both camps, a public debate between Pir Mehr 'Ali Shah and Mirza Ghulam Ahmad never took place. Once in 1900, as pressures were mounting on both sides, a frustrated Pir Mehr 'Ali Shah Golrawi made his way to Lahore in response to a challenge from Mirza Ghulam Ahmad. The dramatic display culminated in an anticlimactic ending when Ghulam Ahmad failed to appear for the debate.[17] The rivalry between Pir Mehr 'Ali Shah Golrawi and Mirza Ghulam Ahmad provides a backdrop for 'Ataullah Shah Bukhari's contempt for Jama'at-i Ahmadiyya. As with Maulvi Nazir Husayn Dehlawi and Maulana 'Abdullah Ghaznavi, it is not surprising that the dispute between Pir Mehr 'Ali Shah and Mirza Ghulam Ahmad was carried forward into the next generation by 'Ataullah Shah Bukhari and Mirza Mahmud Ahmad.[18]

I was unable to locate meaningful biographical information about the final Ahrari spokesperson of note, Mazhar 'Ali Azhar. It is known, however, that Mazhar 'Ali Azhar was born and raised in Batala, which is the closest town to Qadian and was home to Muhammad Husayn Batalwi at the time. This connection may or may not have shaped Mazhar 'Ali Azhar's perception of Jama'at-i Ahmadiyya.

In addition to key figures from the Ahrar and the Ahl-i Hadith, other outspoken critics of Jama'at-i Ahmadiyya included Maulvi Zafar 'Ali Khan, who is typically remembered for his role as editor of the *Zamīndār.* Although Zafar 'Ali Khan attended the formative meeting of the Majlis-i Ahrar, his commitment to the organization wavered for reasons unrelated to his opposition to Jama'at-i Ahmadiyya,[19] which in contrast was rather consistent, as seen in the editorials of the *Zamīndār,* among other works.[20] It is interesting to note that Zafar 'Ali Khan inherited the *Zamīndār* from his father, Maulvi Siraj al-Din, who founded the paper and edited it before his son. Siraj al-Din first met Mirza Ghulam Ahmad in the early 1860s, when Ghulam Ahmad was working as a reader at the Sialkot court during the early part of his career. The extent of their relationship is unclear, which makes it difficult to determine whether they were close. It is known, however, that Maulvi Siraj al-Din paid Ghulam Ahmad a personal visit at his home in Qadian in 1877. From this point forward, the two seem to have established a working relationship once Siraj al-Din was better positioned to offer assistance to Ghulam Ahmad in the form of professional advice regarding the process of publication, which he appears to have done on a number of occasions. Following his passing in 1908, Maulvi Siraj al-Din published a dignified obituary of Mirza Ghulam Ahmad in the *Zamīndār*, which is still quoted by Ahmadi sources today.[21]

Even though Maulvi Siraj al-Din may never have taken *bay'at* with Ghulam Ahmad, it is possible that Zafar 'Ali Khan found the cordial connection to his father to be particularly irritating. Similarly, Zafar 'Ali Khan may have feared that being associated with Mirza Ghulam Ahmad would tarnish his father's reputation. Zafar 'Ali Khan persistently publicized anti-Ahmadi sentiment through the pages of the *Zamīndār*, often during some of the more turbulent periods of Jama'at-i Ahmadiyya's political history. He was succeeded by his son, Akhtar 'Ali Khan, who took over as editor of the *Zamīndār* in the steps of his father and grandfather. Akhtar 'Ali Khan shared a similar role in politicizing anti-Ahmadi sentiment, which was documented by the government of Pakistan following the 1953 disturbances.[22]

Sayyid Abu'l-A'la Mawdudi played a significant role in the spread of anti-Ahmadi activism under the banner of his own political party, Jama'at-i Islami. Jama'at-i Islami's opposition to Jama'at-i Ahmadiyya was less sensationalized than that of the Majlis-i Ahrar, but was nonetheless significant. Maulana Mawdudi's personal connection to the rivalry also stemmed from family lineage. Mawdudi descended from a long line of Chishti *pīr*s who appear to have been authenticated into the order on a hereditary basis. Mawdudi's grandfather may arguably have been the most prominent Sufi master in recent generations and was regarded as a respected figure towards the end of the Mughal era. Seyyed Vali Reza Nasr notes, however, that at present Mawdudi's father, Sayyid Ahmad Hasan, is usually credited with exposing Mawdudi to mysticism.[23] Few are aware that Mirza Ghulam Ahmad once challenged Mawdudi's grandfather, Sayyid Husayn Shah Mawdudi of Delhi, to a *mubāhala* (prayer duel).[24] The details of this dispute between Sayyid Husayn Shah Mawdudi and Mirza Ghulam Ahmad are not known, but the *mubāhala* challenge indicates a sense of animosity between the two.

Considering the family's Sufi affiliation, it is possible that Chishti *sajjāda nishīn*s, *murshid*s, and *pīr*s united against Ghulam Ahmad in an exhibition of fraternal solidarity. According to Ghulam Ahmad, the *mubāhala* challenges were a response to scholars who publicly denounced his views as heretical or deceptive.[25] Some Sufis seem to have resolved their differences with Ghulam Ahmad at a later date. For example, Ghulam Ahmad listed the name of Mian Ghulam Farid Sahib Chishti from Chācharāñ in District Bahawalpur whose association with Ghulam Ahmad is worthy of further discussion, especially since the two seem to have reconciled their differences after earlier strains in their relationship.[26] It is not surprising nonetheless that Mawdudi maintained a negative attitude towards Jama'at-i Ahmadiyya as a result of his grandfather's confrontation with Ghulam Ahmad.

The final cluster of scholars who adopted an anti-Ahmadi platform and had conspicuous connections to Mirza Ghulam Ahmad is centered on Dar al-'Ulum, Deoband. Whereas the opponents mentioned above largely represented individuals or personal spiritual disciples, Dar al-'Ulum represents an educational institution with a structured tradition. Generations of the subcontinent's Muslim preachers have shared in its heritage, adopted its outlook, and espoused its religious methodology. Ghulam Ahmad was opposed by Maulvi Rashid Ahmad Gangohi, Muhammad Qasim Nanautwi, and their mutual *murshid*, Hajji 'Imdadullah Makki, who also shared a Chishti affiliation in terms of Sufism. These scholars played an instrumental role in the founding of the Dar al-'Ulum at Deoband.[27] Mirza Ghulam Ahmad challenged Rashid Ahmad Gangohi to *mubāhala*, but the challenge was never fulfilled.[28] Instead, Ghulam Ahmad wrote a lengthy reply to Gangohi's objections to claims about the coming of the *mahdī* and *masīh* in his supplement (*zamīma*) to part 5 of *Barāhīn-i Ahmadiyya*.[29] The conflict between Ghulam Ahmad and the founders of Dar al-'Ulum filtered down through successive generations of the Deobandi tradition.[30] This sheds light on how the pamphlet written by the Deobandi scholar Shabbir Ahmad 'Usmani came to play a pivotal role in justifying the stoning to death of Ahmadis in Afghanistan in the 1920s.[31] It has also been mentioned that Ahrari leaders later republished the pamphlet to promote anti-Ahmadi sentiment in India, and then in Pakistan after partition. For Deobandis, the peak of tension may have occurred in 1948 when Zafrulla Khan refused to offer the funeral prayer of Muhammad 'Ali Jinnah behind Shabbir Ahmad 'Usmani.

Shortly after partition, Shabbir Ahmad 'Usmani, along with prominent colleagues, including Mufti Muhammad Shafi (1897–1976), established the Dar al-'Ulum, Karachi. Mufti Muhammad Shafi was 'Usmani's cousin and former student, which is why his name is sometimes written as Muhammad Shafi 'Usmani.[32] Since 1948, Muhammad Shafi has been renowned for his dedicated service as the first grand mufti of Pakistan. Accordingly, Mufti Muhammad Shafi had a significant role in the aftermath of the disturbances of 1953 when Muslim leaders of Pakistan were struggling to declare Ahmadis as part of the non-Muslim minority.[33] His influence in the subcontinent remained strong through his demise in 1976 by laying much of the groundwork for the National Assembly decision of 1974.[34] This was despite the decline in his activities by the early 1970s, which opened up opportunities for the next generation. By this point, Mufti Muhammad Shafi's mantle had passed to his son, Mufti Muhammad Taqi 'Usmani (b. 1943), Pakistan's next great Deobandi mufti. Mufti Taqi 'Usmani played a more active role than his father in the constitutional changes of 1974 for this reason.[35] Similarly for Jama'at-i Ahmadiyya, the passage of time meant that in 1974 it was no longer Mirza Ghulam Ahmad or his son, Mirza Mahmud Ahmad, but his grandson, Mirza Nasir Ahmad, who was left to counter the government offensive. At present, Mufti Taqi 'Usmani remains one of Pakistan's leading jurists with an esteemed and active role in society that has extended into retirement.

The Politicization of Ahmadi Identity

The politicization of Ahmadi persecution has hardly been the inevitable consequence of maintaining questionable theology. Over the past century a rather limited group of individuals have promulgated Ahmadi and anti-Ahmadi interests throughout the subcontinent and beyond. The politicization of Ahmadi persecution has been transformed into somewhat of a neo-tribal conflict that extends back multiple generations along hereditary lines, whether physically or spiritually. The allegiances formed towards the end of British colonial rule were passed down from father to son, or teacher to student, from the nineteenth century and into the twenty-first century conflict of today. Each camp has remained faithful to its position and facilitated the transference of loyalties in uncorrupted chains of transmission that can be traced back to the time of Mirza Ghulam Ahmad himself.

A larger pattern appears to be emerging among instigators of the anti-Ahmadi movement. Nearly all of Mirza Ghulam Ahmad's rivals seem to have maintained some connection to the Chishti order at some point in their lives. Although there is not enough evidence at the moment to support a working thesis in this regard, it is an observation that should be duly noted. I can only speculate that this may have its origins in the dubious relationship between Mirza Ghulam Ahmad and Maulana 'Abdullah Ghaznavi.

While these lineages might not offer a satisfactory explanation for the origins of the Ahmadi controversy in the sense that they do not explain why some people hate Ahmadis, they do offer a reason why certain groups of Muslims and community leaders have felt exceedingly passionate about the issue given the cultural context of the time. Ahmadi persecution is not a product of religious lineage. But the politicization of Ahmadi persecution has been facilitated by personal loyalties, which connected narrow segments of scholars who collectively promoted common issues in accordance with mutual interests and affiliations, including an unwritten rule of protecting the honor of spiritual predecessors. This may also explain why the Ahmadi controversy has developed differently—namely under less politicized conditions—in other parts of the Muslim world beyond South Asia, the presumed language barrier aside. The politicization of Ahmadi persecution was in part a direct result of persistent efforts of specific groups of scholars who repeatedly prioritized the issue for the *umma*. Otherwise, there is no reason why Jama'at-i Ahmadiyya should retain any significant influence in mainstream South Asian religion or politics at this time. Negative publicity that reinforces the politicization of Jama'at-i Ahmadiyya, however, remains at the forefront of discussions of religious corruption, deviant Islam, or Islamic authenticity, as well as the purification of South Asia Islam today.

This study has shown that this politicization was only made possible through the lengthy development of the Ahmadi controversy in the nineteenth- and twentieth-century contexts of South Asian religion and politics. Had it taken place in another context or time period, it would likely have yielded different outcomes. In combining religious and political objectives through various phases of the independence movement, Jama'at-i Ahmadiyya slowly crystallized its role in modern South Asia, both as a religious movement and as a political party. This conception of the movement differs from that of most others, who have previously viewed it solely as a religious phenomenon. In choosing to pursue a sectarian outlook, Ahmadis promoted exclusivist conceptions of the world and of themselves, which left many isolated on both sides of the divide. This process eventually placed Ahmadis at the center of religious and political controversies, which increasingly marginalized the movement in accordance with the mainstream's negative response to exclusivity. Mirza Ghulam Ahmad's spiritual claims in this respect only defined the parameters of the controversy once the unfolding issues needed to be clarified. As we have seen, it is certainly conceivable that Ghulam Ahmad's Sufi metaphysics could have been reframed in a more palatable way than was done over the previous century. The way in which Ahmadi doctrine developed, however, reflects the mixed religious and political context of its environment as much as its evolving spiritual self-image.

Since the 1980s, Ahmadi identity has shifted further from its origins and has been transformed under the influence of outsider-imposed perceptions as defined by the constitution of Pakistan. The surge of Ahmadi asylum seekers in Western Europe and North America has underpinned an identity of victimization. This shift has been so dramatic that problems have arisen due to an increasing number of imposters attempting to immigrate to western countries fraudulently by taking advantage of the perception of persecution while claiming asylum as Ahmadis through deceit. Meanwhile, Jama'at-i Ahmadiyya continues to present itself in a way that emphasizes victimization and persecution, since the threat of persecution remains an imminent reality, especially for those residing in rural South Asia. The politicization of the Ahmadi controversy has had a greater impact on the self-image of Ahmadis by broadening the gap with non-Ahmadi Islam under the threat of violence. The development of the Ahmadi controversy, nevertheless, remains a political ploy that emerged from the throes of Muslim politics surrounding the formation of the Islamic state in twentieth-century South Asia, which needed to define a clear boundary between authentic and inauthentic Islam. This shaped the development of Muslim identity in contemporary Islam, as seen in the continuing aftermath of the Ahmadi controversy following partition. From the outside, politicians in search of political gain may scapegoat Jama'at-i Ahmadiyya by blaming Ahmadis for social disparity. Internally, the Ahmadi hierarchy portrays non-Ahmadi Muslims as malicious fundamentalists who are intolerably intent on stamping out Jama'at-i Ahmadiyya of the global *umma* by any means necessary. Ahmadi persecution has spread in recent years, most notably to Bangladesh and Indonesia, where political factions exploit the volatile nature of the controversy to win political favor.[36] Shootings at two Ahmadi mosques in Lahore on May 28, 2010, killed eighty-six people and injured scores more, which indicates that acts of violence may persist in coming years.[37] It is unfortunate in this regard that those who suffer the most tend to come from underprivileged backgrounds.

Providing an explanation for persecution should not be misconstrued with its justification since nothing can adequately justify senseless violence, discrimination, and harassment of religious minorities or any other people with perceived differences. It is rather simplistic and somewhat misleading to conclude—as has so often been done—that the contemporary climate surrounding the Ahmadi controversy, including the role of Ahmadi persecution, was the direct outcome of Mirza Ghulam Ahmad's spiritual claims. Justifications for Ahmadi persecution have clearly varied from case to case, from explanations based solely on jihad to those based solely on *khātam al-nubuwwa*. Still, it is often suggested that Ahmadis bring persecution upon themselves, which in itself is intellectually untenable. But this does not preclude persecution from being an indirect result of the very issues that the Ahmadi hierarchy has diligently pursued over the course of the past century. Jama'at-i Ahmadiyya has made tremendous efforts to publicize the notion of a distinctly Ahmadi version of Islam. The Ahmadi hierarchy has also initiated and sustained campaigns that actively propagate, and thereby politicize, Ahmadi social involvement throughout the world, whether through efforts to provide humanitarian relief, endeavors to alleviate social duress, or even in some cases attempts at political and military mobilization.

A politicized view of Ahmadi Islam has been adopted by both Ahmadis and non-Ahmadis. This image developed as a consequence of mutual interactions and interplay, which in turn facilitated a polarized perception of Jama'at-i Ahmadiyya by creating the alienation necessary for producing an environment conducive to religious persecution. It still may be possible for Ahmadis to help reduce the alienation of their movement through individual interactions and engaged organizational participation in social and religious affairs with non-Ahmadi Muslims. This may eventually help reduce violence and persecution. Otherwise, if the alienation intensifies and the gap with non-Ahmadi Muslims continues to widen, Jama'at-i Ahmadiyya may soon choose to dissociate itself from Islam altogether and create a separate Ahmadi identity, as was done by the Baha'i.

Constructing a New Narrative: A Recap

We have seen that the relationship between Mirza Ghulam Ahmad's family and imperial Britain was consistent with Ghulam Ahmad's political outlook throughout his career. This contributed towards the development of Ghulam Ahmad's religious ideology, namely his polemics against Christianity and his views on violent jihad. Ghulam Ahmad's formal education was limited to language acquisition, and his continued pursuit of religious studies and training with specialist teachers directly influenced the development of Ahmadi interpretations of Islam. This enabled Ghulam Ahmad to foster relationships with spiritual mentors such as Maulana 'Abdullah Ghaznavi, who similarly claimed to be a recipient of divine revelation, and *pīr* Mahbub 'Alam, a celebrated Sufi master of the Naqshbandi order. In addition, the Ahl-i Hadith influence on Ghulam Ahmad's thought, especially that of Maulvi Nazir Husayn Dehlawi, is reflected in Jama'at-i Ahmadiyya's rejection of *taqlīd* of a *madhhab* (or strict adherence to the legalist schools of thought), which is indicative of its unsubstantiated and often arbitrary approach to *fiqh* (jurisprudence).

These influences were also apparent in Mirza Ghulam Ahmad's claims of prophethood. The role of medieval Sufi thought has been connected with Ghulam Ahmad's spiritual claims by previous scholars, most notably Yohanan Friedmann.[38] Ghulam Ahmad's claims were extended beyond the Sufi context in order to be understood in a way that accommodated the development of a distinctively Ahmadi version of Islam. An example of this is the expansion of Ghulam Ahmad's account of Jesus's survival of crucifixion and his subsequent journey with his mother, Mary, to a final resting place in Kashmir. Ghulam Ahmad's fixation on Jesus's natural death stemmed from the need to substantiate his own claim to be the second messiah. In contrast, Ghulam Ahmad also claimed prophethood through a flawless display of perfections of the Prophet Muhammad, which involved imitating the preeminence of the Prophet's example and his virtuous moral character.

Ghulam Ahmad blurred the concept of *walāya* (sainthood) with connotations of *nubuwwa* (prophethood) and sustained an indefinite ambiguity surrounding the notion of revelation, which corresponded to his extraordinary self-image. This appears to have been intended to broaden discussions of Ghulam Ahmad's spiritual claims, which were presented in a way that entailed seemingly contradictory consequences that are arguably beyond the Islamic tradition. We have also seen how the terminology developed by Ghulam Ahmad consistently used descriptive qualifiers to further identify his spiritual rank and place limitations on his prophetic status. The confusion surrounding these claims led Jama'at-i Ahmadiyya to adopt literalist interpretations that draw upon charisma as a means of establishing religious authority.

The ensuing power struggle within the community following Ghulam Ahmad's death shaped the later development of Ahmadi doctrine. This was illustrated by the role of the Lahori-Qadiani split in formalizing Jama'at-i Ahmadiyya's interpretation of Ghulam Ahmad's spiritual mission. The ambiguity regarding Ghulam Ahmad's prophetic status gave way to ambiguities regarding the status of people who rejected his claims, which raised theological questions about the boundaries of *takfīr* (calling someone a nonbeliever). The repercussions of the split led to the formulation of an institutionalized notion of *khilāfat-i ahmadiyya,* which creatively combined sentiment and revelations from Ghulam Ahmad's final will (*al-Wasiyyat*) as justification. This led to a significant departure from Ghulam Ahmad's original conditions of *bay'at,* which were eventually replaced by allegiance to the institution of *khilāfat-i ahmadiyya.* The bureaucratization of Ghulam Ahmad's charisma introduced a hierarchical structure with an explicit chain of authority that connected ordinary Ahmadis to God through the *khalīfat al-masīh.* As this continued to unfold, changes in religious belief led to changes in religious practice, where communal isolation was facilitated by visible sociological distinctions, such as intermarriage and prayer restrictions with non-Ahmadi Muslims, as well as the introduction of a privatized Ahmadi donation system (*chandā*). These developments reinforced the emergent Ahmadi identity by segregating communities and treating newborns of Ahmadi parents as if they belonged to another religion.

These changes took place alongside involvement in many of the most important political challenges facing South Asian Islam during the twentieth century, including the realization of the broader independence movement, the Kashmir crisis, and the partition of India itself with its aftermath. At times, Mirza Mahmud Ahmad's dual roles—such as simultaneously being president of the All-India Kashmir Committee and *khalīfat al-masīh*—created a hybrid platform for Jama'at-i Ahmadiyya, which displayed its religious and political engagements to outsiders. This enabled Jama'at-i Ahmadiyya to expand its mission among members of the general public, but also attracted public scrutiny. Jama'at-i Ahmadiyya's political involvement in Muslim South Asia and its prolonged publicity campaigns in the region came at the cost of the politicization of Ahmadi Islam. The politicization of Jama'at-i Ahmadiyya made it difficult to ignore differences between Ahmadi Islam and the Muslim mainstream. This politicization coincided with the rise of intense opposition movements and internal religious rivalries.

As hostilities increased, the politicization of Ahmadi Islam led to the politicization of Ahmadi persecution. These tensions were subdued, however, until Punjab had formally been partitioned.

The formation of Pakistan as an Islamic state brought to light enduring questions of Muslim identity and Islamic authenticity, which culminated in the disturbances of 1953. This was capped by the 1974 decision of the National Assembly of Pakistan to consider Ahmadis as part of the non-Muslim minority according to constitutional law. Further sanctions in 1984 prompted the migration of Mirza Tahir Ahmad, *khalīfat al-masīh* IV, to London, where his successor, Mirza Masroor Ahmad, continues to publicize the notion of a dichotomy between Ahmadiyyat and Islam to this day. Since then, Jama'at-i Ahmadiyya has largely focused its efforts on Western Europe, North America, and parts of Africa.

Ahmadi theology developed from the mystical visions of Mirza Ghulam Ahmad's messianic mission into the inspiration behind the transnational movement of today. Distinct notions of Ahmadi theology arose in nineteenth-century South Asia and continued to develop under the influence of twentieth-century Muslim politics, until they finally attained the current level of global controversy in contemporary Islam. Both religion and politics shaped this path by enabling the Ahmadi controversy to become politicized and by producing circumstances that made it easier for people to condone religious persecution. It has ultimately been the role of this politicized persecution of Jama'at-i Ahmadiyya that has gradually, over the course of the last century, influenced a continual reassessment of Ahmadi self-identification, which has facilitated the development of the Ahmadi identity and a transformation of the movement from Sufism to Ahmadiyyat.

Appendix

Mirza Ghulam Ahmad's Family Tree

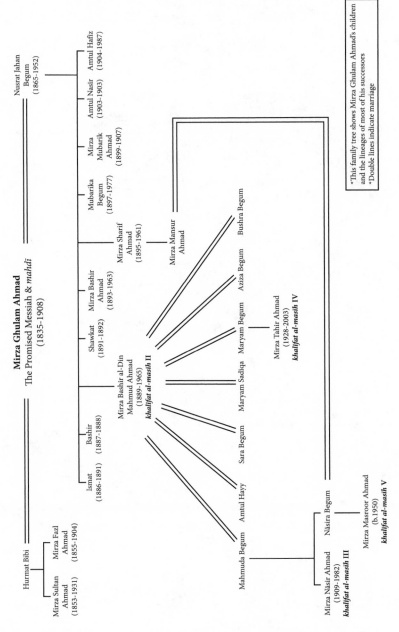

*This family tree shows Mirza Ghulam Ahmad's children and the lineages of most of his successors
*Double lines indicate marriage

Nusrat Jahan Begum (1865-1952)

Amtul Hafiz (1904-1987)

Amtul Nasir (1903-1903)

Mirza Mubarik Ahmad (1899-1907)

Mubarika Begum (1897-1977)

Mirza Sharif Ahmad (1895-1961)

Mirza Mansur Ahmad

Bushra Begum

Aziza Begum

Mirza Tahir Ahmad (1928-2003) *khalifat al-masih* IV

Maryam Begum

Maryam Sadiqa

Sara Begum

Amtul Hayy

Mahmuda Begum

Mirza Bashir Ahmad (1893-1963)

Shawkat (1891-1892)

Mirza Bashir al-Din Mahmud Ahmad (1889-1965) *khalifat al-masih* II

Bashir (1887-1888)

Ismat (1886-1891)

Mirza Ghulam Ahmad
The Promised Messiah & *mahdi*
(1835-1908)

Hurmat Bibi

Mirza Fazl Ahmad (1855-1904)

Mirza Sultan Ahmad (1853-1931)

Nasira Begum

Mirza Masroor Ahmad (b.1950) *khalifat al-masih* V

Mirza Nasir Ahmad (1909-1982) *khalifat al-masih* III

Glossary

abdāl substitutes

achkan a long overcoat common in South Asia as a type of formalwear for men

ahl al-bayt the family of the Prophet Muhammad

akhūndzāda a hereditary designation of a regional religious leader

amīr a leader

ammā jān an affectionate way of referring to one's mother

anjuman an administrative body, such as an assembly, organization, or committee that groups people together

'aqīda an area of Islamic studies focusing on correct orthodox belief, comparable to creed

awliyā Muslim saints who are believed to be close to God spiritually; singular is *walī*

bahishtī maqbara lit. "heavenly graveyard"; signifies where Mirza Ghulam Ahmad and others of the Ahmadi elite are buried, typically after having donated at least one-tenth of their inheritable wealth and assets to Jama'at-i Ahmadiyya

bay'at an allegiance to a teacher, spiritual guide, or leader as well as a process of initiation into a Sufi order or some other exclusive organization

burūzī a manifestation of the original, or manifestational; in an Ahmadi context, it may be more useful to think of this as an imitation of the original

chandā a form of charitable donation

chilla a forty-day spiritual retreat often marked by isolation, fasting, and intense prayer

dajjāl antichrist

darbār a royal court or formal assembly of government officials

fanā a term used to designate a spiritual state in strands of Sufism, describing the complete annihilation of the self or of one's very being

fatwā a religious ruling or opinion about a specific issue

fiqh Islamic jurisprudence

firqa a sect

futūhāt disclosures or illuminations that divulge hidden information in a way that could be associated with revelatory experiences in certain cases

ghawth a mystical title ascribed to one who may be considered a helper of God

ghayb the unseen realm beyond the physical world

hadīth qudsī sacred traditions (hadith) whose chains of transmission may be traced back to God rather than emanating from the Prophet Muhammad

hajj the pilgrimage to Mecca that must be performed once in a lifetime by Muslims who are able to do so; it is considered the fifth pillar of Islam

hakīm a natural medicine doctor who typically prescribes herbal medicines or dietary remedies

hartāl a strike

hikmat lit. "wisdom," but also used in reference to the discipline of philosophy

ijmā' a consensus of opinion in Islamic legal theory which is used as a means of amending Islamic law beyond conventional rulings

ijtihād coming up with new rulings for unprecedented circumstances in Islamic law

ilhām a form of revelation more closely associated with inspiration

irtidād apostasy

jāgīr a large tract of land granted to someone for further development and settlement

jāgīrdār the owner or proprietor of the *jāgīr*; similar to landlord

jalsa sālāna the annual convention of Jama'at-i Ahmadiyya in which Ahmadis gather together for religious activities

jamā'at an organization, community, or congregation

jāmi'a a general term for an institution of higher learning, whether a secular university or a religious seminary

jā-nishīn a term typically used in Sufism to represent the head of the Sufi order or the head's successor

jihād lit. "a struggle," which has an inner spiritual aspect and an outer physical aspect associated with fighting oppression and social injustice

juzwī partial; used by Mirza Ghulam Ahmad in reference to the notion of partial prophethood

kāfir a nonbeliever or an infidel

kalām a form of philosophy closely resembling a type of systematic presentation of speculative theology

kalīm-ullāh an honorary title given to Moses which means the one to whom God speaks

kalima the basic creed of Islam, namely that "there is no god but Allah (God), and Muhammad is his messenger (*lā ilāha illa 'llāh muhammad rasūl allāh*)"

kashf a form of revelatory experience often translated as "unveilings"

khalīfa successor, caliph, or representative

khalīfat al-masīh lit. "successor of the messiah," which refers to Mirza Ghulam Ahmad's successors who took over the movement after his death; the official title of Ahmadi caliphs

khānaqāh mu'allā a late-fourteenth- to early-fifteenth-century mosque complex situated along the Jhelum River of Srinagar in honor of Mir Sayyid 'Ali Hamdani (commonly known as Shah Hamdan), who was a prominent Sufi credited for spreading Islam in Kashmir

khātam al-awliyā lit. "seal of the saints," an honorific title conferred upon some Sufis to designate one as the greatest of the saints

khātam al-nabiyyīn lit. "seal of the prophets," a title conferred upon the Prophet Muhammad in the Qur'an (Sura 33:40)

khatīb one who delivers sermons, usually during the Friday prayer

khilāfat the caliphate

khil'at a land grant given as compensation

khwāb a dream or vision

kufr infidelity; rejection of belief

langar khāna the equivalent of a South Asian soup kitchen which provides food free of charge

madhhab a legal school of thought in Islam

mahdī the guided one who will appear at the end of times alongside the messiah

majlis-i shūrā an advisory council

mantiq the philosophical branch of logic

marham-i 'īsā a special ointment believed to have been applied to Jesus's body when he was removed from the cross after the crucifixion *masīh* the messiah; or sometimes written as *masīh-i maw'ūd,* meaning the promised messiah

maulvi a title of respect conferred upon teachers of Islam or Muslim leaders of prayer

misal usually refers to one of the Sikh confederate states during the eighteenth and nineteenth centuries

mubāhala a lengthy prayer duel in which two religious rivals invoke the wrath of God upon each other as a means of seeking a divine resolution to an unresolved debate. The *mubāhala* was often used to settle opposing claims by praying for the humiliating death of the liar or false claimant.

muballigh an Ahmadi missionary

mubashshirāt glad tidings of forthcoming events

muhaddath someone to whom God speaks or otherwise discloses information through some form of revelatory experience

mujāhidīn those who participate in a jihad

mujtahid one capable of performing *ijtihād* or coming up with new rulings for unprecedented circumstances without appealing to previous authorities

mullā originally an honorific term for a religious leader or scholar, which has taken on a negative connotation in certain contexts

murīd a spiritual disciple, usually associated with members of a Sufi order

mursal someone who is sent with a message, a messenger

murshid a spiritual guide or spiritual teacher, who usually serves as the head of a Sufi order

murtad an apostate, one who renounces one's religion

muslih maw'ūd lit. "the promised reformer" who was foretold by Mirza Ghulam Ahmad; most Ahmadis identify this reformer with Mirza Bashir al-Din Mahmud Ahmad, Ghulam Ahmad's son and second successor

nabī a prophet

nazīr a warner, often used in relation to the duties of a prophet which involve warning people of the day of judgment

nubuwwa prophethood

pesh go'ī an experience such as a vision which may be revelatory in nature and results in the foretelling of future events

pīr a term used to designate a spiritual guide, who usually serves as the head of a particular Sufi order and teaches Sufism to disciples

qādī an Islamic magistrate or judge charged with issuing religious rulings that are legally binding within a given jurisdiction

qutb axis

rasūl lit. "a messenger," commonly used in reference to the Prophet Muhammad

rūh al-quds lit. "holy spirit," a term used in the Qur'an and associated with Gabriel in the Islamic tradition

ru'yā a true dream or vision which could be considered a revelatory experience in certain cases

sajjāda nishīn a term typically used to describe the keeper of a Sufi shrine or the presiding head of a Sufi order

sayyid a term of nobility designating the descendants of the Prophet Muhammad

shahāda the declaration of faith in which one proclaims that there is no god but God (Allah) and that Muhammad is his messenger

shahīd a martyr

shams al-'ulamā lit. "sun of the scholars," a title conferred upon eminent scholars or thinkers

sharī'a a general term used broadly to describe the concept of Islamic law

shūrā see *majlis-i shūrā*

tablīgh lit. "propagation or announcing," but in an Ahmadi context this is synonymous with preaching or other missionary activity

tafsīr a commentary of the Qur'an

tahajjud a voluntary prayer that does not count as one of the five daily prayers but is typically offered before the mandatory dawn prayer

tajdīd renewal, which is most often associated with *tajdīd-i dīn* or religious renewal

takfīr the act of deeming someone a nonbeliever, perhaps by explicitly calling them an infidel

taqlīd the notion of strict adherence to the rulings of a particular legal school of thought

'ulamā religious scholars; plural for *'ālim*, or a scholar

umma the global Muslim community

ummī unlettered; used repeatedly in the Qur'an in reference to the Prophet Muhammd's lack of formal religious education, and often associated with illiteracy

usūl al-fiqh the principles of jurisprudence constituting the theoretical framework for arriving at sound legal rulings in Islamic law

wahy a form of divine revelation in Islam

walāya sainthood

walī see *awliyā*

waqf an endowment

zakat the third pillar of Islam, which stipulates a certain fraction (usually ¹⁄₄₀) of one's wealth and assets to be paid annually as charity for those who are eligible to do so

zillī shadowy or as the image of a shadow

Notes

Introduction

1. See Government of Punjab, *Report of the Court of Inquiry Constituted under Punjab Act II of 1954 to Enquire into the Punjab Disturbances of 1953* (Lahore: Superintendent Government Printing, Punjab, 1954).

2. See *The National Assembly of Pakistan Debates—Official Report*, 5:39 (September 7, 1974), p. 561.

3. See *Ordinance No. XX of 1984* as published in *The Gazette of Pakistan. Islamabad, Thursday, 26 April 1984*.

4. See H. Ritter, "Abū Yazīd (Bāyazīd) Tayfūr b. 'Īsā b. Surūshān al-Bistāmī," in *Encyclopaedia of Islam*, ed. P. Bearman (Leiden: Brill, 2008).

5. See Louis Massignon, *The Passion of al-Hallaj: Mystic and Martyr of Islam* (Princeton, NJ: Princeton University Press, 1994).

6. See Farid al-Din Attar, *Tadhkirat al-Awliyā*, trans. A. J. Arberry as *Muslim Saints and Mystics: Episodes from the Tadhkirat al-Auliya' ("Memorial of the Saints") by Farid al-Din Attar* (London: Arkana Penguin Books, 1966).

7. Annemarie Schimmel, *Mystical Dimensions of Islam* (Chapel Hill: University of North Carolina Press, 1975), p. 200.

8. See Bernd Radtke and John O'Kane, *The Concept of Sainthood in Early Islamic Mysticism: Two Works by al-Hakīm al-Tirmidhī* (Richmond, UK: Curzon Press, 1996).

9. See Khaled El-Rouayheb, "Heresy and Sufism in the Arabic-Islamic World, 1550–1750: Some Preliminary Observations," *Bulletin of the School of Oriental and African Studies* 73:3 (October 2010): 357–380.

10. Carl W. Ernst, *Ruzbihan Baqli: Mysticism and the Rhetoric of Sainthood in Persian Sufism* (Richmond, UK: Curzon Press, 1996), p. 51.

11. Ibid., pp. 24–26.

12. Michel Chodkiewicz, *Seal of the Saints: Prophethood and Sainthood in the Doctrine of Ibn 'Arabi* (Cambridge, UK: Islamic Texts Society, 1993).

13. See Yohanan Friedmann, *Shaykh Ahmad Sirhindi: An Outline of His Thought and a Study of His Image in the Eyes of Posterity* (Oxford: Oxford University Press, 2000).

14. See Shahzad Bashir, *Messianic Hopes and Mystical Visions: The Nurbakhshiya between Medieval and Modern Islam* (Columbia: University of South Carolina Press, 2003).

15. Oliver Scharbrodt, *Islam and the Baha'i Faith* (London: Routledge, 2008).

16. The title *Barāhīn-i Ahmadiyya* literally means "The Proofs of Ahmad" though it may be translated more appropriately as "The Proofs of Islam" or "Ahmad's Proofs of Islam."

17. The original ten-volume edition of *Malfūzāt* has been reissued in five volumes. In addition, *Rūhānī Khazā'in* has been reissued in a newly digitized format for greater clarity in reading the script. At times, the new page numbers vary from the original edition by a fixed margin. For example, page 10 in the original might correspond with page 11 in the newly digitized version. Most references in this study cite the first edition. Both editions are available online through Jama'at-i Ahmadiyya's website at www.alislam.org (accessed June 2014).

18. See Wilfred Cantwell Smith, *Modern Islam in India: A Social Analysis* (New Delhi: Usha Publications, 1985), pp. 367–372, under the heading "A Note on the Ahmadīyah Movement."

19. Ibid., pp. 371–372.

20. Ibid., p. 370.

21. Wilfred Cantwell Smith, "Ahmadiyya," in *Encyclopaedia of Islam*, 2nd ed., ed. P. Bearman (Leiden: Brill, 2008); see also Y. Friedmann, "Ahmadiyya," in *Encyclopaedia of Islam*, 3rd ed., ed. Gudrun Krämer (Leiden: Brill, 2008).

22. Humphrey J. Fisher, *Ahmadiyyah: A Study in Contemporary Islam on the West African Coast* (London: Oxford University Press, 1963).

23. For recent studies, see also John H. Hanson, "Modernity, Religion and Development in Ghana: The Example of the Ahmadiyya Muslim Community," *Ghana Studies* 12/13 (2009/2010): 55–75; see also Denise Brégand, "La Ahmadiyya au Bénin," *Archives de Sciences Sociales des Religions* 135:1 (July–September 2006): 73–90.

24. Humphrey J. Fisher, *Ahmadiyyah: A Study in Contemporary Islam on the West African Coast*, p. 111.

25. Ibid., pp. 35–88; see also H. A. Walter's *The Ahmadiya Movement* (London: Oxford University Press, 1918), which predates the studies by Fisher and Cantwell Smith and devotes considerable attention to the relation between Ahmadi Islam and Christianity. The book is not as balanced as Fisher's study and includes a number of errors and misconceptions. It may prove useful for other reasons, however.

26. Humphrey Fisher, *Ahmadiyyah*, pp. 70–71.

27. Ibid., p. 186.

28. Ibid., pp. 100–102.

29. Ibid., pp. 133–137.

30. Ibid., p. 20.

31. Spencer Lavan, *The Ahmadiyah Movement: A History and Perspective* (Delhi: Manohar Book Service, 1974).

32. A. R. Dard, *Life of Ahmad* (Lahore: Tabshir, 1948).

33. Spencer Lavan, *The Ahmadiyah Movement*, p. 28.

34. Ibid., p. 47.

35. Ibid., p. 29.

36. Dost Muhammad Shāhid, *Tārīkh-i Ahmadiyya*, vols. 1–21 (Rabwah?, 1983). Some volumes may still be forthcoming.

37. See Yohanan Friedmann, *Prophecy Continuous: Aspects of Ahmadi Religious Thought and Its Medieval Background* (Berkeley: University of California Press, 1989), reprinted in 2003 by Oxford University Press.

38. See 33:40, which Friedmann translates in *Prophecy Continuous*, p. 53, as "Muhammad was not the father of any man among you, but the Messenger of Allāh and *khātam* [or *khātim*] *al-nabiyyīn*." The brackets are included in the original text by Friedmann.

39. Yohanan Friedmann, *Prophecy Continuous*, pp. 73–75.

40. Antonio R. Gualtieri, *Conscience and Coercion: Ahmadi Muslims and Orthodoxy in Pakistan* (Montreal: Guernica Editions, 1989).

41. Antonio Gualtieri, *The Ahmadis: Community, Gender, and Politics in a Muslim Society* (London: McGill-Queen's University Press, 2004).

42. Ibid., pp. 145–153.

43. Ibid., p. 148.

44. See Simon Ross Valentine, *Islam and the Ahmadiyya Jama'at: History, Belief, Practice* (New York: Columbia University Press, 2008).

1. Mirza Ghulam Ahmad Qadiani before Prophethood

1. See Mirza Ghulam Ahmad, *Kitāb al-Bariyya*, in *Rūhānī Khazā'in*, vol. 13, pp. 162–313.

2. Ibid., p. 172, in the footnote to the footnote.

3. For more on the ethnography and politics of the Barlas tribe, see Beatrice Forbes Manz, *The Rise and Rule of Tamerlane* (Cambridge: Cambridge University Press, 1999), pp. 27–28.

4. There are multiple narrations of this tradition in both the *kitāb al-tafsīr* of Bukhari (65:4946 or 6:60:420) and the *kitāb al-fadā'il al-sahāba* of Muslim (31:6177–6178 or 45:6661–6662). Bukhari's version states: "*law kāna'l-īmān 'inda l-thurayyā la-nālahu rajul min ha'ūlā'i* (If faith were hung on the Pleiades, still someone from these people [the Persians] would reach it)"; however, Ghulam Ahmad quotes it as "*law kāna'l-īmān mu'allaqa b'l-thurayyā la-nālahu rajul min fāris* (If faith were hung on the Pleiades, [this] a Persian man would return it)." I have not found the source of this version of the narration. The hadith was originally directed at Salman al-Farsi in any case.

5. This is the most common view in both Sunni and Shi'i Islam. For classical conceptions regarding the ancestry of the *mahdī*, see Ibn Khaldun, *The Muqaddimah: An Introduction to History*, trans. Franz Rosenthal and ed. N. J. Dawood (Princeton, NJ: Princeton University Press, 1967), pp. 257–259.

6. For Ghulam Ahmad's revelations regarding his own lineage, see *Haqīqat al-Wahy*, in *Rūhānī Khazā'in*, vol. 22, p. 81, in the footnote and the footnote to the footnote, which include the strong assertion that his lineage is Persian, and not Mughal, as well as the revelation informing him that he descended from Muhammad's daughter Fatima through his paternal grandmothers, who were *sayyids*. Similar revelations appear in *Tiryāq al-Qulūb*, in *Rūhānī Khazā'in*, vol. 15, pp. 272–273, in the footnote; *Tohfa Golrawiyya*, in *Rūhānī Khazā'in*, vol. 17, p. 117, in the footnote; and *Ek Ghalatī kā Izāla*, in *Rūhānī Khazā'in*, vol. 18, p. 212, in the footnote.

7. Sir Lepel H. Griffin and Charles Francis Massy, *The Panjab Chiefs* (Lahore: Civil and Military Gazette Press, 1890), p. 49; see also Mirza Ghulam Ahmad, *Kitāb al-Bariyya*, in *Rūhānī Khazā'in*, vol. 13, pp. 162–163.

8. Mirza Ghulam Ahmad, *Kitāb al-Bariyya*, in *Rūhānī Khazā'in*, vol. 13, pp. 162–164.

9. Ibid., pp. 166–174; see also Muhammad Zafrulla Khan, *Ahmadiyyat: The Renaissance of Islam* (London: Tabshir Publications, 1978), pp. 1–2.

10. Muhammad Zafrulla Khan, *Ahmadiyyat: The Renaissance of Islam*, p. 2.

11. Khushwant Singh, *A History of the Sikhs*, vol. 1, *1469–1839* (Oxford: Oxford University Press, 1999), pp. 188–191; see also G. S. Chhabra, *Advanced History of the Punjab*, vol. 2 (Ludhiana: Parkash [*sic*] Brothers, 1973), pp. 37–39.

12. For example, see Mirza Bashir al-Din Mahmud Ahmad, *Sīrat Masīh-i Maw'ūd* (Rabwah: Majlis Khuddam al-Ahmadiyya Pakistan, 1979), pp. 4–5.

13. Sir Lepel H. Griffin and Charles Francis Massy, *The Panjab Chiefs*, p. 50.

14. See Khushwant Singh, *A History of the Sikhs*, vol. 1, *1469–1839*, pp. 262–265.

15. Sir Lepel H. Griffin and Charles Francis Massy, *The Panjab Chiefs*, p. 50; although Friedmann did not focus on the historical aspects of Ghulam Ahmad's family background, he suggested that the family history "is apparently based on" the accounts in Griffin and Massy's book. It seems more likely that Griffin and Massy based their account on the family's own records—perhaps both oral and written—despite the fact that the family now quotes them to establish a greater sense of historical credibility. This is probably all circular information which was originally based on family records. See also Yohanan Friedmann, *Prophecy Continuous: Aspects of Ahmadi Religious Thought and Its Medieval Background* (Berkeley: University of California Press, 1989), p. 2, in footnote 1; Ghulam Ahmad referenced the original family documents in a number of places, which had been passed down through the generations. For

two such examples, see *Kitāb al-Bariyya*, in *Rūhānī Khazā'in*, vol. 13, pp. 162–163, in the first footnotes; see also *Izāla-i Awhām*, in *Rūhānī Khazā'in*, vol. 3, p. 160, in the footnote.

16. Mirza Ghulam Ahmad, *Kitāb al-Bariyya*, in *Rūhānī Khazā'in*, vol. 13, p. 177, in the first footnote.

17. The most comprehensive account of the variations in Ghulam Ahmad's birthdate may be found in Dost Muhammad Shāhid, *Tārīkh-i Ahmadiyya*, vol. 1 (Rabwah, 1983), pp. 48–50.

18. A. R. Dard, *Life of Ahmad* (Lahore: Tabshir, 1948), p. 27.

19. For example, see Mirza Ghulam Ahmad, *Barāhīn-i Ahmadiyya*, part 1, in *Rūhānī Khazā'in*, vol. 1, p. 1.

20. See Mirza Ghulam Ahmad, *Majmū'a-i Ishtihārāt*, vol. 3, p. 514.

21. It is worth noting that Fazl Ahmad's son, Mubarak 'Ali of Sialkot, later became an Ahmadi. This suggests that the two maintained a good relationship despite Ghulam Ahmad's subsequent conflicts with the Ahl-i Hadith, discussed below.

22. Mirza Ghulam Ahmad, *Kitāb al-Bariyya*, in *Rūhānī Khazā'in*, vol. 13, pp. 179–181, in the footnote.

23. Spencer Lavan, *The Ahmadiyah Movement: A History and Perspective* (Delhi: Manohar Book Service, 1974), p. 28.

24. This view was articulated to me in conversation with Sayyid Mir Mahmud Ahmad Nasir at the Ahmadi seminary in Rabwah, Pakistan, in April 2006. Ghulam Ahmad expressed similar sentiments regarding popular expectations of the promised messiah when he said that the coming messiah would not be taught by anyone other than Allah. In addition, Ghulam Ahmad claimed that he was not taught by any human being, but rather Allah taught him the Qur'an and hadith. See Mirza Ghulam Ahmad, *Ayyām-i Sulh*, in *Rūhānī Khazā'in*, vol. 14, p. 394.

25. I have used "Maulvi" and "Maulana" instead of "Mawlwi" and "Mawlana" because of their common use.

26. Prior to his *bay'at* (allegiance) with Mirza Ghulam Ahmad, Hakim Nur al-Din had taken *bay'at* with Shah 'Abd al-Ghani while studying in Mecca and Medina. He also studied with Maulvi Nazir Husayn Dehlawi and a disciple of Sayyid Ahmad Barelwi. See 'Abd al-Qādir, *Hayāt-i Nūr* (Qadian: Nizārat Nashar-o-Ishā'at, 2003), pp. 54–56; for a less detailed account in English, see also Muhammad Zafrulla Khan, *Hazrat Maulvi Nooruddeen Khalifatul Masih 1* (London: London Mosque, 1983?), pp. 12–13, 24–25.

27. For more on the tension between traditional Islamic learning, classical strands of rationalism, and modernist reform, see Fazlur Rahman, *Islam and Modernity: Transformation of an Intellectual Tradition* (London: University of Chicago Press, 1982).

28. See Francis Robinson, *Islam, South Asia, and the West* (New Delhi: Oxford University Press, 2007), especially chapter 2, "'Ulama of South Asia from 1800 to the Mid-Twentieth Century," pp. 59–98.

29. Mirza Ghulam Ahmad, *Kitāb al-Bariyya*, in *Rūhānī Khazā'in*, vol. 13, p. 181, in the footnote.

30. For more information regarding Ahmadi views on medicine, including specific prescriptions for various ailments, see the book by Ghulam Ahmad's fourth successor, Mirza Tahir Ahmad, *Homeopathy* (Tilford, UK: Islam International Publications, 2005).

31. Spencer Lavan, *The Ahmadiyah Movement*, pp. 28–29.

32. See Mirza Ghulam Ahmad, *Zarūrat al-Imām*, in *Rūhānī Khazā'in*, vol. 13.

33. Dost Muhammad Shahid, *Tārīkh-i Ahmadiyya*, vol. 1, p. 111.

34. Sir Lepel H. Griffin and Charles Francis Massy, *The Panjab Chiefs*, p. 50.

35. See Mirza Ghulam Ahmad, *Kitāb al-Bariyya*, in *Rūhānī Khazā'in*, vol. 13, pp. 4–7. The letter on p. 6 (September 20, 1858) from the Commissioner of Lahore, Robert Cast, stipulates the offer of a *khil'at* (land grant) made to Mirza Ghulam Murtaza worth 200 rupees in return

for the fifty cavalry units provided during the Mutiny. Additional letters are also available in Mirza Ghulam Ahmad, *Kashf al-Ghitā*, in *Rūhānī Khazā'in*, vol. 14, pp. 181–185, and also in *Majmū'a-i Ishtihārāt*, vol. 2, pp. 459–462.

36. Mirza Ghulam Ahmad, *Kitāb al-Bariyya*, in *Rūhānī Khazā'in*, vol. 13, p. 177, in the footnote.

37. See Avril A. Powell, "Contested Gods and Prophets: Discourse among Minorities in Late Nineteenth-Century Punjab," *Renaissance and Modern Studies* 38:1 (1995): 41; see also John McManners, ed., *The Oxford History of Christianity* (Oxford: Oxford University Press, 1990), pp. 511–526; see also E. M. Wherry, *The Muslim Controversy* (London: Christian Literature Society, 1905); see also H. A. Walter, *The Ahmadiya Movement* (London: Oxford University Press, 1918), p. 14.

38. A. R. Dard, *Life of Ahmad*, p. 39.

39. Mirza Ghulam Ahmad, *Barāhīn-i Ahmadiyya*, part 4, in *Rūhānī Khazā'in*, vol. 1, p. 563, in the footnote, and pp. 571–572, in the bottom footnotes; see also *al-Hakam* 10:4 (January 31, 1906): 3, which is available in Muhammad Zafrulla Khan, *Tadhkira* (Tilford, UK: Islam International Publications, 2004), pp. 338–339; see also *al-Hakam* 11:12 (April 10, 1907): 2, in *Tadhkira*, p. 393.

40. Muhammad 'Ali, *The Founder of the Ahmadiyya Movement* (Newark, CA: Ahmadiyya Anjuman Isha'at Islam Lahore, 1984), p. 37.

41. Mirza Ghulam Ahmad, *Barāhīn-i Ahmadiyya*, part 4, in *Rūhānī Khazā'in*, vol. 1, pp. 571–572, in the bottom footnote.

42. Ibid. A similar revelation appears in English in *Haqīqat al-Wahy*, in *Rūhānī Khazā'in*, vol. 22, pp. 316–317.

43. Dost Muhammad Shahid, *Tārīkh-i Ahmadiyya*, vol. 1, p. 92.

44. A. R. Dard, *Life of Ahmad*, p. 39.

45. Bashārat Ahmad, *Mujaddid-i 'Āzam* (Lahore?: Ahmadiyya Anjuman Isha'at Islam Lahore, 1939), p. 45.

46. It is now known as Government Murray College Sialkot. See its website at http://www.gmcs.edu.pk/.

47. Remnants of this position can be found as late as *Barāhīn-i Ahmadiyya*, part 4, in *Rūhānī Khazā'in*, vol. 1, p. 593, which was first published in 1884.

48. A. R. Dard, *Life of Ahmad*, p. 40.

49. There is a critique of Sir Sayyid's concept of revelation in Mirza Ghulam Ahmad, *Izāla-i Awhām*, in *Rūhānī Khazā'in*, vol. 3, pp. 596–602; see also "Sir Sayyad Ahmad of Aligarh and Hazrat Ahmad of Qadian Compared and Contrasted," *Review of Religions* 32:6 (June 1933): 292–297; see also Mirza Ghulam Ahmad, *Barakāt al-Du'ā*, in *Rūhānī Khazā'in*, vol. 6.

50. See Mirza Ghulam Ahmad, *Masīh Hindustān Meñ*, in *Rūhānī Khazā'in*, vol. 15.

51. Bashārat Ahmad, *Mujaddid-i 'Āzam*, p. 60. Ahmad briefly mentions Maulana Mahbub 'Alam and his affiliation with the Naqshbandi order.

52. Dost Muhammad Shahid, *Tārīkh-i Ahmadiyya*, vol. 1, p. 132. Shahid describes a special relationship between the two, but does not mention that Mahbub 'Alam was a Naqshbandi *pīr*; see also A. R. Dard, *Life of Ahmad*, p. 40. Dard mentions that Mahbub 'Alam was "a pious mystic of the Naqshbandi School," but he presents the relationship in a way that implies a light-hearted camaraderie.

53. Arthur Buehler's study of the Naqshbandis in India mentioned Mahbub 'Alam in relation to his position on reciting the *hizb al-bahr* (litany of the sea) of Abu Hasan al-Shadhili without permission, for which Buehler referenced Mahbub 'Alam, *Dhikr-i Kathīr: Mahbūb al-Sulūk* (Lahore: Milli Printers, 1913). See Arthur F. Buehler, *Sufi Heirs of the Prophet: The Indian Naqshbandiyya and the Rise of the Mediating Sufi Shaykh* (Columbia: University of South Carolina Press, 2008), p. 85.

54. Bashārat Ahmad, *Mujaddid-i ʿĀzam*, pp. 46–47.

55. A. R. Dard, *Life of Ahmad*, pp. 40–41.

56. Finding more information on these shrines was particularly challenging, especially from external sources, which makes it difficult to assess their significance, religious affiliations, or influence on Ghulam Ahmad. Dost Muhammad Shahid described them as big Sufi shrines that were frequented by locals. Dost Muhammad Shahid, *Tārīkh-i Ahmadiyya*, vol. 1, p. 132.

57. See the book written by ʿAbdullah Ghaznavi's grandson, who became a leading figure in the Ahl-i Hadith movement, Muhammad Dāʾūd Ghaznavī, *Maqālāt Maulānā Dāʾūd Ghaznavī* (Lahore: Maktaba Nazīra, 1979).

58. A. R. Dard, *Life of Ahmad*, pp. 50–51.

59. Mirza Ghulam Ahmad, *Haqīqat al-Wahy*, in *Rūhānī Khazāʾin*, vol. 22, pp. 250–251.

60. Dost Muhammad Shahid, *Tārīkh-i Ahmadiyya*, vol. 1, pp. 132–134.

61. See Muhammad Dāʾūd Ghaznavī, *Maqālāt Maulānā Dāʾūd Ghaznavī*, pp. 19–22; see also Jānbāz Mirzā, *Kārvān-i Ahrār*, vol. 1 (Lahore: Maktaba-i Tabassira, 1975), pp. 142–143.

62. Dost Muhammad Shahid, *Tārīkh-i Ahmadiyya*, vol. 1, p. 132. Shahid references, Maulānā ʿAbd al-Majīd, *Sīrat al-Sanāʾī* (Amritsar, 1952), p. 369, which apparently discusses the migration from Afghanistan, but was not available to me.

63. See Claudia Preckel, "Ahl-i Hadīth," *Encyclopaedia of Islam*, 3rd ed.

64. Barbara Daly Metcalf, *Islamic Revival in British India: Deoband, 1860–1900* (Oxford: Oxford University Press, 1982), p. 292.

65. In contrast, Maulvi Nazir Husayn Dehlawi had also briefly taught Ghulam Ahmad's first successor, Nur al-Din. See ʿAbd al-Qādir, *Hayāt-i Nūr*, pp. 54–56; see also Muhammad Zafrulla Khan, *Hazrat Maulvi Nooruddeen Khalifatul Masih 1*, p. 12.

66. The original *fatwā* of *kufr* appeared in Muhammad Husayn Batalwi's journal *Ishāʿat-i Sunna* 5:13, which has since been republished several times. For excerpts see Mirza Ghulam Ahmad, *Kitāb al-Bariyya*, in *Rūhānī Khazāʾin*, vol. 13, p. 146.

67. Ghulam Ahmad wrote three companion volumes, *Fath-i Islām*, *Tawzīh-i Marām*, and *Izāla-i Awhām*, in 1891. *Tawzīh-i Marām* and *Izāla-i Awhām* expounded controversial views regarding the death of Jesus, namely that Jesus Christ is not alive in heaven and will not physically return to the world as the orthodox believe.

68. The *fatwā* against Ghulam Ahmad states that he is a *kāfir* (nonbeliever) and the *dajjāl* (antichrist). Ghulam Ahmad's response to the *fatwā* is particularly relevant to this discussion because it inadvertently acknowledges the stature of Maulvi Nazir Husayn among the *ʿulamā* of Delhi. See *Āsmānī Faysala*, in *Rūhānī Khazāʾin*, vol. 4; also available in translation as *The Heavenly Decree* (London: Islam International Publications, 2006).

69. Again, there are slight variations in the various accounts of this encounter. For Ghulam Ahmad's account, see *Haqīqat al-Wahy*, in *Rūhānī Khazāʾin*, vol. 22, p. 251.

70. See M. A. S. Abdel Haleem, trans., *The Qurʾan* (Oxford: Oxford University Press, 2004), p. 33.

71. A. R. Dard, *Life of Ahmad*, pp. 50–51.

72. Dost Muhammad Shahid, *Tārīkh-i Ahmadiyya*, vol. 1, p. 133.

73. A *mubāhala* is a lengthy prayer contest in which two religious rivals curse each other by invoking the wrath of God upon the one who is lying as a means of seeking a divine resolution to unresolved issues. The *mubāhala* was often used between opposing claimants of divine revelation, which was believed to bring about the humiliating death of the liar or false claimant. The textual foundations for the *mubāhala* can be found in the Qurʾan (3:61); see also Yohanan Friedmann, *Prophecy Continuous*, pp. 6–7, n. 20.

74. A. R. Dard, *Life of Ahmad*, pp. 276–279; see also Ghulam Ahmad's book *Tohfa Ghaznawiyya*, which was written as a result of the *mubāhala* and is available in *Rūhānī Khazā'in*, vol. 15.

75. Bashārat Ahmad, *Mujaddid-i 'Āzam*, p. 63.

76. Some examples of these include *Āsmānī Faysala* (1891), *Zarūrat al-Imām* (1898), *Tohfa Ghaznawiyya* (1902), *Tiryāq al-Qulūb* (1902).

77. A. R. Dard, *Life of Ahmad*, pp. 578–584.

78. Ibid., p. 48.

79. See Swami Dayananda Saraswati, *Satyārth Prakāsh* (1875), which is also available in English in a translation by Durga Prasad: *Satyarthaprakasa: An English Translation of the Satyarth Prakash* (Lahore: Virjanand Press, 1908).

80. H. A. Walter, *The Ahmadiya Movement*, pp. 103–104; Dard suggests that similar argumentation led to Dayanand's rewriting of the *Satyārth Prakāsh* in which he omitted the doctrine of *niyoga*, among other things, but I could not confirm the discrepancy between the two editions. See A. R. Dard, *Life of Ahmad*, pp. 112, 330–332.

81. See Kenneth W. Jones, "The Arya Samaj in the Punjab: A Study of Social Reform and Religious Revivalism, 1877–1902," PhD diss., University of California, Berkeley, 1966, pp. 67, 69.

82. Dard provides a full account of the story in A. R. Dard, *Life of Ahmad*, p. 59.

83. See Avril A. Powell, *Muslims and Missionaries in Pre-Mutiny India* (London: Routledge Press, 1993).

84. See Steve Bruce, ed., *Religion and Modernization* (Oxford: Oxford University Press, 1992), especially chapter 2; Roy Wallis and Steve Bruce, "Secularization: The Orthodox Model," pp. 8–30.

85. See Mirza Ghulam Ahmad, *Barāhīn-i Ahmadiyya*, parts 1 and 2 (Amritsar: Safīr Hind Press, 1880).

86. Mirza Ghulam Ahmad *Barāhīn-i Ahmadiyya*, part 1, in *Rūhānī Khazā'in*, vol. 1, p. 3.

87. The Woking mosque, currently known as the Shah Jahan mosque in honor of its benefactress, opened only some months after the Liverpool Muslim Institute, making it the second-oldest mosque in Britain.

88. Humayun Ansari, *"The Infidel Within": Muslims in Britain since 1800* (London: Hurst & Company, 2004), p. 126.

89. A. R. Dard, *Life of Ahmad*, p. 75.

90. In actuality, Ghulam Ahmad said that the difference was just a dot, since the difference between five and fifty (ه and ه٠) in Urdu and Arabic is written as a dot. The same idea might be expressed in English by saying that the difference between 5 and 50 is nothing (i.e., zero). Therefore, Ghulam Ahmad concluded that his five volumes equaled fifty, and hence his promise was complete. The subtle humor in this explanation alludes to a tradition in which the Prophet Muhammad was permitted to reduce the fifty daily prayers to five during the night journey (*isrā* and *mi'rāj*). In Tirmidhi's narration of the hadith, the five daily prayers have the reward of fifty. See Mirza Ghulam Ahmad, *Barāhīn-i Ahmadiyya*, part 5, in *Rūhānī Khazā'in*, vol. 21, p. 9.

91. Mirza Ghulam Ahmad, *Barāhīn-i Ahmadiyya*, part 3, in *Rūhānī Khazā'in*, vol. 1, p. 265, in the bottom footnote.

92. Mirza Ghulam Ahmad, *Izāla-i Awhām*, in *Rūhānī Khazā'in*, vol. 3, p. 193.

93. A. R. Dard, *Life of Ahmad*, pp. 82–84.

94. There is a brief account of this in ibid., pp. 111–114.

95. See Dost Muhammad Shahid, *Tārīkh-i Ahmadiyya*, vol. 1, pp. 274–276; other orders may prefer a similar type of *khalwa* (seclusion) exercise in which forty days are not specified. See also Annemarie Schimmel, *Mystical Dimensions of Islam* (Chapel Hill: University of North Carolina Press, 1975), pp. 103–105.

96. Ghulam Ahmad published a lengthy account of his recollection of the debate as well as the written exchange of arguments in his *Surma Chashm Ārya* (Antimony for Clearing the Obscured Vision of the Arya), in *Rūhānī Khazā'in*, vol. 2.

97. Many classical commentaries of the Qur'an refer to the introductory verses of Sura 54 (*al-Qamar*) as a description of a miraculous event that was witnessed by the companions of the Prophet in which the moon was split in two. Recent commentators, like Muhammad Asad in *The Message of the Qur'an*, suggest that it only appeared to be split, whereas Abdel Haleem in *The Qur'an* says that it refers to one of the signs of the day of judgment. The supernatural and miraculous nature of religions has come under fire since the scientific revolution. One should note that Ghulam Ahmad defended the miracle, even though Jama'at-i Ahmadiyya's position seems to have changed by the time of its fourth successor. For example, see the discussion on evolution in part V of Mirza Tahir Ahmad, *Revelation, Rationality, Knowledge, and Truth* (Tilford, UK: Islam International Publications, 1998).

98. Spencer Lavan, *The Ahmadiyah Movement*, pp. 36–37.

99. Iain Adamson, *Ahmad—the Guided One* (Tilford, UK: Islam International Publications, 1999), p. 84.

100. The details of the relationship between Ghulam Ahmad and his first wife have been scarcely documented by Ahmadi historians. It is clear that the first marriage did not last long. Despite the apparent conflict between the couple, Ghulam Ahmad seems to have continued to support his first family while living in a separated state. Some writings suggest that the marriage was volatile as late as 1891, after the second marriage had taken place; see *Majmū'a-i Ishtihārāt*, vol. 1, pp. 219–221. The eldest son, Mirza Sultan Ahmad, was raised (and possibly even adopted) by Ghulam Ahmad's elder brother Mirza Ghulam Qadir (1828–1883), whose own two children died in infancy. Ghulam Qadir's wife, Hurmat Bibi, should not be confused with Ghulam Ahmad's first wife, even though she shared the same name and raised Sultan Ahmad. The tension between Ghulam Ahmad and his son continued well beyond Ghulam Ahmad's death in 1908. It was only shortly before Mirza Sultan Ahmad's own death in 1931 that he finally became an Ahmadi, after which point most Ahmadi sources overlook their turbulent past. See A. R. Dard, *Life of Ahmad*, p. 72.

101. Mirza Ghulam Ahmad traveled to Delhi for the wedding, where the ceremony was performed by Maulvi Nazir Husayn Dehlawi, which provides an indication of their proximity prior to the first *fatwā* of *kufr* in 1891.

102. Mirza Ghulam Ahmad, *Haqqānī Taqrīr bar Wāqi'a-i Wafāt-i Bashīr*, in *Rūhānī Khazā'in*, vol. 2 (listed on the cover as *Sabz Ishtihār*), pp. 447–470; although there are other publications around the same period concerning the prophecy, this is the most detailed and the most frequently quoted by Ahmadi sources.

103. Kenneth W. Jones, *Arya Dharm: Hindu Consciousness in 19th Century Punjab* (London: University of California Press, 1976), pp. 148–151, as well as the footnotes. Jones provides useful information about the tension between Ghulam Ahmad and Lekh Ram which is not mentioned in Ahmadi sources; see also A. R. Dard, *Life of Ahmad*, pp. 143–144. Dard reproduces some excerpts of Lekh Ram's jeering remarks towards Ghulam Ahmad; see also the collected works of Pandit Lekh Ram, *Kullīyāt Ārya Musāfir* (Sahāranpūr: Sattya Dharam Parchārak Press, 1904).

104. See the pamphlet *Khush Khabrī* (August 7, 1887), in Mirza Ghulam Ahmad, *Majmū'a-i Ishtihārāt*, vol. 1, pp. 141–142.

105. See Mirza Ghulam Ahmad *Haqqānī Taqrīr bar Wāqi'a-i Wafāt-i Bashīr*, in *Rūhānī Khazā'in*, vol. 2 (listed on the cover as *Sabz Ishtihār*), pp. 447–470.

106. See A. R. Dard, *Life of Ahmad*, p. 148, where he briefly mentions the challenges of Mahmud Ahmad's childhood.

107. See *Tablīgh* (December 1, 1888), in Mirza Ghulam Ahmad, *Majmū'a-i Ishtihārāt*, vol. 1, p. 188; it may also be worthwhile to look at Yohanan Friedmann's discussion of the prophecy in *Prophecy Continuous*, p. 5, especially n. 12, which details the composite Qur'anic verses that make up the revelation, such as the excerpt from 48:10 quoted here; see also Dost Muhammad Shahid, *Tārīkh-i Ahmadiyya*, vol. 1, p. 335.

108. See the notice *Takmīl-i Tablīgh* (January 12, 1889), in Mirza Ghulam Ahmad, *Majmū'a-i Ishtihārāt*, vol. 1, pp. 189–192.

109. See the notice *Guzārish-i Zurūrī* (March 4, 1889), in Mirza Ghulam Ahmad, *Majmū'a-i Ishtihārāt*, vol. 1, pp. 193–198; see also A. R. Dard, *Life of Ahmad*, pp. 151–153.

110. For further discussion about the discrepancy in the date, but not the number of disciples, see Dost Muhammad Shahid, *Tārīkh-i Ahmadiyya*, vol. 1, pp. 362–374.

111. The remainder of the original handwritten register is still available in the Khilafat library in Rabwah, Pakistan. For a reproduction of the surviving list, see Dost Muhammad Shahid, *Tārīkh-i Ahmadiyya*, vol. 1, p. 344, in which both March 21, 1889, and its A.H. equivalent, Rajab 19, 1306, have been listed.

112. See A. R. Dard, *Life of Ahmad*, pp. 153–156.

113. See Mirza Bashir al-Din Mahmud Ahmad, *al-Fazl* (February 18, 1959).

114. A. R. Dard, *Life of Ahmad*, pp. 160–161.

115. Mirza Ghulam Ahmad, *Fath-i Islām*, in *Rūhānī Khazā'in*, vol. 3, pp. 17–26, in the footnote.

116. A. R. Dard, *Life of Ahmad*, p. 161, in the footnote.

117. Ibid., pp. 84–85.

118. This is discussed further in the conclusion of this book.

119. A. R. Dard, *Life of Ahmad*, pp. 239–240. Dard states that the original correspondence was published in the *Punjab Gazette*, Sialkot (May 14, 1892); however, I was unable to verify this source.

120. See Mirza Ghulam Ahmad, *Anjām-i Ātham*, in *Rūhānī Khazā'in*, vol. 11, pp. 69–72, where Ghulam Ahmad issued *mubāhala* challenges to over a hundred scholars and *pīr*s by name; see also Mirza Ghulam Ahmad, *Majmū'a-i Ishtihārāt*, vol. 2, pp. 300–303, and pp. 443–451, especially from p. 449, where Ghulam Ahmad issued a pamphlet on July 15, 1897, requesting every opposing scholar in India to seek divine guidance regarding his mission before dismissing his claims. Then, he invited them to receive their own inspirations.

121. A. R. Dard, *Life of Ahmad*, pp. 161–162.

122. All three books make up the third volume of *Rūhānī Khazā'in*.

2. The Prophetic Claims of Mirza Ghulam Ahmad

1. See Avril A. Powell, *Muslims and Missionaries in Pre-Mutiny India* (London: Curzon Press, 1993).

2. These three works constitute the third volume of *Rūhānī Khazā'in*.

3. See Mirza Ghulam Ahmad, *Masīh Hindustān Meñ*, in *Rūhānī Khazā'in*, vol. 15; see also the translation, *Jesus in India* (Tilford, UK: Islam International Publications, 2003).

4. See Nicolas Notovitch, *The Unknown Life of Jesus* (Sanger, CA: Quill Driver Books / Word Dancer Press, 2004).

5. The following account of the Ahmadi belief regarding Jesus is taken from Mirza Tahir Ahmad, *Christianity: A Journey from Facts to Fiction* (Tilford, UK: Islam International Publications, 1994).

6. See verse 4:157 in M. A. S. Abdel Haleem, trans., *The Qur'an* (Oxford: Oxford University Press, 2004), p. 65. The brackets are not part of the original.

7. See verse 4:158 in Malik Ghulam Farid, ed., *The Holy Qur'ān: Arabic Text with English Translation and Short Commentary* (Tilford, UK: Islam International Publications, 2002), p. 225. All italics appear in the original.

8. Mirza Tahir Ahmad, *Christianity: A Journey from Facts to Fiction*, p. 74.

9. Mirza Ghulam Ahmad, *Masīh Hindustān Meñ*, in *Rūhānī Khazā'in*, vol. 15, p. 27; see also *Jesus in India*, p. 30.

10. See verse 4:158 in M. A. S. Abdel Haleem, trans., *The Qur'an*, p. 65.

11. See verse 4:159 in Malik Ghulam Farid, ed., *The Holy Qur'ān*, p. 226.

12. Ibid., pp. 226–227, n. 700.

13. Muhammad Asad, *The Message of the Qur'ān* (Gibraltar: Dar al-Andalus, 1980), pp. 134–135, n. 172.

14. Mirza Ghulam Ahmad, *Masīh Hindustān Meñ*, in *Rūhānī Khazā'in*, vol. 15, pp. 58–59; see also *Jesus in India*, pp. 66–68.

15. See the notice *Dawā'e Ta'ūn* (July 23, 1898), in Mirza Ghulam Ahmad, *Majmū'a-i Ishtihārāt*, vol. 3, pp. 52–54. There is a rare translation of this, listed as *A Revealed Cure for the Bubonic Plague* (Lahore: Victoria Press, 1898), which is available in the British Library Oriental Collections, Shelfmark 14105.e.1.(2.).

16. Humphrey Fisher took issue with the ointment, its sources, and the "swoon theory" regarding Jesus's survival of crucifixion in his study of Jama'at-i Ahmadiyya, but he did not explicitly say how he arrived at his conclusions. See Humphrey J. Fisher, *Ahmadiyyah: A Study in Contemporary Islam on the West African Coast* (London: Oxford University Press, 1963), pp. 69–71.

17. See chapter 13 in J. D. Shams, *Where Did Jesus Die?* (Tilford, UK: Islam International Publications, 1989), pp. 109–117.

18. See chapter 4, section 2, of Mirza Ghulam Ahmad, *Masīh Hindustān Meñ*, in *Rūhānī Khazā'in*, vol. 15, especially p. 82; see also *Jesus in India*, p. 94. Ghulam Ahmad's reference in the original text is mistakenly given as Genesis 3:10, though later Ahmadi publications either cite Genesis 49:10 or 1 Chronicles 16:4–7 as the correction.

19. Mirza Bashir al-Din Mahmud Ahmad presented a detailed explanation of this view in his *Invitation to Ahmadiyyat* (London: Routledge & Kegan Paul, 1980), pp. 30–32.

20. For examples of classical views regarding this position, see Ibn Khaldun, *The Muqaddimah: An Introduction to History*, trans. Franz Rosenthal and ed. N. J. Dawood, (Princeton, NJ: Princeton University Press, 1967), pp. 257–259.

21. Mirza Ghulam Ahmad, *Fath-i Islām*, in *Rūhānī Khazā'in*, vol. 3, pp. 7–8, and the footnote; see also *Victory of Islam* (Tilford, UK: Islam International Publications, 2002), pp. 5–6, and n. 1.

22. Mirza Ghulam Ahmad, *Fath-i Islām*, pp. 8–9, and in the footnote; see also *Victory of Islam*, pp. 7–9, and n. 2.

23. See Mahmoud M. Ayoub, *The Crisis of Muslim History: Religion and Politics in Early Islam* (Oxford: Oneworld Publications, 2006), p. 50, where it is mentioned that the Prophet Muhammad's third successor, 'Uthman, took the title *khalīfat-ullāh*.

24. See Yohanan Friedmann, *Prophecy Continuous: Aspects of Ahmadi Religious Thought and Its Medieval Background* (Berkeley: University of California Press, 1989).

25. Mirza Ghulam Ahmad, *Tawzīh-i Marām*, in *Rūhānī Khazā'in*, vol. 3, p. 59; see also *Elucidation of Objectives* (Tilford, UK: Islam International Publications, 2004), pp. 15–16.

26. Mirza Ghulam Ahmad, *Tawzīh-i Marām*, in *Rūhānī Khazā'in*, vol. 3, p. 60; see also *Elucidation of Objectives*, p. 16.

27. It may useful to consider this claim within the context of the Qur'anic assertion in 22:52, which describes the relationship of God's messages to prophets and Satan's attempts at corrupting them.

28. Mirza Ghulam Ahmad, *Tawzīh-i Marām*, in *Rūhānī Khazā'in*, vol. 3, p. 60.

29. Ibid., p. 61; see also *Elucidation of Objectives*, p. 19.

30. Mirza Ghulam Ahmad, *Ek Ghalatī kā Izāla* in *Rūhānī Khazā'in*, vol. 18, p. 206; see also the English translation, *A Misconception Removed* (Tilford, UK: Islam International Publications, 2007). Translations of this text in particular tend to obscure or mistranslate the subtle implications present in the original.

31. See verse 33:40, which states: "Muhammad is not the father of any one of you men; he is God's Messenger and the seal of the prophets (*mā kāna muhammad abā ahad min rijālikum wa lākin rasūl-allāhi wa khātam al-nabiyyīn*)." M. A. S. Abdel Haleem, trans., *The Qur'an*, p. 269. The phrase *khātam al-nabiyyīn* (seal of the prophets) is interpreted by the Muslim mainstream to mean that Muhammad is the last prophet.

32. Mirza Ghulam Ahmad, *Ek Ghalatī kā Izāla*, in *Rūhānī Khazā'in*, vol. 18, pp. 206–207.

33. Ibid., p. 207.

34. Ibid.

35. See Fazlur Rahman, *Islam* (Chicago: University of Chicago Press, 1979), p. 135; see also "Bakā' wa-Fanā'," in *Encyclopaedia of Islam*, 2nd ed., ed. P. Bearman, (Leiden: Brill, 2008); see also Valerie Hoffman, "Annihilation in the Messenger of God: The Development of a Sufi Practice," *International Journal of Middle East Studies* 31:3 (August 1999): 351–369.

36. See Yohanan Friedmann, *Prophecy Continuous*, especially chapters 2–3; see also Yohanan Friedmann, *Shaykh Ahmad Sirhindi: An Outline of His Thought and a Study of His Image in the Eyes of Posterity* (Oxford: Oxford University Press, 2000).

37. Mirza Ghulam Ahmad, *Ek Ghalatī kā Izāla*, in *Rūhānī Khazā'in*, vol. 18, p. 208.

38. Ibid., p. 210.

39. Ibid., p. 211.

40. See Qur'an 33:40.

41. Mirza Ghulam Ahmad, *Ek Ghalatī kā Izāla*, in *Rūhānī Khazā'in*, vol. 18, pp. 214–215.

42. Ibid., p. 216.

43. See Michel Chodkiewicz, *Seal of the Saints: Prophethood and Sainthood in the Doctrine of Ibn 'Arabi* (Cambridge, UK: Islamic Texts Society, 1993), p. 41.

44. See William A. Graham, *Divine Word and Prophetic Word in Early Islam* (Paris: Mouton, 1977).

45. Humphrey J. Fisher, *Ahmadiyyah: A Study in Contemporary Islam on the West African Coast*, p. 44.

46. See Mirza Ghulam Ahmad, *Haqīqat al-Wahy*, in *Rūhānī Khazā'in*, vol. 22.

47. Ghulam Ahmad's fourth successor and grandson, Mirza Tahir Ahmad, attempted to scientifically justify the act of revelation. Although his book was written nearly one hundred years after Ghulam Ahmad's death, it demonstrates the modernist tendency for Ahmadis to reject miracles. Mirza Tahir Ahmad went to great lengths to show that revelation was a naturally occurring phenomenon which could be used to explain a range of experiences from psychic clairvoyance to prophecy. Ironically, his rationalized explanation of mystical experiences ultimately still depends on divine intervention. See Mirza Tahir Ahmad, *Revelation, Rationality, Knowledge, and Truth* (Tilford, UK: Islam International Publications, 1998), pp. 239–254, and especially the section on "Psychic Experiences Other than Hallucinations."

48. In 42:51, it states that it does not befit God to speak to any human being except through revelation (*wahy*), or from behind a veil, or through a messenger. In this context, *wahy* (revelation) appears to resemble something closer to mere inspiration experienced by ordinary people. This seems distinct from the more robust forms of prophetic communication in Islam,

such as those that make up the verses of the Qur'an, which once again are also believed to be a form of *wahy* received by the Prophet Muhammad, but through the angel Gabriel, and not normative prophetic inspirations.

49. See also Michel Chodkiewicz, *Seal of the Saints*, pp. 165, 179, in note 65.

50. Mirza Ghulam Ahmad, *Fath-i Islām*, in *Rūhānī Khazā'in*, vol. 3, p. 8.

51. See 52:29, 69:42, and 37:36.

52. Mirza Ghulam Ahmad, *Haqīqat al-Wahy*, in *Rūhānī Khazā'in*, vol. 22, p. 406.

53. Ibid.

54. A. R. Dard, *Life of Ahmad* (Lahore: Tabshir, 1948), p. 607.

55. It may also be useful to compare the role of the Ahmadi *khalīfa* to that of the Aga Khan in the Isma'ili tradition. Antonio Gualtieri commented on his experiences with the Ahmadi community and made interesting observations on the essential role of the Ahmadi *khalīfa* "in bridging the divine-human gulf." See Antonio Gualtieri, *The Ahmadis: Community, Gender, and Politics in a Muslim Society* (London: McGill–Queen's University Press, 2004), pp. 38–44. The quotation is taken from p. 38.

56. See *Review of Religions*, 50:7 (July 1956): 503–505, 521–524; see also *Review of Religions* 102:10 (October 2007): 48–51.

57. See Humphrey J. Fisher, *Ahmadiyyah*, p. 20.

58. See *Fiqh-i Ahmadiyya*, 2 vols. (Rabwah: Zia Islam Press, 1983?).

59. In one instance, Ghulam Ahmad provided a bibliographic breakdown of classical sources in terms of their relation to the traditional Islamic sciences. These books essentially represent a cataloguing of the personal library of the first *khalīfa*, Nur al-Din, but are a potential starting place for Ahmadis who may wish to formalize their religious methodology. The list of approved sources are organized according to their respective disciplines, including hadith, *tafsīr*, grammar, history, *fiqh*, *usūl al-fiqh*, *kalām*, logic, Sufism, medicine, and more. It is possible that the choice to list books of hadith before *tafsīr* reflects the influence of Ghulam Ahmad's Ahl-i Hadith background. See Mirza Ghulam Ahmad, *al-Balāgh*, in *Rūhānī Khazā'in*, vol. 13, pp. 458–469.

60. For the full discussion regarding the authority of Ghulam Ahmad's revelations in relation to hadith, see Mirza Ghulam Ahmad, *Izāla-i Awhām*, in *Rūhānī Khazā'in*, vol. 3, pp. 175–177; for a more general commentary that broadly outlines Ghulam Ahmad's position on hadith, see the two books titled *al-Haqq*, in *Rūhānī Khazā'in*, vol. 4.

61. Mirza Ghulam Ahmad, *Tawzīh-i Marām*, in *Rūhānī Khazā'in*, vol. 3, pp. 60–61; see also *Elucidation of Objectives*, pp. 17–18.

62. Mirza Ghulam Ahmad, *Tawzīh-i Marām*, in *Rūhānī Khazā'in*, vol. 3, pp. 60–61.

63. See Yohanan Friedmann, *Prophecy Continuous*, pp. 136–137, in which Friedmann detailed the relation between Ghulam Ahmad's Arabic revelations and the Qur'an, hadith, and other classical sources.

64. See also Michel Chodkiewicz, *Seal of the Saints*, pp. 80–81.

65. See Mirza Ghulam Ahmad, *Haqīqat al-Wahy*, in *Rūhānī Khazā'in*, vol. 22, p. 76, in the footnote.

66. There have already been several examples of inspired figures in Ahmadi Islam. See H. A. Walter, *The Ahmadiya Movement* (London: Oxford University Press, 1918), pp. 45–46; see also the polemic tract, Phoenix, *His Holiness* (Lahore: Sh. Muhammad Ashraf, 1970), p. 151; see also www.alghulam.com/ahmadiyyanews/al-mouslemeen-interview.html (accessed Jan. 2014), for a recent case describing Munir Ahmad Azim, who claimed to be the promised reformer (*muslih maw'ūd*), the same title taken by Mirza Bashir al-Din Mahmud Ahmad. In this interview, Azim discusses the challenges he faced confronting the two most recent Ahmadi *khalīfa*s; see also www.jamaat-ul-sahih-al-islam.com/index.html (accessed June 2014), for an updated website with additional source material.

67. There are numerous passages in Ghulam Ahmad's writing that are capable of justifying future prophets within an Ahmadi framework. In one example, Ghulam Ahmad said that thirty antichrists (*dajjāl*) would appear in Islam, who demanded thirty messiahs to stop them, which in the original passage implied that Ghulam Ahmad was only one of these messiahs. See Mirza Ghulam Ahmad, *Izāla-i Awhām*, in *Rūhānī Khazā'in*, vol. 3, p. 197.

3. Authority, *Khilāfat*, and the Lahori-Qadiani Split

1. Dost Muhammad Shahid, *Tārīkh-i Ahmadiyya*, vol. 3 (Rabwah, 1983), pp. 187–189; Muhammad Zafrulla Khan, *Hazrat Maulvi Nooruddeen Khalifatul Masih 1* (London: The London Mosque, 1983?), pp. 103–108.

2. Muhammad Zafrulla Khan, *Hazrat Maulvi Nooruddeen Khalifatul Masih 1*, pp. 200–201.

3. The term "Qadiani" has developed a negative connotation and is often used in the pejorative with a derogatory tone to insult members of Jama'at-i Ahmadiyya. The followers of Mirza Ghulam Ahmad refer to themselves as "Ahmadis." For our purposes, the term "Qadiani" is only used to distinguish the followers of Mirza Mahmud Ahmad who remained in Qadian from the followers of Muhammad 'Ali who migrated to Lahore and called themselves "Lahoris."

4. See 61:6 in M. A. S. Abdel Haleem, trans., *The Qur'an* (Oxford: Oxford University Press, 2004), p. 370.

5. See John 12:13, 14:16–17, 15:26, and 16:7.

6. Muhammad Asad noted in his commentary that the Biblical account used the Greek word *paráklētos*, which is often translated as "the Comforter." He believed this to be a corruption of the word *períklytos*, "the much praised," which was more appropriate as an exact translation of the original Aramaic *mawhamana*. Asad argued that the Aramaic *mawhamana* clearly resembles the two Arabic words, *muhammad* and *ahmad*, both of which are derived from the same root, *hamida*, meaning "to praise." See Muhammad Asad, *The Message of the Qur'ān* (Gibraltar: Dar al-Andalus, 1980), p. 861.

7. Maulana Muhammad 'Ali, *The Split in the Ahmadiyya Movement* (Columbus, OH: Ahmadiyya Anjuman Isha'at Islam Lahore, 1994), pp. 19–20.

8. See Mirza Bashir al-Din Mahmud Ahmad, *Ā'ina-i sadāqat* (Lahore, 1921) in *Anwār al-'Ulūm*, vol. 6 (Tilford, UK: Islam International Publications, n.d.), which is also available in translation as *Truth about the Split* (Tilford, UK: Islam International Publications, 2007), pp. 56–61, under the section "Alleged Innovations."

9. See Maulana Muhammad 'Ali, *The Split in the Ahmadiyya Movement*, pp. 50–78.

10. For Mahmud Ahmad's elaboration on this issue, see Mirza Bashir al-Din Mahmud Ahmad, *Haqīqat al-Nubuwwa*, in *Anwār al-'Ulūm*, vol. 2, §10, pp. 345–613.

11. Mirza Ghulam Ahmad, *Ek Ghalatī kā Izāla*, in *Rūhānī Khazā'in*, vol. 18, p. 207.

12. See Fazlur Rahman, *Islam* (London: University of Chicago Press, 1979), pp. 85–99; see also W. Montgomery Watt, *The Formative Period of Islamic Thought* (Oxford, UK: Oneworld Publications, 2006).

13. Maulana Muhammad 'Ali, *The Split in the Ahmadiyya Movement*, p. 79.

14. A. R. Dard, *Life of Ahmad* (Lahore: Tabshir, 1948), pp. 178, 374.

15. Maulana Muhammad 'Ali, *The Split in the Ahmadiyya Movement*, pp. 81–83.

16. Ibid., p. 79.

17. See Bukhari, hadith 6045 or 8:73:71, and hadith 6103 or 8:73:105.

18. This is all from an interview with Ghulam Ahmad during his final visit to Lahore in the weeks before his death. See *Badr* on May 24, 1908, which is available in Mirza Ghulam Ahmad, *Malfuzāt*, vol. 10 (Rabwah: Zia al-Islam Press, 1967), pp. 376–377.

19. Mirza Ghulam Ahmad, *Tiryāq al-Qulūb* (1902), in *Rūhānī Khazā'in*, vol. 15, pp. 258–259.

20. Mirza Ghulam Ahmad, *Barāhīn-i Ahmadiyya*, vol. 5 (1905), in *Rūhānī Khazā'in*, vol. 21, p. 82.

21. Mirza Ghulam Ahmad, *Haqīqat al-Wahy*, in *Rūhānī Khazā'in*, vol. 22, pp. 120, 163–165, 178.

22. Maulana Muhammad 'Ali, *The Split in the Ahmadiyya Movement*, pp. 79–80.

23. See Mirza Bashir al-Din Mahmud Ahmad, *Truth about the Split*, pp. 134–179, particularly the sections related to his article on "Kufr-o-Islam."

24. See Mirza Bashir al-Din Mahmud Ahmad's article under Hazrat Khalifatul Masih II, "Are Non-Ahmadis Kafirs?," *Review of Religions* 34:7 (July 1935): 241–256.

25. Maulana Muhammad 'Ali, *The Split in the Ahmadiyya Movement*, p. 10.

26. Maulana Muhammad 'Ali cited the original letter of expulsion as appearing in *Badr* (July 11, 1912). He provided an excerpt of the original in ibid., pp. 10–11.

27. Maulana Muhammad 'Ali cited the follow-up letter as originally appearing in *Badr* (August 1, 1912) in *The Split in the Ahmadiyya Movement*, p. 11.

28. Maulana Muhammad 'Ali, *The Split in the Ahmadiyya Movement*, p. 11.

29. Ibid., pp. 11–12.

30. The full response is available in Mirza Bashir al-Din Mahmud Ahmad, *Truth about the Split*, pp. 96–120, in the section "Factors Relating to Zahiruddin's Expulsion," and also pp. 121–123, under "Zahiruddin's Second Expulsion."

31. For the biography of Maulana Muhammad 'Ali, see Mumtaz Ahmad Faruqui, *Muhammad Ali: The Great Missionary of Islam* (Lahore: Ahmadiyya Anjuman Isha'at-i Islam, 1966).

32. Maulana Muhammad 'Ali, *The Split in the Ahmadiyya Movement*, p. 2.

33. Mirza Ghulam Ahmad, *al-Wasiyyat*, in *Rūhānī Khazā'in*, vol. 20, pp. 315–317.

34. Ibid., p. 316.

35. Ibid., p. 319.

36. There is a common misconception among Ahmadis and non-Ahmadis that burial in *bahishtī maqbara* guarantees one's entrance into paradise, even though Ghulam Ahmad explicitly rejected this view in *al-Wasiyyat*. Contrary to popular belief, Ghulam Ahmad clearly stated that there was no inherent quality in the land that automatically grants one entrance into paradise. He said that no one would enter paradise simply by being buried in the graveyard, but rather only those Ahmadis who were already bound for heaven would be permitted to be buried in the *bahishtī maqbara*. See the footnote in Mirza Ghulam Ahmad, *al-Wasiyyat*, in *Rūhānī Khazā'in*, vol. 20, p. 321.

37. Ibid., p. 318.

38. Ibid., p. 330.

39. Mirza Ghulam Ahmad, *al-Wasiyyat*, in *Rūhānī Khazā'in*, vol. 20, p. 326.

40. The size of the Sadr Anjuman Ahmadiyya was never predefined by Mirza Ghulam Ahmad. The minutes and attendance of the first meeting (January 29, 1906) of the *majlis-i mu'tamidīn-i sadr anjuman ahmadiyya* (Organization of the Trustees of the Executive Ahmadiyya Committee) are available in ibid., pp. 330–332.

41. Mirza Ghulam Ahmad, *al-Wasiyyat*, in *Rūhānī Khazā'in*, vol. 20, p. 325.

42. Ibid., p. 306, in footnote.

43. Annemarie Schimmel, *Mystical Dimensions of Islam* (Chapel Hill: University of North Carolina Press, 1975), p. 236.

44. Mirza Ghulam Ahmad, *al-Wasiyyat*, in *Rūhānī Khazā'in*, vol. 20, p. 326, in section 15 and also in the footnote.

45. Ibid., pp. 306–307, 318–319.

46. Ibid., p. 306.

47. Ibid., p. 305.

48. Ibid.

49. Ibid.

50. Mirza Bashir al-Din Mahmud Ahmad, *Anwār-i Khilāfat* (Qadian, 1915), pp. 91–93; see also Spencer Lavan, *The Ahmadiyah Movement: A History and Perspective* (Delhi: Manohar Book Service, 1974), p. 114.

51. See Zahid Aziz, *The Qadiani Violation of Ahmadiyya Teachings* (Columbus, OH: Ahmadiyya Anjuman Isha'at Islam Lahore, 1995).

52. Mirza Bashir al-Din Mahmud Ahmad, *Barakāt-i Khilāfat* (Qadian, 1914), in *Anwār al-'Ulūm*, vol. 2, p. 220; see also *al-Fazl* (May 23, 1914), p. 8. Although the original *al-Fazl* article was not available to me, excerpts are often quoted in various sources by Ahmadis and non-Ahmadis regarding Mahmud Ahmad's dictate on marriage.

53. Peter Hardy, *The Muslims of British India* (Cambridge: Cambridge University Press, 1972), p. 173.

54. Spencer Lavan, *The Ahmadiyah Movement*, p. 92.

55. Ibid., p. 42, in n. 48.

56. Mirza Ghulam Ahmad, *Malfūzāt*, vol. 5, p. 388.

57. Ibid., vol. 3, p. 372. This specific question and answer was dated August 26, 1902.

58. Sayyid Mir Mahmud Ahmad Nasir, "Positions Taken by the Ahmadiyyah Anjuman-e-Isha'at-e-Islam after March 13, 1914 on Nubuwwat and Khilafat in the Ahmadiyyah Muslim Jama'at," in Munawar Ahmed Sa'eed, trans., *Nubuwwat & Khlilāfat: Prophethood and Its Successorship* (Tilford, UK: Islam International Publications, 2006), pp. 51–59.

59. See Zahid Aziz, *The Qadiani Violation of Ahmadiyya Teachings*, especially the section called "M. Mahmud Ahmad Usurps Anjuman's Authority," from p. 37.

60. I am greatly indebted to Maulana Abdul Mannan Tahir—who was then a missionary at the Fazl Mosque, London—for his detailed explanation of the inner structure of Jama'at-i Ahmadiyya. He was kind enough to meet with me at his office on April 1, 2005, and a number of times thereafter. The knowledge he shared serves as the primary source of information for the following section.

61. These issues are discussed in detail in the next two chapters.

62. *Review of Religions* 97:2 (February 2002): 19.

63. *Review of Religions* 98:4 (April 2003): 22.

64. *Review of Religions* 97:2 (February 2002): 19.

65. Ibid., pp. 7–23.

66. Mirza Ghulam Ahmad, *al-Wasiyyat*, in *Rūhānī Khazā'in*, vol. 20, p. 306, in the footnote.

67. Mirza Ghulam Ahmad, *Sabz Ishtihar*, in *Rūhānī Khazā'in*, vol. 2, pp. 447–470; see also Mirza Ghulam Ahmad's pamphlet from February 20, 1886, p. 21, in the footnote; see also Muhammad Zafrulla Khan, *Tadhkira* (Tilford, UK: Islam International Publications, 2004), pp. 85–86.

68. Maulana Sheikh Mubarak Ahmad, "Khilāfat-e-Ahmadiyyah and the Pledge of Allegiance to Khilāfat," in Munawar Ahmed Sa'eed, trans., *Nubuwwat & Khlilāfat*, pp. 27–45; see also *Review of Religions* 50:10 (October 1956): 503–505, 510–511, 519–524; see also *Review of Religions* 102:10 (October 2007): 49–51, 58, 59.

69. See Mirza Bashir al-Din Mahmud Ahmad's speech *"Da'wā Muslih Maw'ūd ke Muta'alliq Pur-Shawkat E'lān"* (February 20, 1944), which was delivered in Hoshiarpur and is available in *Anwār al-'Ulūm*, vol. 17, pp. 138–170.

70. The original pamphlet containing the ten conditions of *bay'at* was published as *Takmīl-i Tablīgh* (January 12, 1889). See Mirza Ghulam Ahmad, *Majmū'a-i Ishtihārāt*, vol. 1, pp. 189–192.

71. Spencer Lavan appears to have been the first to comment on the simplicity of the ten conditions of *bay'at*, but his discussion is limited to Ghulam Ahmad's lack of emphasis on the zakat and the hajj. Lavan noted that Ghulam Ahmad never made the pilgrimage to Mecca due to a life of chronic illness. Lavan's discussion is more interesting if one treats Jama'at-i Ahmadiyya as a new religious movement with a new religious identity. Otherwise, if one accepts that Jama'at-i Ahmadiyya belongs within the fold of Islam, then being a Muslim clearly presupposes the ten conditions listed above. There is no evidence to suggest that one could be an Ahmadi without first being a Muslim, since being an Ahmadi is contingent upon one's Islam. In addition, the basic tenets of Islam, such as the five pillars, are implicitly included in the sixth condition's emphasis on the Qur'an and sunna, as well as the eighth condition's emphasis on giving precedence to Islam in one's life. For some unknown reason, Ghulam Ahmad specifically emphasized the observance of prayer in his second condition, but this may have been intended to facilitate his additional requirement of imposing the voluntary *tahajjud* prayer upon his followers. For Lavan's comments, see Spencer Lavan, *The Ahmadiyah Movement*, p. 37, especially his comments in n. 48.

72. See 33:40.

73. See Francis Robinson, *Islam, South Asia, and the West* (New Delhi: Oxford University Press, 2007), p. 69.

74. There are a few important counterexamples which are worth mentioning here. Considering current trends in Jama'at-i Ahmadiyya, most people presume that a child born to Ahmadi parents is automatically Ahmadi, which more closely resembles a new religion, or at least an exclusivist religious movement, rather than a traditional Sufi order. A traditional Sufi order would typically require each member to take *bay'at* individually upon reaching maturity. Mirza Bashir al-Din Mahmud Ahmad, however, was not formally initiated at the hand of his father until March 10, 1898. See A. R. Dard, *Life of Ahmad*, p. 148; in addition, Ghulam Ahmad's second wife, Nusrat Jahan Begum (*ammā jān*), never took her husband's *bay'at*, which implies that the *bay'at* might not have been necessary in exceptional cases. Dost Muhammad Shahid argued that it was not necessary for her to take her husband's *bay'at* since her allegiance to him was already implicit in their marriage, which seems reasonably convincing. This particular case, however, is contrary to Mahmud Ahmad's views on marrying non-Ahmadi women, as mentioned above. See Dost Muhammad Shahid, *Tārīkh-i Ahmadiyya*, vol. 1, p. 342.

75. The "declaration form" is available online in both Urdu and English on the official Jama'at-i Ahmadiyya website, www.alislam.org/introduction/initiation.html (accessed June 2014).

76. For the beginnings of such a study see Antonio Gualtieri, *The Ahmadis: Community, Gender, and Politics in a Muslim Society* (London: McGill–Queen's University Press, 2004).

4. Politics and the Ahmadiyya Movement under Mirza Bashir al-Din Mahmud Ahmad

1. The title *Rangīlā Rasūl* has a variety of offensive connotations. Although it literally means the "Colorful Prophet," it more appropriately connotes the "Queer" or "Gay Prophet." In addition to the *Rangīlā Rasūl* pamphlet, Ahmadi responses to the attacks on the Prophet Muhammad often refer to another polemic tract published in the *Risāla Vartamān*, an Amritsar-based monthly periodical.

2. See Mirza Bashir al-Din Mahmud Ahmad, *Kitāb "Rangīlā Rasūl" kā Jawāb* (July 1, 1927) in *Khutbāt-i Mahmūd*, vol. 11 (Islamabad, Surrey, UK: Islam International Publications, n.d.), pp. 168–178.

3. Excerpts from the response are available in Dost Muhammad Shahid, *Tārīkh-i Ahmad-iyya*, vol. 4 (Rabwah?, 1983), pp. 596–598.

4. Spencer Lavan, *The Ahmadiyah Movement: A History and Perspective* (Delhi: Manohar Book Service, 1974), p. 136, and also n. 44 for the government's concern regarding the poster.

5. The letter from July 5, 1927 is available in *Review of Religions* 26:10 (October 1927): 22.

6. *Review of Religions* 26:10 (October 1927): 22–27.

7. The *Rangīla Rasūl* incident was brought to the attention of the undersecretary of state for India, Earl Winterton, also called Edward Turnour, on two occasions in the House of Commons. Captain Foxcroft raised the question on July 27, 1927, and Sir Frank Sanderson raised the issue again on July 29, 1927. See *Parliamentary Debates House of Commons Official Report, Fifth Series*, vol. 209 (Hansard), for July 27, 1927, pp. 1258–1259, and also July 29, 1927, p. 1651.

8. *Review of Religions* 26:10 (October 1927): 27.

9. Ayesha Jalal, *Self and Sovereignty: Individual and Community in South Asian Islam since 1850* (London: Routledge, 2001), p. 296.

10. *Review of Religions* 26:10 (October 1927): 21.

11. Mridu Rai, *Hindu Rulers, Muslim Subjects: Islam, Rights and the History of Kashmir* (London: Hurst & Company, 2004), p. 26.

12. Ayesha Jalal, *Self and Sovereignty*, pp. 352, 215–216.

13. India Office Records (henceforth IOR) R/1/1/2154 in the *Report of the Srinagar Riot Enquiry Committee* (September 24, 1931), p. 17.

14. Ayesha Jalal, *Self and Sovereignty*, p. 354.

15. IOR R/1/1/2064 in the *Fortnightly Report for the First Half of June 1931 from the Resident in Kashmir* (June 19, 1931). The Riot Enquiry Committee later found that the Muslim constable had in fact exaggerated the event. Officially, the Muslim constable was reprimanded for failing to put away his bedding in the early morning hours, as it was past the permissible time, and not for his recitation of the Qur'an. Nevertheless, the head constable's reaction was to grab the wad of bedding and crassly throw it away. Wrapped up in the bedding was a copy of the *panj sūra*, a booklet containing five chapters of the Qur'an. The outcome of the incident resulted in the retirement of the head constable and the dismissal of his Muslim subordinate officer. For the official report, see IOR R/1/1/2154 in the *Report of the Srinagar Riot Enquiry Committee* (September 24, 1931), p. 20.

16. Ayesha Jalal, *Self and Sovereignty*, pp. 354–355.

17. IOR R/1/1/2154, see *Telegram R. no. 2017-S from the Viceroy (Foreign and Political Department) Simla to the Secretary of State for India, London* (August 13, 1931).

18. The date recorded in the *Report of the Srinagar Riot Enquiry Committee* for the speech is June 21, 1931, whereas the *Fortnightly Report for the First Half of July 1931 from the Resident in Kashmir* states that the arrest was made on July 1, 1931.

19. IOR R/1/1/2064 *Fortnightly Report for the First Half of July 1931 from the Resident in Kashmir* (July 17, 1931).

20. Although this account was taken largely from government documents, it differs from Spencer Lavan's independent reading of the same reports. Lavan said that "the [Riot Enquiry] Commission upheld the actions of the Maharajah and commended his prompt dispatching of troops to prevent further troubles." See Spencer Lavan, *The Ahmadiyah Movement*, p. 161, in n. 8; however, the report also criticized the attitude of the police and their implementation of these orders, see IOR R/1/1/2154 in the *Report of the Srinagar Riot Enquiry Committee* (September 24, 1931), pp. 4–5.

21. See IOR R/1/1/2154 in the *Report of the Srinagar Riot Enquiry Committee* (September 24, 1931) for the official report of the riots. Dost Muhammad Shahid's *Tārīkh-i Ahmadiyya*, vol. 5, contains rare photographs in an insert between pp. 406 and 407, depicting disturbing scenes of

victims, including children, amid the bereaved at the Jāmʿi Masjid in Srinagar, where the bodies were taken following the riots. He has also included photographs of large crowds of women protesters demonstrating and the maharaja's troops surrounding the mosque in the weeks following the riots. Most Muslim accounts indicate substantially higher death tolls, including Shahid's own account, which numbers the injured in the low hundreds.

22. IOR R/1/1/2155(1) in Telegram no. 60–6 (September 24, 1931) from the resident in Kashmir.

23. Ibid. This contains a booklet of the ordinance entitled *Notification of no. 19-L of 1988.*

24. Ibid.

25. IOR R/1/1/2064 *Fortnightly Report for the Second Half of September 1931 from the Resident in Kashmir, F.9-C/30* (October 3, 1931); see also IOR R/1/1/2155(1).

26. See IOR R/1/1/2064 *Fortnightly Report for the Second Half of September 1931 from the Resident in Kashmir, F.9-C/30* (October 3, 1931) for the full account, including the above quotations; in contrast, see also Ian Copland, "Islam and Political Mobilization in Kashmir, 1931–1934," p. 239, which seems to suggest that Muslims were willingly displaying patriotism.

27. The above accounts present an image of the critical situation in Kashmir from the perspective of a disenfranchised Muslim population. A comprehensive historical analysis is beyond the scope of this study. See Mridu Rai, *Hindu Rulers, Muslim Subjects* (2004); Ayesha Jalal, *Self and Sovereignty* (2001); Spencer Lavan, *The Ahmadiyah Movement* (1974); Ian Copland, "Islam and Political Mobilization in Kashmir, 1931–1934" (1981); and David Gilmartin, *Empire and Islam: Punjab and the Making of Pakistan* (London: University of California Press, 1988).

28. The Khilafat Movement was based primarily in India and sought to prevent the demise of the Ottoman *khilāfat* after the First World War by appealing to pan-Islamic sympathies as a means of uniting Muslims globally. The movement collapsed after the Ottoman *khilāfat* was abolished in 1924. See Gail Minault, *The Khilafat Movement: Religious Symbolism and Political Mobilization in India* (New York: Columbia University Press, 1982).

29. See H. A. Walter, *The Ahmadiya Movement* (London: Oxford University Press, 1918), pp. 78, 90–94; see also Humphrey J. Fisher, *Ahmadiyyah: A Study in Contemporary Islam on the West African Coast* (London: Oxford University Press, 1963), pp. 68–71.

30. See Mirza Ghulam Ahmad, *Masīh Hindūstān Meñ*, in *Rūhānī Khazā'in*, vol. 15 (Rabwah, 1984).

31. See Mirza Tahir Ahmad, *Christianity: A Journey from Facts to Fiction* (Tilford, UK: Islam International Publications, 1994); see also J. D. Shams, *Where Did Jesus Die?* (Tilford, UK: Islam International Publications, 1989).

32. Muhammad Zafrulla Khan, *Hazrat Maulvi Nooruddeen Khalifatul Masih 1* (London: The London Mosque, 1983?), p. 39. It appears as though Nur al-Din's status as the royal physician is what earned him the title *hakīm*, which typically precedes his name. Although Nur al-Din served as the royal physician from 1877 to 1893 under Ranbir Singh and Pratap Singh, Dost Muhammad Shahid's account suggests that Nur al-Din was asked to leave Kashmir under seemingly unfavorable circumstances; see *Tārīkh-i Ahmadiyya*, vol. 5, p. 369.

33. Nawab Sir Zulfiqar ʿAli Khan had a particularly impressive profile which may appear to be overshadowed by other eminent figures in the committee, such as Iqbal and Mian Fazl-i Husain. Among other things, he was the chief minister of Patiala (1910–1913), a participant for the Simon Commission (1928–1929), and an Indian delegate to the League of Nations (1930). His brother, Nawab Muhammad ʿAli Khan, married Mirza Ghulam Ahmad's daughter, Nawab Mubaraka Begum, which made both Nawabs the brothers-in-law of Mirza Mahmud Ahmad, *khalīfat al-masīh* II. In addition, Ghulam Ahmad's other daughter, Amtul Hafiz Begum, married Nawab Muhammad ʿAli Khan's son, Nawab ʿAbdullah Khan.

34. See Dost Muhammad Shahid, *Tārīkh-i Ahmadiyya*, vol. 5, pp. 415–416, for an account of the committee's formation, and pp. 419–421 for the full list of members.

35. Shimla traditionally belonged to the region of mountain states associated with the people of the Himalayas rather than the Punjab, until the British became acquainted with the town and made it their summer capital in 1864. Shimla continued to function as India's summer capital until partition in 1947. In 1972, the Indian government redefined state borders along more traditional lines and made Shimla the capital of the new state of Himachal Pradesh.

36. This spelling commonly appears in English works, instead of Shaykh Muhammad 'Abdullah, which would be more consistent with the transliterations in this book.

37. For a sketchy autobiographical account, see Sheikh Mohammad Abdullah, *Ātish-i Cinār*, trans., *Flames of the Chinar* (New Delhi: Penguin, 1993).

38. For more on the Majlis-i Ahrar, see Janbaz Mirza, *Kārvān-i Ahrār*, 8 vols. (Lahore: Maktabah-i Tabassira, 1975); see also his *Hayāt-i Amīr-i Sharī'at* (Lahore: Maktabah-i Tabassira, 1970).

39. David Gilmartin, *Empire and Islam*, pp. 96–97; see also Ayesha Jalal, *Self and Sovereignty*, p. 349, where she comments on how the appeal of the early Ahrar attracted "communitarian bigots of varying measure."

40. IOR R/1/1/2155(1) in the *Letter from Chief Secretary to the Government of the Punjab* (October 10, 1931), p. 12.

41. Waheed Ahmad, ed., *Diary and Notes of Mian Fazl-i Husain* (Lahore: Research Society of Pakistan, University of the Punjab, 1977), p. 141.

42. Ayesha Jalal, *Self and Sovereignty*, p. 293.

43. Ibid., p. 296.

44. Most scholars oversimplify the Ahmadi position by concluding that Mahmud Ahmad rejected the Khilafat Movement outright, which is incorrect. For instance, see Yohanan Friedmann, *Prophecy Continuous*, pp. 35–36. This ignores certain subtleties in Mahmud Ahmad's position, which Zafrulla Khan attempted to explain in Wayne Wilcox and Aislie T. Embree (interviewers), *The Reminiscences of Sir Muhammad Zafrulla Khan* (Maple, Canada: Oriental Publishers, with permission from Columbia University, 2004), p. 8.

45. Dost Muhammad Shahid, *Tārīkh-i Ahmadiyya*, vol. 5, p. 433.

46. Ibid., pp. 444–445.

47. Ibid., p. 445. Dost Muhammad Shahid did not provide the names of the individuals in question, but his account implies that they were all reasonably young activists who were already making a name for themselves in Jammu and Kashmir.

48. Ibid., pp. 446–447. Despite the absence of this story from Sheikh Abdullah's autobiography (which is the only other source capable of verifying or denying its authenticity), it is consistent with the development of the subsequent history of Kashmir with regard to Sheikh Abdullah's close political affiliation with Jama'at-i Ahmadiyya throughout the early part of his career.

49. See Francis Robinson, *Islam and Muslim History in South Asia* (Oxford: Oxford University Press, 2000), especially chapter 3, "Islam and the Impact of Print in South Asia."

50. Mridu Rai, *Hindu Rulers, Muslim Subjects*, p. 261.

51. Dost Muhammad Shahid, *Tārīkh-i Ahmadiyya*, vol. 5, p. 447. There are also several photocopies of handwritten letters from Sheikh Abdullah to Mirza Mahmud Ahmad detailing other donations, which have been inserted at the end of vol. 5 between pp. 630 and 631; see also Ian Copland, "Islam and Political Mobilization in Kashmir," p. 237. Copland's account is vague but reasonably consistent with that of Dost Muhammad Shahid, but he did not provide sources for this specific information; see also Janbaz Mirza, *Kārvān-i Ahrār*, vol. 1, p. 369, which expresses a similar belief regarding financial ties.

52. IOR R/1/1/2164 in the *Fortnightly Report for the Second Half of October 1931 from the Resident in Kashmir*, F.9-C/30 (November 3, 1931); see also IOR R/1/1/2531 in *File no. 91-Political*

(January 17, 1934), in which a warning was sent to B. J. Glancy (of the Glancy Commission) cautioning that Sheikh Abdullah was an Ahmadi even though he may say that he is not. The conclusion of the report is that the authenticity of the source is dubious and likely to be linked to the opposition (i.e., the Ahrar), who were threatening to publish the fraudulent letter when "it suits them," as was repeatedly the case throughout Sheikh Abdullah's career. It is surprising that his affiliation with Jama'at-i Ahmadiyya continued to be an issue with the *darbār* as late as 1934, even though both Ahmadi officials and Sheikh Abdullah himself consistently denied his religious commitment to the movement.

53. Sheikh Abdullah, *Flames of the Chinar*, p. 39. A *kāngrī* is a warming device that was traditionally used by indigenous Kashmiris. It consists of a clay bowl filled with hot coals or cinders, which are typically kept in a wooden pail throughout the winter months as a means of staying warm. The pail is small enough and light enough to be carried in one's hands, usually underneath a thick Kashmiri shawl, which makes it a portable heat source for people who are outdoors in inclement weather.

54. See Dost Muhammad Shahid, *Tārīkh-i Ahmadiyya*, vol. 5, p. 433, where he provides citations from Maulana Zafar 'Ali Khan's anti-Ahmadi newspaper, *Zamīndār*, which criticized Mahmud Ahmad's scheme to promote Sheikh Abdullah by repeatedly referring to him as the *sher-i kashmīr*.

55. Ibid., p. 448.

56. Ibid., pp. 470–471.

57. According to the old system of currency, there were 3 *pāī'* in 1 *paysā* and 64 *payse* in 1 rupee.

58. Dost Muhammad Shahid, *Tārīkh-i Ahmadiyya*, vol. 5, p. 436. It is unclear when the fund ceased to exist. It is likely that the scheme was eventually absorbed into broader initiatives of the Ahmadi donation system (*chandā*) that continue to this day under various names.

59. See the ordinance booklet *Notification of no. 19-L of 1988* in IOR R/1/1/2155(1), particularly pp. 5–7, which deal with the legalities of seizure of private property.

60. Mirza Ghulam Ahmad received revelations informing him that all languages were derived from Arabic, which was sacred because of its relation to the Qur'an. See his book *Minan al-Rahmān*, in *Rūhānī Khazā'in*, vol. 9, pp. 126–248. Muhammad Ahmad Mazhar expanded this thesis and wrote numerous lexicons which traced the words of various languages back to their allegedly original Arabic roots. This involved an elaborate system of phonetic substitutions, which he devised himself. Many of his works are still available in the library of the School of Oriental and African Studies (SOAS), University of London; see *Arabic: The Source of All the Languages* (1963); *English Traced to Arabic* (1967); *Yoruba Traced to Arabic* (1976); *Hausa Traced to Arabic* (1977); and *Sanskrit Traced to Arabic* (1982).

61. Dost Muhammad Shahid, *Tārīkh-i Ahmadiyya*, vol. 5, pp. 535–554. This section is further subdivided by each individual attorney and their respective legal contributions.

62. Ayesha Jalal, *Self and Sovereignty*, pp. 352–353.

63. Ibid., p. 356; Ian Copland, "Islam and Political Mobilization in Kashmir," p. 236.

64. See Ayesha Jalal and Anil Seal, "Alternative to Partition: Muslim Politics between the Wars," *Modern Asian Studies* 15:3 (1981): 415–454; see also Ian Talbot, *Khizr Tiwana: The Punjab Unionist Party and the Partition of India* (Oxford: Oxford University Press: 2002), pp. 84–87; see also Ian Talbot, *Pakistan: A Modern History* (London: Hurst & Company, 2005), pp. 71–73.

65. Waheed Ahmad, ed., *Diary and Notes of Mian Fazl-i Husain*, p. 36, where Fazl-i Husain mentions this in regard to visiting Muhammad 'Ali's house in Lahore for a dinner party (Monday, October 27, 1930).

66. Janbaz Mirza, *Kārvān-i Ahrār*, vol. 1, p. 238.

67. Wayne Wilcox and Aislie T. Embree (interviewers), *The Reminiscences of Sir Muhammad Zafrulla Khan*, pp. 36–38.

68. Waheed Ahmad, ed., *Diary and Notes of Mian Fazl-i Husain*, p. 137, under Thursday, May 12, 1932.

69. Wayne Wilcox and Aislie T. Embree (interviewers), *The Reminiscences of Sir Muhammad Zafrulla Khan*, pp. 49–50.

70. Dost Muhammad Shahid, *Tārīkh-i Ahmadiyya*, vol. 5, p. 452.

71. Spencer Lavan, *The Ahmadiyah Movement*, p. 149.

72. IOR R/1/1/2154, see *Telegram: From the President of the All-India Kashmir Committee to His Excellency the Viceroy*, which is underneath *Telegram R. no. 2017-S from the Viceroy (Foreign and Political Department) Simla to the Secretary of State for India, London* (August 13, 1931).

73. There were eight founding members of the Majlis-i Ahrar: 'Ataullah Shah Bukhari, Chaudry Afzal Haqq, Maulana Habib al-Rahman, Mazhar 'Ali Azhar, Zafar 'Ali Khan, Khwaja 'Abd al-Rahman Ghazi, Shaykh Haysam al-Din, and Maulana Da'ud Ghaznavi. See Janbaz Mirza, *Kārvān-i Ahrār*, vol. 1, p. 82.

74. Although Da'ud Ghaznavi and his brothers are most often associated with the Ahl-i Hadith movement, their father, Maulana 'Abdullah Ghaznavi, had close ties to Mirza Ghulam Ahmad. See 'Abd al-Qādir, *Hayāt-i Nūr* (Qadian: Nizārat Nashr-o-Ishā'at Qadian, 2003), p. 79; see also Janbaz Mirza, *Kārvān-i Ahrār*, vol. 1, p. 319.

75. Dost Muhammad Shahid, *Tārīkh-i Ahmadiyya*, vol. 5, p. 432.

76. Janbaz Mirza, *Kārvān-i Ahrār*, vol. 1, p. 190. The article in question appeared in the *Inqilāb* (September 22, 1931). Mahmud Ahmad expressed similar sentiments in a *Siyāsat* article from Lahore (October 31, 1931), which is available in translation in IOR R/1/1/2155(1); see *Demi-Official Letter From C. C. Garbett, ESQ, CMG, CIE, Chief Secretary, Government Punjab no. 15267-S.B. Dated the 2nd/3rd Nov. 1931.*

77. Janbaz Mirza, *Kārvān-i Ahrār*, vol. 1, pp. 149–150, which details the registration form and conditions for membership.

78. Dost Muhammad Shahid, *Tārīkh-i Ahmadiyya*, vol. 5, pp. 445–446.

79. Janbaz Mirza, *Kārvān-i Ahrār*, vol. 1, p. 278.

80. Jama'at-i Ahmadiyya split into two branches in 1914 following the death of Ghulam Ahmad's first successor, Nur al-Din. This is discussed in detail in the previous chapter.

81. See Sheikh Abdullah, *Flames of the Chinar*, pp. 32–33, in which Sheikh Abdullah described an instance where he confronted Mahmud Ahmad about his intentions for propagating Ahmadi Islam in Kashmir.

82. Spencer Lavan and Dost Muhammad Shahid provided differing accounts of Mahmud Ahmad's resignation from the All-India Kashmir Committee. See Dost Muhammad Shahid, *Tārīkh-i Ahmadiyya*, vol. 5, pp. 641–644, in contrast to Spencer Lavan, *The Ahmadiyah Movement*, pp. 154–156, 172. Spencer Lavan focused more on the external pressure which influenced the resignation, whereas Dost Muhammad Shahid was more concerned with preserving Mahmud Ahmad's legacy. It is unlikely that the tension within the All-India Kashmir Committee produced a stalemate, since the committee never revoked Mahmud Ahmad's membership or prevented Ahmadis from participating in the organization following his resignation.

83. Dost Muhammad Shahid, *Tārīkh-i Ahmadiyya*, vol. 5, p. 643; see also Ayesha Jalal, *Self and Sovereignty*, pp. 364–365.

84. Dost Muhammad Shahid, *Tārīkh-i Ahmadiyya*, vol. 5, pp. 644–662; in contrast, see also Ian Copland, "Islam and Political Mobilization in Kashmir," p. 249.

85. This was the sentiment expressed in Iqbal's letter of resignation as interim president of the All-India Kashmir Committee on June 20, 1933. See Syed Abdul Vahid, ed., *Thoughts and Reflections of Iqbal* (Lahore: Sh. Muhammad Ashraf, 1964), pp. 301–303.

86. See Ian Copland, "Islam and Political Mobilization in Kashmir," pp. 240–245; see also Government of Punjab, *The Munir Report.*

5. Religion and Politics after Partition

1. Mridu Rai, *Hindu Rulers, Muslim Subjects: Islam, Rights and the History of Kashmir* (London: Hurst & Company, 2004), p. 275.
2. See Mirza Ghulam Ahmad, *al-Wasiyyat*, in *Rūhānī Khazā'in*, vol. 20, pp. 315–317, 326, in section 15 and also in the footnote.
3. IOR L/PJ/7/12415 in a letter dated November 13, 1947.
4. See 23:50 in M. A. S. Abdel Haleem, trans., *The Qur'an*, p. 217, which reads, "We made the son of Mary and his mother a sign; We gave them shelter on a peaceful hillside with flowing water"; see also Yohanan Friedmann, *Prophecy Continuous: Aspects of Ahmadi Religious Thought and Its Medieval Background* (Berkeley: University of California Press, 1989), p. 39.
5. See Wayne Wilcox and Aislie T. Embree (interviewers), *The Reminiscences of Sir Muhammad Zafrulla Khan* (Maple, Canada: Oriental Publishers, with permission from Columbia University, 2004).
6. Ibid., p. 170.
7. Ibid., p. 171.
8. Ibid.
9. Ibid., pp. 170–172, has the full discussion including a breakdown of the first UN Security Council resolution.
10. Ibid., pp. 172–174.
11. Ibid., p. 175.
12. Ibid., p. 176.
13. Ibid., p. 177.
14. See Mridu Rai, *Hindu Rulers, Muslim Subjects*, p. 37, where she provides a lucid breakdown of castes and social classes in her section "The Social Structure of Kashmir." She takes these specific figures from the *Census of India*, Jammu and Kashmir, 1941.
15. Wayne Wilcox and Aislie T. Embree (interviewers), *The Reminiscences of Sir Muhammad Zafrulla Khan*, pp. 178–179.
16. Ibid., pp. 180–181.
17. Dost Muhammad Shahid, *Tārīkh-i Ahmadiyya*, vol. 5, p. 699; see also IOR L/PJ/7/12415 in a letter to the Under Secretary of State, Colonial Office (October 3, 1947), which notes that there were press reports of large amounts of illegal weapons and ammunition being stockpiled in Qadian. The letter also notes that these charges are probably baseless, but cites an article from the *Hindustan Times* (September 18, 1947) as a reference. In this sense, the timing of the report suggests that the rampant violence and insecurity of partition itself may have initiated the reevaluation of Ghulam Ahmad's ban on jihad. In any case, I have personally met with Ahmadis who were present in Qadian during partition, who claim that the *khalīfat al-masīh* made appeals to Jama'at members to loan personal hunting rifles, ammunition, and other weapons during this period. Indeed, one such Ahmadi was still bitter about the experience and protested that the borrowed weapon was never returned as promised.
18. Dost Muhammad Shahid, *Tārīkh-i Ahmadiyya*, vol. 5, pp. 699–703.
19. Ibid., p. 705. The name seems peculiar to me and could possibly be an acronym, considering it was capitalized this way in the original source.

20. See ibid., in which there is a reproduction of the letter as well as a photocopy of the original letter by General Gracey, which appears as a picture insert between pp. 710 and 711. There are also pictures of members of the Furqan Battalion in the same location.

21. See Mirza Ghulam Ahmad, *Government Angrēzī Awr Jihād*, in *Rūhānī Khazā'in*, vol. 17, pp. 1–34.

22. Mirza Ghulam Ahmad, *Arba'īn*, in *Rūhānī Khazā'in*, vol. 17, p. 443, in the footnote. For an analysis of certain aspects of Ghulam Ahmad's concept of jihad, see Yohanan Friedmann, *Prophecy Continuous*, pp. 165–180; see also John H. Hanson, "Jihad and the Ahmadiyya Muslim Community: Nonviolent Efforts to Promote Islam in the Contemporary World," *Nova Religio* 11:2 (November 2007): 77–93.

23. Mirza Ghulam Ahmad, *Tuhfa Golarawiyya*, in *Rūhānī Khazā'in*, vol. 17, pp. 77–78, 80, though the entire poem runs from pp. 77 to 80, which corresponds to 41–44, at the bottom of the page.

24. Mirza Bashir al-Din Mahmud Ahmad, *Kalām-i Mahmūd* (Amritsar: Nazārat-i Nashr-o-Ishā'at Qadian, 2002), p. 195, poem no. 120 is listed under the heading *ta'rīf kē qābil hayñ yā rab tere dīvāne*. The footnote states that the poem originally appeared in the January 2, 1946, issue of *al-Fazl*.

25. Dost Muhammad Shahid, *Tārīkh-i Ahmadiyya*, vol. 5, p. 699.

26. See Yohanan Friedmann, *Prophecy Continuous*, pp. 165–180; see also Spencer Lavan, *The Ahmadiyah Movement*, pp. 145–185, which includes a discussion of the initial stages of the Kashmir crisis, including the riots, since his study ends shortly thereafter in 1936.

27. This claim is an important aspect of Jama'at-i Ahmadiyya's presentation of Ghulam Ahmad's prophethood, which is based on the idea that he was a non-law-bearing prophet (*lā tashrī' nabī*). Ghulam Ahmad advanced this claim and elaborated it in several works throughout his career. For two such examples, see Mirza Ghulam Ahmad, *Tiryāq al-Qulūb*, in *Rūhānī Khazā'in*, vol. 15, pp. 258–259; and *Ek Ghalatī kā Izāla*, in *Rūhānī Khazā'in*, vol. 18, p. 211.

28. For example, just prior to the outbreak of riots in 1931, Maharaja Hari Singh was immersed in a controversy surrounding the legality of slaughtering cows for meat. This politicized debate was a major source of communal tensions between Hindus and Muslims in the days leading up to the riots. See IOR R/1/1/2064, *The Jammu and Kashmir Government Gazette*, July 9, 1931; see also Ayesha Jalal, *Self and Sovereignty*, pp. 302, 353, 355; and Mridu Rai, *Hindu Rulers, Muslim Subjects*, pp. 278–279.

29. K. K. Aziz, *The All India Muslim Conference, 1928–1935: A Documentary Record* (Karachi: National Publishing House, 1972), pp. 33, 35.

30. Dost Muhammad Shahid, *Tārīkh-i Ahmadiyya*, vol. 5, p. 311. Zulfiqar 'Ali Khan was the elder brother of Maulana Muhammad 'Ali and Shawkat 'Ali. The brothers are more commonly known by their pen names (*takhallus*), Zulfiqar 'Ali Gawhar and Muhammad 'Ali Jawhar.

31. Ibid., p. 240.

32. Maulana Hafiz Sher Muhammad, *Dr. Sir Muhammad Iqbal and the Ahmadiyya Movement* (Columbus, OH: Ahmadiyya Anjuman Isha'at Islam Lahore, 1995), pp. 8–9; see also Syed Abdul Vahid, ed., *Thoughts and Reflections of Iqbal* (Lahore: Sh. Muhammad Ashraf, 1964), p. 297, where Iqbal expresses his early optimism about the Ahmadiyya movement prior to 1911; see also Spencer Lavan, *The Ahmadiyah Movement*, p. 172. Lavan based his information on a citation of Dost Muhammad Shahid, which I could not find in the specified location.

33. Maulana Hafiz Sher Muhammad, *Dr. Sir Muhammad Iqbal and the Ahmadiyya Movement*, p. 11.

34. Mirza Ghulam Ahmad, *Malfūzāt* (in 5 vols.), vol. 5, pp. 283–285, 635–636; see also *Payghām-i Sulh* in *Rūhānī Khazā'in*, vol. 23, p. 488.

35. *Review of Religions* 26:10 (October 1927): 28–29, with a picture of Sir Mian Fazl-i Husain on the inside cover. See also Adil Hussain Khan, "The Big and the Old: Ahmadi Mosques in South London," *The Middle East in London* 6:9 (April 2010): 8.

36. Waheed Ahmad, ed., *Diary and Notes of Mian Fazl-i Husain*, pp. 59–60; the entry is under Friday, May 1, 1931.

37. See Humayun Ansari, *"The Infidel Within": Muslims in Britain since 1800* (London: Hurst & Company, 2004), p. 126.

38. Dost Muhammad Shahid, *Tārīkh-i Ahmadiyya*, vol. 5, p. 438.

39. There are multiple versions of a hadith which states that anyone who wrongfully calls a believer a *kāfir* is surely a *kāfir*. For example, see the *kitāb al-adab* in Bukhari, hadith 6045 or 8:73:71; and hadith 6103 or 8:73:105.

40. Aside from his editorials in the *Zamīndār*, Zafar 'Ali Khan wrote anti-Ahmadi poetry as well. See Zafar 'Ali Khan, *Bahāristān* (Lahore: Urdu Academy Punjab, 1937), pp. 543–578 in the section *"Qādiyānī Khurāfāt"* (Qadiani Nonsense).

41. Mirza Ghulam Ahmad, *Haqqānī Taqrīr bar Wāqi'a-i Wafāt-i Bashīr*, in *Rūhānī Khazā'in*, vol. 2 (listed on the cover as *Sabz Ishtihār*), pp. 447–470.

42. See Mirza Bashir al-Din Mahmud Ahmad, *Truth about the Split*, pp. 134–179, particularly the sections dealing with his article on "Kufr-o-Islam"; see also his article listed under Hazrat Khalifatul Masih II, "Are Non-Ahmadis Kafirs?," *Review of Religions* 34:7 (July 1935): 241–256; see also Maulana Muhammad 'Ali, *The Split in the Ahmadiyya Movement*, pp. 79–80.

6. Early Opposition and the Roots of Ahmadi Persecution

1. There are three main versions of these events which loosely overlap: Mirza Ghulam Ahmad in *Tazkirat al-Shahādatayn* (Qadian: Riyaz Hind Press, 1903); Mirza Tahir Ahmad in his Friday Sermon (July 14, 1989); and the compilation of accounts given by 'Abd al-Latif's students and family members detailed in B. A. Rafiq's *The Afghan Martyrs* (London: Raqeem Press, 1995); see also Yohanan Friedmann, *Prophecy Continuous: Aspects of Ahmadi Religious Thought and Its Medieval Background* (Berkeley: University of California Press, 1989), pp. 26–27.

2. See Bijan Omrani, "The Durand Line: History and Problems of the Afghan-Pakistan Border," *Asian Affairs* 40:2 (2009): 177–195.

3. See Mirza Ghulam Ahmad, *Ā'īna-i Kamālāt-i Islām*, which makes up vol. 5 of *Rūhānī Khazā'in*.

4. This Sayyid 'Abd al-Sattar Shah should not be confused with Sayyid 'Abd al-Sattar Shah, the Ahmadi doctor from Rawalpindi whose daughter, Mariam (Umm Tahir), married Mirza Bashir al-Din Mahmud Ahmad, *khalīfat al-masīh* II, and became the mother of *khalīfat al-masīh* IV, Mirza Tahir Ahmad.

5. Mirza Ghulam Ahmad, *Tazkirat al-Shahādatayn*, in *Rūhānī Khazā'in*, vol. 20, p. 48.

6. Ibid., pp. 47–48.

7. Frank A. Martin, *Under the Absolute Amir* (London: Harper & Brothers, 1907), pp. 132–133.

8. See Mirza Ghulam Ahmad, *Tazkirat al-Shahādatayn*, in *Rūhānī Khazā'in*, vol. 20, pp. 49–60, which contains Ghulam Ahmad's account of 'Abd al-Latif's martyrdom, but for the full booklet see pp. 1–128.

9. See Mirza Ghulam Ahmad in *Badar* (January 8, 1904), as quoted in B. A. Rafiq, *The Afghan Martyrs*, p. 33.

10. B. A. Rafiq, *The Afghan Martyrs*, p. 36.

11. See ibid.; see also Francis Robinson, *The 'Ulama of the Farangi Mahall and Islamic Culture in South Asia* (New Delhi: Permanent Black, 2001), pp. 88, 109–110.

12. B. A. Rafiq, *The Afghan Martyrs*, p. 37.

13. Senzil Nawid, "The State, the Clergy, and British Imperial Policy in Afghanistan during the 19th and Early 20th Centuries," *International Journal of Middle East Studies* 29:4 (November 1997): 593.

14. Frank A. Martin, *Under the Absolute Amir*, p. 299.

15. Senzil Nawid, "The State, the Clergy, and British Imperial Policy in Afghanistan during the 19th and Early 20th Centuries," p. 593.

16. Frank A. Martin, *Under the Absolute Amir*, pp. 269–270, and also chapter 10, "Tortures and Methods of Execution," pp. 157–172.

17. Senzil Nawid, "The State, the Clergy, and British Imperial Policy in Afghanistan during the 19th and Early 20th Centuries," p. 593.

18. For a contrasting view which argues that Ahmadis rightly deserved to be executed, see Sirdar Ikbal Ali Shah, *Afghanistan of the Afghans* (London: Diamond Press, 1928), pp. 211–215.

19. Whereas the word *mullā* should be an honorific term used with dignity and veneration, it has increasingly acquired a derogatory usage among Punjabis, including Ahmadis, who use it almost exclusively in the pejorative. See the poem by *khalīfat al-masīh* IV Mirza Tahir Ahmad on *mullās* in his book, *Kalām-i Tāhir* (Tilford, UK: Islam International Publications, 2001), p. 104, 106, or poems §41 and §42.

20. The extent of Mirza Ghulam Ahmad's exposure to traditional Islamic scholarship is debatable, despite the fact that the community contends that he was *ummi* (unlettered), as discussed in chapter 1.

21. 'Abd al-Qādir, *Hayāt-i Nūr* (Qadian: Nizārat Nashar-o-Ishā'at, 2003), pp. 54–56; for a less detailed account in English, see also Muhammad Zafrulla Khan, *Hazrat Maulvi Nooruddeen Khalifatul Masih 1* (London: London Mosque, 1983?), pp. 12–13, 24–25.

22. See Yohanan Friedmann, *Prophecy Continuous*, pp. 28–29.

23. There is a good discussion of these efforts in ibid., pp. 24–25.

24. *Review of Religions* 30:11 (November 1931): 290–291, with a picture of Maulvi Abu'l 'Ata Jalandhari after the title page.

25. *Review of Religions* 30:11 (November 1931): 290; see also Bashir Ahmad, *The Ahmadiyya Movement: British-Jewish Connections* (Rawalpindi: Islamic Study Forum, 1994), p. 65.

26. *Review of Religions* 31:1 (January 1932): 30, with a picture of Maulvi Jalal al-Din Shams after the title page.

27. IOR L/P.S./11/263 in a letter from the undersecretary of the government of India, Foreign and Political Department, under tab 4399.

28. Ibid., in a letter addressed to the Right Honourable Sir Austin Chamberlain, Foreign Secretary (June 26, 1928), under tab 4399.

29. Ibid., in the letter from Mufti Muhammad Sadiq under tab 4399.

30. *Review of Religions* 33:9–10 (September-October 1934): 402–403.

31. Ibid., pp. 403–404. The italics were included in the original. The reference to the text *'ain-uz-zia* is difficult to assess, even though it was expanded earlier in the same article as *"'ain-uz-zia-fir-rad-i-'ala' Kashfil Ghata* (the Fountain of Light in refutation of "a misconception removed" [*'ain al-ziyā fī radd 'alā kashf al-ghitā*])," which actually translates as "The Fountain of Light in Refutation of 'The Unveiling of the Covering.'" This may have been a reference to something written about one of Ghulam Ahmad's less popular books, *Kashf al-Ghitā* (The Unveiling of the Covering), which is available in *Rūhānī Khazā'in*, vol. 14, pp. 177–226. However, Ghulam Ahmad had also written a book called *Ek Ghalatī kā Izāla*, which has fre-

quently been translated and publicized by the Jama'at under a title similar to "A Misconception Removed." See Mirza Ghulam Ahmad, *Ek Ghalatī kā Izāla*, in *Rūhānī Khazā'in*, vol. 18, pp. 205–216. It is not clear which obscure booklet the *khatīb* was referring to in his letter.

32. Abu'l-'Ata Jalandhari, *The Cairo Debate*, 4th ed. (Rabwah: The Maktaba-al-Furqan, 1963), p. iii.

33. Yohanan Friedmann, *Prophecy Continuous*, p. 24.

34. Humayun Ansari, *"The Infidel Within": Muslims in Britain since 1800* (London: Hurst & Company, 2004), p. 127.

35. Sufi 'Abd al-Qadīr and Mirza Bashir Ahmad, *The Family of the Founder of the Ahmadiyya Movement* (Qadian: Book Depot Talif-o-Isha'at, 1934), p. 33, and also pp. 32–36, for other letters and notes about the war.

36. For a counterexample where Muslims are portrayed as the defenders of Empire, see Muslim Council of Britain, *Remembering the Brave: The Muslim Contribution to Britain's Armed Forces* (London: Muslim Council of Britain, 2009), p. 6.

37. For example, see Bashir Ahmad, *The Ahmadiyya Movement: British-Jewish Connections* (Rawalpindi: Islamic Study Forum, 1994).

38. See also M. Naeem Qureshi, *Pan-Islam in British Indian Politics: A Study of the Khilafat Movement, 1918–1924* (Leiden: Brill, 1999).

39. See Gail Minault, *The Khilafat Movement: Religious Symbolism and Political Mobilization in India* (New York: Columbia University Press, 1982).

40. Yohanan Friedmann, *Prophecy Continuous*, pp. 35–36.

41. Wayne Wilcox and Aislie T. Embree (interviewers), *The Reminiscences of Sir Muhammad Zafrulla Khan* (Maple, Canada: Oriental Publishers, with permission from Columbia University, 2004), p. 8.

42. Yohanan Friedmann, *Prophecy Continuous*, pp. 35–36.

43. Government of Punjab, *Report of the Court of Inquiry Constituted under Punjab Act II of 1954 to Enquire into the Punjab Disturbances of 1953* (Lahore: Superintendent Government Printing, Punjab, 1954), p. 196. Henceforth *The Munir Report*.

44. Jānbāz Mirzā, *Kārvān-i Ahrār*, vol. 1 (Lahore: Maktabah-i Tabassira, 1975), p. 238.

45. Wayne Wilcox and Aislie T. Embree (interviewers), *The Reminiscences of Sir Muhammad Zafrulla Khan*, pp. 36–38.

46. Government of Punjab, *The Munir Report*, p. 12.

47. Spencer Lavan, *The Ahmadiyah Movement: A History and Perspective* (Delhi: Manohar Book Service, 1974), p. 165.

48. Government of Punjab, *The Munir Report*, p. 12.

49. Spencer Lavan, *The Ahmadiyah Movement*, p. 165.

50. Government of Punjab, *The Munir Report*, p. 12.

51. Spencer Lavan, *The Ahmadiyah Movement*, p. 166.

52. This was from a letter from C. C. Garbett to M. G. Hallett (November 1, 1934), as quoted in Spencer Lavan, *The Ahmadiyah Movement*, p. 166.

53. Spencer Lavan, *The Ahmadiyah Movement*, p. 166. Lavan spelled Qadian as Qadiyan.

7. Persecution in Pakistan and Politicization of Ahmadi Identity

1. See Sugata Bose and Ayesha Jalal, *Modern South Asia: History, Culture, Political Economy* (Lahore: Sang-e-Meel Publications, 1998), especially chapter 15, pp. 156–164.

2. See David Gilmartin, "Religious Leadership and the Pakistan Movement in the Punjab," *Modern Asian Studies* 13:3 (1979): 485–517.

3. See *al-Fazl* (November 13, 1946), as quoted in Maulānā Allāh Wasāyā, *Tārīkh-i Khatm-i Nubuwwat 1974: Qawmī Assembly meñ Qādiyānī Muqaddama,* vol. 2 (Multan: 'Ālamī Majlis Tahaffuz-i Khatm al-Nubuwwat, 1994), p. 162.

4. Maulānā Allāh Wasāyā, *Tārīkh-i Khatm-i Nubuwwat 1974,* vol. 2, pp. 162–163.

5. Government of Punjab, *Report of the Court of Inquiry Constituted under Punjab Act II of 1954 to Enquire into the Punjab Disturbances of 1953* (Lahore: Superintendent Government Printing, Punjab, 1954), pp. 196–197. Henceforth *The Munir Report.*

6. See Mian Muhammad Sadullah, ed., *The Partition of the Punjab 1947: A Compilation of Official Documents,* vol. 2 (Lahore: National Documentation Centre, 1983), pp. 244–252.

7. It is worth noting that Zafrulla Khan represented the Muslim League, but not Jama'at-i Ahmadiyya, before the Boundary Commission. This suggests that the Ahmadi position was different from the Muslim League's position, which represented the Muslim mainstream. Considering that Zafrulla Khan was a key spokesperson for Jama'at-i Ahmadiyya, Mirza Mahmud Ahmad could have taken advantage of the opportunity to demonstrate his solidarity with Muslims by compromising on a solution with the Muslim League in order to present a unified Muslim front. Instead, Jama'at-i Ahmadiyya sent a different representative to the Boundary Commission. For the full account of Zafrulla Khan's arguments, see Mian Muhammad Sadullah, ed., *The Partition of the Punjab 1947: A Compilation of Official Documents,* vol. 2, pp. 252–538.

8. Official reports of the number of Ahmadis are not released by the Ahmadi hierarchy. Jama'at-i Ahmadiyya boasts that its total membership is around 200 million worldwide. According to available census figures, I would estimate that there are currently no more than 2 to 5 million Ahmadis worldwide, which may be generous. For example, see *Review of Religions* 98:4 (April 2003): 4, 25–26. On page 26, there is a graph charting the alleged number of Ahmadi conversions from 1994 to 2002.

9. Ayesha Jalal, *Self and Sovereignty: Individual and Community in South Asian Islam since 1850* (London: Routledge, 2001), pp. 374–375.

10. Government of Punjab, *The Munir Report,* p. 11.

11. Ibid., pp. 11–12.

12. Ibid., pp. 12–13.

13. Ibid., p. 199.

14. Yohanan Friedmann, *Prophecy Continuous: Aspects of Ahmadi Religious Thought and Its Medieval Background* (Berkeley: University of California Press, 1989), p. 29.

15. Government of Punjab, *The Munir Report,* p. 18.

16. For more on 'Usmani and the religious politics of the Jam'iyyat-i 'Ulama-i Islam, see Ayesha Jalal, *Self and Sovereignty,* p. 454; see also David Gilmartin, "Religious Leadership and the Pakistan Movement in the Punjab," *Modern Asian Studies* 13:3 (1979): 511–512.

17. For the details of the above account, see Government of Punjab, *The Munir Report,* pp. 15–17.

18. Ibid., p. 17.

19. Ibid., p. 24.

20. Ibid., p. 30.

21. Ibid., p. 57.

22. Ibid., p. 75.

23. Ibid.

24. Ibid., pp. 75–76.

25. Ibid., p. 76.

26. Ibid., p. 105.

27. See the official website at www.khatm-e-nubuwwat.com (accessed June 2014).

28. See Government of Punjab, *The Munir Report*, p. 111, for Akhtar ʿAli Khan's role in campaigning for Majlis-i Tahaffuz-i Khatm-i Nubuwwat.

29. F. C. R. Robinson, "Mawdudī, Sayyid Abuʾl-Aʿlā," in *Encyclopaedia of Islam*, 2nd ed., ed. P. Bearman.

30. Seyyed Vali Reza Nasr, *Mawdudi and the Making of Islamic Revivalism* (Oxford: Oxford University Press, 1996), pp. 35–36.

31. Ibid., p. 42.

32. Ibid.

33. See Seyyed Vali Reza Nasr, *The Vanguard of the Islamic Revolution: The Jamaʿat-i Islami of Pakistan* (Berkeley: University of California Press, 1994), pp. 131–141.

34. I have only had access to reprints of this text, in which the copyright date for the first edition is listed as 1953. *The Munir Report* states that *Qādiyānī Masʾala* was published on March 5, 1953; see Government of Punjab, *The Munir Report*, p. 250. However, the publication for the first edition is listed as 1951 in the bibliography of Seyyed Vali Reza Nasr, *Mawdudi and the Making of Islamic Revivalism*, p. 199.

35. Government of Punjab, *The Munir Report*, p. 155.

36. Ibid., p. 153.

37. Ibid., p. 157.

38. Ibid., p. 176.

39. Ibid., p. 172.

40. Ibid., p. 166. This is the same Shaykh Bashir Ahmad mentioned above as the Ahmadi advocate who represented the Jamaʿat before the Punjab Boundary Commission prior to partition.

41. Government of Punjab, *The Munir Report*, p. 160.

42. For other considerations regarding Daultana's disinterest in the Majlis-i ʿAmal and its demands, see Ian Talbot, *Pakistan: A Modern History* (London: Hurst & Company, 2005), p. 141.

43. Seyyed Vali Reza Nasr, *Mawdudi and the Making of Islamic Revivalism*, p. 43.

44. Ibid., p. 44.

45. Ian Talbot, *Pakistan: A Modern History*, p. 141.

46. Ayesha Jalal, *The State of Martial Rule* (Cambridge: Cambridge University Press, 1990), p. 152.

47. Government of Punjab, *The Munir Report*, p. 115.

48. Even if Ahmadis were indeed exploiting influence for their own nefarious reasons, it would not be an act of *kufr* in traditional Sunni Islam. The charge of *kufr* can only be linked to problems of theology as discussed below.

49. Dost Muhammad Shahid, *Tārīkh-i Ahmadiyya*, vol. 17 (Rabwah, 1983). The police report is on pp. 21–37 and Shahid's account is on pp. 230–234.

50. This is a difficult situation to assess, since so little has been written about the attack on Mahmud Ahmad. Perhaps the absence of these accounts is itself the result of a conscious decision by Jamaʿat-i Ahmadiyya to preserve what many Ahmadis consider to be a dignified memory of their beloved *muslih mawʿūd* (promised reformer). I have therefore prioritized the oral accounts of those Ahmadi elders who witnessed Mahmud Ahmad's condition and the sentiment of Rabwah throughout various stages of the latter part of his life.

51. For more biographical information concerning Nur al-Din, including his marriages and children, see ʿAbd al-Qādir, *Hayāt-i Nūr* (Qadian: Nizārat-i Nashar-o-Ishāʿat, 2003).

52. *Review of Religions* 49:1 (January 1955): 57.

53. *Review of Religions* 50:7 (July 1956): 395.

54. *Review of Religions* 49:3 (March 1955): 192.

55. *Review of Religions* 49:5 (May 1955): 294. One may question to what extent these statements reflect Mahmud Ahmad's apprehensions or the views of Mian Nasir himself.

56. For examples of articles that illustrate the insecurities of the Ahmadi hierarchy, see *Review of Religions* 50:10 (October 1956): 503–505, 510–511, 519–524; *Review of Religions* 50:11 (November 1956): 579–581.

57. The article in question is in *The Times* of Karachi (August 20, 1956), and was rebutted in *Review of Religions* 50:10 (October 1956): 548.

58. When 'Abd al-Mannan 'Umar left the Qadiani branch, he began offering his services to the Lahoris. He claimed never to have taken formal *bay'at* with either side, which may in fact be true. It is irrelevant to his active participation in both communities, however. 'Abd al-Mannan 'Umar most notably appeared before the National Assembly on behalf of the Lahoris during the 1974 inquiry. Unfortunately, I was unable to speak to him before his death on July 28, 2006, in the United States. Prior to his passing he published a new translation of the Qur'an and compiled a dictionary of Qur'anic words based on his father's notes, both of which are readily available. See *The Holy Qur'an* (Hockessin, DE: Noor Foundation International, 2002); see also *Dictionary of the Holy Qur'an* (Hockessin, DE: Noor Foundation International, 2004).

59. See Iain Adamson, *A Man of God: The Life of His Holiness Khalifatul Masih IV* (Bristol, UK: George Shepherd Publishers, 1991), pp. 92–96.

60. Yohanan Friedmann, *Prophecy Continuous*, pp. 41–42.

61. Seyyed Vali Reza Nasr, *Mawdudi and the Making of Islamic Revivalism*, p. 45.

62. *The National Assembly of Pakistan Debates—Official Report*, vol. 4, no. 26 (June 30, 1974), pp. 1302–1309.

63. The names of the National Assembly members who voted on the motion were recorded in the government's official report. Normally, this would not be worth mentioning, however, there is a popular misconception among Ahmadis that is worth elaborating briefly. Ahmadis insist that there were 72 members of the National Assembly who unanimously voted against the one true Jama'at-i Ahmadiyya, which hence provided literal fulfillment of a hadith narrated by Tirmidhi regarding a chosen sect in the latter days that would be opposed by the remaining 72 sects of the *umma*, who had gone astray. Neither the members of the National Assembly nor the members of the National Assembly's special committee consisted of 72 members. Furthermore, neither group represented 72 different sects in Islam. For the full list of names of members who voted, see *The National Assembly of Pakistan Debates—Official Report*, vol. 5, no. 39 (September 7, 1974), pp. 571–574. Although this belief is based on false information, the source of the erroneous claim seems to have stemmed from two newspaper articles that mistakenly drew a literal connection between the vote of the National Assembly and the alleged fulfillment of the hadith. It is most likely that some Ahmadi spokesperson initially connected the vote to the hadith and then provided the information to journalists, perhaps even correctly. At some point, irrespective of who is responsible, there was some confusion regarding the supposed fulfillment of the hadith and the actual number of National Assembly members who participated in the vote. Since then, numerous Ahmadis have quoted the two newspaper articles as proof of literal fulfillment of the hadith, since the journalist either misunderstood or misreported the connection. See *The Guardian* (September 9, 1974); see also *Nawa-i-Waqt* (October 10, 1974). One Ahmadi author wrote, "In 1974, some newspapers published headlines that seventy two sects of Islam had agreed in this declaration about Ahmadis. We are proud and happy to be the minority 73rd sect as predicted by the Holy Prophet, peace be upon him." See Aziz Ahmad Chaudhry, *The Promised Messiah and Mahdi* (Tilford, UK: Islam International Publications, 1996), p. 171. In addition, the fourth *khalifa*, Mirza Tahir Ahmad, discussed the

literal fulfillment of the hadith in a question and answer session at the Fazl Mosque, London (August 23, 1984).

64. *The National Assembly of Pakistan Debates—Official Report*, vol. 5, no. 39 (September 7, 1974), p. 561.

65. See the official website at www.federalshariatcourt.gov.pk (accessed June 2014).

66. It may be useful to see a classical perspective, such as al-Ghazali's work on issues related to *kufr* and *takfīr* in *Faysal al-Tafriqa bayn al-Islām wa'l-Zandaqa*, which is available in translation in Richard Joseph McCarthy, trans., *Deliverance from Error: An Annotated Translation of al-Munqidh min al-Dalāl and Other Relevant Works of al-Ghazāli* (Louisville, KY: Fons Vitae, 1980); see also Sherman A. Jackson, *On the Boundaries of Theological Tolerance in Islam* (Karachi: Oxford University Press, 2002).

67. *The National Assembly of Pakistan Debates—Official Report*, vol. 5, no. 39 (September 7, 1974), p. 561.

68. Yohanan Friedmann, *Prophecy Continuous*, p. 45.

69. See *Ordinance no. XX of 1984* as published in *The Gazette of Pakistan. Islamabad, Thursday, 26 April 1984*.

70. See Section 298B of *Ordinance no. XX of 1984*.

71. Antonio R. Gualtieri, *Conscience and Coercion: Ahmadi Muslims and Orthodoxy in Pakistan* (Montreal: Guernica, 1989), pp. 49, 57–58.

72. Iain Adamson, *A Man of God: The Life of His Holiness Khalifatul Masih IV*, pp. 198–199.

73. Mirza Masroor Ahmad was elected *khalīfat al-masīh* V in London on April 22, 2004. He is the great-grandson of Mirza Ghulam Ahmad, but unlike his two predecessors he is not a descendant of the second *khalīfa*, Mirza Bashir al-Din Mahmud Ahmad. Instead, he is the grandson of Mirza Bashir al-Din Mahmud Ahmad's youngest brother, Mirza Sharif Ahmad.

Conclusion

1. For an elaboration of the German context see Michael Nijhawan, "'Today, We Are All Ahmadi': Configurations of Heretic Otherness between Lahore and Berlin," *British Journal of Middle Eastern Studies* 37:3 (2010): 429–447.

2. See *Review of Religions* 98:4 (April 2003): 22.

3. See Oliver Scharbrodt, *Islam and the Baha'i Faith* (London: Routledge, 2008); see also Shahzad Bashir, *Messianic Hopes and Mystical Visions: The Nurbakhshiya between Medieval and Modern Islam* (Columbia: University of South Carolina Press, 2003).

4. Once again, Mirza Ghulam Ahmad expounded some of his more controversial views regarding the death of Jesus in *Tawzīh-i Marām*, namely that Jesus Christ is not alive in heaven and will not physically return to Earth in the same corporeal flesh as many Muslims believe.

5. Barbara Daly Metcalf, *Islamic Revival in British India: Deoband, 1860–1900* (Oxford: Oxford University Press, 1982), p. 292.

6. A. R. Dard, *Life of Ahmad* (Lahore: Tabshir, 1948), pp. 276–279.

7. Muhammad Dā'ūd Ghaznavī, *Maqālāt Maulānā Muhammad Dā'ūd Ghaznavī* (Lahore: Maktaba Naziriyya, 1979), p. 19. The account describes Da'ud Ghaznavi as the *sachcha jā-nishīn* (true successor) of his father, 'Abd al-Jabbar Ghaznavi, which is a peculiar way of describing their relationship in that it might be taken to imply that 'Abd al-Jabbar had a false *jā-nishīn* (successor).

8. See 'Abd al-Qādir, *Hayāt-i Nūr* (Qadian: Nizārat Nashr-o-Ishā'at Qadian, 2003), p. 79; this was confirmed by Jānbāz Mirzā in his *Kārvān-i Ahrār*, vol. 1, p. 319.

9. Like his brothers, 'Abd al-Wahid Ghaznavi was also challenged to a *mubāhala* (prayer duel) by Mirza Ghulam Ahmad. See Mirza Ghulam Ahmad, *Anjām-i Ātham*, in *Rūhānī Khazā'in*, vol. 11, p. 70.

10. Jānbāz Mirzā, *Kārvān-i Ahrār*, vol. 1, p. 319.

11. Ibid., vol. 1, p. 143.

12. Jānbāz Mirzā, *Hayāt-i Amīr-i Sharī'at* (Lahore: Maktabah-i Tabassira, 1970), p. 37.

13. There are a number of leaflets pertaining to Pir Mehr 'Ali Shah Golrawi under various headings in Mirza Ghulam Ahmad, *Majmū'a-i Ishtihārāt*, vol. 3, pp. 325–341, 346–355.

14. See Mirza Ghulam Ahmad, *Haqīqat al-Wahy* in *Rūhānī Khazā'in*, vol. 22, p. 356.

15. All of these texts are available in *Rūhānī Khazā'in*, vols. 17–18.

16. Mirza Ghulam Ahmad, *Anjām-i Ātham*, in *Rūhānī Khazā'in*, vol. 11, p. 71.

17. A. R. Dard, *Life of Ahmad*, pp. 592–593.

18. In personal correspondence (March 7, 2006) Dost Muhammad Shahid listed the name of a Chishti scholar, Hazrat Imam al-Din Gujrati (possibly from a place called Goliki?), who took *bay'at* with Mirza Ghulam Ahmad. Prior to his *bay'at* with Ghulam Ahmad, Imam al-Din Gujrati was a *murīd* of the Chishti Shaykh Shams al-Din Siyālwī, who was the *murshid* (spiritual guide and teacher) of Pir Mehr 'Ali Shah Golrawi.

19. Jānbāz Mirzā, *Kārvān-i Ahrār*, vol. 1, p. 83.

20. For example, see the anti-Ahmadi poetry in the section *"Qādiyānī Khurāfāt"* [Qadiani nonsense], in Zafar 'Ali Khan, *Bahāristān* (Lahore: Urdu Academy Punjab, 1937), pp. 543–578.

21. Maulana Muhammad Ali, *The Founder of the Ahmadiyya Movement*, 3rd ed. (Wembley, UK: Ahmadiyya Anjuman Lahore Publications, UK, 2008), pp. 11, 104–105; the original obituary, which I have not been able to access, is cited as *Zamīndār* (June 8, 1908).

22. See Government of Punjab, *The Munir Report*, for numerous accounts of the role of Akhtar 'Ali Khan and the *Zamīndār* during the disturbances.

23. Seyyed Vali Reza Nasr, *Mawdudi and the Making of Islamic Revivalism*, p. 10. For a more thorough account of Mawdudi's father and childhood, see also Seyyed Vali Reza Nasr, "Mawlāna Mawdūdī's Autobiography," *The Muslim World* 85:1–2 (January–April 1995): 53–56.

24. Sayyid Husayn Shah Sahib Mawdudi's name is listed in the section of *sajjāda nishīns* whom Ghulam Ahmad challenged to *mubāhala*. See Mirza Ghulam Ahmad, *Anjām-i Ātham*, in *Rūhānī Khazā'in*, vol. 11, p. 71.

25. Ibid., p. 69.

26. See ibid., p. 71, in the *sajjāda nishīn* section.

27. For a biographical account of the three scholars that describes their relations, see Barbara Daly Metcalf, *Islamic Revival in British India: Deoband, 1860–1900*, pp. 75–80.

28. Mirza Ghulam Ahmad, *Anjām-i Ātham*, in *Rūhānī Khazā'in*, vol. 11, p. 69.

29. See Mirza Ghulam Ahmad, *Barāhīn-i Ahmadiyya*, part 5, in *Rūhānī Khazā'in*, vol. 1, pp. 371–410.

30. Dost Muhammad Shahid expressed these ideas to me during my visit to Rabwah in March 2006. I also have personal correspondence from him, dated March 7, 2006, in which he included the name of Maulvi Ashraf 'Ali Thanwi with those of Rashid Ahmad Gangohi, Muhammad Qasim Nanautwi, and Hajji 'Imdadullah Makki as opponents of Jama'at-i Ahmadiyya.

31. Government of Punjab, *The Munir Report*, p. 18.

32. Maulana Shabbir Ahmad 'Usmani was the son of the sister of Mufti Muhammad Shafi's father.

33. Government of Punjab, *The Munir Report*, pp. 77–78, 133, 136.

34. See Muhammad Anwar Shah Kashmiri, *al-Tasrīh bi mā Tawātara fī Nuzūl al-Masīh* [The explanation of the most repeated reports about the advent of the messiah] (Aleppo:

Maktab al-Matbū'āt al-Islāmiyya, 1965), in which Mufti Muhammad Shafi apparently wrote a lengthy refutation of Jama'at-i Ahmadiyya's beliefs regarding the death of Jesus in the foreword. Although I did not have access to the original source, this work and several others written in response to Jama'at-i Ahmadiyya have been outlined in Yunoos Osman, "Life and Works of 'Allāma Muhammad Anwar Shāh Kashmīrī" (PhD diss., University of Durban–Westville, 2001), pp. 71–78.

35. See Muhammad Taqi Usmani and Maulana Samiulhaq, *Qadianism on Trial: The Case of the Muslim Ummah against Qadianis Presented before the National Assembly of Pakistan* (Karachi: Idaratul-Ma'arif, 2006).

36. Anti-Ahmadi rioting and demonstrations intensified in Bangladesh following a government ban on the publication of Ahmadi literature in January 2004. See http://news.bbc.co.uk/1/hi/world/south_asia/3985785.stm (accessed June 2014). Similarly, anti-Ahmadi demonstrations in Indonesia intensified in 2008. See http://news.bbc.co.uk/1/hi/world/asia-pacific/7370650.stm (accessed June 2014). For an Ahmadi website with general information and current incidents of Ahmadi persecution, see www.thepersecution.org (accessed June 2014); see also www.persecutionofahmadis.org, (accessed June 2014).

37. Although eighty-six were killed during the attacks, at least one more person was killed in related attacks shortly thereafter. See Mirza Masroor Ahmad, *Shuhadā-i Lāhore kā Zikr-i Khayr* (Tilford, UK: Islam International Publications, 2010). For media coverage of the shootings, see "Pakistan Mosque Attacks in Lahore Kill Scores" (May 28, 2010), available at www.bbc.co.uk/news/10181380 (accessed June 2014); see also "Pakistan Ahmadis Bury Lahore Mosque Attacks Victims" (May 29, 2010), available at http://www.bbc.co.uk/news/10190389 (accessed June 2014); and Declan Walsh, "Ahmadi Massacre Silence Is Dispiriting" (June 7, 2010), available at www.guardian.co.uk/commentisfree/belief/2010/jun/07/ahmadi-massacre-silence-pakistan (accessed June 2014); and "Death Toll Rises to 98 after Lahore Attacks" (May 29, 2010), available at www.cnn.com/2010/WORLD/asiapcf/05/28/pakistan.violence/index.html (accessed June 2014).

38. See Yohanan Friedmann, *Prophecy Continuous*, especially chapters 2 and 3.

Bibliography

Mirza Ghulam Ahmad's Major Works

The majority of Mirza Ghulam Ahmad's works have been collected into twenty-three volumes known as *Rūhānī Khazā'in* (Spiritual Treasures). This collection was published in Rabwah, Pakistan, in 1984, then reprinted in 2008 following a process of digitization of the Urdu script. Some tracts were unfinished manuscripts or otherwise unpublished works that only appeared in print after Ghulam Ahmad's death. Other works have been known by multiple names and appear with title pages listing two or three alternative titles for the same work. Jama'at-i Ahmadiyya later published excerpts from larger works as independent books, even though *Rūhānī Khazā'in* includes all major works of Ghulam Ahmad from 1880 until his death in 1908. I have tried to include, wherever possible, the date each tract was written rather than the date of publication, even though *Rūhānī Khazā'in* itself appears to have largely been organized in chronological order, which provides a sense of the sequence of publication.

Volume 1

Barāhīn-i Ahmadiyya (The Proofs of Islam [or Ahmad's Proofs of Islam]), vol. 1 (1880)
Barāhīn-i Ahmadiyya, vol. 2 (1880)
Barāhīn-i Ahmadiyya, vol. 3 (1882)
Barāhīn-i Ahmadiyya, vol. 4 (1884)

Volume 2

Purānī Tahrīreñ (A Collection of Previous Writings: Three Tracts on the Arya) (1879)
Surma Chashm Aryā (Antimony for Clearing the Obscured Vision of the Arya) (1886)
Shehni-i Haqq (Guardians of the Truth) (1894)
Sabz Ishtihār (Green Pamphlet) (1888)

Volume 3

Fath-i Islām (Victory of Islam) (1891)
Tawzīh-i Marām (Elucidation of Objectives) (1891)
Izāla-i Awhām (Removal of Suspicions) (1891)

Volume 4

al-Haqq (Ludhiana) (The Truth) (1891)
al-Haqq (Delhi) (The Truth) (1891)
Āsmanī Faysala (Heavenly Decree) (1891)
Nishān-i Āsmānī (Heavenly Sign) (1892)

Volume 5

Ā'īna-i Kamālāt-i Islām (Reflections of Islam's Perfections) (1893)

Volume 6

Barakāt al-Duʿā (The Blessings of Prayer) (1893)
Hujjat al-Islām (The Proof of Islam) (1893)
Sachchāʾī kā Izhār (Appearance of Truth) (1893)
Jang-i Muqaddas (Holy War) (1893)
Shahādat al-Qurʾān (Testimony of the Qurʾan) (1893)

Volume 7

Tohfa Baghdād (A Gift for Baghdad) (1893)
Karāmāt al-Sādiqīn (Miracles of the Righteous) (1893)
Hamāmat al-Bushrā (Dove of Good News) (1893)

Volume 8

Nūr al-Haqq (Light of Truth) (1894)
Itmām al-Hujjat (Perfection of Proof) (1894)
Sirr al-Khilāfa (The Secret of Succession) (1894)

Volume 9

Anwār al-Islām (Lights of Islam) (1894)
Minan al-Rahmān (Blessings of the Most Merciful) (1895)
Ziyā al-Haqq (Light of Truth) (1895)
Nūr al-Qurʾān (Light of the Qurʾan, parts 1 and 2) (1895)
Meʿyār al-Madhāhib (The Standard of Religions) (n.d.)

Volume 10

Āryā Dharam (Arya Customs) (1895)
Satt Bachan (Acknowledging the Truth) (1895)
Islāmī Usūl kī Falāsafī (The Philosophy of the Teachings of Islam) (1896)

Volume 11

Anjām-i Ātham (The End of Atham) (1897)

Volume 12

Sirāj-i Munīr (Illustrious Lamp) (1897)
Istiftā (Seeking a Legal Ruling) (1897)
Hujjatullah (Proof of God) (1897)
Tohfa Qaysariyya (A Gift for the Queen) (1897)
Mahmūd kī Āmīn (Upon Mahmud's First Completion of the Qurʾan) (1897)
Sirāj al-Din ʿĪsāʾī ke Chār Suʾāloñ kā Jawāb (Siraj al-Din the Christian's Four Questions Answered) (1897)

Volume 13

Kitāb al-Bariyya (The Book of Exoneration) (1898)
al-Balāgh (Eloquence) (1898)
Zarūrat al-Imām (The Need for an Imam) (1898)

Volume 14

Najm al-Hudā'e (Star of Guidance) (1898)
Rāz-i Haqīqat (Keeper of Truth) (1898)
Kashf al-Ghitā (The Unveiling of the Covering) (1898)
Ayyām al-Sulh (Days of Reconciliation) (1899)
Haqīqat al-Mahdī (The Reality of the Mahdi) (1899)

Volume 15

Masīh Hindustān Meñ (Jesus in India) (1899)
Sitāra Qaysara (Victorian Star) (1899)
Tiryāq al-Qulūb (Antidote for Hearts) (1899)
Tohfa Ghaznawiyya (A Gift for the Ghaznavis) (1900)
Rū'edād-i Jasla Du'ā (An Eyewitness Account of the Jalsa Gathering Prayer) (1900)

Volume 16

Khutba Ilhāmiyya (Revealed Sermon) (1901)
Lujjat al-Nūr (Abyss of Light) (1900)

Volume 17

Government Angrezī awr Jihād (The British Government and Jihad) (1900)
Tohfa Golrawiyya (A Gift for the People of Golra) (1900)
Arba'īn (Forty Proofs) (1900)

Volume 18

I'jāz al-Masīh (Miracles of the Messiah) (1901)
Ek Ghalatī kā Izāla (The Correction of an Error) (1901)
Dāfe'u'l-Balā'i (Repelling Misfortunes) (1902)
al-Hudā (Guidance) (1902)
Nuzūl al-Masīh (The Descent of the Messiah) (1902)
Gunnā se Nijāt kyoñ kar Mil Saktī hay (How to Be Liberated from Sin) (1902)
'Ismat-i Anbiyā (Integrity of the Prophets) (1902)

Volume 19

Kashtī Nūh (Noah's Ark) (1902)
Tohfa al-Nadwa (A Gift for the People of Nadwa) (1902)
I'jāz-i Ahmadī (Miracles of Ahmad) (1902)
*Mawlwī Abū Sa'īd Muhammad Husayn Batalwī awr Mawlwī 'Abdullāh Sāhib Chakrālwī
    ke Mubāhasa par Masīh Maw'ūd Hakam Rabbānī kā Review* (A Review of the De-
    bate between Maulvi Abu Sa'id Muhammad Husayn Batalwi and Maulvi 'Abdul-
    lah Chakralwi by the Divine Arbitrator, the Promised Messiah) (1902)
Mawāhib al-Rahmān (Gifts of the Most Merciful) (1903)

Nasīm-i Da'wat (The Gentle Breeze Inviting People to Islam) (1903)
Sanātan Dharam (Perennial [Hindu] Customs) (1903)

Volume 20

Tazkirat al-Shahādatayn (Memoirs of the Two Martyrs) (1903)
Sīrat al-Abdāl (Biographies of the Virtuous) (1903)
Lecture Lahore (1904)
Lecture Sialkot (1904)
Lecture Ludhiana (1905)
al-Wasiyyat (The Will) (1905)
Chashm Masīhī (The Christian Perspective) (1906)
Tajalliyāt-i Ilāhiyya (Divine Manifestations) (1906)
Qādiyān ke Āryā awr Ham (The Arya of Qadian and Us) (1907)
Ahmadī awr Ghayr Ahmadī meñ kyā Faraq hay? (What Is the Difference between
    Ahmadis and Non-Ahmadis?) (1905)

Volume 21

Barāhīn-i Ahmadiyya, vol. 5 (The Proofs of Islam) (1905)

Volume 22

Haqīqat al-Wahy (The Reality of Revelation) (1907)

Volume 23

Chashma-i Ma'rifat (The Spring of Gnosis) (1908)
Payghām-i Sulh (Message of Peace) (1908)

Other Works by Mirza Ghulam Ahmad:

Majmū'a-i Ishtihārāt (Collected Pamphlets), 3 vols. (Rabwah, 1984)
Malfūzāt (Collected Sayings), 10 vols. (Rabwah: Zia al-Islam Press, 1967), republished in
    5 vols.

Select Bibliography of Related Source Material

Some works have only been cited in the footnotes, such as those found in the India Office
Records of the British Library, which are listed as IOR. Most of the larger anthologies
of Ahmadi works, including the works of Mirza Ghulam Ahmad's successors, such as
Anwār al-'Ulūm in nineteen volumes, or the works of the Lahoris, are available through
these websites: www.alislam.org and www.aaiil.org.

'Abd al-Qādir. Hayāt-i Nūr. Qadian: Nizārat Nashr-o-Isha'at Qadian, 2003.
'Abd al-Qadīr, Sufi, and Mirza Bashir Ahmad. The Family of the Founder of the Ahmad-
    iyya Movement. Qadian: Book Depot Talif-o-Isha'at, 1934.
Abdel Haleem, M. A. S. trans. The Qur'an. Oxford: Oxford University Press, 2010.
Abdullah, M. Islam, Jesus, Mehdi Qadiyanis, and Doomsday. New Delhi: Adam Publish-
    ers, 2004.
Abdullah, Sheikh Mohammad. Flames of the Chinar: An Autobiography. New Delhi:
    Penguin Books, 1993.
Abou El Fadl, Khaled, ed. The Place of Tolerance in Islam. Boston: Beacon Press, 2002.

Adamson, Iain. *Ahmad—the Guided One*. Tilford, UK: Islam International Publications, n.d.

———. *A Man of God: The Life of His Holiness Khalifatul Masih IV*. Bristol, UK: George Shepherd Publishers, 1991.

Ahmad, Basharat. *Mujaddid-i 'Āzam*. Lahore?: Ahmadiyya Anjuman Isha'at Islam, Lahore, 1939.

Ahmad, Bashir. *The Ahmadiyya Movement: British-Jewish Connections*. Rawalpindi: Islamic Study Forum, 1994.

Ahmad, Mirza Bashir al-Din Mahmud, *Invitation to Ahmadiyyat*. London: Routledge & Kegan Paul, 1980.

Ahmad, Waheed, ed. *Diary and Notes of Mian Fazl-i Husain*. Lahore: Research Society of Pakistan, University of the Punjab, 1977.

Ahmed, Asad A. "The Paradoxes of Ahmadiyya Identity: Legal Appropriation of Muslim-ness and the Construction of Ahmadiyya Difference." In *Beyond Crisis: Re-evaluating Pakistan*, ed. Naveeda Khan, 273–314. New Delhi: Routledge India, 2010.

Ahmed-Ghosh, Huma. "Ahmadi Women Reconciling Faith with Vulnerable Reality through Education." *Journal of International Women's Studies* 8:1 (November 2006): 36–51.

'Ali, Muhammad. *The Founder of the Ahmadiyya Movement*. Newark, CA: Ahmadiyya Anjuman Isha'at Islam, Lahore, 1984.

———. *The Founder of the Ahmadiyya Movement*. 3rd ed. Wembley, UK: Ahmadiyya Anjuman Lahore Publications, UK, 2008.

Allāh Wasāyā, Maulānā. *Tārīkh-i Khatm-i Nubuwwat 1974: Qawmī Assembly meñ Qādiyānī Muqaddama*. Vol. 2. Multan: 'Ālamī Majlis Tahaffuz-i Khatm-i Nubuwwat, 1994.

Anonymous. "A Short Sketch of the Ahmadiyya Movement." *Revue du Monde Musulman* 1:4 (February 1907).

Anonymous. *Fiqh-i Ahmadiyya*. 2 vols. Rabwah: Zia al-Islam Press, 1983?

Ansari, Humayun. *"The Infidel Within": Muslims in Britain since 1800*. London: Hurst & Company, 2004.

Archer, John Clark. *The Sikhs in Relation to Moslems, Christians, and Ahmadiyyas*. Princeton, NJ: Princeton University Press, 1946.

Ayoub, Mahmoud M. *The Crisis of Muslim History: Religion and Politics in Early Islam*. Oxford, UK: Oneworld Publications, 2006.

Aziz, K. K. *The All India Muslim Conference, 1928–1935: A Documentary Record*. Karachi: National Publishing House, 1972.

Aziz, Zahid. *The Qadiani Violation of Ahmadiyya Teachings*. Columbus, OH: Ahmadiyya Anjuman Isha'at Islam Lahore, 1995.

Baird, Robert D., ed. *Religion in Modern India*. New Delhi: Manohar Publishers, 2001.

Balogun, Ismail. *Islam versus Ahmadiyya in Nigeria*. Beirut: Dar al Arabia Publishing, 1974.

Balzani, Marzia. "Dreaming, Islam and the Ahmadiyya Muslims in the UK." *History & Anthropology* 21:3 (September 2010): 293–305.

Bashir, Shahzad. *Messianic Hopes and Mystical Visions: The Nurbakhshiya between Medieval and Modern Islam*. Columbia: University of South Carolina Press, 2003.

Bose, Sugata, and Ayesha Jalal. *Modern South Asia: History, Culture, Political Economy*. Lahore: Sang-e-Meel Publications, 1998.

Brégand, Denise. "La Ahmadiyya au Bénin." *Archives de Sciences Sociales des Religions* 135:1 (July–September 2006): 73–90.

Buehler, Arthur F. *Sufi Heirs of the Prophet: The Indian Naqshbandiyya and the Rise of the Mediating Sufi Shaykh.* Columbia: University of South Carolina Press, 2008.

Burhani, Ahmad Najib. "Hating the Ahmadiyya: The Place of 'Heretics' in Contemporary Indonesian Muslim Society." *Contemporary Islam* 8:2 (May 2014): 133–152.

———. "Treating Minorities with Fatwas: A Study of the Ahmadiyya Community in Indonesia." *Contemporary Islam* (November 2013): 1–17. doi: 10.1007/s11562-013-0278-3. Accessed June 2014.

Cantwell Smith, Wilfred. *Modern Islam in India: A Social Analysis.* New Delhi: Usha Publications, 1985.

Chaudhry, Aziz Ahmad. *The Promised Messiah and Mahdi.* Tilford, UK: Islam International Publications, 1996.

Chodkiewicz, Michel. *Seal of the Saints: Prophethood and Sainthood in the Doctrine of Ibn 'Arabi.* Cambridge, UK: Islamic Texts Society, 1993.

Copland, Ian. "Islam and Political Mobilization in Kashmir, 1931–1934." *Pacific Affairs* 54:2 (Summer 1981): 228–259.

Crouch, Melissa. "Judicial Review and Religious Freedom: The Case of Indonesian Ahmadis." *Sydney Law Review* 34:3 (September 2012): 545–572.

Dard, A. R. *Life of Ahmad.* Lahore: Tabshir, 1948.

Del Re, Emanuela. "Approaching Conflict the Ahmadiyya Way: The Alternative Way to Conflict Resolution of the Ahmadiyya Community in Haifa, Israel." *Contemporary Islam* 8:2 (May 2014): 115–131.

El-Rouayheb, Khaled. "Heresy and Sufism in the Arabic-Islamic world, 1550–1750: Some Preliminary Observations." *Bulletin of the School of Oriental and African Studies* 73:3 (October 2010): 357–380.

Ernst, Carl W. *Ruzbihan Baqli: Mysticism and the Rhetoric of Sainthood in Persian Sufism.* Richmond, UK: Curzon, 1996.

———, trans. *The Unveiling of Secrets: Diary of a Sufi Master.* Chapel Hill, NC: Parvardigar Press, 1997.

Faruqui, Mumtaz Ahmad. *Muhammad Ali: The Great Missionary of Islam.* Lahore: Ahmadiyya Anjuman Isha'at-i Islam, 1966.

Fisher, Humphrey. "The Concept of Evolution in Ahmadiyyah Thought." *The Muslim World* 49:4 (October 1959).

———. *Ahmadiyyah: A Study in Contemporary Islam on the West African Coast.* London: Oxford University Press, 1963.

Friedmann, Yohanan. *Prophecy Continuous: Aspects of Ahmadi Religious Thought and Its Medieval Background.* Berkeley: University of California Press, 1989.

———. *Shaykh Ahmad Sirhindi: An Outline of His Thought and a Study of His Image in the Eyes of Posterity.* Oxford: Oxford University Press, 2000.

Fuchs, Stephen. *Godmen on the Warpath: A Study of Messianic Movements in India.* New Delhi: Munshiram Manoharlal, 1992.

———. *Rebellious Prophets.* London: Asia Publishing House, 1965.

Garcia-Arenal, Mercedes. *Messianism and Puritanical Reform: Mahdis of the Muslim West.* Leiden: Brill, 2006.

Ghaznavī, Muhammad Dā'ūd. *Maqālāt Maulānā Dā'ūd Ghaznavī.* Lahore: Maktaba Nazīra, 1979.

Gilmartin, David. *Empire and Islam: Punjab and the Making of Pakistan.* London: Oxford University Press, 1988.

———. "Religious Leadership and the Pakistan Movement in the Punjab." *Modern Asian Studies* 13:3 (1979): 485–517.

Government of Punjab. *Report of the Court of Inquiry Constituted under Punjab Act II of 1954 to Enquire into the Punjab Disturbances of 1953.* Lahore: Superintendent Government Printing, Punjab, 1954. Cited as *The Munir Report.*

Graham, William A. *Divine Word and Prophetic Word in Early Islam.* Paris: Mouton, 1977.

Griffin, Sir Lepel H., and Charles Francis Massy. *The Panjab Chiefs.* Lahore: Civil and Military Gazette Press, 1890.

Gualtieri, Antonio. *The Ahmadis: Community, Gender, and Politics in a Muslim Society.* London: McGill–Queen's University Press, 2004.

———. *Conscience and Coercion: Ahmadi Muslims and Orthodoxy in Pakistan.* Montreal: Guernica Editions, 1989.

Haddad, Yvonne Yazbeck, and Jane Idleman Smith. *Mission to America: Five Islamic Sectarian Communities in North America.* Gainesville: University Press of Florida, 1993.

Halm, Heinz. *Shi'ism.* Edinburgh: Edinburgh University Press, 2004.

Hanson, John H. "Jihad and the Ahmadiyya Muslim Community: Nonviolent Efforts to Promote Islam in the Contemporary World," *Nova Religio* 11:2 (November 2007): 77–93.

———. "Modernity, Religion and Development in Ghana: The Example of the Ahmadiyya Muslim Community." *Ghana Studies* 12/13 (2009/2010): 55–75.

Hardy, Peter. *The Muslims of British India.* Cambridge: Cambridge University Press, 1972.

Hasan, Mushirul. *Nationalism and Communal Politics in India, 1885–1930.* New Delhi: Manohar, 2000.

Hermansen, Marcia K., trans. *The Conclusive Argument from God: Shāh Walī Allāh of Delhi's Hujjat al-Bāligha.* New Delhi: Kitab Bhavan, 2013.

Hoffman, Valerie. "Annihilation in the Messenger of God: The Development of a Sufi Practice." *International Journal of Middle East Studies* 31:3 (August 1999): 351–369.

Houtsma, M. Th. "Le Mouvement Religieux des Ahmadiyya aux Indes Anglaises." *Revue du Monde Musulman* 1:4 (February 1907).

Ibn Khaldun. *The Muqaddimah: An Introduction to History.* Trans. Franz Rosenthal. Ed. N. J. Dawood. Princeton, NJ: Princeton University Press, 1967.

Iqbal, Muhammad. *Islam and Ahmadism: A Reply to Questions Raised by Pandit Jawahar Lal Nehru.* New Delhi: Media & Publishing, 1995.

Jalandhari, Abu'l-'Ata. *The Cairo Debate.* 4th ed. Rabwah: Maktaba al-Furqan, 1963.

Jalal, Ayesha. *Self and Sovereignty: Individual and Community in South Asian Islam since 1850.* Lahore: Sang-e-Meel Publications, 2001.

———. *The Sole Spokesman: Jinnah, the Muslim League and the Demand for Pakistan.* London: Cambridge University Press, 1985.

———. *The State of Martial Rule.* Cambridge: Cambridge University Press, 1990.

Jalal, Ayesha, and Anil Seal. "Alternative to Partition: Muslim Politics between the Wars." *Modern Asian Studies* 15:3 (1981): 415–454.

Jones, Kenneth W. *Arya Dhram: Hindu Consciousness in 19th Century Punjab.* London: University of California Press, 1976.

———. "The Arya Samaj in the Punjab: A Study of Social Reform and Religious Revivalism, 1877–1902." PhD diss., University of California, Berkeley, 1966.

Kaushik, Surendra Nath. *Ahmadiya Community in Pakistan: Discrimination, Travail and Alienation.* New Delhi: South Asian Publishers, 1996.

Khan, Adil Hussain. "The Kashmir Crisis as a Political Platform for Jama'at-i Ahmadiyya's Entrance into South Asian Politics." *Modern Asian Studies* 46:5 (September 2012): 1398–1428.

———. "The Big and the Old: Ahmadi Mosques in South London." *The Middle East in London* 6:9 (April 2010): 8.

Khan, Amjad Mahmood. "Persecution of the Ahmadiyya Community in Pakistan: An Analysis under International Law and International Relations." *Harvard Human Rights Journal* 16 (2003): 217–244.

Khan, Ashrafuzzaman, and Mrinmoy Samadder. "Struggling Insecurity: Ahmadiyya Community in Bangladesh." *International Journal on Minority & Group Rights* 20:3 (June 2013): 371–379.

Khan, Muhammad Zarulla. *Hazrat Maulvi Nooruddeen Khalifatul Masih 1.* London: London Mosque, 1983?

———. *Tadhkira.* Tilford, UK: Islam International Publications, 2004.

Khan, Naveeda. *Muslim Becoming: Aspiration and Skepticism in Pakistan.* Durham, NC: Duke University Press, 2012.

Khan, Zafar 'Ali. *Bahāristān.* Lahore: Urdu Academy Punjab, 1937.

Lathan, Andrea. "The Relativity of Categorizing in the Context of the Ahmadiyya." *Die Welt des Islams* 48:3 (2008): 372–393.

Lavan, Spencer. *The Ahmadiyah Movement: A History and Perspective.* Delhi: Manohar Book Service, 1974.

———. "Polemics and Conflict in Ahmadiyya History: The 'Ulama', the Missionaries, and the British (1898)." *The Muslim World* 62:4 (October 1972): 283–303.

Malik, Atif M. "Denial of Flood Aid to Members of the Ahmadiyya Muslim Community in Pakistan." *Health and Human Rights* 13:1 (July 2011): 70–77.

Mawdudi, Abu'l-'Ala. *The Qadiani Problem.* Lahore, 1979.

Mazhar, Muhammad Ahmad. *Arabic: The Source of All the Languages.* Rabwah: Review of Religions, 1963.

———. *English Traced to Arabic.* Lahore: Sunrise Art Printers, 1967.

———. *Yoruba Traced to Arabic.* Lagos: Ahmadiyya Bookshop, 1976.

———. *Hausa Traced to Arabic.* Lagos: Ahmadiyya Bookshop, 1977.

———. *Sanskrit Traced to Arabic.* Faisalabad: Sheikh Aziz Ahmad, 1982.

McCarthy, Richard Joseph, trans. *Deliverance from Error: An Annotated Translation of al-Munqidh min al-Dalāl and Other Relevant Works of al-Ghazāli.* Louisville, KY: Fons Vitae, 1980.

Metcalf, Barbara Daly. *Islamic Revival in British India: Deoband, 1860–1900.* Oxford: Oxford University Press, 1982.

———, ed. *Islam in South Asia in Practice.* Princeton: Princeton University Press, 2009

Minault, Gail. *The Khilafat Movement: Religious Symbolism and Political Mobilization in India.* New York: Columbia University Press, 1982.

Mirzā, Jānbāz. *Kārvān-i Ahrār.* 8 vols. Lahore: Maktabah-i Tabassira, 1975–1986.

———. *Hayāt-i Amīr-i Sharī'at.* Lahore: Maktabah-i Tabassira, 1970.

Mohammad, Maulana Hafiz Sher. *The Ahmadiyya Case: Famous Religious Court Case in Capetown between Lahore Ahmadiyya Muslims and Sunni Muslim Religious Bodies.* Newark, CA: Ahmadiyya Isha'at Islam Lahore, 1987.

Momen, Moojan. *An Introduction to Shi'i Islam: The History and Doctrines of Twelver Shi'ism.* London: Yale University Press, 1985.

Mukul, Kazi, ed. *Rise of Islamic Militancy, Minority Persecution, and Human Rights in Bangladesh.* Dhaka: Nirmul Committee, 2005.

Nasr, Seyyed Vali Reza. *Mawdudi and the Making of Islamic Revivalism.* Oxford: Oxford University Press, 1996.

———. *The Vanguard of the Islamic Revolution: The Jama'at-i Islami of Pakistan.* Berkeley: University of California Press, 1994.

Nawid, Senzil. "The State, the Clergy, and British Imperial Policy in Afghanistan during the 19th and Early 20th Centuries." *International Journal of Middle East Studies* 29:4 (November 1997): 581–605.

Nijhawan, Michael. "'Today, We Are All Ahmadi': Configurations of Heretic Otherness between Lahore and Berlin." *British Journal of Middle Eastern Studies* 37:3 (2010): 429–447.

Noori, Yahya. *Finality of Prophethood and a Critical Analysis of Babism, Bahaism, Qadiyanism.* Tehran: Maidane Shohada, Madresa-e-Shohada, 1981.

Osman, Yunoos. "Life and Works of 'Allāma Muhammad Anwar Shāh Kashmīrī." PhD diss., University of Durban–Westville, 2001.

Otten, Henry J. *The Ahmadiyya Doctrine of God.* Hyderabad: Henry Martyn Institute of Islamic Studies, n.d.

Phoenix. *His Holiness.* Lahore: Sh. Muhammad Ashraf, 1970.

Powell, Avril A. *Muslims and Missionaries in Pre-Mutiny India.* London: Routledge Press, 1993.

———. "Contested Gods and Prophets: Discourse among Minorities in Late Nineteenth-Century-Punjab." *Renaissance and Modern Studies* 38 (1995): 38–59.

———. "'Duties of Ahmadi Women': Educative Processes in the Early Stages of the Ahmadiyya Movement." In *Gurus and Their Followers: New Religious Reform Movements in Colonial India,* ed. Antony Copley. New Delhi: Oxford University Press, 2000.

———. "'Pillar of a New Faith': Christianity in Late-Nineteenth-Century Punjab from the Perspective of a Convert from Islam." In *Christians and Missionaries in India,* ed. Robert Eric Frykenberg. London: Routledge Curzon, 2003.

Qasmi, Ali Usman. *The Ahmadis and the Politics of Religious Exclusion in Pakistan.* London: Anthem Press, 2014.

Qureshi, M. Naeem. *Pan-Islam in British Indian Politics: A Study of the Khilafat Movement, 1918–1924.* Leiden: Brill, 1999.

Radtke, Bernd, and John O'Kane. *The Concept of Sainthood in Early Islamic Mysticism: Two Works by al-Hakīm al-Tirmidhī.* Richmond, UK: Curzon Press, 1996.

Rafiq, B. A. *The Afghan Martyrs.* London: Raqeem Press, 1995.

Rahman, Fazlur. *Islam and Modernity: Transformation of an Intellectual Tradition.* Chicago: University of Chicago Press, 1982.

———. *Revival and Reform in Islam.* Oxford, UK: Oneworld Publications, 2000.

Rai, Mridu. *Hindu Rulers, Muslim Subjects: Islam, Rights and the History of Kashmir.* London: Hurst & Company, 2004.

Ram, Pandit Lekh. *Kullīyāt Ārya Musāfir.* Sahāranpūr: Sattya Dharam Parchārak Press, 1904.

Rashid, Qasim. "Pakistan's Failed Commitment: How Pakistan's Institutionalized Persecution of the Ahmadiyya Muslim Community Violates the International Covenant on Civil and Political Rights." *Richmond Journal of Global Law and Business* 11:1 (Winter 2011): 1–42.

Robinson, Francis. *Islam and Muslim History in South Asia.* Oxford: Oxford University Press, 2000.

———. *Islam, South Asia, and the West.* New Delhi: Oxford University Press, 2007.

———. "Prophets without Honour: Ahmad and the Ahmadiyya," *History Today* 40:6 (June 1990): 42–47.

———. *The 'Ulama of the Farangi Mahall and Islamic Culture in South Asia.* New Delhi: Permanent Black, 2001.

Sadullah, Mian Muhammad, ed. *The Partition of the Punjab 1947: A Compilation of Official Documents.* 4 vols. Lahore: National Documentation Centre, 1983.

Saeed, Sadia. "Pakistani Nationalism and the State Marginalisation of the Ahmadiyya Community in Pakistan." *Studies in Ethnicity and Nationalism* 7:3 (December 2007): 132–152.

Sa'eed, Munawar Ahmed, trans. *Nubuwwat & Khlilāfat: Prophethood and Its Successorship.* Tilford, UK: Islam International Publications, 2006.

Sanyal, Usha. *Devotional Islam and Politics in British India: Ahmad Riza Khan Barelwi and His Movement, 1970–1920.* New Delhi: Yoda Press, 1996.

———. *Ahmad Riza Khan Barelwi: In the Path of the Prophet.* Oxford: Oneworld, 2005.

Seth, H. L. *The Khaksar Movement: And Its Leader Allama Mashraqi.* Delhi: Discovery, 1985.

Scharbrodt, Oliver. *Islam and the Baha'i Faith.* London: Routledge, 2008.

Schimmel, Annemarie. *Mystical Dimensions of Islam.* Chapel Hill: University of North Carolina Press, 1975.

Shah, Sirdar Ikbal Ali. *Afghanistan of the Afghans.* London: Diamond Press, 1928.

Shāhid, Dost Muhammad. *Tārīkh-i Ahmadiyya.* 21 vols. (perhaps with additional volumes forthcoming). Rabwah, 1983.

Siddiq, M. Nadeem Ahmad. "Enforced Apostasy: *Zaheeruddin v. State* and the Official Persecution of the Ahmadiyya Community in Pakistan." *Law and Inequality* 14:1 (December 1995): 275–338.

Sirriyeh, Elizabeth. *Sufis and Anti-Sufis: The Defense, Rethinking and Rejection of Sufism in the Modern World.* Richmond, UK: Routledge Curzon Press, 1999.

Suvorova, Anna. *Muslims Saints of South Asia: The Eleventh to Fifteenth Centuries.* London: Routledge Curzon, 2004.

Talbot, Ian. *Pakistan: A Modern History.* London: Hurst & Company, 2005.

———. *Region and Partition: Bengal, Punjab and the Partition of the Subcontinent.* Oxford: Oxford University Press: 1999.

———. *Khizr Tiwana: The Punjab Unionist Party and the Partition of India.* Oxford: Oxford University Press: 2002.

Troll, Christian W., ed. *Muslim Shrines in India.* 2nd ed. New Delhi: Oxford University Press, 2004.

Vahid, Syed Abdul, ed. *Thoughts and Reflections of Iqbal.* Lahore: Sh. Muhammad Ashraf, 1964.

Valentine, Simon Ross. *Islam and the Ahmadiyya Jama'at: History, Belief, Practice.* New York: Columbia University Press, 2008.

———. "Prophecy after the Prophet, Albeit Lesser Prophets? The Ahmadiyya Jama'at in Pakistan." *Contemporary Islam* 8:2 (May 2014): 99–113.

Walter, Howard Arnold. "Islam in Kashmir." *The Moslem World* 4:4 (October 1914).

———. *The Ahmadiya Movement.* London: Oxford University Press, 1918.

Watt, W. Montgomery. *The Formative Period of Islamic Thought.* Oxford: Oneworld Publications, 2006.

Weitbrecht, H. U. "A Moslem Mission to England." *The Moslem World* 4:2 (April 1914).

Wherry, E. M. *The Muslim Controversy.* London: Christian Literature Society, 1905.

Wilcox, Wayne, and Aislie T Embree. *The Reminiscences of Sir Muhammad Zafrulla Khan.* Maple, CA: Oriental Publishers, with permission from Columbia University, 2004.

Zaman, Muhammad Qasim. *The Ulama in Contemporary Islam: Custodians of Change.* Princeton, NJ: Princeton University Press, 2002.

———. *Modern Islamic Thought in a Radical Age: Religious Authority and Internal Criticism.* Cambridge: Cambridge University Press, 2012.

Index